Contours of the Heart

South Asians Map
North America

Edited by
Sunaina Maira and
Rajini Srikanth

THE ASIAN AMERICAN WRITERS' WORKSHOP · NEW YORK

Contours of the Heart: South Asians Map North America
© 1996 by Rajini Srikanth and Sunaina Maira
Library of Congress Number 96-078960
ISBN 1-889876-00-3
Published by the Asian American Writers' Workshop, 37 St.
Mark's Place, New York, NY 10003. All rights reserved.
Except for brief quotations in critical articles and reviews, no
part of this book may be reproduced in any manner without
prior written permission from the author or publisher.

Copyrights and Acknowledgments are continued at the back
of the book and constitute a continuation of the copyrights
page.

Design by Wendy Lee
Cover art: "Play in Grace" by Shakti Maira
Distributed by Rutgers University Press
Printed in the United States of America

Publication of this book was made possible through the generous
support of The Lannan Foundation.

The Asian American Writers' Workshop is a not-for-profit lit-
erary organization devoted to the creation, development and
dissemination of Asian American literature, and is supported
by the National Endowment for the Arts, the New York State
Council on the Arts, the Department of Cultural Affairs,
Jerome Foundation, Bay Foundation, Greenwall Foundation,
Axe Houghton Foundation, New York Foundation for the
Arts,   AT & T, Anheuser-Busch, Avon Corporation,
Consolidated Edison, and Two St. Marks Corporation.

For

Netra and Vanita—as you navigate these and other contours and

Miguel, in memory of the White Elephant and a very hot summer

Acknowledgments

We would like to thank the following people who worked with us in the Boston area for assisting with soliciting submissions and raising funds: Sonia Arora, for her tireless work in helping the project get off the ground; Mrinalini Rajwar, for being tech-queen, maker of energizing chai, and fount of clear-headed advice; Manish Bapna, for helping to organize a fabulous benefit dinner and navigate bureaucratic mazes; Anjali Kataria, without whom the Cambridge benefit would not have been as successful; and Gayathri Arumughan, for giving us her time and gracious assistance.

We are immensely grateful to the following people, from around the country, for their support and encouragement: Sucheta Mazumdar, for her inspirational guidance and continual encouragement; Sandip Roy, for his astute editorial advice and thoughtful comments; Ginu Kamani, Agha Shahid Ali, and Hema Nair, deep gratitude for traveling to support us at the Cambridge benefit reading; David Jenkins, for playing Spanish guitar; Chitra Divakaruni, for her unflagging encouragement and assistance, and for saving the day; Arvind Kumar, for his support; Michael Kemp, for his enthusiastic assistance in organizing a benefit at A Clean Well Lighted Place For Books in Cupertino, CA; Mahesh Ram, for sponsorship of the New York City fundraiser; and Roshni Rustomji-Kerns, for letting us benefit from her pioneering experience and advising us at many a turning point.

Many thanks to our friends and colleagues at the Asian American Writers' Workshop: Curtis Chin and Eric Gamalinda, for visionary leadership and for making this happen; Parag Khandhar, for his input and assistance; Anantha Sudhakar, for cheerfully managing the tediousness of typesetting; Kiran Jain for help with proofreading, and Peter Ong for masterful publicity.

And thank you to our families who supported us through all the phases of the project and bore with us as we burrowed into manuscripts and monopolized the telephone.

This book would not have been possible without the
generous contributions of the following individuals and corporations:

The Lotus Foundation

Rajat Gupta

K.S. Sriram & family

Arun Maira

Ashok Mehta, Tata Inc.

Center for South Asian Studies,
University of California at Berkeley

Arvind Kumar

Anoop Garg

A Clean Well Lighted Place for Books, Cupertino, C.A.

Naren Chawla

Poonam and Naren Patni

Chitra Divakaruni

Manisha Roy

Bishwapriya Sanyal

Youmna Sfeir

Café of India, Cambridge, Massachusetts

Thali, New York City

Contours of the Heart:
South Asians Map North America

Table Of Contents

Unrolling the Map

Finding the Natives

Sounding the Challenge

Inventing Territories

Returning to Camp

Redrawing the Contours

Photographs by (in order of appearance):

Jaishri Abichandani

Vivek Bald

Naheed Islam

Amitava Kumar/Impact Visuals

Nisma Zaman

Nupu Chaudhuri

Foreword

I am sitting down on a Sunday morning in El Paso, Texas, writing this foreword. On my lap is a half poodle-half chihuahua (a "poochie" if you will) who insists on occupying that spot whenever I type. VH1 is playing Melissa Etheridge in the background on the big screen. I can hear the whir of the hair dryer upstairs. Later I must go out and get the Sunday New York Times to find out what I am thinking about the state of the world, the state of business, the state of the arts and the state of literature.

But for now the poochie looks out from my lap onto my tiny yard where the breeze blowing through the arroyo is rustling the jasmine plant that I have carefully nurtured outside my window. Any day now it will bloom; every morning I walk out there with my coffee hoping that this will be the day.

The old Mexican gardener employed by the condo is, even on Sunday, raking dead leaves. He, a non-American, a crosser-of-borders just like me, seems to understand the religious nature of labor; he needs no seminar on total-quality-management or swimming-with-the-sharks. Radio headphones are clamped on his ears. It makes for an incongruous sight: his greying temples, weathered brow, faded hat with the bright yellow headphones holding the hat down. The small antenna protrudes skyward; he is undoubtedly tuned to a Spanish station broadcasting from across the border in Juarez. I wave hello. When we talk, it is usually of general matters and we are limited by the paucity of my Spanish verbs. But I feel a kinship with him, with the way he has come to the States and has rooted himself through this job, using it as the base from which to make things better for his children, his folks back home. It's an unwritten unspoken contract with America that I recognize in him and in myself. I have seen it in the face of the Bangladeshi cabbie I spoke with at length in New York recently, I see it in the faces of other South Asians whose paths cross mine at airports and on city streets. Perhaps this is a wishful projection on my part, painting my emotions and motives on others. But as I watch the gardener inspect the jasmine, pluck off a dead leaf or two, ascertain that I have watered it, I think this jasmine is as important to him as it is to me; he has read my mind, understood my motives, even as I presume to understand his.

This xeriscaped west Texas world is now my world. It resembles in no way other lands and continents I have lived in. But physical geography is of no longer much importance to me (as long as it isn't cold). I have never met the contributors to Contours of the Heart—except through their writing—but I can sense our commonalities, our experience (if not comfort) with the transit lounges and the immigration booths of other nations, our chameleonlike adaptation to the cultures of Hoboken or west Texas, our quickness to pick up the steaks-on-the-barbie ritual, or the potato-salad pot-luck ritual, or even the ritual of the local community Diwali get-together.

Naipaul, in one of his books on India (and I extrapolate his comments to South Asia in general) said that there are two Indias: one, the physical India, the India of that first arrival into Bombay, the India of choking exhaust fumes and stifling crowds and, of course, dirt and poverty. And the other India is a glorious one; it is the historical, mythical India, with saints and maharajahs and glittering elephants and unspoiled forests. The trick to living in the physical India according to Naipaul—and perhaps he derives this sense from not having lived in India—is to let the body pass through the physical India while the mind plays only the grand-historical-India movie. Perhaps Naipaul simplifies South Asia, strives to reduce it to a simple algorithm, one that explains to the traveller the phenomena he observes. I was brought up largely outside India, but in an Indian community; I went to college and medical school in India; I know my motherland better than Naipaul, but I still feel the need to define what that native place is, what it represents to me. This activity occupies me more than I suppose it should, it colors my every interaction, makes me look for xenophobia in situations too ridiculous for that to be an issue.

I'm tempted to extend Naipaul's metaphor: there is, I think, a third South Asia, a continent that hovers in space over North America, supported by massive pillars in New York/New Jersey, Toronto, but with columns thrusting up from every other city, and little struts shooting up from the smaller burgs. This South Asia's connection with Naipaul's secular or mythical South Asia is increasingly tenuous; it is a continent with its own abbreviations (like NRI, FMG, FLEX, ECFMG, USMLE), its own matrimonial syntax (J-1 waiver, H-1 visa, "innocently divorced," "traditional eastern values with western outlook") and its visible personalities running for Congress or Senate, making it in business or film or otherwise fulfilling Andy Warhol's prediction that everyone will have their ten seconds of fame.

Contours of the Heart, then, is the literature of that third South Asia. You will find it all here: tender poems, thoughtful essays, poignant short stories, raunchy pieces that, whether you are gay or straight, should get your engine running (and if it doesn't you will need to be examined—check Urology listings in India Abroad.) The titles of the contributions alone read like a roadmap of this third South Asia.

So enjoy. The poochie and I wait for the jasmine to bloom. Why? So that one morning when I go out there and see the white flowers and smell the jasmine I can call up the image of an evening in Madras, call up the memory of strolling past the glittering sari shops in Mambalam, and the shops selling stainless steel ware and the jewelry shops, and the freshly swept and watered pavements where, every few yards women are selling jasmine by the foot, where the sea breeze finds its way from Marina and staunches the heat of a city, pushes everyone into this dreamy, soporific state, where all you do is walk and breathe in jasmine, buy jasmine even if you have no woman to give it to. These images, this nostalgia, is the brick and mortar of the South Asia we immigrants carry with us in North America. I recognize it is a nostalgia specific to the immigrant; but these images are vaguely familiar even to our children, the second-generation South Asians who in their writing still carry strong echoes of that other subcontinent, even when they deny its influence. The second generation, I think, either embraces their tradition—sometimes almost to excess with the zeal of a new convert—or else they reject it out of hand, claiming to be free of the cultural schizophrenia that I can't escape. Perhaps the logical choice for us is something in between, some accommodation of masala with MacDonalds, the bhangra-disco sort of adjustment that seems to satisfy and to come about regardless of what the purist says.

This morning, as the old Mexican gardener goes about his work, headphones on, everything in my world seems to depend on the jasmine blooming.

—Abraham Verghese
El Paso, Texas

Introduction

What is the map of one's home? Is a map still useful, or even necessary, if it fails to encompass the imaginings of a person who locates herself in multiple spaces? Consider, for instance, a Japanese American woman who identifies with the Vietnamese immigrant community yet who sent us her work because the boundaries between "South-East Asia" and "South Asia" in her mind were still fluid and shifting. We did not accept her submission, even though her transcending of geography and biology made us realize the tenuousness of cartography. We cite this story as an instance of inventiveness that disrupted our complacent assumptions. In our rejection, we revealed our own uneasiness with jettisoning all geographic parameters and cultural boundaries of identity; but in resorting to "South Asian" as a marker of collective belonging, we still acknowledge the paradoxes within the possibilities of building a pan-ethnic identity. Given the problem of both being seen, and seeing oneself, as South Asian, how does this influence the ways in which we traverse the North American terrain of racial politics? In a country in which socio-political or pan-ethnic allegiances are emphasized, how do these forces collide with the compulsion to identify with very specific local, regional, and religious communities?

Sojourner, expatriate, immigrant, American, Canadian, South Asian American/Canadian—these labels signify varying degrees of comfort with the adopted land. First-, second-, and in-between generations negotiate these constructions of belonging in different ways. One of the most significant moments in the life of an immigrant community is the coming of age of its children—a second generation raised in the new country. As has been well-documented, it is a time when inter-generational tensions abound; challenges of cultural preservation intensify; gender, class, and racial boundaries begin to shift; and career expectations come into conflict.

The majority of first-generation South Asians share a nostalgia for the old countries. However, their memories may not resonate with many second- and 1.5-generation South Asians. Yet, these younger South Asians are still fed with these images of nostalgia, leading them to construct "a place out there" that serves as sanctum, haven, the polar opposite to North America, and the backdrop against which the younger generation can better define and understand itself. The relationship between the generations is complex and nuanced. Second-generation South Asians, having come of age in a post-Civil Rights era, often refuse to be treated as "other" by the mainstream culture; at the same time, many question the uncritical acceptance of the need for assimilation. The resulting political involvement of the second generation, in its building of alliances with other people of color, often conflicts with the first generation's political agenda, which is typically more rooted in home-country interests.

For first-generation South Asians, issues of belonging become increasingly complicated the longer they stay in North America, and even more profoundly complex as they bring up children here, children who are socialized in the North American context—its schools, its movie theaters, its bars, its malls, its streets. For the second generation, questions of identity provide a continual undercurrent to the day-to-day business of living. Boundaries between ethnicities, class, gender, and religion dissolve and re-emerge, as second-generation South Asians move from home to school and college, to workplace, and to peer groups. In the fissures of these topographies of consciousness arise the ingredients of contested identities and complex forms of belonging (or not belonging) in North America. *Contours of the Heart* is a distillation of the powerful creative activity of South Asian American/Canadian communities. It is a testament to the increasingly critical articulations of identity and belonging among first- and second-generation South Asians and their refusal to remain invisible.

A year ago, in the fall of 1995, we sat in an Au Bon Pain café in Boston and thought about the need for this book. Both of us had been impressed and intrigued by pioneering collections of writings by South Asian Americans/Canadians, books that each of us had used in our work at the time— Rajini, in her American literature courses at Tufts University; and Sunaina, in her research on second-generation Indian Americans for a doctoral thesis at Harvard. Yet we also thought the time had come to challenge monolithic constructions of South Asian identities and to begin to reveal the complexities and subtleties of class, gender, sexual orientation, national or regional origin, religion, and generation. These nuances needed to be explored, we felt, because of narrow definitions of South Asian-ness by both the larger society and our own communities. The majority culture is pervaded by stereotypical images of model minority professionals and caricatures of shopkeepers. In South Asian communities, those who are gay, lesbian, or bisexual; or those who work in blue-collar jobs; or those who challenge traditional gender roles are often silenced or rendered invisible.

The contributors to this book challenge the notion that we South Asians merely follow the terrain already charted for us—leading our lives as unobtrusively as possible. They show how we are, instead, clearing new ground and imprinting ourselves on North American landscapes in unmistakable terms—as cab drivers demanding an end to racist treatment; as doctors working to cure AIDS; as gays, lesbians, and bisexuals fighting for social change; as teachers introducing students to diasporic South Asian literature; as feminists redefining heterosexual relationships between South Asian men and women.

Early on in the editorial process, we wondered about the North American context in which this book would be located. As a South Asian anthology, the book is expected to focus solely on the experiences of being South Asian; but this criterion is somewhat problematic because it limits the expressions of writers and relegates them to a specific niche. Multiculturalism, while fostering the expansion of the literary canon, has, nevertheless created a narrow genre of ethnic literature to be consumed by voyeuristic readers sampling from different ethnic experiences. Moroever, the publishing world has reinforced these constricted spaces for ethnic writing. We hope that in the future the possibilities for ethnic writers will be more varied and less restricted. It was with this hope in mind that we invited Abraham Verghese to write the foreward for this anthology. His memoir, *My Own Country*, has in many ways resisted the parameters already in place for ethnic writing.

An additional layer of complexity in shaping this book was the issue of representation of writers of diverse South Asian origins—Bangladesh, Bhutan, India, the Maldives, Nepal, Pakistan, and Sri Lanka. The dominance of contributions by Indian Americans can be attributed to our own extended networks in this community. As Indian American academics, we are also caught within the divisions in our communities along lines of class and nationality. We were forced to confront the fact that we had limited access to networks in other South Asian communities and therefore made targeted efforts to make the submissions more representative. At the same time, in making these efforts we were aware of the danger of appearing to make only token acknowledgments of some points of view in the attempt to be inclusive. We did not undertake the task of translating writing in the vernacular into English, and this decision may have further constricted the available pool of submissions. Furthermore, the majority of works are by writers from the United States rather than Canada, a condition that reflects our residence and networks in the United States.

Despite these difficulties in soliciting submissions, we were nevertheless gratified that we received over a hundred contributions. But it became increasingly apparent to us that the issues of greatest concern to artists and activists in our communities are often alien to successful South Asians in business and the professional bourgeoisie, or even to prominent community leaders and elite intellectuals. The Asian American Writers' Workshop, as a non-profit collective, needed our assistance in raising funds toward the publication of the book. In the course of our fundraising efforts, we encountered countless rejections of our plea for support from those who were more than well-equipped to contribute, reflecting the all-too-common attitude that the arts are incidental, not essential, to the well-being of our communities. Yet there were inspiring exceptions—generous and gracious patrons—from owners of a small Indian restaurant who made possible a benefit dinner, to supportive management executives we had not even met, to tireless students who planned, pleaded, and postered.

As we received our submissions, it became clearer to us that the space we were trying to enlarge was alive with paradoxes and conflicts. Some of the writers challenge the notion of an "authentic" South Asian identity that dismisses those who were born in overseas communities with long histories of migration. The insertion of images of working-class South Asians highlights the struggles for justice that underlie the mythology of the promised land. These images also raise questions of exploitation as those in privileged positions seek to represent the experiences of less affluent compatriots. Issues of representation and political/ethnic allegiances are equally complex, if not controversial, in the writings that explore the search for a "suitable" partner. The perception that feminist solidarity and ethnic loyalty are at odds with each other is questioned in explorations of inter-racial relationships. Romantic and sexual choices are further examined by gay and lesbian writers who are engaged in defining themselves both in South Asian and mainstream lesbigay communities.

As the table of contents indicates, we organized the selected pieces into six sections, trying to achieve a balance among fiction, poetry, essays, and photography. The titles of the sections seek to convey a sense of initiative and agency, emphasizing the spirit of adventure that characterizes a diasporic people. South Asians encounter North America on their terms—they unroll the map, find the natives, sound the challenge, invent territories, and return to camp to reflect on their experiences and redraw the contours of the land.

In the first section, "Unrolling the Map," the writings throw open the vastness of North American social and cultural landscapes; they explore the influences of race and ethnicity, and hint at the immense diversity of the South Asian diaspora. The pieces in "Finding the Natives" play with representation: who sees whom as "native"; who gazes at whom in order to define and understand both "self" and "other." "Sounding the Challenge" contests predefined and prescribed roles. The writers in this section question the validity of boundaries of class, gender, ethnicity, and cultural traditions and call for new ways of politicizing identities. In "Inventing Territories," the writings discover new social and cultural landcapes, new ways of bringing together North American and South Asian influences. "Returning to Camp" signals a time of reflection and analysis in order to absorb the lessons of actively engaging with the landscape to come to a better understanding of experiences and strategies. In the final section, "Redrawing the Contours," the writers re-position old boundaries and territorial lines, by highlighting new North American social and cultural topographies. South Asians pick up the cartographic instrument and etch themselves into the terrain.

Sunaina Maira   Rajini Srikanth

August, 1996
Lexington, Massachusetts
"The Birthplace of American Liberty"

I am a twenty six year old photographer living in New York. About a month after I bought my camera in Jan 1993, I found myself exclusively photographing my family and South Asian neighbors. Looking through my lens, I discovered the ways my family was recreating our old environment in India. We are working class people in both countries. The camera changed my interaction with my extended family, as I found myself attending family functions with greater frequency. I also began to haunt the streets of Jackson Heights, the largest South Asian neighborhood in Queens. Now, the shopkeepers, hip-hop styled teenagers and paan vendors have all come to recognize me. I started on a personal quest to document my transformation from a teenager from India into an Indian-American woman. I found myself making a visual history of the community I have been entrenched in for eleven years.

—*Jaishri Abichandani*

Unrolling the Map

The Spelling Bee

Anuradha M. Mitra

On some days, I wake up with the jangled edges of letters from various alphabets colliding with great fury in the pit of my stomach. I don't understand the intensity of my anger. Neither do I know where it will take me. My paranoia is simple. On certain days, I just fear that in the process of arranging these spaghetti-o's of jumbled letters into meaning, I will perform irreversible surgery on myself.

My anger, I firmly believe, emerges from getting down to the level of the alphabet, the *matrika shakti*, and doing all the scrub work, all day, every day. Don't be mistaken. It's not as if I loathe this work. On the contrary, my particular seat in the house is hard to come by. I am paid handsomely to do what I love best: to polish each syllable of a word to make it authentic, to make it be, to write with power, then write some more—this time with less bravado, and then to rewrite what I have just written, with meaning. To write as myself. To feel the nuances of my broken skin in the landscape of words. To lose myself in my creation till I feel that I have finally been nirvanized. Even if it is for a brief countdown of minutes. All day, most days, I deal with the power and delight of language, the meaning that it is capable of containing, the intelligibility that is derived from words sometimes strung seamlessly across a page.

I continue the process of becoming "chilled." Of becoming frozen in the word so there is no difference between it and me. Of becoming one with the text so that word and blood type match up perfectly. There is no dissonance.

But my deficiencies grow sharper by the day. At times they seem so large that even those with perfect myopia can sense my presence in jarring word after each word. What I seem to lack is not skill as a writer, but as a speaker of words. I lack mastery over the right pronunciation and the right accent. I give myself away in an instant. At that point, the vulnerable parts of me are forced out of the soup bowl in one heap of linguine, revealing an aspect of myself that is not particularly attractive to behold.

Every so often, this multiple-choice testing of my abilities shows up as a simple spelling bee. You would think that because my accent is different, the mainstream would want to correct my pronunciation or rectify my speaking patterns. But that is not so. Because I speak differently, others assume that my knowledge of the language is just plain deficient, less than, my comprehension is questionable, and my hearing abilities are on the wane. Many are the times when I have had an immaculately mannered white person come up to me and blast out his generosity: "Welcome to the United States of America. We hope that you like it here." All this at a pitch that I swear even the deaf can hear.

From dentist's office to hair-cutting salon, from library clerk to the serviceperson in the garage, every one seems intent on making me prove myself. "How do you spell your first name?" the serviceperson asks politely. The first initial is an "A," A for acrylic. How much more generic can I get? "What is your first name, ma'am?" he asks with an authoritative air, with the intention of making me feel stupid. "How much does it matter to you?" I think aloud, as I begin the long, tortuous road to the end of the fourth syllable that constitutes my name. Which prompts the next comment, "What a different name. Where are you from? You speak differently?" and out spews the flood of questions which conceals more than it reveals. For under the critical gaze of these half-questions, I shrink into my old, inarticulate, inexpressive self, the self that is defined by the chaos of different alphabets rather than one uniformly recognizable one.

It is the same story wherever I go. "How do you spell your child's name, your daughter's name, the child whose lashes are long enough to sweep the floor?" Are these descriptors necessary? I reply back with a question. Would they describe one of their own with such poetic abilities? Would they ask for the correct spelling of Marcia's name with a panegyric to her freckles? I begin spelling my daughter's name because I have kept the nurse's assistant waiting too long. Her name begins with a "P," a "P as in Psychology." The assistant looks at me again, half-annoyed and fully impatient at my innate stupidity, sarcasm, or erudition. She cannot make out which. "Okay," I have resolved the issue for the time being. "I give up," I say with resignation. "My daughter's name begins with a 'P,' as in Paul," and then I rattle off the three remaining syllables that run through the geography of her name. If it is vanilla-flavored homogeneity that is desired, then so be it.

I become reconciled to spelling my way through the syntax of my life as I make myself comfortable in the new grammar of America. I realize that my anger is mostly self-directed because I try so very hard to find my place. And I don't. Yet, in some, undefined corner of my self, I stand tall because of my difference. I train myself to be upbeat about these spelling bees. For all I know, it is because of the consistent efforts of these well-intentioned people that I know how to spell eleemosynary without even so much as consulting a dictionary.

San Andreas Fault

Meena Alexander

'And if I cried, who'd listen to me in those angelic orders?'

—Rilke

I: The Apparition

Too hard to recall each grass blade, burn of cloud
in the monsoon sky, each catamaran's black sail.
Nor very easily, could we make ourselves
whole through supplication,
before and after—the jagged rasp of time,
cooled by winds brushing the Pacific.
The brown heart, rocking, rocking,
ribs dashed to the edge of San Andreas Fault.

Suddenly I saw her, swathed in silk
seemingly weightless, nails prised into rock,
rubber boots dangling over the gorge:

'This morning light over water
drives everything out of mind, don't you agree?
I know the Ganga is like nothing else on earth
but now I fish here.
San Andreas suits me: salmon, seaperch, striped bass.'

Montara, Moss Beach, Pescadero, Half Moon Bay,
North American names quiver and flee, pink shrubs,

stalks of the madrone, speckled heather rooting in clumps
and under it all the fault her voice worked free:
'Saw him walking with you, holding hands in sunlight
two of you against a wall: hands, face, eyes, all shining
he had a brown paper bag you nothing. How come?'

Feet hot against madrone roots, veins beating indigo
to the rift where her thighs hung, musically,
unbuckling gravity, I set my face to her squarely:

'Come to America so recently
what would you have me carry in my hands?
In any case why bring in a man I hardly see anymore?

II: Flat Canvas

Once, waiting for him in the parking lot
right by the tap and muddied pool
where wild dogs congregate
—he was often late—I let the sunlight bathe my face.
Stared into water, saw myself doubled, split
a stick figure, two arms bloodied with a bundle
racing past parked cars of third world immigrants.

Then I saw him sprinting by my side:
'Teeth, Teeth, Teeth'
he cried his body bolted down, a dream
by Basquiat, flat canvas, three pronged heart, broken skull
laced with spit, skin stretched over a skeleton pierced with nails,
Gray's Anatomy in one hand, in the other, the Bible.

In Malayalam, Hindi, Arabic, French he cried out
turning to English last, babbling as the continental coast

broke free riveting Before and After, jumpstarting reflection.
The Angel of Dread, wings blown back
neck twisted over mounds of rubble
doorposts with blood of the lamb smeared on.
And faintly visible under jarring red
words like 'Progress' 'Peace' 'Brotherly Love'
'One Nation under God' all that stuff.'

III: Funeral Song

I sensed his breath on my neck
he needed to suck me into eternity
press thumbs against my throat, set a paper bag
against my thighs, warm with the hot dog he got on the cheap
from the corner store by the supermarket wall.
'A real American hot dog, sauerkraut and all' he boasted
till tears took hold.

He pressed me tight against a tree,
in full sight of an Indian family
struggling with their groceries, thrusting
harder as breath came in spurts—
a funeral song he learnt from his mother
the words from Aswan filling me:

'You have crossed a border, never to return.
Stranger in this soil, who will grant you burial?
Neck of my beloved, who will grant you burial?
Eyes, lips, nose who will shield you from sight?'

Tighter and tighter he squashed me
till the fruits of the fig tree broke loose
and fit to faint I thrust my fist
through his blue cotton shirt, cast myself free.

IV: Package of Dreams

Late at night in Half Moon Bay
hair loosed to the glow of traffic lights
I slit the moist package of my dreams.
Female still, quite metamorphic
I flowed into Kali ivory tongued, skulls nippling my breasts
Durga lips etched with wires astride an electric tiger
Draupadi born of flame betrayed by five brothers stripped
of silks in the banquet hall of shame.

In the ghostly light of those women's eyes
I saw the death camps at our century's end

A woman in Sarajevo shot to death
as she stood pleading for a pot of milk,
a scrap of bread, her red scarf swollen
with lead hung in a cherry tree.

Turks burnt alive in the new Germany,
a grandmother and two girls
cheeks puffed with smoke
as they slept in striped blankets
bought new to keep out the cold.

A man and his wife in Omdurman
locked to a starving child, the bone's right
to have and hold never to be denied,
hunger stamping the light.

In Ayodhya, in Ram's golden name
hundreds hacked to death, the domes
of Babri Masjid quivering as massacres begin—
the rivers of India rise mountainous,

white veils of the dead, dhotis, kurtas, saris,
slippery with spray, eased from their bloodiness.

V: San Andreas Fault

Shaking when I stopped I caught myself short
firmly faced her 'What forgiveness here?'
'None' she replied 'Every angel knows this.
The damage will not cease and this sweet gorge
by which you stand bears witness.

'Become like me a creature of this fault.'

She said this gently, swinging to my side
body blown to the fig tree's root.

'Stop,' I cried 'What of this burden?
The messy shroud I stepped into?
Ghostly light? Senseless mutilations?'

Her voice worked in my inner ear
sorrow of threshed rice,
cadences of my mother tongue loosed in me:

'Consider the glory of the salmon
as it leaps spray to its own death,
spawn sheltered in stone under running water.
That's how we make love—Can you understand?
Each driven thing stripping itself
to the resinous song of egg and sap
in chill water.

'Sometimes I think this is my mother's country
she conceived me here, legs splayed, smoke in her eyes
in the hot season when gold
melts from chains, beads, teeth
and even the ceremonials of the dead
dwelt on in Upper Egypt, dissolve away.

'We are new creatures here.
Hooking fish in San Andreas we return them to the fault
perch, black salmon, the lot.
'When the walls of your rented room
in Half Moon Bay fall away
consider yourself blessed.

'The snows of the Himalayas
glimpsed in your mother's songs
once came from rainclouds high above this coast
cradling the rafters of the seven heavens.'

For James And Buffalo—
Who Launched Me Off

Rajini Srikanth

The spring of 1977 to the winter of 1978 was a sensational period. Even while I lived through it, I realized it was exceptional, that I would return to it years later, like a quilter who saves certain pieces of fabric, knowing that one day they will form the central motif of her design.

That was the time when Buffalo, NY dug itself out from fifteen feet of snow and bid goodbye to the National Guard, who'd come to help shovel. Buffalonians danced around fountains in shorts and T-shirts in a desperate and frenzied propitiation to the sun. In the spring of 1977, I first met James, in the dingy stone building of the Media Studies department.

In the summer of 1978, I drove down from Buffalo to Houston in a flame-red Volkswagen Beetle. With me were two other Indian women, friends of mine from Bombay. We'd all had a hard semester and looked, as my husband said, "like dried and shriveled chilli peppers." When we entered Texas from Arkansas, I remember feeling relieved. In Texas, we were at least identifiable as Mexicans; in Arkansas, we were unrecognizable, entirely foreign.

Later that summer, after my friends had left Houston, disc jockey John Jenkins and I climbed into a patrol car of the Houston Police Department, Super 8 camera and mike in hand, to ride for three weeks, sometimes at 2 and 3 a. m., with a police officer as he made his daily rounds. We were trying to find out, Studs Terkel style, just what the officer felt about his job and the effect of that feeling on how he did his work. One night, outside a bar in the Mexican part of town, an angry young man put his hand over my camera lens and told me in Spanish to stop filming. That night, the patrol officer didn't get out of his car until a backup arrived, and Jose Campes Torres was partially vindicated.

My husband worked in Houston; I studied in Buffalo. In those years of our commuter marriage, we should have bought stock in AT&T. We didn't know it then, but Houston was to be the springboard of my husband's career; Buffalo, we joked, is where we would retire. James, coincidentally, was the link between the two cities. He'd come from Houston to Buffalo, a filmmaker-activist, glowing with the success of his recent exposé of the Houston city government and its systematic neglect of a black downtown neighborhood. He'd been enticed to come to Buffalo so he could teach young would-be filmmakers how to use the camera as an instrument of social change.

James was a good cameraman and a great storyteller, two skills that don't often coexist. A lot of people can take good shots, because they recognize the aesthetic quality of a moment or situation. But James had a story in his head *before* he took the shot, before he lifted his 16mm or Super 8 camera to his shoulder. In any context, he could discern almost immediately who the key players were, who would be most likely to speak, who would move across the room, who would get angry, who would break down. He had the uncanny ability to make people feel comfortable enough to reveal themselves. This was because the minute he walked into a situation, he entered totally into the lives of the people there. He'd joke about himself, how he'd be speaking with a person from England and within minutes find himself replicating the English accent; and the same thing would happen when he was with someone from Mississippi, or New York. He could do the South Indian head roll with ease, if he gave himself a few minutes to re-enter the world of Madras that he'd visited when he worked as a filmmaker for the USAID.

Before I came to know James well, I thought he was somewhat presumptuous, particularly because he'd stride into people's lives with his camera and assume they would welcome him or even want to speak with him. I was putting him in the same category as a news cameraman, who one minute thrusts his camera into the most private moments in a superficial show of interest and empathy, and the next minute walks away, abandoning the individuals in their grief and rage. A few days after I had registered for James's class, he told me about his work in India with the USAID. He was delighted to find out that I was South Indian, and proceeded to describe for me his experience of eating sambar and rice with his fingers off a plantain leaf. This was in the days before multiculturalism, and as he spoke with gusto in front of the class, his voice booming with laughter, I cringed inwardly, wondering if all my classmates were thinking how uncivilized and backward Indians were. It wasn't until later that I realized that James had been laughing at himself, at his own ineptitude in curving his fingers and guiding them accurately into his mouth.

He probably looked ridiculous, food dribbling down the sides of his mouth and down the length of his arm, while all around him the experts sat, dextrously consuming their meal.

I made a similar mistake with another of his stories about India. This one had to do with Delhi. He was speaking of the dhobis at the Red Fort and marveling at how they dried sarees. One person holds the saree at one end, while another runs, unfurling the saree in the air, flapping the open garment until it dries. I remember thinking, "How typical! Just like a westerner to romanticize what must be very hard work." Sure, the sarees look brilliant under the blue sky, arching into the wind. Sure, they provide a breathtaking foreground to the Red Fort, a band of colors in an undulating rainbow, perfect camera material. I said as much to James, how I was irritated that he should glorify the harshness of the washermen's lives, fail to see that the sarees screen the unrelenting repetitiveness of their labor. James conceded my point gracefully, and I know now that he did it because he knew that I would eventually understand his perspective. I did. It didn't take me long to find myself re-evaluating my every preconception about James. His fascination with the dhobis had less to do with the cinematographic value of their labor, I realized (although that did play a part), and more to do with his desire to understand what they felt about their work. The spectacularr visual images were the accompaniment to something he thought he detected in them—perhaps an indomitability of spirit, perhaps a defiant gesture at the unchanging nature of their lives, perhaps the few moments everyday in which they abandoned reason and responsibility and became again young boys flying homemade kites.

Today it is deemed incorrect to speak of universality of feeling; specificity is called for. Would James have felt as comfortable today walking in to a black neighborhood or a dhobi ghat, movie camera in hand, assuming that his presence would be accepted? This tall white Oklahoman with a radio announcer's rich and deep voice could glide into any situation because he refused to remain on the outside. Easy for a white man, you say, part of his arrogant ownership of the world. Maybe. But what redeemed James was his expectation that all his students—black, white, brown— would come to feel the same way, and would feel the same way not because of arrogance but because of their genuine desire to step out of their own selves and enter into the selves and lives of the people they were filming. In the eighteen months between the spring of 1977 and the winter of 1978, this is the attitude I tried to develop.

Buffalo was a dying city when I first entered it, in 1976. The potholes were as long as hockey sticks, as deep as basketballs, and as wide as half a dozen footballs laid end to end. It was a city eaten by snow and ice, where brick turned the color of slate and even new window panes had short-lived gleams. People walked and drove slowly in Buffalo. The students at the University were a hardy bunch. Many of us became experts at steering our cars with one hand and scraping the frost off the insides of our windscreen and windows with the other. We learned to wiggle our toes and blow on our fingers for warmth as we made the turns and peered through thick drifts of blowing snow.

James came to Buffalo from the heat and boom of Houston. He came perhaps to settle in Buffalo, for this is where he bought a house, and nobody in his right mind bought a house in the depressed economy of Buffalo unless he was planning to stay. He bought a house and filled it with students—itinerant young men and women with dreams of community involvement through filmmaking—who threw down their rolled up sleeping bags and claimed a corner of James's home. They'd come in sleepy-eyed from hours of night-time editing in rooms and on equipment borrowed from the local media cooperative. James's presence in the house was unpredictable, but his kitchen was open to all to stock as they pleased and use when they could. He'd hung a bunch of dried chillis on a beam, a reminder of his Southern roots. On a cold Buffalo winter day, snowed in from a blizzard, James could make a masterful chilli, thick and full of fire, deep red, rich with meat and onions and charged with streaks of tongue-turning flavor. The smell filled the bare rooms, settling solidly in huge clouds, cloaking the students in their wine-drenched conversations on the frustrations and highs of making films.

In the days before cooperative learning, before multiculturalism, before diversity training, and cross-cultural sensitivity awareness, James took four of us, threw us together, expected we would work as a team and told us to make a documentary—tell a story about Buffalo's laid-off steelworkers. There we were: one twenty-year old woman, newly arrived from India; one New York City-raised black woman with a wry sense of humor; one Stamford, Connecticut-raised Jewish woman who considered herself Jewish first and American second; and one local man, white, born and brought up in Buffalo, who played ice hockey and was sensationally handsome. Two of us were married, the other two regaled us with stories of their amorous affairs. We spent hours together, sometimes entire days, nights even.

One morning, at 5:00 a.m., we decided to take a break. We'd been through an entire night of editing. We'd looked at hours of footage: talking head interviews, shots of abandoned buildings, rusty and dented cars in driveways marred by frost heaves, poorly-lit living rooms. We had yards of footage where people stood in non-aesthetic clusters, and floral wallpaper patterns clashed with someone's foregrounded plaid shirt. One person's hat completely blocked another's face. We were so tired, we were turning knobs too far on the editing console—to "fast forward" when we needed to rewind, or the other way round, not hitting the stop button soon enough.

There was no lounge to sit in and relax; we were editing in a large warehouse-like structure, and the only spaces were rooms fitted with editing equipment and closets for storing cameras, tripods, and lights. There was one screening room, but this was also strictly utilitarian: a large stack of folding metal chairs leaned against a wall. In one corner sat a wide wooden table. The rest of the room was bare. This is where we went.

None of us had had the foresight to bring sleeping bags. We had envisioned a delirious night of editing, adrenalin pumping high; we had expected to emerge from long productive hours with a dramatic segment of skilfully edited moments. Fatigued, we looked around. Joe opened up a few chairs, arranged them in a long line, and stretched himself out on them. I chose the top of the table. Rebecca and Joan found a wall with a sliver of early morning sun, slid down to the floor with their backs against the wall, their legs extended into the empty center of the room. We tried to sleep.

Spread out like a hunk of meat on a butcher block, I felt the shape of more bones in my body than I cared to think about, the table's hard surface pressing against my tired muscles. Just what was the point of this exercise, I wondered. Did I really want to spend the rest of my life lying on table tops and probing lives I had no business questioning; after all, what did I know of steel mills and steelworkers' lives; what was it to me that Buffalo was once a bustling mill town and today was decrepit flotsam on the Niagara River? I may have dozed off fitfully.

When we pulled ourselves up an hour later, the diner across the street was open. Not being a coffee drinker, I braced myself for what I knew would be most unsatisfactory tea. The water was barely hot, the teabag a generic brand whose tag said only "Orange Pekoe." Sipping the lukewarm fluid, the tea that was not quite tea, I felt myself drift in and out of consciousness. What connection did our badly shot footage have to the reality of the steelworkers' situation? What did they think of us, four multicolored faces, bursting in upon their lives, gazing at their pain and anger from behind a camera lens, asking them questions that to us were only an intellectual exercise. We hadn't lost jobs, we didn't have to tell children that once again they couldn't have a new bicycle for their birthday, we didn't have to economize on an only sister's wedding present. They knew we were just students, so why did they even bother to speak with us? To kill time? To amuse themselves? Because they were willing to explore every avenue of possible redress, however slim?

"Go get more footage," was all James said when we told him of our wasted hours. He smiled slightly, as if our predicament were not entirely unexpected.

"You mean, find other laid-off steelworkers who'll want to talk to us?"

"Sure. You have a list."

The thought was horrifying. More living rooms, more confused stares at our strangely mixed crew. Months later, I carried those looks with me on my drive down to Houston and found them replayed at the Waffle House and Jefferson Davis Steak Barn and Hoagie's Sandwiches we'd stop at to eat. By then, however, I had learned how to return fire with fire. Or at least had trained myself to do it. An eye for an eye. A stare for a stare. But in Buffalo, it was more complicated.

I don't remember names, but let's call them the Parkers: a steelworker who'd recently lost his job, his wife, who worked part-time at a local grocery store, and two sons, ten and twelve. A black family. We climbed up a narrow staircase to their second-floor apartment. They were all sitting on a long couch, mother and father at either end, children in between. The room was narrow, and I remember thinking, how are we going to get enough distance from them so that we don't get a distorted image? I wanted to get behind the camera, for reasons of my own, but Joe, for reasons of his own had already hoisted it up to his shoulder and was safely wedded to the eyepiece. I was stuck doing the lights. As the Parkers blinked in the white glare, I felt intrusive, like a hostile force illuminating a target for attack.

Joan decided to remain silent. Later, when I asked her about it, she told me quite firmly that just because she was black she was not going to be used as the entry into the Parkers' lives. It was up to Rebecca to do the talking. Mr. Parker had been laid off for three weeks. He didn't hold much hope for finding reemployment as a skilled machinist. "They're saying us steelworkers have to learn new types of jobs—service jobs, they're calling them. They're talking about the new hotels that are going to open up. But who'll give a person like me a job in a hotel?" I wondered if Rebecca would follow up with her usual "What do you mean?" She liked having everything clearly spelled out. Not that she didn't believe in subtlety, but she wanted people to speak their minds completely; she was ever ready to help them do that. Then I heard her ask, "Why? Because you're black?"

Rebecca, you're an ass, I thought. How could you? You just earned yourself an earful from Joan. And Joan, I knew, was never sparing with her words. (She had chastised Rebecca and me for not having sent her a condolence card after she had told us about a tragedy in her family that happened a year ago.) But surprisingly, Mrs. Parker began to talk. Yes, that was exactly it, she said. Bill didn't want to have to yessir and yesmaam to hotel customers, and it showed in the way he spoke and carried himself. "He's proud to be a machinist; he knows how to work a piece of machinery. He treats it well, it works well. With people, it's not like that. You don't know how they're going to react. It's always a guessing game."

What had given Rebecca the gumption to ask that question? I could never have done what she did. In the first place, I didn't know enough then about the racial dynamics of the United States, didn't know about the nuances of inter-racial experiences and interactions. It had seemed to me to be a rude question, no different from the insensitive queries of the evening news reporter who thrusts a microphone into a grieving person's face. But Rebecca had perceived something that I hadn't. Perhaps she had seen in Mr. Parker's phrase "a person like me" a desire to speak about his feelings as a black man, and she had taken him up. And once Mrs. Parker said what she did, speaking for her husband, everyone felt more comfortable. Joe relenquished his behind-the-lens position to me and Joan started to speak to the young boys about their school.

But the entire experience could have ended up a disaster. "I can't believe you did that," Joan said to Rebecca when we left the Parkers. Rebecca herself was surprised. "It just came out that way; I don't know what happened to me." We owed it to Mrs. and Mr. Parker that the situation had resolved itself as happily as it had. Yet, I had to recognize Rebecca's courage in not trying to cover up her initial awkwardness with follow-up questions. She had let the silence challenge all of us.

In those moments when all you could hear was the low hum of the camera motor, it suddenly became very clear to me that this was what James was trying to do—to have us understand that an artificially created situation can lead to a point at which the players involved are made to confront hard questions about themselves. Paradoxically, Rebecca's very intrusive query both facilitated and inhibited revelation from the Parkers. They could have chosen to remain silent or evade the question, and either of those would have been a perfectly understandable response. But they chose to speak, chose to welcome the intrusiveness of that question and used it to voice their perspective and frustration. This is what the city officials needed to hear as they blissfully went ahead and theorized about the growth of the service industry as an easy fix for laid-off steelworkers. Rebecca's question and the Parkers' response put the issue of race smack into the center of the retraining and re-employment blueprints the officials were drafting.

Years later, when I was deep in the middle of writing my dissertation on William Faulkner and steeping myself in the history of the South, that scene of Rebecca and the Parkers came back to haunt me as I read of the complex alliances between Blacks and Jews in the Civil Rights movement. Without goodwill and trust and courage, that morning at the Parkers could have merely given us some more uninteresting footage; instead, what we got was not just a compelling drama on film, but the realization in each of us of the intricate interplay of personal, social, and historical forces as they impinge on our lives. I was beginning to understand the ways in which my life would be shaped here in this country.

There were other instances. One older man, in his mid fifties, an owner of a small factory manufacturing machine parts, spoke to us about how he had hired several laid-off steelworkers and given them jobs on his shop floor. He looked at a person's skill, he told us. I noticed that Joan asked him a lot of questions, almost as if she were deliberately leading him to say something objectionable. "I've got colored people working here," he said. "They're good workers." Of course, the minute we stepped outside, she exploded. "Did you hear that! He's still talking like it's the '50s. 'Colored.' And what does he mean, they're good workers. What did he expect." Joe responded by saying that while he thought Mr. Galton was archaic in his choice of words, he didn't appear to be racist. Joan would not be placated. "He should pay attention to what's happening around him. Where was he in the '60s?" But Joe would not give up, either. He insisted that Mr. Galton, if he were racist, would have shut the doors of his factory on black workers. Joan pointed out that he probably would have done just that if it hadn't been for affirmative action legislation. Rebecca was uncertain what she felt; she understood Joan's outrage, but she was also willing to concede a fundamental kindness in Mr. Galton.

I was baffled, entirely ignorant of the nuances and subtleties of discrimination and racism. What had Joan detected in Mr. Galton's demeanour that led her almost to bait him to implicate himself? The Ku Klux Klan variety of racism I could recognize, but I had no clue, it appeared, to less-obvious verbal and bodily signals of racism. I was as yet unschooled in identifying the numerous genres of discrimination, as yet a novice in reading the many varieties of racist script. Perhaps my limitations had something to do with my recent life of relative privilege in India. The interchange among Joan, Rebecca, and Joe left me feeling foolish and humbled. I wonder today what Joan thought of me then. Did she see me as an ally, and was she disappointed that I said nothing? Did she think that I, like all other newcomers to this country, was guilty of being insensitive to and ignorant of the historically defined predicament of African Americans? Or did I not even figure in her thinking; was I just too insignificant a player, someone she could dispense with because I was too foreign, too Indian, too un-American.

James was delighted with the debate. He saw the argument as evidence of a developing bond among us. We were becoming so comfortable with one another through our hours of work together that we were beginning to toss caution and diplomacy to the wind in our conversations, even about the most controversial and volatile of subjects. That such intimacy and honesty existed among his student groups is entirely to James' credit—he believed implicitly in people's ability to come together. He had taken part in the 1963 March on Washington, and it was the possibilities of those times that influenced his teaching. People can step into each other's shoes, he insisted, even if the shoes don't fit perfectly and you stumble as you walk.

I tried to remember that message on my long drive down from Buffalo to Houston. When the middle-aged slightly rotund man in the lounge of the Nashville Holiday Inn came up to the table where I sat with my two friends from

Bombay and invited himself to sit down with us and offered to buy us a drink, I tried not to think of him as arrogant and sexist, seeking to stoke his waning sense of western male power by flirting with three Eastern women. Maybe he was just a friendly guy looking for some conversation, and we appeared to be able to offer him something other than the usual fare of local talk; maybe he wanted to learn about the unfamiliar places we came from, perhaps he was planning a trip eastward; or maybe he was just trying on a different pair of shoes. He told us how fortunate we were to be in God's own country, and I thought, well, maybe we do look tired and undernourished, after all we've been on the road ten hours, and maybe this is his welcome speech to us. At least he's not telling us we don't belong.

When the young man in the green pick-up truck followed us through much of Arkansas, I tried very hard not to see him as a potential rapist who could force my little Beetle off the road and take his three-fold pleasure. Perhaps he was just some farm boy hungry for diversion, never having seen faces other than white and black. Maybe he had no clue he was terrifying us because he was, like Faulkner's Benjy, a full-grown idiot incapable of thought. Just before we crossed into Texas, he took the last exit in Arkansas, waving to us and screaming wild whoops into the air; he seemed like a well-trained animal that knows not to stray past its designated running area. We didn't wave back.

And when the very overweight state trooper, gun at his hip striking his solid thigh, held open the door for us as we entered the restaurant in Texarkana, I felt a thrill of friendship for all the Chicanos who'd taught a Texas cop that to be Mexican was to be a person. Or perhaps the cop's parents raised him to treat everyone with courtesy, or maybe he raised himself to be that way.

But James would have been most proud of me that night in Houston outside the Mexican bar, where Jenkins and I sat in the patrol car with the sergeant waiting for a backup officer to arrive. A brawl was on in full swing, but we didn't leave the car. I understood what the sergeant was feeling. "I'm not getting out and going there on my own," he said. As he stated and displayed his fear, he was passing on to us—not in anger, not in pain, not even in frustration, but in total comprehension—the long history of interactions between the Houston police and the city's Hispanic community; he was acknowledging and accepting the danger and tension in their encounters. A few months earlier, a young Hispanic man, Jose Campes Torres, had been found beaten and floating in a bayou. Police brutality was suspected. The Hispanic community erupted, and police officers' lives were in danger. So there I was, both sympathizing with the officer, because here was one more instance of his having to risk his life to preserve the public peace, and, at the same time, thinking that he had partly brought this on himself. This is how racism recoils on its perpetrator. When we finally did go outside after the backup car arrived, I understood, too, why a man from the bar walked up to me and firmly blocked my camera lens, telling me angrily to get back in the car. As I wore all those shoes, it's a wonder I didn't just collapse from their weight. But surprisingly, it seemed as if I were soaring up, being lifted up magically and held aloft the scene below—two white officers holding apart two drunken Hispanic men, but doing so within a circle of other Hispanic men looking inward at them, watching their every move to see if law enforcement would step over its limits. And I saw how we were all living and acting within concentric circles, endlessly spiralling inward and outward, into and out of and into each other's lives.

• • •

James died in 1981, swiftly. A stomach cancer tore through him in six months stripping the flesh off his bones, hurling his wasted body again and again onto hospital beds and operating tables. After the funeral service, we went back to his house where his dear friend Adele fed us souffles and pies, which we ate with our tears.

I have never really left Buffalo. By some good fortune, because my husband's brother has continued to live there and his two daughters and my two are close friends, I visit the city almost every year in April. It is a comforting place, because the landmarks don't change. The street corners look like they did ten years ago; the buildings on the old campus are as weather-beaten as they always were; the Niagara river is eternally and magnificently predictable as it tumbles over into its crashing falls.

Months before James was diagnosed with cancer, while the four of us were still editing our documentary, we crossed the Peace Bridge to Canada to have a Chinese meal. When we were done eating, it was twilight outside. We stopped for a while on the bank of the river, watching the water ripple. We had no schedule to keep, nothing pressing to complete that moment. From where we sat we saw an islet with a young tree on it about a hundred yards into the river. I can't remember who it was who said, "Let's swim." But the next thing I knew, the three of them were tossing their clothes onto the bank and plunging into the water, completely naked, shouting out to me to join them in their strokes to the islet. I hesitated. But only for a few minutes. When I entered the river, the cold water froze my limbs. I'm usually a strong swimmer, but at that moment, the chill that locked my arms and legs tightly against my body was a force I couldn't break. My head went under and I must have flailed in reflex. Then I felt an arm hooked around my neck pulling me toward the bank. All three of them slapped the warmth back into my muscles, speaking to me all the time, their words drifting down, blanketing me like layers and layers of silk.

When I visit Buffalo today, I don't make pilgrimages to the sights of my filmmaking days. I know they're there. James is not buried in Buffalo, but that hardly seems to matter. The corner restaurant across campus where he would often join us for dinner still looks the same, at least from the outside, as it did all those years ago. The closed steel plants still stand, memorials to lost promises. The roads are still ravaged by the salt and ice of winter. But in this desolate city in upstate New York I renew myself, scattering this carefully held together person I carry—motherwifeteacherdaughterwriter—and becoming for a few days the chaotic nineteen-year old I was when I first came to this country wondering if the confusion I was feeling was pleasurable or painful intoxication and only dimly suspecting that it was perhaps both and always would be.

Michigan Basement II

Saleem Peeradina

Above the ground another life goes on: my life
As seen from below. In which

Children barge in and out
Of my mind's swivel door. They knock, pummel

And pulverize my consciousness. They own it.
They know its uses. A funhouse

To set up and populate with props
That never stop talking. Their shrieks

Can drill holes in the head.
In deep conversation, my legs are pillars

To negotiate: my thread of thought is snapped.
Dislodged from its hook, the heart is tossed

Like a ball. The body at rest is good
For tramping: safe, and to them, entirely un-

Breakable. They curl up in its dark
Hollows and lead my eyes to the window

To gaze at the magic of the ordinary world.
Too plain in my view, I flee into my own

Bubble. Scoldings, threats, harsh words arrest
Their step but for a second. Recognizing no barrier

In their blessed, gifted state, they breach
Nothing. I am what I appear

To them: a country without borders. My space
Is their turf. I surface, with no place to hide

Except just below the skin.
Remaining whole is no longer the point:

It's staying divided, attaining equipoise.

The Great American Movie Script

Roshni Rustomji-Kerns

For Betty Parent:
"We are one people
tied by the buried bones of antepasados"
Nina Serrano
Antepasados/Ancestors

—from *In Other Words: Literature by Latinas of the United States* edited by Roberta Fernandez

Annie Foster and I met in 1967. During an anti-war march in Berkeley. But we really didn't become good friends until we exchanged our stories about green Jell-O. Specifically, green Jell-O with fruit cocktail. That happened in the '80's. By "good friends," I mean the type of friends who become a family unit. With special shared rituals for celebrations and mournings. With an acceptance of language that doesn't need to explain the spaces between words nor demand the fine tuning of grammar. With the possibility of unembarrassed, unapologetic discussions about dreams and ghosts. The type of friends who reach a level of comfort that allows for the intensity of disagreements or love only family members can usually afford to indulge in.

From the '60's to the '80's, Annie Foster and I used our separate birth places, hers being her Aunt Mabel's home in Bethel, Alaska, U.S.A. and mine being the Parsi Lying-In Hospital in Bombay, India; our mother-languages, hers being Yupik Eskimo, mine being Gujarati; and our supposedly insurmountable cultural differences to keep us from forming a not-bonded-by-blood family unit. Although she and I were both born on October 31, she in 1934 and I in 1936, although both of us considered the very land of Northern California our home, and although very soon after we met, she and I did become related by one of the most traditional methods, marriage, we didn't really feel at home with one another until at least twenty years after we met.

When Annie and I found ourselves walking next to one another during that anti-war march, we looked at the placard that each of us was carrying as we marched along Telegraph Avenue. Right there in front of God and everybody. And of course, in front of the Berkeley cops and the FBI agents. Annie and I burst out laughing. Both placards said, "An Indian Woman Against America's War Against Vietnam."

"You," said Annie, "are from India. I am from Alaska."

"I," I said "was born in India but have lived in America since I was five years old. My name is Rhoda, short for Rhodabeh Sohrabji, and I am against this war. My sister is not against the war at all. In fact, she is there, in Vietnam, right now. As an army nurse. She would have preferred to go there as a combatant. She is quite ferocious, this sister of mine. A healer who would rather be a warrior."

Annie smiled and her eyes turned from black to gold and back again to black. I found out later that her eyes change black-gold-black in any emotional situation.

"My name is Annie Foster. I am against any and all wars. I don't know if my brother is against or for the war. But he too is there. My brother is actually a very gentle, quiet man. He should have been a healer or at least a teacher. At one time he had wanted to become a priest. But now he is a warrior." Annie smiled at me again.

I tried to explain, as best as I could, as we marched and shouted and waved our placards, that India was not the real, authentic, ancient, self-given name of the country I came from.

I didn't tell Annie that from the day my sister had left for Vietnam, my mother had called me every morning. To tell me that she had just awakened from a dream that assured her that her daughter, my sister, was still alive and unharmed. And Annie didn't mention to me until much later that she kept an eye on her brother's welfare in Vietnam through her dreams. One doesn't talk about such things in America. When I refuse to tell my mother about my dreams, she shakes her head sadly and says, "Rhoda, if we were still at home, in India, you would tell me your dreams. No one there thinks that such discussions are private or silly or crazy." I am not sure if this is true of India today. Neither my mother nor anyone else in our small family has returned to India, even as a visitor, since 1944. We had made that visit for the Navjote ceremony in Bombay in which my sister and I were officially initiated into our Zoroastrian faith. I really don't have many memories from that visit. Except that it was in Bombay, that I, brought up in Dallas, Texas, fell in love with the ocean.

When Annie and I left the march, we exchanged addresses and made vague noises about keeping in touch.

About three weeks after we met, Annie sent me a cartoon she had cut out of a newspaper. Some people in a version of Hollywood style "Indian costumes" were welcoming Christopher Columbus to their island. The leader of the welcoming party was saying, "We thank the Great Spirit for sending you to us. Ever since the Great Spirit created our land and our people, we have been lost because we have never known what to call ourselves. Now we know! We are Indians. What can we do for you who have at last told us who we are?" Annie had written, on top of the cartoon, "Hallelujah! Hallelujah! And Adam named the animals etc. This is one movie script I don't want to have anything to do with!" She also wrote a letter of appreciation to the cartoonist, met him, married him and lived relatively happily after that. But that is another story. And anyway it happened many years later. In another country. Peru.

I phoned Annie to ask about her movie script statement and found out that her ambition was to write the Great American Movie Script. It is still her ambition. She uses references to that future movie script to comment on events that surprise, disgust, please, pain or bewilder her.

After she sent me the cartoon, we met for coffee every few weeks to exchange news about our lives as graduate students at U.C. Berkeley. We discussed the war in South East Asia in general terms but we never spoke about the presence of our siblings in that area of the world. Until the day I received the following note from her: "We need to meet. Soon. Can you please meet me at the Student Union tomorrow morning? Early?" She received a note from me the same day which said, "Annie, we must meet as soon as possible. Tomorrow at 9 a.m. in the Student Union lobby?"

We both turned up at the Union steps at 8.30 the next morning. Both with two letters in our hands. She said, "What is your sister's name?" "Shireen," said I. She gave me one of her letters. I had already started with, "What is your brother's . . ." "Max," said she and I handed her one of my letters. And yes, of course, my sister and her brother had met and married. Annie and I were informed, she by her brother, I, by my sister that they had met two months ago, somewhere in Vietnam. We were further informed that at that first meeting, Shireen had yelled at Max that neither he nor she were Indians, they were Americans. He had smiled and quoted from the *Bhagvadgita*. Shireen had never read the *Gita* and was immediately impressed by its code of duty. Max had tried to explain the complications which could arise from such a code. Shireen had disagreed with him and in the process fallen in love with him. And he with her. The two of them of course, had no idea that Annie and I had met. In an effort to end the war. To bring them home to the States. As soon as possible.

Annie and I grinned at one another. Her eyes turned from black to gold to black. I said, "We are sisters-in-law, or some such thing. We should celebrate. Exchange gifts. I'll get you a sari."

But then we both stopped grinning. She and I exchanged the second letters we had received.

Hers was from her father. It said: "Dear Annie, By now Max must have written to you to tell you that he has married an Indian woman. From India. In Vietnam. Why couldn't he, my only son, have married a real American woman? There are American women even in Vietnam.

"I have nothing against Indians from India but what will happen to my grandchildren? Max's children? What will Max's wife know anything about us? About our ways? What will happen if her family looks down upon us and thinks that we exist only in history books or movies?

"You know that our Max will have exceptionally wonderful children. Beautiful, healthy, smart. And I am afraid that his wife's family will not let us keep my grandchildren. And even if I will be allowed to teach them our ways, they will insist on making them as Asian as possible. The Asians don't like to lose their children to other cultures. And I don't blame them. And in that other war, when I went to Japan, did I marry an Asian woman? No. I came back and married a woman of my own people! We can't afford to lose—in any way—any more of our children. You of all people know that better than most others. Why couldn't your brother have just married an American? If not from our own people, at least a born-in-America American. Some of those younger people are getting interested in our culture and our ways.

"Your Aunt Mabel is very happy about the marriage. She keeps on talking about how she has dreamed that Max will have twins. A son and a daughter. I am glad about that but I would have been happier if he had married an American woman. And if I were assured that my grandchildren will be counted among us. Alaska Natives. Yupik Eskimos. Love, Dad"

I turned to Annie and said, "But Shireen is an American. She came here when she was four. She is more American than most of my born-in-the-United States of America friends! At one time, when she was about seven-years old, she was so insistent about proving herself, and us, her family, as being American that she forced us to recite the Pledge of Allegiance every Friday evening. Before dinner. We pledged allegiance for about three weeks before we rebelled. To compensate for our rebellion and to assure her that we were Americans, my parents bought an American flag and stuck a flag pole in the middle of our front lawn. And they hoisted that flag not only on all the patriotic holidays but also on Shireen's birthday. They still fly that flag on special occasions."

Annie shook her head. "I hear they do such things in Texas. That is a movie script I didn't write! But I don't know about our fathers, Rhoda. Our siblings are barely married and our fathers are already talking about grandchildren. Oh well! It will be my job to begin educating my father about Indians, from India, in America. Somehow I will persuade him that Shireen is an American. I am not sure if the Pledge of Allegiance will quite work out. Even though he was in the army and all that, he has mixed feelings about the American government and their continuing insistence on presenting us with the American flag."

"Frances Scott Key composed 'The Star Spangled Banner' on the *Minden* . . ."

"I know that."

"But you didn't know that the ship was built for the British Royal Navy in Bombay. By the Wadias. Parsi master shipbuilders."

Annie looked mildly interested. "I don't know if that will help either. But I know that your sister being a warrior—a healer and a warrior—will work well. But what about your father, Rhoda? Red Indians?? Some educating of your parents is needed there!"

My father had written to me that he was extremely upset about Shireen's marriage to Max. He said that he was proud and happy to be in America. The best place on earth. But what was the use of being in America, in the New World, with two healthy children when one, namely I, was turning out to be a *nimak-haram*, a betrayer of the salt of the country which had taken us in and given us so much? The last of course, was in reference to my anti-war stand and my never-quiet criticism of the US government. My father had copies of signed pictures of every single President of the United States, from George Washington onwards, on the walls of the waiting room of his dental office. In those days, he refused to listen to me when I told him that I wouldn't take the trouble to try and change the US of A if I didn't consider it my country.

After expressing his disappointment in me, my father went on to write about Shireen's marriage. He was extremely proud of her for having volunteered to take care of "our boys in Vietnam" who were protecting democracy and America in that far away Asian land. But now she had gone ahead and gotten married. Without telling her parents about her plans. That didn't upset him as much as the fact that she had married not a Parsi, as was expected of her, but an outsider. Were there Parsis in the American forces in Vietnam? Most probably. But she had not found a Parsi to marry there in Vietnam nor had she waited to come back home, to America, to find a Parsi husband.

My father wrote, "I would have taken her to Bombay and Karachi, to find a good Parsi boy for her, if she so desired. It is an offer I have made so often to you. An offer you won't even consider. But Rhodabeh, if Shireen chose to marry outside our faith, outside our community, why didn't she marry a real, regular American? I don't think your mother and I have ever even met a Red Indian. Annie says he is a Yupik Eskimo. A Native American. Why is this man in Vietnam? I thought they all live on reservations. I do honor him for fighting for his country and I am sure he is a very nice man. He wrote a very respectful letter to us about how much he loved Shireen and how he will take care of her.

"But I ask you, Rhodabeh, who will perform the Navjote ceremonies for Shireen's children? You know that it is hard enough to find a *mobed* who will perform the Navjote for a child of a Zoroastrian Parsi woman married to a non-Zoroastrian. Your mother and I think that is not at all correct. After all, your mother's great-great-grandmother was a Chinese lady who married your great-great-grandfather. He of course, was a Parsi and so his children were counted as Parsis. But Shireen will obviously not be a Parsi father! Some of our Parsis are getting so conservative about our girls marrying outside the community and the Navjotes for their children and all that. And if there are no Navjotes for the children born to our Shireen, will her children, my grandchildren, be counted as Parsis, Jarthoshtis? Even if you, Rhodabeh, don't care about our dwindling numbers—less than 10,000 of us and getting fewer! . . . I care very much. I am very disturbed by all this, I tell you. And even if we do find a *mobed* who will be willing to perform the Navjote ceremony for Shireen's children, will he still go ahead and perform our ancient Iranian, Jarthoshti *sudreh-kusti* ceremony for my grandchildren when he finds out that the father is a Red Indian? We don't know what religion he follows. Will Shireen's husband and his family allow the children to become Zoroastrians?

"I tell you Rhodabeh," my father never calls me Rhoda when he is upset, "I try to be tolerant and open-minded. After all, we are all children of God but we can't afford to lose our ancient faith and our children.

"Your mother, as usual, is not worried. She says she is happy for Shireen and that Max Foster sounds like a very nice man. She wants to meet his family as soon as possible. I don't want to go to Alaska. So please persuade your mother not to go overboard about this marriage. I will try to make the best of this situation. We will just tell people that Shireen has married a soldier in the American army in Vietnam. When we see what he looks like and find out what he believes in, we will decide if we need to tell people that he is not quite a real, regular American. Love, Daddy."

Annie's Aunt Mabel and my mother persuaded the two fathers to calm down. They assured the two men that their children's children would learn about both cultures, that my mother would find a *mobed* to perform the Navjote for each and every child Shireen and Max had and that they could see no reason, legal or otherwise, why the children couldn't be numbered among their mother's ethnic, racial and religious community as well as their father's ethnic, racial and religious community. Practical women that they are, they made the two future aunts, Annie and myself, promise that we would see to it that our nieces and nephews were taught to state, "Alaska Native-Yupik Eskimo/Asian Indian-Parsi-Zoroastrian" (alphabetical order) in the appropriate spaces about religion and ethnicity on all and every form and questionnaire they had to fill out. Throughout their lives. In the United States or elsewhere.

My mother went to Alaska before Shireen and Max returned from Vietnam. Aunt Mabel came to Dallas to see her great-niece and -nephew a year later when Max and Annie came to the States for the birth of the twins. Max and my sister went back to Vietnam leaving the twins in the care of Aunt Mabel and my mother. Aunt Mabel stayed with my parents in Dallas for the next two years.

Shireen was killed in Vietnam only two months before America got out of there. I don't think any of us have quite accepted that fact even now. But we have managed to live with the information about her death that we received from the army. Her body was never found. But we did get a flag.

My mother or Annie consistently report dreams in which Shireen is still alive. Somewhere in Asia. Trying to remember who she is so she can return home. I try not to pay too much attention when either my mother or Annie tell me about their Shireen dreams. As far as I am concerned, dreams are messy, inelegant, and undependable.

When we got the news about Shireen, Annie's eyes turned from black to gold. They turned back to black seven months later. When she began to dream that Shireen was still alive. In the short time that she and Shireen had been together, after the birth of the twins, the two women had become very good friends. Something that I didn't quite understand and, yes, was a bit jealous about.

I was the one who had to call Annie about Shireen's death. Annie demanded, "Who wrote this movie script anyway? Don't they know the rules? Haven't they seen enough Hollywood movies? In a marriage across racial, ethnic lines, the man or woman of non-white color is to die and leave the spouse-lover behind ONLY if the other person in the couple is white." Annie wasn't crying. She was shouting. "It's not every day that one gains a sister. Especially if one has only one brother. And we know that he will not marry again. And anyway, Shireen wasn't my sister-in-law, she was my sister."

I tried to comfort her by pointing out that I was still her sister-in-law of sorts and that we did have the twins and Max.

Shireen's death brought Max's father to Texas to be with my father. And the two men remain close friends to this day although my father has yet to go to Alaska. They write long letters to one another about the importance of keeping up traditions and the old ways. Max says that the two men should go down in history. His father-in-law as the only Parsi who knows as much as a non-Alaska

Native could know about Yupik Eskimos and his father as the first Yupik Eskimo scholar of Zoroastrianism.

The twins were named by my mother and Aunt Mabel. Aava, Sacred Water, is our niece. Zaal, Young Warrior with White Hair, is our nephew.

After the war, Max became a travel writer specializing in the United States and Canada and took the two children with him wherever he went. The three of them have always spent long vacations in Dallas or Alaska or the San Francisco Bay Area.

After we graduated, Annie became a free lance journalist and writer of mystery novels. She recently bought a condo in San Francisco. I was hired as Assistant Professor in the mathematics department at Sierra College in San Mateo and have lived in Pescadero over the last fifteen years. The Pacific Ocean is only a ten minute walk from my home. My mother did find a *mobed* in Texas to perform the Navjote for Aava and Zaal when they were eight years old. She still refuses to allow anyone to include Shireen's name among the list of our dead ancestors and relatives during our annual family ceremonies and prayers of thanksgiving.

After graduating from high school, Zaal joined the airforce. Aava decided to do her undergraduate work at Sierra College. She graduated, in Environmental Sciences, with honors, a year ahead of schedule. Since she hadn't bothered to inform any of us until the last moment about her early graduation, Annie and I were delegated by the two families to be their representatives at the Commencement Exercises. Annie and I decided to take Aava to her favorite restaurant, Duarte's Tavern, in Pescadero, after the ceremony.

But Annie didn't show up either at the Commencement or at the restaurant. I got her answering machine every time I called her that evening and late into the night. Aava who has inherited a belief in dreams and a dexterity in paranormal skills from her maternal grandmother and her paternal aunt, told me that she was sure her Auntie Annie was all right. We weren't overly worried because Annie's work, both journalism and mystery writing, often forces her to take off to strange places at a moment's notice. And Annie has been known to forget an appointment with family or friends when she is starting a new book.

Annie called me the next day. At 11 a.m. She had just been discharged from the hospital where she had spent the night after an accident on her way to the Commencement. She had been too drugged and too much in pain to call me earlier. I told her not to move from her bed until I arrived at her door and asked if I could do anything for her on my way over.

"Yes," she said, "Can you please bring me something to eat? I am very hungry and there is nothing of great interest in my refrigerator. And I am not bedridden. Just a bit shaken up."

"What would you like to eat?" I asked her.

"If it isn't too much trouble, that spicy chicken you make. Or any other type of chicken. Except the Colonel's. Any spicy food. And Green Jell-O with fruit cocktail. Actually what I want the most right now is that Green Jell-O with fruit in it."

I didn't say anything.

When my silence continued, Annie sounded somewhat irritated. "What's the matter? Do you have something against Jell-O with fruit cocktail?

"No. It's just that I have never made it. I don't like it."

"Rhoda! Jell-O is the easiest thing in the world to make. You can also buy it in that deli near your house. You don't have to eat it. Bring yourself some cookies or something. Right now, your company and Green Jell-O with fruit cocktail will go a long way to make me feel better. My special comfort food and another Indian is what I need now. That stupid car just plowed right into me."

I took the chicken *dhan-sak* I had frozen for emergencies. Both Aava and Zaal have a habit of turning up at my house and saying, "Rhodabeh Masi, I am dying for good, hot, spicy, Parsi food."

The green Jell-O with fruit cocktail that I bought at the deli was actually quite pretty and festive. Christmasy green. Perfectly molded with precisely placed curves. Yellow, green, and red fruit appeared at careful intervals inside the Jell-O and four bright red maraschino cherries perched outside on the crown. The lady at the deli gave me a container of whipped cream to go with the whole production.

After we ate, I insisted on Annie coming with me to my house and staying with me for a few days. I wanted to keep an eye on her. She brought the leftover portion of the green Jell-O to my house together with her typewriter and a change of clothes. She spent a week with me, and one afternoon taught me how to make Jell-O with fruit cocktail. It was red, not green, Jell-O.

Two days after that cooking lesson, Annie woke up looking quite upset and retreated into my office. I heard her typing for at least four hours. Later that evening she showed me what she had written. It was an article about her accident in which she credited her quick recovery to me, her sister-in-law-of sorts, Rhodabeh, Rhoda for short, Sohrabji and green Jell-O with fruit cocktail. And then she discussed, not quite briefly, how she, who prided herself on always being alert to cultural differences had blown it with me. She, Annie, had demanded her own culturally defined comfort food, green Jell-O with fruit cocktail, from me who apparently didn't have the same comfort foods. I who obviously didn't even like that dessert, had to first buy the Jell-O from a deli and then be forced to learn how to make it. In my own kitchen. Annie wrote that she had forgotten that Jell-O, a food that is basic, easy to prepare and pretty good to eat as far as many Americans are concerned, may not be basic, easy or tasty for many other Americans. Americans such as her "transported from India" friend and relative, Rhoda Sohrabji.

"I couldn't of course include the dream I had the night before the accident. One doesn't do such things in newspaper articles." Annie said to me. "I saw Shireen sitting with you and Aava at Duarte's Tavern. All three of you were eating. Shireen turned to me and said, 'Annie, don't worry too much when you miss my Aava's graduation. Very soon you will be on your way to Asia.' What do you think about that. Rhoda? As you know, I really don't like to travel much. I leave that to Max."

As I have mentioned, I am uncomfortable around insubstantial subjects. Except of course, some forms of mathematics. When Annie asked me what I thought about her dream, I wanted to talk about more tangible matters. Such as the two egrets I had seen in the Pescadero marsh the week before. Such as my looking forward to the annual visit of the red-tailed hawk that swoops down— once, twice, three times—in my backyard at the beginning of fall. Such as the astonishing green-gray color of the ocean the day before as it retreated from Pescadero Beach at low tide. As I began to talk about these matters of the earth and the ocean, I got a picture of Shireen. Shireen and myself as young girls, sitting at a table, staring at a bowl of green Jell-O with fruit.

I decided it was time to tell Annie the story about Shireen, myself and green Jell-O with fruit cocktail. A story from Texas transported to California. I had not told that story to anyone before. And as far as I know, nor had Shireen.

"Do you want to know why I don't like green Jell-O, with or without fruit?" I asked Annie.

"Not your ethnic, cultural comfort food. And you didn't grow up on US Government Issue food the way I did."

"Yes," I said. And then I told Annie the following story.

When I was eight years old and Shireen was about seven, before we went to India for our Navjote, my best friend of that year, Judy Taylor, invited both of us to spend a weekend, a Saturday and Sunday, with her and her family.

Shireen and I didn't know that we were expected to attend church with the Taylors on Sunday or that Mr. Taylor was a Minister. My sister and I of course knew something about the Christian story. And we were vaguely aware that in Christian churches the Minister preached and prayed and everybody in the church prayed and sang. But neither of us had ever attended a church before. Our first experience was in a church where we were the only two non-white people in the congregation. The church was presided over by Mr. Taylor. A friendly, funny, gentle man at home, he became a born-again, fire-and-brimstone preacher in that church. And he pitched his sermon at us. Two little heathen girls. He said—and he said it very loudly—he couldn't believe it! Heathens in America! In American schools! His heart wept for us. He knew that his little daughter, Judy, had befriended us because God had sent a message to her heart to befriend us and to bring us to her father's church. Judy whispered to me that she had befriended me because we both liked math. Mr. Taylor of course, didn't hear her. He went on to state that his mission in life was to save people such as the two little visitors in his church. He wanted to save two such sweet, well-behaved little girls from the terrors of hell.

Mr. Taylor spoke. The congregation prayed with him and then all of them stood up and sang hymns. Shireen and I also stood up but of course neither of us knew the songs. I tried to hum along because I really liked the sound of some of the songs. I had stopped listening to Mr. Taylor after about the first five minutes. He was so loud that I couldn't understand him and I was fascinated by the hat the lady in front of me was wearing. It had birds and flowers and a huge yellow bow. I wondered what my mother, who always wore saris, would look like in such a fantastic hat. Judy whispered to me that the hat was ugly and old-fashioned.

Shireen had paid attention to every single word of that sermon and was terrified. Since I hadn't really heard much more after Mr. Taylor's statement about saving us from the terrors of hell, and since I rather liked Mr. Taylor and wasn't particularly terrified by hell, I didn't know what to say or do to make Shireen lose that look of a hunted rabbit as we came out of the church.

Mr. Taylor's sermon continued during lunch at Judy's house. But now, Mr. Taylor was back to his gentle, sweet self. He spoke softly. He patted our heads and hands while he spoke. And Shireen became more and more terrified. She pushed her mashed potatoes all around her plate. She barely ate the fried chicken as she listened to Mr. Taylor. She stopped eating completely when he pulled out a dollar bill and said, "America is God's country. A Christian country. See? Young lady, read out what it says here!" He held the dollar under Shireen's nose and pointed a bit above the picture of George Washington. Shireen read aloud, "In God We Trust."

"Yes," said Mr. Taylor. "One God. The God. The God of our fathers. Jesus Christ the Son of God died so we, all of us, can be saved. And this is a good, Christian country. And the two of you are very good little girls. But how can you be true Americans if you are not Christians?" And he put another piece of chicken and another dollop of mashed potatoes on Shireen's plate. He didn't seem to notice that she had tears running down her face as he asked his wife for a cup of coffee.

Mrs. Taylor went off to the kitchen to get the coffee and I tried to distract Shireen by pointing at the dessert in the middle of the round table covered with a pale blue, very delicate lace table cloth. Shireen loved desserts and the color blue. Any and all desserts. Any and all shades of blue. The dessert in the middle of the table was green Jell-O with pieces of bright colored fruit stuck inside it.

Shireen, Judy and I watched in awe, as Judy's baby sister who was sitting on a high chair, began to take advantage of her mother's absence. She reached over and started to pull off globs of that green Jell-O. Some of it did find its way into the little girl's mouth but most of it was smeared, with immense concentration and satisfaction, all over her face and into her hair. Mr. Taylor didn't seem to notice anything his little daughter was doing.

Mrs. Taylor returned to the dining table and looked at her baby daughter and my sister with dismay. She picked up a napkin and began wiping the Jell-O from the little girl's face who set up quite a lamentation. Then Mrs. Taylor tried to dry my sister's tears with the same napkin. My sister continued to cry silently. While she was wiping off the Jell-O and the tears, Mrs. Taylor tried to talk to her daughter and Shireen. "There, there, Shireen. You naughty little girl . . . not you Shireen . . . But Shireen there is nothing to cry about honey! Don't be afraid. Mr. Taylor is trying to help you and Rhoda. He is trying to give you a wonderful gift. Just listen to him, honey. There is nothing to fear about Christianity. No, you may not have any more Jell-O." That last part was for her little daughter.

Mrs. Taylor didn't realize that it wasn't Christianity that was terrifying Shireen into tears. It was the whole question of being an American, a good American, a real American that was scaring her.

Shireen had become obsessed by the idea of being an American a week before that lunch at the Taylors. The Monday before that Sunday lunch, Shireen had come home covered with mud, her clothes torn, a bruise on her cheek—the right one—and dried blood around her nose. One of her classmates, Gloria Allen, had told her that she wasn't a real American. Because she was dark and wasn't a Christian. Gloria had suggested that if Shireen drank lots and lots of milk and took at least three showers a day, her complexion might improve. She also suggested that Shireen tell our parents to look for a Christian church where we could worship. Her church didn't allow "colored people," or foreigners. Shireen didn't mind the milk part but she hated water in the form of showers, baths, swimming pools. She didn't know what to make about the church part.

Shireen didn't begin the fight until Gloria told her that we, all of us, were uncivilized. We didn't always speak English in our home and my mother wore strange clothes. Apparently Shireen hit out when Gloria told her that her uncle said that all of us foreigners should be deported.

Shireen started crying as soon as she came home. "Mummy," she sobbed, "where will we go when they deeeport us? I don't want to go anywhere else. I like Dallas. I like Texas. I like America." And then she hid her face in our mother's lap and said, "Please, please Mummy, please don't wear saris anymore. Not outside the house. I love you very much but please don't wear saris! And I promise I will take two showers a day. Every day." I don't know who won the fight but I do know that it took my mother at least three hours to clean and calm my sister.

But to return to that Sunday lunch at Judy's house, Shireen's terror about being "deeported" was being intensified by Mr. Taylor's efforts to help us with his official and unofficial sermon about Christianity and America.

Mr. Taylor looked at his wife with the napkin in her hand and noticed Shireen's tears. "Little girl," he said, "Don't cry. Don't you like chicken and potatoes? Don't worry. You don't have to eat them. Here take some Jell-O. It's really good."

Mrs. Taylor carefully carved us Jell-O servings from the side that had not been demolished by her daughter. Judy said that the gouged-out side reminded her of Mount Rushmore. Shireen stopped crying and did eat the dessert. It may have been the last time that she and I ate green Jell-O with fruit cocktail.

Annie laughed at my story. "What a script! I don't blame you. Definitely not in the comfort food category for you and Shireen."

I told her that there was more to the story.

A few days later, while Shireen was still trying to get over her fear of hell and "deeeportation," the Allens visited us. Mr. and Mrs. Allen had just heard about the fight and had brought Gloria to apologize to Shireen. Mr. Allen who was in the army, assured Shireen that he thought of us as Americans, very good Americans. He didn't agree with Gloria's uncle at all. That night Shireen announced at the dining table, "I am going to be the best American from India. I'll be the best American in the whole world." And demanded that we recite the Pledge of Allegiance every Friday but instead got a flag which was flown on our front lawn on her birthdays. Gloria and Shireen became good friends. They both became nurses and both went to Vietnam. Shireen met Max, married him, had twins, reenlisted and died in the service of her country.

Annie said, "Who wants to writes such scripts anyway?"

And then she told me why green Jell-O with fruit cocktail is her most important comfort food.

"As you know," Annie said, "my mother died when I was five. A few weeks after Max was born. Max and I were brought up by our father and his sister, Aunt Mabel."

I knew that. I also knew that the first time Max met my mother when she welcomed him and Shireen into our house with the ceremony of an egg, a coconut, and a handful of rice, Max leaned down, hugged my mother and said, "I have waited a long time to find a woman I can call 'mother.' Hello Mom."

Annie didn't often speak about her mother. Or her mother's death.

"During my mother's funeral, I heard one of the women say, 'Shouldn't someone inform Mr. and Mrs. Richardson about Ellie's mother's death?' 'No,' said

Aunt Mabel, 'Part of the deal was that we would not have anything more to do with Ellie. And anyway she is only five years old.' I was trying to find anything that would help me move away from the pain of my mother's death. I said, 'I too am five years old!' And the woman who had spoken earlier said, 'Of course dear, Ellie after all is your twin sister.' And that is when I found out that I had a twin sister who had been adopted out the day we were born.

"I went to my father and demanded that since he said he couldn't bring back my mother, at least he should bring back my sister. She wasn't dead. And a sister would help me stop hurting so much inside my eyes, chest and stomach. That is where, I told him, I missed my Mom the most. My father went to his bedroom, carried Max to me and put him in my arms and then walked out of the house.

"To this day, neither my father nor Aunt Mabel will tell me anything more about my twin sister's adoption. Except that they had promised that no one in the family would ever try to contact Ellie.

"That first time I heard about my twin sister, at my mother's funeral, I could not stop crying. And I wouldn't let anyone come near me. I sat down on the floor, holding Max, and I cried and cried. I let my father take Max when he promised me that no one would take Max away from us. But I refused to eat anything. For at least three days. Until I saw my Aunt Mabel crying. When I asked her if she were crying because of my mother and my twin sister, she said, 'No, I am crying because I don't know what to do to make you eat. What to do to make your pain go away.' And I said, 'OK, I'll eat. But something nice and special. Something sweet!' And since the US Government always provided us with lots of Jell-O and canned fruit cocktail, Aunt Mabel made me a big bowl of green Jell-O with fruit cocktail. She held me on her lap and fed me that whole bowl of Jell-O herself. And she sang me songs and told me stories and kissed me at least four times. As you know, Aunt Mabel is not into overt demonstrations of affection. I stopped crying and sometimes it seems as if I haven't stopped eating since that day! And green Jell-O with fruit cocktail always reminds me that I do have people who love me. And it nearly always comforts me. It didn't when we got the news about Shireen's disappearance."

"Death." I corrected her. Half-heartedly.

At that point, the telephone rang. It was Aava. She said, "I have great news for you and Auntie Annie."

"She's right here." I informed our niece. Annie picked up the extension across the room.

"Here's the news. Zaal and I are applying for all kinds of fellowships and scholarships and whatever. Because he and I have decided that we want to go to India. Work there. Live there. At least for some time. And Dad, the grandparents, plus of course, Aunt Mabel have promised to visit us there. What do you think of that? Zaal and I want to see where our mother and you, Rhodabeh Masi, were born. Oh yes, and on our way to India we are going to stop off in Vietnam. To see where our mother died."

When we hung up the telephone, Annie turned to me.

"This, Rhodabeh, is a script I want to write! What about following our niece and nephew to their mother's motherland? It will be my Great American Movie Script. About two middle-aged Indian women detectives who go from America to Asia. In search of their sister who supposedly died in Vietnam. But in reality she got lost on her way to America from Vietnam and ended up in India. And since she can't quite figure out who she is, where's home, she sends messages through dreams to the people who can rescue her. To the two sisters who live in Northern California. What do you think about that, Rhoda? Shall we go and check out locations for the movie? In Vietnam? India?"

I sat myself down behind my California Mission-style desk, looked straight at Annie and told her that ever since her accident I had been dreaming of India and America. Indian trains and Indian monsoons in America. The Grand Canyon and the Taos pueblo in India. And I had been dreaming of ancestors. Ancestors long dead in Iran, in India, in China. Our sister Shireen, dead in Vietnam. The death—in the future—of my parents, her father, her aunt, her brother, herself and myself. In America. And of course, that was the beginning of our real friendship. In my living room in Pescadero, California.

I don't know if the world is ready for Annie's Great American Movie, but I told her I would go with her to Asia.

"In Search of Evanescence"

Agha Shahid Ali

"It was a year of brilliant water."

—Thomas De Quincey

2

It was a year of brilliant water
in Pennsylvania that final summer
seven years ago, the sun's quick reprints

in my attaché case: those students
of mist have drenched me with dew, I'm driving
away from that widow's house, my eyes open

to a dream of drowning. But even
when I pass—in Ohio—the one exit
to Calcutta, I don't know I've begun

mapping America, the city limits
of Evanescence now everywhere. It
was a year of brilliant water, Phil,

such a cadence of dead seas at each turn:
so much refused to breathe in those painted
reflections, trapped there in ripples of hills:
a woman climbed the steps to Acoma,
vanished into the sky. In the ghost towns
of Arizona, there were charcoal tribes

with desert voices, among their faces
always the last speaker of a language.
And there was always thirst: a train taking me

from Bisbee, that copper landscape with bones,
into a twilight with no water. Phil,
I never told you where I'd been these years,

swearing fidelity to anyone.
Now there's only regret: I didn't send you
my routes of Evanescence. You never wrote.

3
When on Route 80 in Ohio
I came across an exit
to Calcutta

the temptation to write a poem
led me past the exit
so I could say

India always exists
off the turnpikes
of America

so I could say
I did take the exit
and crossed Howrah

and even mention the Ganges
as it continued its sobbing
under the bridge

so when I paid my toll
I saw trains rush by
one after one

on their roofs old passengers
each ready to surrender
his bones for tickets

so that I heard
the sun's percussion
on tamarind leaves

heard the empty cans of children
filling only with the shadows
of leaves

that behind the unloading trucks
were the voices of vendors
bargaining over women

so when the trees
let down their tresses
the monsoon oiled and braided them

and when the wind again parted them
this was the temptation
to end the poem this way:

The warm rains have left
many dead on the pavements

The signs to Route 80
all have disappeared

And now the road is a river
polished silver by cars

The cars are urns
carrying ashes to the sea

4

Someone wants me to live   A language will die with me

                      (once
spoken by proud tribesmen
in the canyons east
of the Catalinas   or much farther north

in the Superstition Mountains)   It will die with me

(Someone wants me to live)

It has the riches consonants   exact
for any cluster of sorrows

that haunt the survivors of Dispersal   that country
which has no map

but it has histories   most
of them forgotten
scraps of folklore   (once

in mountains   there were silver cities
with flags   on every rooftop
on each flag a prayer   read

by the wind   a passer-by forgiven all
when the wind became his shirt)

Someone wants me to live
so he can learn

those prayers
that language   he is asking me
questions

He wants me to live

and as I speak he is freezing
my words   he will melt them
years later

to listen   and listen
to the water   of my voice

when he is the last
speaker of his language

10

Shahid, you never
    found Evanescence.
        And how could

you have? You didn't throw
    away addresses from
        which streets

departed, erasing
    their names. Some
        of those streets,

lost at junctions, were
            run over by trains.
                        At stations

where you waited, history
            was too late:
                        those trains

rushed by and disappeared
            into mirrors
                        in which

massacres were hushed.
            No reporters
                        were allowed

in. You waited to hear
            the glass break,
                        but no train

came back. And then
            on those mirrors
                        curtains

were drawn. You didn't
            throw away addresses,
                        and some

of those streets
            were picked up
                        at exits

that took them
          in cities miles
                    under the ocean

from where postcards came
          with Africa washed
                    off them.

You didn't throw away
          addresses from which
                    streets

departed. There's
          no one you know
                    in this world.

11
"Phil was afraid of being forgotten."
It's again that summer, Phil, and the end
of that summer again. Good-bye, I am

saying to those student of mist, leaving
Pennsylvania with the sun's reprints.
Ahead is a year of brilliant water—

there's nothing in this world but hope: I have
everyone's address. Everyone will write:
And there's everything in this world but hope.

Snow on the Desert

Agha Shahid Ali

"Each ray of sunshine is seven minutes old,"
Serge told me in New York one December night.

"So when I look at the sky, I see the past?"
"Yes, Yes," he said. "especially on a clear day."

On January 19, 1987,
as I very early in the morning
drove my sister to Tucson International,

suddenly on Alvernon and 22nd Street
the sliding doors of the fog were opened,

and the snow, which had fallen all night, now
sun-dazzled, blinded us, the earth whitened

out, as if by cocaine, the desert's plants,
its mineral-hard colors extinguished,
wine frozen in the veins of the cactus.

•   •   •

The Desert Smells Like Rain: in it I read:
The syrup from which sacred wine is made

is extracted from the saguaros each
summer. The Papagos place it in jars,

where the last of it softens, then darkens
into a color of blood though it tastes

strangely sweet, almost white, like a dry wine.
As I tell Sameetah this, we are still

seven miles away. "And you know the flowers
of the saguaros bloom only at night?"

We are driving slowly, the road is glass.
"Imagine where we are was a sea once.

Just imagine!" The sky is relentlessly
sapphire, and the past is happening quickly:

the saguaros have opened themselves, stretched
out their arms to rays millions of years old,

in each ray a secret of the planet's
origin, the rays hurting each cactus

into memory, a human memory—
for they are human, the Papagos say:

not only because they have arms and veins
and secrets. But because they too are a tribe,

vulnerable to massacre. "It is like
the end, perhaps the beginning of the world,"

Sameetah says, staring at their snow-sleeved
arms. And we are driving by the ocean

that evaporated here, by its shores,

the past now happening so quickly that each

stoplight hurts us into memory, the sky
taking rapid notes on us as we turn

at Tucson Boulevard and drive into
the airport, and I realize that the earth

is thawing from longing into longing and
that we are being forgotten by those arms.

.   .   .

At the airport I stared after her plane
till the window was

again a mirror.
As I drove back to the foothills, the fog

shut its doors behind me on Alvernon,
and I breathed the dried seas

the earth had lost,
their forsaken shores. And I remembered

another moment that refers only
to itself:

in New Delhi one night
as Begum Akhtar sang, the lights went out.

It was perhaps during the Bangladesh War,
perhaps there were sirens,

air-raid warnings.
But the audience, hushed, did not stir.

The microphone was dead, but she went on
singing, and her voice

was coming from far
away, as if she had already died.

And just before the lights did flood her
again, melting the frost

of her diamond
into rays, it was, like this turning dark

of fog, a moment when only a lost sea
can be heard, a time

to recollect
every shadow, everything the earth was losing,

a time to think of everything the earth
and I had lost, of all

that I would lose,
of all that I was losing.

Out on Main Street

Shani Mootoo

1.

Janet and me? We does go Main Street to see pretty pretty sari and bangle, and to eat we belly full a burfi and gulub jamoon, but we doh go too often because, yuh see, is dem sweets self what does give people like we a presupposition for untameable hip and thigh.

Another reason we shy to frequent dere is dat we is watered-down Indians — we ain't good grade A Indians. We skin brown, is true, but we doh even think 'bout India unless something happen over dere and it come on de news. Mih family remain Hindu ever since mih ancestors leave India behind, but nowadays dey doh believe in praying unless things real bad, because, as mih father always singing, like if is a mantra: "Do good and good will be bestowed unto you." So he is a veritable saint cause he always doing good by his women friends and dey children. I sure some a dem must be mih half sister and brother, oui!

Mostly, back home, we is kitchen Indians: some kind a Indian food every day, at least once a day, but we doh get cardamom and other fancy spice down dere so de food not spicy like Indian food I eat in restaurants up here. But it have one thing we doh make joke 'bout down dere: we like we meethai and sweetrice too much, and it remain overly authentic, like de day Naana and Naani step off de boat in Port of Spain harbour over a hundred and sixty years ago. Check out dese hips here nah, dey is pure sugar and condensed milk, pure sweetness!

But Janet family different. In de ole days when Canadian missionaries land in Trinidad dey used to make a bee-line straight for Indians from down South. And Janet great grandparents is one a de first South families day exchange over from Indian to Presbyterian. Dat was a long time ago.

When Janet born, she father, one Mr. John Mahase, insist on asking de Reverend MacDougal from Trace Settlement Church, a leftover from de Canadian Mission, to name de baby girl. De good Reverend choose de name Constance cause dat was his mother name. But de mother a de child, Mrs. Savitri Mahase, wanted to name de child sheself. Ever since Savitri was a lil girl she like de yellow hair fair skin and pretty pretty clothes Janet and John used to wear in de primary school reader – since she lil she want to change she name from Savitri to Janet but she own father get vex and say how Savitri was his mother name and how she will insult his mother if she gone and change it. So Savitri get she own way once by marrying this fella name John, and she do a encore, by calling she daughter Janet, even doh husband John upset for days at she for insulting de good Reverend by throwing out de name a de Reverend mother.

So dat is how my girlfriend, a darkskin Indian girl with thick black hair (pretty fuh so!) get a name like Janet.

She come from a long line a Presbyterian school teacher, headmaster and headmistress. Savitri still teaching from de same Janet and John reader in a primary school in San Fernando, and John, getting more and more obtuse in his ole age, is headmaster more dan twenty years now in Princes Town Boys' Presbyterian High School. Everybody back home know dat family good good. Dat is why Janet leave in two twos. Soon as A Level finish she pack up and take off like a jet plane so she could live without people only shoo-shooing behind she back . . . "But A A! Yuh ain't hear de goods 'bout John Mahase daughter, gyul? How yuh mean yuh ain't hear? Is a big thing! Everybody talking 'bout she. Hear dis, nah! Yuh ever see she wear a dress? Yes! Doh look at mih so. Yuh reading mih right!"

Is only recentish I realize Mahase is a Hindu last name. In de ole days every Mahese in de country turn Presbyterian and now de name doh have no association with Hindu or Indian whatsoever. I used to think of it as a Presbyterian Church name until some days ago when we meet a Hindu fella fresh from India name Yogdesh Mahese who never even hear of Presbyterian.

De other day I ask Janet what she know 'bout Divali. She say, "It's the Hindu festival of lights, isn't it?" like a line straight out a dictionary. Yuh think she know anything 'bout how lord Rama get himself exile in a forest fourteen years, and how when it come time for him to go back home his followers light up a pathway to help him make his way out, and dat is what Divali lights is all about? All Janet know is 'bout going for drive in de country to see light, and she could remember looking forward, around Divali time, to the lil brown paper-bag packages full a burfi and parasad that she father Hindu students used to bring for him.

One time in a Indian restaurant she ask for parasad for dessert. Well! Since den I never go back in dat restaurant, I embarrass fuh so!

I used to think I was a Hindu *par excellence* until I come up here and see real flesh and blood Indian from India. Up here, I learning 'bout all kind a custom and food and music and clothes dat we never see or hear 'bout in good ole Trinidad. Is de next best thing to going to India, in truth, oui! But Indian store clerk on Main Street doh have no patience with us, specially when we talking English to dem. Yuh ask dem a question in English and dey insist on giving de answer in Hindi or Punjabi or Urdu or Gujarati. How I suppose to know de difference even! And den dey look at yuh disdainful disdainful– like yuh disloyal, like yuh is a traitor.

But yuh know, it have one other reason I real reluctant to go Main Street. Yuh see, Janet pretty fuh so! And I doh like de way men does look at she, as if because she wearing jeans and T-shirt and high-heel shoe and make-up and have long hair loose and flying about like she is a walking-talking shampoo ad, dat she easy. And de women always looking at she beady eye, like she loose and going to thief dey man. Dat kind a thing always make me want to put mih arm round she waist like, she is my woman, take yuh eyes off she! and shock de false teeth right out dey mouth. And den is a whole other story when dey see me with mih crew cut and mih blue jeans tuck inside mih jim-boots. Walking next to Janet, who so femme dat she redundant, tend to make me look like a gender dey forget to classify. Before going Main Street I does parade in front de mirror practicing a jiggly-wiggly kind a walk. But if I ain't walking like a strong-man monkey I doh exactly feel right and I always revert back to mih true colours. De men dem does look at me like if dey is exactly what I need a taste of to cure me good and proper. I could see dey eyes watching Janet and me, dey face growing dark as dey imagining all kinda a situation and position. And de women dem embarrass fuh so to watch me in mih eye, like dey fraid I will jump up and try to kiss dem, or make pass at dem. Yuh know, sometimes I wonder if I ain't mad enough to do it just for a little bacchanal, nah!

Going for a outing with mih Janet on Main Street ain't easy! If only it wasn't for burfi and gulub jamoon! If only I hadlearned how to cook dem kind a thing before I leave home and come up here to live!

2.

In large deep-orange Sanskrit-style letters, de sign on de saffron-colour awning above de door read "Kush Valley Sweets." Underneath in smaller red letters it had "Desserts Fit For The Gods." It was a corner building. The front and side was one big glass wall. Inside was big. Big like a gymnasium. Yuh could see in through de brown tint windows: dark brown plastic chair, and brown table, each one de length of a door, line up stiff and straight in row after row like if is a school room.

Before entering de restaurant I ask Janet to wait one minute outside with me while I rumfle up mih memory, pulling out all de sweet names I know from home, besides burfi and gulub jamoon: meethai, jilebi, sweetrice (but dey call dat kheer up here), and ladhoo. By now, of course, mih mouth watering fuh so! When I feel confident enough dat I wouldn't make a fool a mih Brown self by asking what dis one name? and what dat one name? we went in de restaurant. In two twos all de spice in de place take a flying leap in our direction and give us one big welcome hug up, tight fuh so! Since den dey take up permanent residence in de jacket I wear dat day!

Mostly it had women customer sitting at de tables, chatting and laughing, eating sweets and sipping masala tea. De only men in de place was de waiters, and all six waiters was men. I figure dat dey was brothers, not too hard to conclude, because all a dem had de same full round chin, round as if de chin stretch tight over a ping-pong ball, and dey had de same big roving eyes. I know better dan to think dey was mere waiters in de employ of a owner who chook up in a office in de back. I sure dat dat was dey own family business, dey stomach proudly preceding dem and dey shoulders throw back in de confidence of dey ownership.

It ain't dat I paranoid, yuh understand, but from de moment we enter de fellas dem get over-animated, even armorously agitated. Janet again! All six pair a eyes land up on she, following she every move and body part. Dat in itself is something dat does madden me, oui! but also a kind a irrational envy have a tendency to manifest in me. It was like I didn't exist. Sometimes it could be a real problem going out with a good-looker, yes! While I ain't remotely interested in having a squeak of a flirtation with a man, it doh hurt a ego to have a man notice yuh once in a very long while. But with Janet at mih side, I doh have de chance of a penny shave-ice in de hot sun. I tuck mih elbows in as close to mih sides as I could so I wouldn't look like a strong man next to she, and over to de l-o-n-g glass case jam up with sweets I jiggle and wiggle in mih best imitation a some dem gay fellas dat I see downtwon Vancouver, de ones who more femme dan even Janet. I tell she not to pay de brothers no attention, becuase if any a dem flirt with she I could start a fight right dere and den. And I didn't feel to mess up mih crew cut in a fight.

De case had sweets in every nuance of colour in a rainbow. Sweets I never before see and doh know de names of. But dat was alright because I wasn't going to order dose ones anyway.

Since before we leave home Janet have she mind set on a nice thick syrupy curl a jilebi and a piece a plain burfi so I order dose for she and den I ask de waiter-fella, resplendent with thick thick bright-yellow gold chain and ID bracelet, for a stick a meethai for mihself. I stand up waiting by de glass case for it but de waiter/owner lean up on de back wall behind de counter watching me like he ain't hear me. So I say loud eneough for him, and everybody else in de room to hear, "I would like to have one piece a meethai please," and den he smile and lift up his hands, palms open-out motioning across de vast expanse a glass case, and he say, "Your choice! Whichever you want, Miss." But he still lean up against de back wall grinning. So I stick mih head out and up like a turtle a say louder, and slowly, "One piece a meethai – dis one!" and I point sharp to de stick a flour mix with ghee, deep fry and den roll up in sugar. He say, "That is koorma, Miss. One piece only?"

Mih voice drop low all by itself. "Oh ho! Yes, one piece. Where I come from we does call dat meethai." And den I add, but only loud enough for Janet to hear, "And mih name ain't 'Miss.'"

He open his palms out and indicate de entire panorama a sweets and he say, "These are all meethai, Miss. Meethai is Sweets. Where you from?"

I ignore his question and to show him I undaunted, I point to a round pink ball and say, "I'll have one a dese sugarcakes too please." He start grinning broad broad like if he half-pitying, half-laughing at dis Indian-in-skin-colour only, and den he tell me, "That is called chum-chum, Miss." I snap back at him, "Yeh, well back home we does call dat sugarcake, Mr. Chum-chum."

At de table Janet say, "You know, Pud [Pud, short for Pudding; is dat she does call me when she feeling close to me, or sorry for me], it's true that we call that 'meethai' back home. Just like how we call 'siu mai' 'tim sam.' As if 'dim sum' is just one little piece a food. What did he call that sweet again?

"Cultural bastards, Janet. cultural bastards. Dat is what we is. Yuh know, one time a fella from India who living up here call me a bastardized Indian because I didn't know Hindi. And now look at dis, nah! De thing is: all a we in Trinidad is cultural bastards, Janet, all a we. *Toutes bagailles*! Chinese people, Black poeple, White people. Syrian. Lebanese. I looking forward to de day I find out dat place inside me where I am nothing else but Trinidadian, whatever day could turn out to be."

I take a bite a de chum-chum, de texture was like grind-up coconut but it had no coconut, not even a hint a coconut taste in it. De thing was juicy with sweet rose water oozing out a it. De rose water perfume enter mih nose and get trap in mih cranium. Ah drink two cup a masala tea and a lassi and still de rose water perfume was on mih tongue like if I had overdosed on Butchart Gardens.

Suddenly de door a de restaurant spring open wide with a strong force and two big burly fellas stumble in, almost rolling over on to de ground. Dey get up, eyes red and slow and dey skin burning pink with booze. Dey straighten up so much to over-compensate for falling forward, dat dey find deyself leaning backward. Everybody stop talking and was watching dem. De guy in front put his hand up to his forehead and take a deep Walter Raleigh bow, bringing de hand down to his waist in a rolling circular movement. Out loud he greet everybody with "Alarm o salay koom." A part a me wanted to bust out laughing. Another part make mih jaw drop open in disbelief. De calm in de place get rumfle up. De twos fellas dem, feeling chupid now because nobody reply to dey greeting, gone up to de counter to Chum-chum trying to make a little conversation with him. De same booze-pink alarm-o-salay-koom-fella say to Chum-chum, "Hey, howaryuh?"

Chum-chum give a lil nod and de fella carry right on, "Are you Sikh?" Chum-chum brothers converge near de counter, busying deyselves in de vicinity. Chum-chum look at his brothers kind a quizzical, and he touch his cheek and feel his forehead with de back a his palm. He say, "No, I think I am fine, thank you. But I am sorry if I look sick, Sir."

De burly fella confuse now, so he try again.

"Where are you from?"

Chum-chum say, "Fiji, Sir."

"Oh! Fiji, eh! Lotsa palm trees and beautiful women, eh! Is it true that you guys can have more than one wife?"

De exchange make mih blood rise up in a boiling froth. De restaurant suddently get a gruff quietness 'bout it except for a woman I hear whispering angrily to another woman at de table behind us, "I hate this! I just hate it! I can't stand to see our men humiliated by them, right in front of us. He should refuse to serve them, he should throw them out. Who on earth do they think they are? The awful fools!" And de friend whisper back, "If he throws them out all of us will suffer in the long run."

I could discern de hair on de back a de neck a Chum-chum brothers standing up, annoyed, and at de same time de brothers look like dey was shrinking in stature. Chum-chum get serious, and he politely say, "What can I get for you?"

Pinko get de message and he point to a few items in the case and say,

"One of each, to go please."

Holding de white take-out box in one hand he extend de other to Chum-chum and say, "How do you say 'Excuse me, I'm sorry' in Fiji?"

Chum-chum shake his head and say, "It's okay. Have a good day."

Pinko insist, "No, tell me please. I think I just behaved badly, and I want to apologize. How do you say 'I'm sorry' in Fiji?"

Chum-chum say, "Your apology is accepted. Everything is okay." And he discreetly turn away to serve a person who had just entered the restaurant. De fellas take de hint dat was broad like daylight, and back out de restaurant like two little mouse.

Everybody was feeling sorry for Chum-chum and Brothers. One a dem come up to de table across from us to take a order from a woman with a giraffe-long neck who say, "Brother, we mustn't accept how these people think they can treat us. You men really put up with too many insults and abuse over here. I really felt for you."

Another woman gone up to de counter to converse with Chum-chum in she language. She reach out and touch his hand, sympathy-like. Chum-chum hold the one hand in his two and make a verbose speech to her as she nod she head in agreement generously. To italicize her support, she buy a take-out box a two burfi, or rather, dat's what I think dey was.

De door a de restaurant open again, and a bevy of Indian-looking women saunter in, dress up to weaken a person's decorum. De Miss Universe pageant traipse across de room to a table. Chum-chum and Brothers start smoothing dey hair back, and pushing de front a dey shirts neatly into dey pants. One brother take out a pack a Dentyne from his shirt pocket and pop one in his mouth. One take out a comb from his back pocket and smooth down his hair. All a dem den converge on dat single table to take orders. Dey begin to behave like young pups in mating season. Only, de women dem wasn't impress by all this tra-la-la at all and ignore dem except to make dey order, straight to de point. Well, it look like Brothers' egos were having a rough day and dey start roving 'bout de room, dey egos and de crotch a dey pants leading far in front dem. One brother gone over to Giraffebai to see if she want anything more. He call she "dear" and put his hand on she back. Giraffebai straighten she back in surprise and reply in a not-too-friendly way. When he gone to write up de bill she see me looking at she and she say to me, "Whoever does he think he is! Calling me dear and touching me like that! Why do these men always think that they have permission to touch whatever and wherever they want! And you can't make a fuss about it in public, because it is exactly what those people out there want to hear about so that they can say how sexist and uncivilized our culture is."

I shake mih head in understanding and say, "Yeah. I know. Yuh right!"

De atmosphere inde room take a hairpin turn, and it was man aggressing on woman, women warding off a herd a man who just had dey pride publicly cut up a couple a times in just a few minutes.

One brother walk over to Janet and me and he stand up facing me with his hands clasp in front a his crotch, like if he protecting it. Stiff, stiff, looking at me, he say, "Will that be all?"

Mih crew cut start to tingle, so I put on mih femmest smile and say, "Yes, that's it, thank you. Just the bill please." De smart-ass turn to face Janet and he remove his hands from in front a his crotch and slip his thumbs inside his pants like a cowboy 'bout to do a square dance. He smile, looking down at her attentive fuh so, and say, "Can I do anything for you?"

I didn't give Janet time fuh his intent to even register before I bolldoze in mih most un-femmest manner, "She have everything she need, man, thank you. The bill please." Yuh think he hear me? It was like talking to thin air. He remain smiling at Janet, but she, looking at me, not at him, say, "You heard her. The bill please."

Before he could even leave de table proper, I start mih tirade. "But A A! Yuh see dat? Yuh could believe that! De effing so-and-so! One minute yuh feel sorry fuh dem and next minute dey harassing de heck out a you. Janet, he crazy to mess with my woman, yes!" Janet got vex with me and say I overreacting, and is not fuh me to be vex. Is she he insult, and she could take good enough care a sheself.

I tell she I don't know why she don't cut off all dat long hair, and stop wearing lipstick and eyeliner. Well, who tell me to say dat! She get real vex and say dat nobody will tell she how to dress and how not to dress, not me and not any man. Well I could see de potential dat dis fight had coming, and when Janet get fighting vex, watch out! It hard to get a word in edgewise, yes! And she does bring up incidents from years back dat have no bearing on de current situation. So I draw back quick quick but she don't waste time; she was already off to a good start. It was best to leave right dere and den.

Just when I stand up to leave, de doors dem open up and in walk Sandy and Lise, coming for dey weekly hit a Indian sweets. Well, with Sandy and Lise is a dead giveaway dat dey not dressing fuh any man, it have no place in dey life fuh man-vibes, and dat in fact dey have a blatant penchant fuh women. Soon as dey enter de room yuh could see de brothers and de couple men customers dat had come in minutes before stare dem down from head to Birkenstocks, dey eyes bulging with disgust. And de women in de room start shoo-shooing, and putting dey hand in front dey mouth to stop dey suprise, and false teeth, too, from falling out. Sandy and Lise spot us instantly and dey call out to us, shameless, loud and affectionate. Dey leap over to us, eager to hug up and kiss like if dey hadn't seen us for years, but it was really only since two nights aback when we went out to dey favorite Indian restaurant for dinner. I figure dat de display was a genuine happiness to be seen wit us in dat place. While we stand up dere chatting, Sandy insist on rubbing she hand up and down Janet back — wit friendly intent, mind you, and same time Lise have she arm around Sandy waist. Well, all cover get blown. If it was even remotely possible dat I wasn't noticeable before, now Janet and I were over-exposed. We could a easily suffer from hypothermia, specially since it suddenly get cold cold in dere. We say goodbye, not soon enough, and as we were leaving I turn to acknowledge Giraffebai, but instead a any recognition of our buddiness against de fresh brothers, I get a face dat look like it was in de presence of a very foul smell.

De good thing, doh, is dat Janet had becomed so incensed 'bout how we got scorned, dat she forgot I tell she to cut she hair and to ease up on de make-up, and so I get save from hearing 'bout how I too jealous, and how much I inhibit she, and how she would prefer if I would grow my hair, and wear lipstick and put on a dress sometimes. I so glad, oui! dat I didn't have to go through hearing how I too demanding a she, like de time, she say, I prevent she from seeing a ole boyfriend when he was in town for a couple hours en route to live in Australia with his new bride (because, she say, I was jealous dat ten years ago dey sleep together). Well, look at mih crosses, nah! Like if I really so possessive and jealous!

So tell me, what yuh think 'bout dis nah, girl?

Finding the Natives

Taxi Meters and Plexiglass Partitions

Vivek Renjen Bald

The following are excerpts from the documentary video, Taxi-vala/Auto-biography, by Vivek Renjen Bald. Sections in plain text are voiceovers written by Bald, and those in italics are portions of interviews with three of the drivers in the video, Jasvinder Singh, Irfaan R., and Saleem Osman.

It's 2 a.m. I flag down a taxi to go back uptown to my apartment near Columbia University. I get in, looking as usual at the name on the hack license up front—Ahmed Khan: I make a guess he's from Pakistan.

After sitting a few minutes in silence, I begin speaking in the best Urdu I can manage, asking Ahmed where he is from. He turns all the way around to look at me. I'm sitting in the back seat with my shaggy dark hair, light skin and eyes, American clothes, voice, mannerisms, speaking in Urdu, and he asks me how it is that I know this language.

I tell Ahmed that my mother is from India. He asks about my father, and I say that he's from Australia, that my parents met and married here, that I was born in Los Angeles and grew up in California.

Ahmed is only two years older than me, and has been driving a yellow-cab 12 hours a day, 7 days a week for the past three years. I find out he's from Lahore, and excitedly tell him its the city where my mother was born. But he just looks at me in the rear view mirror and nods.

I tell Ahmed I have this idea about making a documentary about South Asian taxi drivers in New York. I say that I've noticed the division in our communities here. On the one hand are the people who came in the 50's and 60's—professionals who settled quietly and comfortably in the suburbs. And on the other hand the thousands of mostly young men who came in the mid 1980's after shifts in the world economy and the closing of borders in Europe—people from smaller towns and less privileged backgrounds, who are working at restaurants and newsstands or driving taxicabs to survive. I tell Ahmed that I want to make a film about the new immigrants—what they are experiencing, what kind of problems they are having. Ahmed is not impressed or enthusiastic—more than anything he seems suspicious.

Two years after our first meeting, I get back in touch with Ahmed and ask if I can interview him. And I should know by now that I'm also part of the story. With my shaky Urdu, my light skin and mixed family origins, and the privilege that puts me in the back seat of the cab, not the front, I can't escape that I'm part of the story. But there's a tense silence as I sit with the camera in my hands—the camera my parents bought me. I won't admit that while my mother and Ahmed share a birthplace, Ahmed and I may not share anything at all. Or that my few words of Urdu, because they're spoken here in New York, don't suddenly make us part of the same community. As I start to shoot, I want to believe we're connected, though we grew up in different nations, religions, histories, and here in New York, we're separated by a taximeter and a plexiglass partition.

Jasvinder: If you see in Third World countries, its very hard to make money. If you're rich, then its fine . . . but if you're an average person in that {country}, then a college degree doesn't mean anything. You don't even get a job if you have a college degree . . . You can't

get a job unless you know somebody somewhere, or you're rich . . . So for them, the only way they've seen is that a lot of people have gone out.

Irfaan: We used to think that when we go over there, we will make enough money. So we don't have to worry—we just need to go to America and then everything will be okay. We just work eight hours and every day we will get $100 or something like that. And we were happy that we're gonna make more and more money . . . {But} when I came here and it was a recession period—and still it is—many people were jobless, and I was also jobless. I had a lot of wishes that I will do this and that, but after three months I did nothing—I stayed at home or just roamed about. I couldn't get any job . . . Then I realized its very hard to live in America.

When I first came to New York, I only planned to stay for two or three years. Since I was eighteen or nineteen years old, I had planned to go back to India, where most of my mother's family still lived. Yes, I was born in the U.S., but I didn't want to call myself American. In my mind, America stood for violence, arrogance, hypocrisy, greed. So ignoring my birth here, my whole childhood here, and a much-loved side of my own family which was from California, Australia, and before that Scotland, I chose India as my "place of origin." I imagined India as America's polar opposite. I saw it as the place of my true roots, my true politics, my true home. So all I had to do was "go back" and everything would be alright.

When Ahmed first came to New York, he also only planned to stay for two or three years. He tells me every movie, magazine, and rumor seemed to say the same thing—that all he had to do was come to America, work hard for a while, and he could become rich. He could return to Pakistan in just a couple years with dollars in his pocket, then open his own business there, start something solid, and everything would be alright.

The truth is, we were running from opposite directions, chasing two sides of the same myth. And we intersected, collided, in this city. Now it's five years later and we're both still in New York. There was no magic India, no miracle America. So the question is: what are we making here in this place to which we've come?

Jasvinder: In my college, there is this fraternity, I think its HKN or whatever, and whenever you become a member in that, like one of the brothers, you're assigned a brother and whatever he says to you, you gotta do it. That's like, part of joining. And one of my friends, when he joined this group, he was asked to wear a turban for a week. I mean they can tell you anything they want, they can tell you that you have to wear your shorts over your pants or you have to wear your pants the other way around, or whatever. But he was asked to wear a turrban. He's from Pakistan. He's never worn a turban in his life. But he was asked to wear a turban and a t-shirt saying "Cab Driver."

As I begin to shoot and edit, talking to more drivers and cutting interviews into neat little segments, the absence running through the video becomes obvious.

Among taxi drivers, I'm in an all-male part of the community. And off camera, time after time, I'm remaining silent, avoiding discussions and confrontations that might jeaopordize my own inclusion.

One night a driver turns to me and asks: Do you have a girlfriend? Is she Indian? Is she American? Do you live together? I could answer plainly: "Yes, I have a girlfriend. No, she's not Indian, she's African American, Italian American, Native American and Chinese American. Yes we plan to live together." But instead of answering, I'm uncomfortable, I evade the questions. Is this a desire for privacy or a fear of judgement?

Then he continues, complaining that American women are too promiscuous, that in America South Asian women become spoiled, and they need to be restricted. And through all of this I don't say a thing—not a word of argument, not a word of protest. In my silence, I'm thinking about my girlfriend and other close friends, my feminist Indian American mother, and my grandmother from Lahore who used to rise each morning against her husband's wishes to go sing protest songs in front of British colonial jails. But still I don't speak a word.

So with each new interview, I try to bring the issues on camera, asking drivers questions: Why is it only men who come here on their own, I ask. Why can young men do what they please, go where they please, work and grow up here, but young women are restricted? I ask: Don't we have a chance, in our generation, to criticize and change what's given to us? But my simplistic questions fall flat—they fail to say anything about the complexities of South Asian or U.S. sexisms. They shift attention away from my own silences and exclusions; and, at worst, they make the drivers look foolish in front of American eyes, while I hide conveniently behind the camera.

Saleem: A lot of people are so ill-informed about cab drivers' income, and when you talk to them, they will say, "Oh, cab drivers make more than me and I'm an attorney, I'm a doctor." This is not true.

Mostly people now work on a shift basis—either the day shift or the night shift—and you have to pay about eighty to ninety dollars lease per shift. So first of all, you are worried about that eighty or ninety dollars—to come to equal—because you have already paid him, the owner, eighty or ninety dollars. And now, after making that eighty or ninety dollars, you are worried about the gas money. After all, you are burning the gas also, which will be not less than fifteen to twenty dollars per shift. And the gross money is around a hundred and sixty or seventy dollars per good shift. So if you have to pay a hundred and ten to a hundred and twenty dollars to the owner, including the gas money and the lease money, you are not making more than forty to fifty dollars for yourself. And I'm talking of good days . . .

• • •

Saleem: This is the history of this world. If you go into recent history, you're gonna see all those white people going to all our areas, conquering those countries, taking the wealth out of that and making us slaves. Or forcing all these people from Africa to be brought up to those places where they can work for the benefit of these white people and they can help them in making money . . . So, with the passage of time, people started getting education and everything, then these guys started thinking about themselves, "Oh that's not fair—people are now blaming {us} for all this slave trade." So they smartly have formulated a system, which is the Green Card—now we are the slaves of our own choice.

I'm sitting with Kym, my best friend and lover, in a Pakistani restaurant on our block. We are joined by Aziz, a former driver himself, who opened the restaurant after four years behind the wheel. Aziz asks Kym half-jokingly to find him a girlfriend, and Kym responds, also half- jokingly, by asking Aziz what kind of woman he is looking for. He says any kind of woman, except a black woman. He says he cannot trust black women. Kym, who is herself a black woman, looks at me, and I look at Aziz, trying to think of the words in Urdu to respond to what he has just said. But once again I remain silent and he goes on casually to another topic as if nothing has happened. Kym's anger is as much about my convenient silence as it is about Aziz's prejudice.

Saleem: A lot of people who come to this country are told the stories, which are stereotypes, which are not correct, about people of color — that people of color are mostly criminals, or telling them stereotyped stories, or {that} you should stay away. This is one of their ways to control a lot of things, which is very successful . . .

I'm sitting with Saleem, a driver who has become a friend and political ally. We are talking about the "right" which many drivers are demanding to refuse passengers they think look dangerous. Saleem has long opposed this "right of refusal," saying that it's a racist measure which drivers would aim at African Americans and Latinos. But when I begin telling my own stories about different friends of color who, no matter what time of day, no matter what their age, dress, or physical appearence, have all been passed by empty yellow-cabs, Saleem explodes in anger. He says I'm in no place to speak. He says I can stand behind my camera or sit comfortably at my desk and call him and his friends racist, but until I drive a cab on the streets seven days a week to support my family, I don't know a thing.

• • •

Sometimes when I use the word "white" to refer to other people, I wonder about myself. I wonder if I'm wearing this video as a badge of brownness — as a proof of my political loyalties in a world which looks at me and sees white. I wonder, at these times, whether I'm denying not only my own privilege, but the fact that I've learned as much about love, justice, and politics from my father and his side of the family as from my mother and hers. And in this am I accepting the easy racial divisions of this society even as I claim to be fighting them?

After three years, maybe all I know is how complex and fraught with problems my own relation to community and history is. During my Indian grandparents' time, the Divide and Rule of the British was strengthened by the kind of silences I've been keeping, strengthened by the kind of narrow definitions of community we could now again be making on this soil . . .

Saleem: Your country is going through this kind of oppression where people of color are dying of hunger and other stuff. But, on the other hand, every year they're gonna announce one-hundred thousand, two-hundred thousand immigrant visas for all those people to apply. And you're gonna see people from Third World countries and elsewhere applying in millions. The number is always more than a million applicants applying for 100,000 immigrant visas. If you don't have anything, why are you giving every year 100,000 visas?

Every new immigrant group that comes to the United States is taught that the first step towards success in this country is the step away from—or on the backs of—other people of color. We are not taught the histories that have transpired here before us—histories to which we are connected, histories which we share . . . So whose American Dream is this? What kind of Americans are we expected to become? Who are we expected to ignore, and betray? And who is it who gains when our communities fight against each other in this country, instead of fighting side by side?

Saleem: Yeah, I have seen a lot of friends of mine after living in this country four or five years will come to understand what actually the people of color are. They will understand and will know the history of their struggle. . . .

A Difference of Background

Litu Kabir

Is life ever free of problems? If your worries are waved away with a magic wand, just wait, your mind will create new problems out of thin air for you. Thus I never thought being a taxi cab driver was as pitiful a fate as many of my compatriots thought. Like anything in life, one must make the best of it. There were ill-mannered passengers, robbers in the heart of the night, and perhaps, yes, not so much money at the end of the week to compensate for the loneliness in which I drove through endless circles. But that was okay. If you knew the impossible situation I was in in another land far away and the chance that brought me to this country, like the kindly ocean current washing a weary swimmer to a desolate shore, you would understand right away. Without a soul to welcome me in this vast teeming metropolis, with the heels of my shoes worn out by my search all over the great city for work—any kind of work—life as a taxi cab driver was simple and blessed, a precious love found after a lifetime of wandering. I meant to be forever grateful to the fellow countryman through whose intercession this came to be, Saladin.

Saladin, dear friend! How fragile is gratitude! It shatters one day into pieces and becomes dust. Vengeance lives longer. I look at Saladin across the table as he wolfs down another dish of murag biriyani. He asks why is it that I cook so well for him, so much, and he asks this in a light way because he actually believes that this is his due. He does not go very deep into any matter these days, he never suspects the trap he has fallen in. Revenge, I tell you, is indeed sweet. And let me tell you, it takes many forms. There is revenge you take after much planning and waiting, like medicine in one gulp, and there is revenge that requires no effort on your part, that Fate hands you on a platter. If the latter be yours, take care of the gift well, for it is as pleasurable as the quenching of daily thirst, as long-lasting as your life.

When my eyes first set on him I saw a handsome young man, possessed of qualities which would never be mine. He was studying at a great university, and at the party in his house he was surrounded by others as glamorous as himself. I had never been to any such event before. Mine were the modest get-togethers the people of my background have, simple people who never erase from their hearts the memories of other lives in the homeland far away. Men sit around in a room warmed by their camaraderie and exchange their tales and the women gather in another room with their housewives' talk. Many were the cold nights when I returned home late from such gatherings to my single bare room, the awareness of fellowship in my heart like a candlelight in the darkness.

Saladin's party was different, I could tell straight away. The women and men were in the same hall, talking, drinking wine, laughing, as if it was completely natural for everybody to be together. They were mostly foreigners, and by that I don't mean white Americans, because of course everybody knows some Americans. They are easier to befriend than many compatriots even though the friendships with them are far less likely to last as long. Well, in Saladin's house there were men and women from all four corners of the globe. Foreign students, professors, artists, filmmakers. In the midst of these people was Saladin himself, the center of attention in the distinguished crowd. Elegantly dressed in a black silk shirt and black slacks, a brown leather belt around his waist, he was of medium height and slim, had sharp features and a mass of curly hair. A dark complexion on such a handsome figure accentuated his serious mien, his grave and deliberate manner of conversing. Of such a person mothers back at home would say to their daughters, "He comes from a fine family."

I hesitated between entering the crowd of people and leaving quietly when I caught Saladin's eyes. He paused in his talk to a beautiful foreign woman to throw me a look. It was not quite a greeting, but the hint of a nod that acknowledged my existence. Soon he came to meet me. He came over and measured me with a look that went from feet to head. We made our introductions.

"Have you had dinner? Would you like a sandwich?" he asked in a voice made soft with grace.

The sandwiches on the big trays were delicate, perfect, like items of show in glass cases. But how was I to have one here in front of these people? "I ate." I replied.

Saladin gave me a glance of unease. He helped himself to a sandwich and resumed questioning me. Did he not already know all about me? Soon he came to the point.

"You have looked for work?" He asked, as he threw me another sideways look and his lips played out a faint smile. Or was it a sneer?

"From the day I landed."

"Do you have a degree?"

"A student in the polytechnic."

"No papers?"

"I hear you can get by," I offered. Indeed I knew *deshis* who got by very well without documents, working around the clock with no more than six hours of sleep. I could do that, yes.

"Difficult." Saladin replied, looking away at the crowd in the middle of the hall.

"You can do nothing?" I asked in anxiety, nagged by fresh worries. The hope with which I had come to him was very high; I had been told that Saladin could get me work even without the "papers."

He bent his head without replying. A young man with very short, very blond hair came near us and Saladin greeted him warmly, as if they had not met in a long time. I was forgotten.

Well, Saladin got me my taxi job soon after that meeting. How happy I was then! Just this foothold is what I needed to succeed in this country. My boss, the owner of several cars, didn't speak much with me even though he was a *deshi*, but I could see he thought well of me because of my connection with Saladin. He could have given the job to anybody else. He gave it to me because he had a respect for learned people like Saladin. He noticed, I think with a bit of fear, that I too read books. I am not the average high-class Bangladeshi who goes from the university to a cushy job, but I like to pick up a book here and there and try to learn something from it. Driving a taxi cab is thus quite a good occupation because you can read in the cab when waiting for customers. Often I would pull off to some side road to be away from passengers and just read.

On one such night none other than Saladin came up to my cab and surprised me while I was reading a book. I think he thought a bit better of me from that point on. Previously he may have thought that I was completely outside of his cultured society. We chatted a little on that drive. He took my phone number. Soon thereafter I got calls from him inviting me to come to his parties. I went a couple of times even though it was hard to get time off from my taxi cab shifts, even for critical matters. Each time I went I marveled at how Saladin, a fellow countryman, mixed so easily with women and foreigners. This was not something I could do, nor could my other *deshi* friends. An inexplicable hesitation stood in my way even when I knew what to say. It was different with the brown people from Mexico, Puerto Rico, and other Spanish-speaking countries who also lived in this city in great numbers, ordinary people like me, taxi cab drivers, construction workers, building cleaners. Through a halting foreign language I sensed a familiarity and an equality that loosened my tongue and made easy the affectionate slap on the back. They conveyed a warmth that I never expected from the upper-class *deshi* or Indian. Pakistanis I never liked anyway. They come to me as if we are brothers but they already forget what their army did in Bangladesh in 1971 in the name of religion.

So with the taxi cab work and my getting to know people like Saladin, I began to feel settled in the USA. I was bringing home a steady income and no longer lived off my card. Soon I would be able to send some money back home. Soon there would be other things. . . Things looked so good that one day I gave Saladin a phone call inviting him to dinner at my house. He accepted my invitation and I was truly happy. I had moved up in life by my friendship with so great a character. I was okay, like any one of those young well-heeled people I saw chatting away at the cafés, like Saladin himself. I had never gone in to any café but with my new found confidence I felt I could go in one day and sit at a table in an elegant café, just like that.

We had indeed become closer. At Saladin's insistence I used his first name only, dropping the respectful "Bhai" after the name. A rose is a not rose by any other name, otherwise why do people who come here change names? Without the appellation Saladin indeed appeared as someone like me, born under the same sun. He was someone with a better start, but still no more than another human being looking at the world through windows that were perhaps no clearer or wider than my own.

"Why are you here?" he asked me shortly after we began our meal.

"Why is anybody here? To survive."

"Money?"

"Yes," I hesitated, feeling trapped and yet convinced of my innocence.

"Why are you here?," I asked back.

"Me?" he replied taken aback. "The university I go to has the best film department in this country."

"You want fame?"

"You don't understand. I plan to make movies. Good ones."

He was different because he was a student. He was not here just to get a job. He was going to make movies. Movies with great messages that would change people's way of thinking, give them new dreams, offer solace in life through epic stories. He would be an "America-returned" movie maker in Bangladesh, living and conversing with other gifted people like himself. Sometime in the future.

I looked at him and could think of nothing good to say. Doubt grows insidiously and I was no longer secure about my little happiness. "A job is to survive, no matter what you do . . . ," I offered in a weak defense.

"You should not be so content. People do not respect a cab driver." He replied in a silky voice.

"You can not see their worth?" Anxiety was clouding my mind like a cold fog. Someone had applied a cold wet towel to my temple.

"Me? With me it is different. Why, in Bangladesh my family always accepted the servant as our own family member." Saladin replied quickly, with a note of irritation.

"The servant is a family member?" Can this be true? "Does he eat from the same table as everybody else?" I asked.

Saladin's face contorted in an ugly expression of anger. He stared at me under clenched brows. "Just what do you mean by that?" he whispered with a quiet vehemence.

Did I exceed my limits? But how could I back down?

I realized soon that we were not talking about the situations we each happened to find ourselves in at the moment, but about faceless fears that lurked deep inside our souls and the clashing philosophies of life they gave seed to. From the heights of his future glory, Saladin saw me without ambition, content with the little I had achieved and irritatingly incapable of comprehending the greatness of his dreams and of himself. I had missed his point, probed too deep on chance remarks, challenged assumptions he was not prepared to question and, somewhere, a raw nerve was touched. He was now speaking to another untiring and loyal, invisible listener, defending before an unknown judge his image that I had put on the dock. He had me in mind but he was no longer talking to me. He talked with a quiet violence about people who fall unawares into American banality, ignorant people who apply American norms to our culture without understanding "the parameters," who waste away their life amounting to nothing more than fodder for American materialism. I chewed small mouthfuls of my food slowly while he went on talking. "What irks me most, after the unthinking slide into degeneracy," he continued, "is that it is for no great cause, for no goals worth speaking of, that *deshis* shamelessly exploit the goodwill of others, as if help from other expatriates is a God-given right that can never be denied but must come unconditionally, no matter what, as if by virtue of a common nationality all personal deficiencies must be forgiven and forgotten." I had long finished eating and given up trying to reply honestly to anything he said; neither was I interested in agreeing and saying nice things just to placate Saladin. Instead I filled and refilled my glass with water and sipped it while Saladin talked away in a monotone, his mind stalking the woods and forests of a world none but he was familiar with. I sipped the water and looked askance at him trying hard to conceal my growing impatience. I only wanted him to leave.

That evening with Saladin may have faded from my mind long ago if it was not for a curious thing that happened afterwards. I lost my job in a week's time.

Now, I can not prove this but I am convinced that it was because of Saladin. I don't know just what he told my boss but it could easily have been any number of well-known secrets about me. I have no doubt everything he said was true. My boss didn't have to explain. The coldness in his voice, the paucity of his words, the averted look all told me that nothing I could do or say to him would change the decision. He no longer "needed me." He had made up his mind well before he talked with me. The only person who could help would have been Saladin, but Saladin never returned my calls. Now, if you think Saladin was not behind my getting fired, do you think he didn't even know about what had happened to me? He knew! My boss would respond to just a vibe from him! He knew very well!

I kept phoning Saladin and always his answering machine took my anxious messages. That he never got back to me was proof enough that he was the man responsible. Suspicion became bitterness, became a dull hatred that profiled Saladin and all he stood for. To drop me like that! I wanted to tell him what I thought of his speeches, his fancy parties, his high culture. For days I walked alone in the streets looking for work and thinking of nothing else but Saladin.

He didn't care. I will make him care. He will not see me. I will pin him down. I will make him admit a thousand times over and more, he is false, false, false.

Arrogant, know-it-all who knows nothing!

I never got him. Life began to overtake me again, and yes, I had to give up trying to see him. But the desire for hitting him, attacking him in some way, that did not go away. Do you like being the lowly bug that somebody can just walk over without even a thought? What does it matter that I had no higher education, that I did not throw big parties, that I was only a cab driver? Is my worth less as a human being? From a hot gas that enveloped my brain the desire for revenge sublimated and condensed and became part of my beating heart. It was responsible for the new, stronger person I became, it was a source of strength in hard times. It was indeed a gift from Saladin that I cherished and did not want to see eroded by time, a talisman against despair. I worked harder, I saved every penny, I made new friends. And yet a certain lightness of spirit ebbed away and disappeared. Secretly, in rare moments by myself in the cab, in my bare room late at night, looking at the far sky through the small window, I would remind myself that life was not given for enjoyment but for becoming strong and to grow so nobody could demean me. The stars up there in the darkness would be my guide, their constancy my inspiration. Like them, I would live by my own truth. I had no need of praise or appreciation from the world. If others looked at me and saw nothing more than a taxi driver, I would still know all the good hidden by that label. Without university degrees I could still learn; shut in a taxi cab or in this little room I would travel infinite vistas. I would know myself, find my truth, make peace with my life, and I would let the disdain of others fall at my feet like flightless spears.

Time is an anomaly. The minutes slide grudgingly but the years fly by. They fly by and their gifts are removed, away from sight, till a long way along life's path they are unveiled in the very bosom of the present. More than a decade had gone by when one pleasant summer evening I found myself walking along a peaceful street lined with low offices placed between shops and residences. The blue of the sky had deepened to a purple and a beautiful full moon rested low on the horizon just above the houses. The yellow street lights had come on above my head. One of the windows was of a small real estate office, with color photographs of properties to be sold on the glass pane. I do not know what mysterious hand of fate made me pause to look at these photos, but I did. My glance went past them and fell on a brown face inside. There in that room was Saladin, working late, all by himself in this street corner real estate office! My heart beat fast and my throat became dry. I went in.

Ah! The unease of his eyes when they meet mine! "Saladin. How are you!" I said in a joy only half-affected.

"Quite well. What can I do for you?" He gave me a hard stare. He remembered me, but he did not want to.

I persisted. "You are working late, and all by yourself!"

"As you can see."

"Don't you make movies?"

"No. I work here, no time for movies."

How I admired his practical sense!

"Are you married and with children?"

"None of those things for me."

He had expected to hear worse things. I saw before me the very same arrogance and I remembered perfectly well my resolutions, but I was a small boy tip toeing to catch the most desired butterfly in an open field. Fear of losing him calmed my feverish mind. I gave up any thought of talking about the past. A strange idea that I had never anticipated took hold of me. I had to go back to the scene of the crime, to the past, and I had to take him back there with me! The terrible accusations and the insults I had phrased and rephrased in my mind for precisely this encounter were pitiful drops of water that would never slake my thirst for revenge. That demanded life—warm, living blood. It required friendship.

Yes, I found out about how Saladin came to where he was today. With care and affection and patience, between visits he accepted reluctantly at first and then with resignation and habit, in light comments and masked excuses, he traced out the path from the great movie-maker he was to have been, the mover and shaker of society, the beacon of enlightenment, to the real estate agent he is today. I didn't need him to tell me the ending, for it was written all over him: his face, harassed by the real estate deals narrowly missed; his eyes, glazed by the late hours over boring descriptions of houses he wanted rich people to buy through him; his body, soft and bloated beyond recognition by virtue of the sedentary life he led; his mind, swimming in schemes to snatch away closures from his colleagues and incapable now of passions other than the square footage and location of houses, their prices, mortgage payments. This real estate agent was very far from the man whom I had one day met with trepidation and awe. This man was quite middle-class, harmless.

We come from different backgrounds and we meet today in another land, more equal than twins. This friendship is perfidy, you say? Yes, it is. I have no remorse. But know that it is a faithful friendship. No brotherhood is stronger than mine for Saladin. Friendship takes many forms and flows from many fountains, and who is to say that ours was not destined to be this? The human heart is mysterious. Like the photo developed from a negative, its source can be the inverse of what the eyes see. Revenge can be the seed of love, from which grows a fruit of exquisite taste, no less true than friendship from any other tree, all the more true because vengeance requires precisely that.

Flushing Meadows Park

Sunita Sunder Mukhi

I love picnicking families
They reek of forgiveness
Laughing at each other's silly jokes
Lolling about on the dog poo grass
Swaying their hips to salsa
Barbecuing slabs of meat
And even if it's pumped up with chemicals
or the marinade's really not that great
Everyone's really hungry
and say it's yummy.

I love picnicking families
Children romp about
while the breeze balloons out
their kurta pajamas
Convinced that the turtle sludging through
that murky lake does love it
will live long, will win that race.
It doesn't.

I love picnicking families
Couples lay facing one another
their coffee thighs entwined,
exchanging sighs and glances
forgetting at least for now that
last night she faked her orgasm
and he's been laid off again
because of his bad english.

I love picnicking on families
The sun numbs them
into lethargic bliss
at least for these few hours
they reek of forgiveness.

Signs of Belonging

Naheed Islam

*A walk through almost any of today's large modern cities in
Western Europe or the U.S. leaves one with the impression that each
contains many cities: the corporate city of high-rise office buildings; the
old, dying industrial city; and the immigrant city. It is a space of
power, a space of labor and machines, and a Third World space.*

—*Saskia Sassen, 1993*

Major demographic shifts have been taking place in the United States, particularly in urban centers like Los Angeles and New York that epitomize the
immigrant, multi-racial landscapes that Saskia Sassen evokes.   These demographic shifts, as well as changing political contexts and the emergence of the city
as center for Pacific Rim trade, make Los Angeles a "metropolis in motion," a rising "technopolis" (Chang, 1994; Davis, 1992; Soja, 1989).   The immigrant
spaces within the city of Los Angeles have a striking, yet often subtle, visual character.   Bangladeshi entrepreneurs or business community project public images
of their identities through the use of street signs and store names.   It is in this
public space that Bangladeshis assert their national and ethnic identity, and illustrate their encounters with Latino/Chicano, Black, Asian, Muslim, and poor
White communities in an urban landscape.

After the 1965 Immigration Act, Asians have become the fastest growing
minority group in the U.S.[1] and are a part of the racial recomposition and transformation of Los Angeles.   The multiracial population of Los Angeles is composed of 10% Asians, 36% Latinos, 10% Blacks, and 41% Whites.   Los Angeles
has emerged as the home of the single largest Asian population in the United
States; between 1970 and 1990, the proportion of Asian Americans in Los
Angeles county grew from two percent to over ten percent.   The Asian popula-

tion itself is extremely diverse and most are foreign born.

Los Angeles has also been undergoing major shifts in its economic structure; there has been an increase in high-technology industry employment and in low-paying service and manufacturing jobs (Mollenkopf and Castells, 1992; Soja, 1989). The labor market has mostly boomed in low-paying, part-time work, and an informal or underground economy has created sweatshops, particularly in the garment industry. These changes are accompanied by the intensification of residential segregation in what has always been the a highly segregated city (Davis, 1992; Mollenkopf and Castells, 1992; Soja, 1989); there is a fragmentation based on the axes of race, ethnicity, immigrant status, gender, and class. Bangladeshi immigrants display their arrival and build a home for themselves within this complex socio-economic landcape.

The small initial Bangladeshi immigration between 1915 and the late 1960's was by a small number of merchant marines to the ports of New York, Los Angeles, and San Francisco, and by a few students or professionals. Until the 1970's immigration continued to be by professionals and by beneficiaries of family reunification visas. But since 1985, the growth in immigration is also a result of arrivals under visa lottery programs, immigrants who entered the country on visitors' visas and stayed on in undocumented status, and some working-class and lower-middle class migrants who undertook border crossings through Mexico.

Today, Los Angeles has the second largest Bangladeshi community in the U.S. and the immigrants' occupations have changed over the years. In the early 1900's, Bangladeshi immigrants worked almost exclusively in restaurants, as agricultural workers, or as extras in Hollywood films playing Indian or 'generic foreign other' roles. Most of the downtown residents now work in the service industry as fast food restaurant or convenience store workers, gas station and parking lot attendants, and cab drivers, while some are professionals and a few own businesses. In this daily work sphere, women's attire (saris and shalwar kameez) and the language spoken on the streets become identifiers of Bangladeshi immigrants. Stores with signs in Bengali are further testimony to their growing visibility within Latino and Asian neighborhoods.

Approximately five thousand Bangladeshis live in a downtown cluster of apartments. This 3rd Street/Vermont area is referred to by most as the *deshi para*.[2] Bangladeshis also live beyond this neighborhood, in the valleys and suburbs of Los Angeles, creating a dispersed yet interconnected network of families and communities. While the cultural and geographic space of the city is new and initially unfamiliar to immigrants, they are trying to recreate a sense of community by invoking and transforming the social and communal space of a *para* within private spaces.

Although socializing is made difficult by geographic dispersal, time constraints, and new norms of interaction, many Bangladeshis use the telephone and weekend gatherings to maintain ties to their community. Videos of Bangladeshi and Indian movies and theater productions also become critical facilitators of community and cultural boundaries. For many immigrants, the telephone becomes an especially crucial link to others' lives, not only in Los Angeles and the United States but also in Bangladesh, thus helping to maintain transnational connections between families and communities. There is a real sense of emotional urgency in being able to utilize the phone to maintain family ties. The telephone becomes the medium through which experiences are shared and created in conversations with relatives in Bangladesh. There are single men who get married over the phone, and married men who retain their marriages and contact with children over periods of many years with the help of the phone because they cannot leave the country due to lack of immigration documentation. Immigrants also share information about their lifestyles here, about ways of thinking, new gadgets, music, and other consumer goods. Women are instructed about the rituals of childbearing, parenting, and household duties by mothers and sisters in Bangladesh; these rituals are then modified for pragmatic reasons and performed within the immigrant community. Requests are made to perform religious ceremonies in Bangladesh, such as making offerings to religious sites. A transnational family is maintained and reshaped through this telephone system, cultural information is shared and transformed, and political ties are maintained and utilized to impact local immigrant politics as well as the politics in Bangladesh.

These communications not only have emotional, cultural, religious, and political implications, but also an economic impact. Men who have left behind spouses claim to make hundreds of dollars worth of calls to Bangladesh and, in fact, list it as their single largest expenditure after rent. There is both a courting, and capitalizing on the needs, of these clients by telephone companies as epitomized by recent AT&T television advertisements. A vast underground market flourishes for stolen phone cards and other means of calling because of the steep costs of telephone services. Furthermore, transnational ties are also supported by economic remittances, or the immigrant savings that are sent to Bangladesh to support extended families. The arrangements and negotiations over how the money will be spent and who will be the recipient make the immigrant an active participant in the dynamics of the transnational family.

In the local in Los Angeles context, businesses owned by Bangladeshis provide services that build the community. Most Bangladeshi businesses are either restaurants or "convenience" stores and serve two different clientele: stores on streets such as Melrose or Sunset are aimed at middle-class and more affluent groups; those around Vermont or in South Central target Bangladeshis and a working-class Black, Asian, Latino, and White population. Restaurants provide a venue for quick meals to single men and cater food for large gatherings. Convenience stores stock Bangladeshi fish, spices, fruits and other specialities, as well as videos.

Videos of the Bangladesh Television Drama Series and of Indian films deeply impact the communities by continually feeding them cultural images from South Asia. These videos become the focal point of peoples' entertainment and transmit a particular view of Bangladesh and construction of Bangladeshi culture to both the immigrants and their children. The Indian film industry also exports fashions and symbols of culture to immigrants, who in turn feel connected to their families in Bangladesh as they exchange the names of the latest movies and fashions. Immigrants are thus able to convey to their families that they still share a common world. The Bangladeshi culture that is articulated to second-generation immigrants is also shaped largely by Hindi films from India. This influence is seen in the cultural shows and performances arranged by local organizations. The music, dances, and clothing diplayed are transposed from the "latest" films. An interesting phenomenon that has arisen in the South Asian diaspora is the move towards a definition of Bangladeshi culture that transgresses national boundaries. This has emerged as a result of these interactions via technology and commerce within, and between, the sites of Bangladesh, India, and the U.S.

The crossing of national boundaries may also have an underlying economic motivation as immigrants try to position themselves most profitably in the marketplace. Bangladeshi businesses often utilize the more recognizable identifier of

"Indian" names to present themselves to the outside community. Older Bangladeshi restaurants bear names such as "Tandoori Nights," or "Gate of India," for they reach out to a clientele who can not, or does not, distinguish between peoples of different South Asian nations and commonly mis-identifies most of them as Indian. Bangladeshis play on such mistaken identities but at the same time—as in the case of the restaurant, "Gate of India," where a Bangladeshi artist has painted a mural of a "typical" scene in Bangladesh—they find ways to assert their own construction of identity. The mural in this restaurant, for example, depicts a portrait of village in Bangladesh, which is a particular notion and depiction of home as peaceful, rural life. This imagined place draws on the nostalgia for the "real" Bangladesh in urban, middle-class Bangladeshis. Yet it is also an attempt to claim a distinct ethnic identity through symbols that may only be recognizable for those within the community.

Naheed Islam

Recently, the presence of a larger Bangladeshi community base has led to store signs that proclaim their national and linguistic background. Bangladeshi businesses often display bilingual signs, showing the duality of belonging. Store signs also reflect attempts to connect with Spanish-speaking groups through the usage of Spanish words, with other Muslim communities through advertisements of availability of Halal (kosher) meat, or with Black communities through images of African Americans (although those are more scarce). These signs and images illustrate the creation of the multiethnic/racial space within which (im)migrant communities interact. In a city where communities are residentially segregated and socially isolated from one other, public spaces such as the corner 'convenience store' are where they meet in co-operation and silence, co-existence and conflict.

As a rather new immigrant community, Bangladeshi immigrants are just beginning to insert themselves into this multi-ethnic/racial urban setting. The emergence of the larger community provides a base for business owners who control the assertion of Bangladeshi images within public spaces and interact with multi-ethnic/racial/linguistic communities. They utilize certain mis-identifications to negotiate the urban space and yet assert their own national/linguistic identity to build community and home within Los Angeles.

Notes

[1] Between 1921 and 1960, Asians comprised 4 percent of immigration to the U.S.; between 1971 and 1980, 35%; and between 1981-1989, 42%. Primarily from China (including Hong Kong and Taiwan), India, Korea, the Philippines and Vietnam, the Asian American population grew five-fold between 1970-1990, from 190,000 to 926,000 in Los Angeles (Ong, Bonacich, and Cheng).

[2] *Para* is a Bengali word meaning a spatial and social boundary within which residents create a community. In urban and rural Bangladesh, the composition of *paras* vary depending on their socio-economic make-up and location. Their fluid borders are defined by social networks among women and families who create boundaries within private spaces, and young men who hang out at local tea stalls and playing fields, surveying and maintaining the public space of the community.

Bibliography

Chang, Edward T. And Russell Leong. Eds. *Los Angeles—Struggles Toward Multiethnic Community.* University of Washington Press, Seattle. 1994.

Davis, Mike. *City of Quartz: Excavating the Future in Los Angeles.* Vintage Books, New York. 1992.

Light, Ivan & Edna Bonacich. *Immigrant Entrepreneurs: Koreans in Los Angeles.* University of California Press, Los Angeles. 1988.

Mollenkopf and Manuel Castells. Eds. *Dual City: Restructuring Los Angeles.* Russell Sage Foundation, New York. 1992.

Ong, Paul, Bonacich, Edna, and Lucie Cheng. *The New Asian Immigration In Los Angeles and Global Restructuring.* Temple University Press. 1994.

Sassen, Saskia. "Rebuilding the Global City: Economy, Ethnicity, and Global Cities," *Social Justice,* Vol. 20, Nos. 3–4, 1993.

Soja, Edward W. *Postmodern Geographies: The Reassertion of Space in Critical Social Theory.* Verso, London. 1989.

In the Office, the Florescence of Computers Blinds Me

Purvi Shah

This is a day of no poems. In my cubicle
I am a lion in hibernation, a butterfly
before the coming of cocoon. I know
the caterpillars must crave the chewing

through of that thread, the unraveling
of their boundaries until freedom,
until they can crawl. Bound

to a limb, fall turns to flight
and open air is more precious after
the drowsy gestation of captivity.

I Want to Give you Devotion

Ameena Meer

I was ten the year my mother started the Center for Internal Healing. You must have heard of it. Before that, she was just Bina, a young Indian woman who taught yoga classes in the afternoons to amuse herself. Like a lot of women in Connecticut, her husband was a banker in the city. Vijay joined all the other men in blue suits on the platform every morning, while we sat watching from the front seat of the car, the heater whirring and the motor running. From there, we'd often go to the shopping center to pick up the drycleaning and groceries for dinner. Believe it or not, in those days, my mother was a normal suburban housewife in blue jeans, pushing a shopping cart down the aisles of the supermarket, looking for sales on tuna fish.

So I do have a father, actually, a perfectly normal man. In those days, I called her "Mama," but no one else did. She became "Ma-ji" much later.

Even my mother admits, in the beginning, she didn't have her powers. Well, she says she had them, but she fought them. She fought them and that kept her from using them. Sometimes, someone from her yoga group would linger in the pools of sunlight in her yellow kitchen, waiting to unburden themselves of some problem to this softspoken woman. She would make cups of tea. Normal black tea in those days. Strong and milky, with as many spoons of sugar as she could toss in until you restrained her.

As my mother relaxed, she would let flow a stream of advice. A cooling stream, the sound of which had the effect of calming and soothing the listener. Of course, people started coming for more. They started telephoning during the evenings to hear her gentle matter-of-fact voice. Then they started arriving in groups. So my mother added some words of wisdom between stretches during her yoga classes. Eventually, she started teaching. Teaching about Life. My mother taught Life the same way she'd taught yoga. She taught it as she learned herself, going partly on instinct and partly on books from the library. She rode on the acceptance of most Americans that Indians had an innate knowledge of spirituality by virtue of their race. They believed her. They believed the clothes, the accent, the long dark hair and melting brown eyes. They believed, because my mother is simply a good person. Myself, I believe that last quality to this day.

When my mother started her life-healing classes regularly, I was three or four, running here and there between her students. I chattered, helped myself to candy or pens I found in their pockets. I tried on all their shoes while they grunted through complicated movements on our living room carpet. I pretended I was a kitten and rubbed against their flailing limbs, purring. They would smile indulgently or pat my head, even if such behavior did not come easily to them. My mother taught them tolerance.

So I became a Child of Love much later, at eight-years old. Before that I was just a little Indian kid with scrawny brown knees amidst the big healthy American ones. My two sisters, on the other hand, were born already healed. Their immortality was predestined. It's not surprising, given that start, that they didn't last long in the real world. Can a hothouse rose survive a hedgerow? I think that was one of my mother's "paths of wisdom," printed on a red background beside a picture of her smiling face, on a laminated card to keep on your bedside table. My sisters were princesses. We all were. By the time there were three of us, my mother's divinity had been revealed. We were then, as blood daughters of this guru, this goddess, the real Children of Love.

Her followers built her that beautiful retreat in the Catskills. It was actually more like a country club. I remember standing in a muddy field, watching my mother's followers—doctors, lawyers, scientists—sitting behind the wheels of cranes and tractors, digging foundations and hammering nails, doing their *seva*, to show their devotion to my mother. Everyone knows the place, it's a resort now, I think. It was designed by a well-known architect who swallowed my mother's words as fast as she could get them out. There, amidst rolling green hills, tennis courts and riding stables and immense electronically-operated halls of audience, we grew up. Protected, spoiled and indulged like orchids. I was the only one who remembered being mortal.

I remember at five, coming back to the United States after visiting my grandmother in Delhi. Miss Miller made me stand up in show-and-tell. She said, "Anu's just come back from her trip to India."

Everyone asked, "What's India like?"

I said, "It's really hot. You just go outside for five minutes and you have to come back in and have a bath and change your clothes." I said, " I changed all my clothes three times a day." I remembered the color of the sunlight—a heavy, dusky yellow like the matted coat of a lion, sleeping in the sand. I said, "Cows walk around all over the place. There are animals everywhere." Sad little puppies and bony cats. Donkeys with big eyes and long black lashes like girls on fashion magazines. Huge, white humpbacked cows wandering the streets like ghosts in the night. After I told the class about India, I lost the spotlight. Anne-Marie, the girl with a face like a Raggedy Ann doll pulled up her dress. She showed everyone her new underwear and wasn't even embarrassed when the whole class started laughing. I was just an ordinary kid then, so I laughed too.

Anyway, I wasn't a very popular child. Not unpopular either. But nothing special. On the day of the bake sale in first grade, one girl said, "What's your mother bringing?" I said I didn't know, maybe cookies. She said, "Well, we don't want none of your honky-monkey Chinese cookies here!" Everyone laughed at me, including Anne-Marie.

So my first experiences made it a lot easier for me when I had to go back down. Funny that phrase. That's what people in the ashram, the Children of Love, called it when they left the Center and returned to their lives and jobs in the real world. "Going down." Down to the world of mortals.

When they were with my mother, they felt enlightened. Almost at the same level as me and my sisters. We, on the other hand, required no special education. Occasionally, one of my mother's devotees, often some of the most brilliant minds of the time, would attempt to teach us math or science or grammar. But no discipline restricted our freedom. We could come and go as we chose. Nothing was ever forced upon us by ordinary people. My sisters and I were born to our elevated positions. Our divinity was not our choice. It was the result of our good actions in our previous lives. One of my sisters remembers clearly that she was a healer in the middle ages, caring for the sick during the bubonic plague.

I was often told that I had been a cat. As a tiny baby, I used to awake from dreams saying, "Meow." It was my cat-like indifference that led to the downfall of the entire ashram.

When the Center of Internal Healing collapsed, my mother had fourteen Rolls Royces, three Mercedes convertibles, and one little MG—a gift from a poorer devotee—all in the same hot pink Diana Vreeland called, "the Navy Blue of India." She had houses in France, Switzerland, India and the Maldives. She had thousands of faithful followers. Her Center in New York included a school and housing for a hundred children of her followers, as well as resort-style accommodations for any follower who preferred, and could afford, to stay there. A rotating group of three handsome young men, her personal consorts, attended to her every whim and accompanied her to the ends of the earth. They even insisted on being incarcerated with her, in the same prison cell, despite the fact that they had been found innocent of any crimes and allowed to go free.

When I think about those days now, it's in those same blotchy black-and-white images that were printed in scores of tabloid newspapers. My face was young, cool and impassive, despite the destruction around me. My sisters were tearful, innocent: beautiful green-eyed children with honey-colored hair. My mother maintained her calm and beatific smile, still inspiring faith and trust in the people she encountered. During the case, while her sloppy financial records were plundered, and she was accused of everything from killing dozens of helpless children, to seducing teenage boys to creating an arsenal big enough to destroy the state of New York, she continued to convert people to her cause. In one dramatic court session, the lawyer for the Federal government, a hard-nosed man in a grubby gray suit with ink on his fingers and bits of fuzz caught in his badly-shaved face, leaped out of his chair and joined the defense. At that, a number of people rushed forward from the audience to grasp his hand in welcome.

Whenever called upon, I refused to comment. My mother, in the public eye, grew still more beautiful and charismatic. It was as if the eye of camera saw something in her that no one else could. And in the glow of the halogen, she blossomed, became more herself, and still more good. Somehow she began to embody everyone's ideal woman. From the start, males of all ages swooned when they saw my mother, something any daughter would be envious of, and they came in swarms to the Center, in the hopes of attracting my mother's attention. Women wanted to embrace her—she became their mother, their twin sister, their best friend—they adored her. Her open attitude toward love and sex among her followers did mean that early converts misunderstood the instructions and went crazy. Their behavior gave the Center its reputation for wild promiscuity. The image was not improved by mother's everchanging consorts, always golden-haired men who resembled Greek statues in both looks and bearing. However, the resulting children of her disciples' indiscretions were welcomed and treated royally, little dukes and duchesses to our princesses. They were taught by the best instructors in their own school, all dressed luxuriously in my mother's signature fuschia clothing. Even I knew that my apricot-skinned sisters were the daughters of her various consorts, though their actual paternity was too complicated to ever solve.

As for her tax evasion, my mother, who had not managed to learn about the IRS in her studies of yoga and Life, had left everything to her accountants when her reign grew too big. They were volunteers from her followers and they all tended to cheat a little, for the better good of their guru, they thought. Previously, she had no real records, because she'd not known she needed any, leaving them first to my father and then to divine supervision. As for the arsenal, it was true that we had a huge collection of guns, ammunition, bombs, and grenades. The reality was that we'd welcomed any sort of weapons, from any source. We believed we were "disarming" them, by using the butts to hold up shelves, or the barrels of guns as bud vases, or to poke in the ground while planting seeds. Bombs and grenades were used as borders for gardens. No one really knew what we had, or that anything worked until the day the stables and schoolhouses exploded. My sisters screamed, tears pouring down their cheeks, trying to throw themselves into the flames, "along with the other children of the cult, in an act of selfless solidarity," the newspapers reported. However, my sisters were too isolated from the others to even think of them as the same species. They sobbed for their friends: their horses, dogs, monkeys and birds, wanting to rescue them from the burning wreckage.

I refused to watch any television coverage of it. I couldn't stand the thought of all of us being dragged into police cars, the sound of crashing fires and loudspeakers, a second or third time, in living color.

Fortunately, for me and my sisters, there was a trust in each of our names, that couldn't be plundered no matter how ill-gotten the funds were. We were not due to come into it until we were thirty, my mother's theory being that the momentous age was when a woman gained wisdom. Unfortunately, when the ashram collapsed, I was just twenty, one of my sisters was sixteen and the other was twelve. We were on our own.

After the months of court appearances ended, we all were sent to my grand-mother's in Delhi until the newspapers and television stations lost interest. Occasionally, one of my sisters was accosted by microphones and cameras while walking in a daze through Lodhi Gardens. But even in their distraught state, their previous life had left them so haughty and imperious that the most aggressive reporters were repelled. It didn't take long for my grandmother to get fed up with the three of us, though. Occasionally, she demanded that one of us make tea or serve drinks for visiting relations. My sisters simply refused, flat out, and stalked out of the room. They couldn't ever imagine serving anyone, not even one of their hundreds of pets, their huge menagerie of exotic animals.

Needless to say, we had no pets in India. My grandmother grumbled that she had enough problems, just with the three of us princesses, without adding to her burden. She'd decided that the only way to solve everything would be to get us girls back on the right track. So my youngest sister was sent off to the Convent of Jesus and Mary school to get properly educated—her flowing silk garments traded for salwars and t-shirts. The next was enrolled at Lady Shri Ram University for Women, given a cottage industry woven shoulder bag full of books and a ballpoint pen and relieved of her diamond bracelets. Both my sisters suffered miserably, trying to navigate their way on and off the public buses through Delhi's smog-choked streets and inevitably ended up back at home with an irate taxi driver banging on the gate demanding to be paid. Because neither of them spoke a word of Hindi, they could simply ignore the drivers and march into the house. It didn't bother them that, after a few days, they were ostracized by their classmates. They thought it below them to share books or erasers with mere mortals anyway.

In my case, my grandmother opened every avenue of communication, visiting friends and relations long since forgotten, taking every phone call that got through, even during her afternoon siesta. There were daily tea parties, lunches, drinks, dinners, and wedding after wedding to attend. My portrait was taken by a local society photographer and then circulated in the right circles. These were all preparations to find me a husband who could brave my checkered past. My grandmother thought that if she could get me married, me being the most pliable of three, she might have a chance at giving a respectable life to the other two as well.

Right from the start, my grandmother had been skeptical of my mother's enterprise. My mother and grandmother would have passionate phone conversations over the crackling phone lines between India and Connecticut which forced them to shout intimacies and always ended with both of them hysterical and sobbing. My grandmother sent my mother weighty missives, double-wrapped in worn blue aerogramme paper, the watery blue ink blotched with tear drops. And my mother would answer her, packing up handfuls of her booklets and cards into padded envelopes, making me write endless letters while she dictated, alternately self-righteous and pleading. I was the only one who knew how complicated her relationship was with my grandmother. The one who knew that no matter how powerful she became, she could never convert the one person whose approval she wanted more than anything else. Because, after all, my mother was just a dutiful, ordinary Indian daughter in the end. Just as I am.

The lowest point in my mother's relationship with her own mother was probably during her divorce. My grandmother begged my mother to stay with her husband. She reminded my mother of what she should have been learning in all her books. That the good Hindu wife treats her husband like her lord and master. But my mother, like Meera who knew she'd been betrothed to another, knew she had a higher calling. And an immortal master.

My father was angry. When she picked him up at the train station in the evening, always sitting in the passenger seat so he could drive home, he slammed the door of the car shut behind him. He threw his briefcase violently over his shoulder. I was always relieved that his aim was so good. It bounced off the vinyl seat beside me. Then, with equally violent, jerking motions, he raced the car home, screeching to a halt in our driveway. There was nothing he could really complain about. Nothing to put a finger on, without embarrassing himself. His wife had been replaced by a sort of a saint. She spent all her time caring for her followers and had no time for the intimacies required of a wife.

On the other hand, my mother never neglected her duties. There was a hot dinner waiting for her husband every night, homecooked Indian food and handmade chapatis, no matter what the events of the day. When the doctor asked him to lower his cholesterol, she found clever recipes to remake his favorites leaving out the oil and fat. His shirts were always perfectly ironed and starched in the morning, so he had a large selection to choose from before he dressed for work. His breakfast, no longer two fried eggs and parathas, but now a lighter chapati and vegetable curry or hot margerined toast, was waiting the minute he appeared from his shower. The house was always immaculate. And she was always there to pick him up when his train roared in from the city. He had never waited a minute, forced to reread his newspaper impatiently on the platform, like the other neglected fathers.

Despite all that, my father found his wife had nothing to say to him. She had left the immediate world and drifted amongst her philosophies, trying to make sense of the world while he watched the football game on television. I would have to guess that she was equally detached in more private moments. And though there was never a single one of her followers left in the house when he entered, he felt their presence. Certainly, the state of the house was a partial result of their efforts. My mother's students cleaned and polished and cooked and repaired in their search for wisdom. And, in payment for their devotion, she gave them part of herself. By the time my father came home, there was nothing left.

The divorce was relatively simple. My father couldn't really explain it to anyone. He was too modern to care that the first child his wife had presented him with was a daughter. But old-fashioned enough not to be too worried about who would have custody of a girl child. My mother didn't ask him for money or the house, there was enough coming in. In fact, all she asked was that he disappear. He signed a paper, drawn up by one of her lawyer followers, saying that he had no rights to her or her estate whatsoever and that he would never defile or libel her publicly or begin any sort of proceedings against her based on their relationship. And that was to his advantage as well, because he quickly remarried and returned to a normal middle-class Indian-American suburban life. I think I have two brothers, the sons he was hoping for, somewhere on the East Coast. But even now, my grandmother believes my mother should seek her husband's forgiveness.

When the explosion—physical and legal—at the ashram hit the papers, my grandmother was unflinchingly loyal to her daughter. My grandmother said that her daughter had only tried to help others. To this day, even I would swear upon the head of which ever god you want that my mother's real desire was only to better the lives of others. Of course she enjoyed the luxuries given to her by her followers, anyone would. Given the choice of an airconditioned ride in a Rolls

Royce, who would choose the subway? Even if you know the material world is ethereal—wouldn't you want the best, most functional and attractive objects to be the ones you use and leave behind rather than clumsy, flimsy junk? That's how it was. She didn't want everything. She really believed that she was doing her followers a favor by accepting their gifts. She was allowing them to express their devotion to her. She was letting them get some relief from taxes and accountants. And, of course, she had to use her gifts, in an obvious way. Anything else would have been rude.

Of course, her followers kept increasing as fast as her fame and her possessions. She even had Indian followers, rich and powerful ones, though few of them will admit to it today.

So how did it all come crashing down? It was more than the explosion and the fire. It was more than the accidental deaths of her followers entombed in the burning wreckage, that could simply have been a tragedy. I changed everything.

It all started when I, my head buried in a science book as usual, crashed into one of her followers bringing tea to her room one morning. It was a clear, early summer morning and the sun had buttered the corridor a soft yellow. I was nineteen, but a skinny, shy nineteen, more like fifteen for the way I had been sheltered from the world. I was all long, gangly limbs and as I untangled myself from him, I realized that he was one of my mother's chosen consorts. He was tall, about a foot taller than I was, and his golden hair glistened in the beams of sunlight. Even though my blush was invisible under my brown skin, my face burned and I broke into a sweat. He apologized profusely, his handsome, symmetrical face more attractive for the look of concern that distorted it. He looked at me with eyes as cool and blue as the Caribbean sea and I wanted to dive into them. My nerves hummed. My ears buzzed. I lost my voice. He began to wipe the spilled milk from my clothes. I was frozen. Immobile. The book I'd picked up again slipped from my fingers, slapping the polished floor. Neither my science books or my mother's teachings had prepared me for what was happening.

As the tea towel reached my neck, he stopped. The air sparked with electricity around us. I barely dared breathe. I think he saw my mother's face for a moment in my own. Or the frantic rush of hormones in my body had aroused his own. Or perhaps it was the juxtaposition of a child-woman, impossibly vulnerable and naive, with my mother, a strong, selfwilled woman in possession of the wisdom of the ages. Whatever it was, he bent down. His lips pressed into mine, his tongue pushed them open. I gasped. I almost lost consciousness. But fear kept me alert. I was terrified that another one of her followers would catch us.

Then he stroked my trembling cheek and continued on down the hallway. I stood stock still. I felt I would disintegrate if I moved so much as a muscle. My eyes were glued to him as he walked through the swinging doors of the kitchen to make another pot of tea.

From that moment on, my life changed. While I had always been jealous of her followers for the way they got my mother's attention, for the first time, I began to envy my mother her popularity. I ached every time I saw him at my mother's side. He was my golden flax dream boy, the blue sea sailor who could navigate the sun-warmed waters of my imagination. I longed for him. During the day, as I wandered about the grounds, played games with my sisters or read my science books, I allowed myself only a fraction of a second to imagine his touch. Just to let a deep shiver pass over my body and then, just as quickly, dismiss all thoughts of him from my mind. Only at night, as I lay in my bed, embraced by dense damask sheets, did I unfold the memory of that kiss. Then I luxuriated in every detail, reliving it, over and over again, so that each sensation—the taste of him, the smell of his skin, the feel of his lips, his fingers, the way my body vibrated afterwards—was recorded in my memory as if carved into stone tablets.

But, for all that, I never dreamed it would happen again. My mother, like all good Indian mothers, made sure that I was well-protected. Despite all her modern trappings, she couldn't keep from wanting to safeguard her daughters' reputations as well as our chastity. We were always carefully observed and—while every whim was indulged—we were sheltered from any of life's harsh realities. To be honest, I don't know what she thought would become of us in the end. Did she ever think about whether we would marry? Or choose a calling? As I said, she spent her time worrying about greater things. While she adored all three of us, of that there is no question, the immediate care of a family and children was finally too pedestrian for such an enlightened mind.

I knew I was lucky. Because I had her in the days when she just belonged to me. In those days, she was just the mother of a little girl, living in a quiet

Connecticut town, without much more than me to distract her. By the time my sisters came along, she was the wife of a god and the mother to a whole tribe of people. So I knew that an encounter like that—for the daughter of an immortal leader—was unlikely to ever happen again. And, though I was envious of my mother, I was ashamed of that envy and I couldn't imagine wanting to hurt her in any way.

Despite all that, I found myself alone with him a second time. Perhaps it was he who arranged it. Found some reason to be in the library in the afternoon, knowing it was my hiding place. But, of course, I am the one who must be held responsible. I am the one with stronger powers. Or so I have been told. He was only a young man. I was a Child of Love. It must have been my will, which I was too weak to control, that brought him there.

I was buried deep amongst the bookshelves as usual. I lay on the floor, inhaling the scent of paper and printed pages, the sweet smell of books. I lay on my stomach, a cushion under my elbows and a heavy book, as usual, propped up in front of me. At the moment, I was interested in genetics. Even though I haven't had much formal education, I am proud to say I am an autodidact, and what I know I learned from books, rather than from experience in laboratories and operating rooms. That knowledge is what helped me find my career, allows me to do my research now with the consent of the university, without having a formal degree. So the fact that most of my childhood was spent reading rather than doing, in the purely theoretical, was finally quite practical.

But this was real life. When he came upon me, I was so engrossed in my book that I didn't even look up. In fact, the first thing I remember was being about to turn a page and seeing a sandal beside the book cover. Then I saw that there was a foot in the sandal. I looked up and there he was. Again, I gulped. Almost choked on the lump in my throat. He smiled.

He said how surprised he was to see me again. I smiled back. I would be lying if I said that in that mix of emotions—terror, anticipation and foreboding—that filled me, a great joy didn't leap up inside me as well. Perhaps I had reached a new level of self-knowledge, as my mother says in her teachings, and my excitement came from that. It was an epiphany. Because there is almost no other way to describe the thrill of the pleasure I felt. It was as if every dream I had ever had up till now had come true. Again, I was speechless. I found myself almost unable to breathe. When the words finally did come, they were unintelligible and nonsensical, my breath, hoarse and strained. I mumbled. Tried to stand and found I could not. So I stayed where I was.

He sat down beside me. My mother had told him a lot about me. He told me he was a student in his last year of medical school, so we had a common interest. He discussed the book with me. I was overwhelmed by his knowledge. Afterwards, I found out that he was an extremely gifted student. A sort of child prodigy and budding genius. Light years beyond his peers, he was already engaged in serious research as well as performing experimental surgery with some of the best doctors of the previous generation. It was all in the newspapers later. How such a brilliant mind could have been duped, swallowed up by a cult. But, like most of my mother's followers, he was much brighter and more educated than the average person. That's why her teachings appealed to him. He could understand the abstract. He could sense the idea of a greater plan in the making of the earth. He truly loved other beings, human and otherwise, and wanted to help them. And, like all the others, he found what made him stay with her. Above all, my mother made sense.

That afternoon, I might have harnessed my strength. I might have breathed and relaxed and tried to find the right path in my mind, before I went any further. But I did not. I was so unnerved that I forgot everything I had learned. And so, I suppose, did he.

As he spoke, I calmed down. I could talk to him. And as long as our bodies didn't touch or his breath brush my skin, I could maintain my composure. We talked for what seemed like a few minutes, but it must have been longer because—in the middle of the rush of words that poured out of us—he leapt to his feet and said he had to go finish his *seva*—his manual work that would lead to his enlightenment—before the sunset. Then he bent again and kissed me.

Again, I felt that flood of perception. A wave of sensation washed over me. I was overwhelmed. Submerged. When I came up for air again, he was already gone.

After that, we met often. In the early mornings, in the meadow, first crouched in the tall grasses and then lying amidst the wildflowers. The sugary smell of crushed plants filling our noses as we talked, our fingers wound into each other. When we got up, our clothes were striped with green chlorophyll smears. Or we hid in the library, using the bookshelves as cover. When we were together, we talked incessantly. Both of us were quiet types, restrained and taciturn, in ordinary company. But together, we erupted, our words and ideas gushing out over each other like molten lava. As usual, I found myself thrilled by him—my mind and body overstimulated—so I was beyond my own controls.

Gradually, though, I began to realize that something was not right. I started to find my path again and I realized that I was straying. This man belonged to my mother. My relationship with him was compromising her and her teachings. Every time we met, he seemed to be planning the next meeting. I looked forward to it as well, but the sense of wrongdoing increased in me to the extent that I now felt sick after every encounter. While my body still thrilled to him, my mind was returning to me.

The last afternoon, the last real day at the Center, I demanded he tell me what his relationship was with my mother. I told him to stop deceiving her. I told him he had to decide what was really important. Again, my emotions rose out of control. I was angry and the anger stopped me from being able to see the path I should have taken.

We were in the stables then. He had made the excuse of coming to check up on one of my sisters' horses, who was acting up. It was not just me. He had a magical touch with all living creatures, this man. Just a soft word and they seemed to instantly calm, just a touch and they were soothed. He would have been a miraculous doctor if he had lived out his life. He was surprised at my behavior. He became pale. How could we stop seeing each other, he whispered. It would kill him. He had to whisper because the adjoining school and petting zoo was full of children having their lessons. My sisters, of course, were not there because they preferred to take naps in the afternoon, having been up until all hours at night. They found school superfluous anyway. And who was going to force the children of heaven to learn the rules of the material world?

He came toward me. To touch me, I think. I stepped back. I knew the minute his fingers touched my body, I would lose. My strength lay in the invisible wall between us. I bent down and dug a grenade out of the ground. It was half-buried in the dirt, having been there for years and my fingernails ached from the soil pushed underneath them. That can't possibly work anymore, he said. I pulled out the pin, just as I'd seen them do on television, years ago, when I was an ordinary girl. He looked still paler. He took a step toward me again. I ran back, towards the meadow and then I stopped. He was still standing in the door of the stables, watching me. His beautiful, kind face was crumbling. I realized then that it was worse than I thought. He loved me. He had transferred the love that should have been my mother's, should have been devoted to a higher goal, to me. I had to run to him. To hold him. To soothe him, the way he soothed the animals and children.

I threw the grenade. I was surprised that my aim was so good. When it hit the ground in front of him, it exploded and burst into flames, setting off a series of enormous explosions as the entire arsenal blew up—like someone throwing a match into a box of fireworks. Bullets and missiles shot sparks all around them. Fortunately, someone in the main building saw smoke and pulled the alarm. The emergency system went into effect and within minutes all the nearby buildings were evacuated. Unfortunately, all the people in the stables, school and zoo were killed, including the children and animals.

At the same time that the fire trucks and television crews roared into the area, my sisters ran screaming down the hill to throw themselves into the burning wreckage. I watched as they were restrained. I joined the followers in bringing my hysterical sisters to my mother, who had been moved to the luxury hotel down the road. Then all of a sudden, there were helicopters and policemen and SWAT teams everywhere. It seemed that they'd been watching us all along. There were rumors that my old friend had been an informer, but nothing was ever really clear and I don't believe it. Then again, you never know.

No one ever pressed me to tell what really happened. So I didn't. When I was questioned, I told them I was concerned about the financial state of the place. I asked idiotic questions about the government. I led them to the tax evasion and treason charges. I blamed the followers for losing their heads and their children. I wanted the government to take it all away. I wanted them to release my mother.

You might be the only person who knows the whole story. Fortunately, they dropped most of the charges against my mother, saying that they were based on circumstantial evidence—mostly because the entire courtroom seemed to take her side—and she was released from prison after a few years, under orders not to practice her teachings again on United States soil. My sisters and I were all sent to India, to my grandmother, and she did manage to find me a husband, amazingly enough.

It's Sunil, actually. His grandmother went to school with mine and she knew my mother since she was a little girl. Sunil did his graduate work here in Michigan so that's why we moved here after we got married. He has never met my mother, but he's heard about her, over the years, and is quite impressed with her books. My mother lives in the Maldives and she still writes her teachings there, publishing book after book. But she is no longer interested in living in this world and she was happy to be freed from it when the Center burned down. She speaks to no one, save her publishers, I would think. No one is ever invited to visit her. She doesn't see or have contact with any members of her family, but I'm sure she'd be happy if she knew how my life turned out.

I only have one sister now. The younger one found life in the mortal world too much. Eventually, she retreated to her bed. She had stopped moving because she couldn't bear the thought of serving a mere mortal. She stopped eating as well because food wasn't really necessary for a divinity. She couldn't understand that she had been returned to the world, that the Goddess had been dethroned. Finally, she found no reason to continue breathing either and she expired.

My older sister still lives with my grandmother. She adjusted more to her new position and the remains of her imperious attitude serve her well as the mistress of my grandmother's now wealthy household. However, she could never see her way to bending to the will of a man and for that reason, she never married and does not have a job.

As for me, I guess I knew I was just an ordinary girl all along. I was playing at being a goddess. I was just a skinny Indian girl from Connecticut with a smart, beautiful mother. So I never really crashed down to earth. It was a game, being important, and I never cared one way or the other, except if my mother thought I should. The only person I was really loyal to was her. I was just a good daughter. Like all of us, I guess.

Do you want some more tea?

Passage to North America

S. Shankar

1

Thirunelveli, South India

Creaking in a bullock cart to a village
long unseen, my family finds the past
peeled away, and learns the grief of the bereaved.
Steel and glass have elbowed out brick and wood.
A canal we remember brown and green
has been poisoned, made a lurid red.
Chemical effluent has now left it dead.
There is no returning to a place.
Every past is but a once-known face,
a lost book frozen in the mind,
a reverie of ghosts that refuse to die.

2

Morapanadu Temple, South India

Now and then my family returns here,
though many of the records are gone.
We desire this temple of our ancestors,
this broken crone from a different era,
penurious, batscented, senile.

The carved dancing figures watch us from the walls,
observe with stony gaze our coming.
Yet I imagine their awakening,

the bowed legs of stone slowly straightening,
the heads nodding, the frozen lips straining to go
beyond the well-rehearsed smiles of dancers
and adventure into forgotten speech.
I let my eager fingers touch and trace
the flaring nostrils, the slowly ripening gaze.
I imagine I let them bravely calm
the heaving too round breasts of the dancing girls,
the too flat chests of the dancing boys.
The nipples are hard against my fingers.

In his white cloth, his head half-shaven,
the priest hurries towards us, sending dust
into the air. We stand, unsure, shoes dangling
from fingers, sunglasses filtering sunlight,
feet itching in the dust of our ancestry.
We do not belong. We do not find
our names here in the half-destroyed records.
We have trickled away, unhappy moderns,
seepage from a ruptured moss-green temple tank.

Yet, we strain to defy gravity.

3
New Delhi, North India

And here in monumental Delhi
there is the political economy
of memory. Soldiers are in the airports
encouraging happy forgetfulness,
their expressionless faces like the walls
of Tihar Jail. In polite khaki,
policemen stop unordinary men

who look like they remember too much,
too differently, much too violently.
Children have died at a birthday party.
Just trade in your memories, the soldiers' guns
are saying. Only trade in your memories.
But here memory is a commodity
beyond exchange. One is what one remembers,
and these men who inhabit other histories
will not remember what others remember.
They wish only to remember the future.

4

Transit Lobby, Zurich Airport

This is nowhere land. Nothing ever
happens here but spectral wandering
between worlds, a soundless coming and going
of aircraft beyond dirty glass windows.
Within, passengers drift past one another,
swirling and eddying through duty-free shops
with books in many strange languages,
shoulders bag-burdened with little bits of worlds
that have just been left behind—lost, all,
and tentative as unclaimed baggage
on an ever returning conveyor belt.
We are all waiting, beyond impatience,
waiting to be sucked back into history,
into some world's whirlpool existence,
waiting to be efficiently whooshed away
through steel and glass exit gates and be ferried
to uncertain new jobs, old spouses.
Meanwhile in my mind, shadowy figures
beckon out of the mist, whispering:

From India to North America,
the journey takes more than time. You pay for it
in more than money, you fathom more than space.
Do you know that? Do you realize that at all?

5

Outside Austin, Texas

Summer becomes the season of remembering,
of Texas turning India for me
one night in a McDonald's parking lot.
The smell of heated concrete in my nose
turns a sudden transplanted scent from across
half the world. This is the floor of the car-shed
in Madras come wafting over without
ticket or visa. Soon other ghosts follow:
Tamil voices of tv newscasters
chase out golden oldies on the radio.
On the billboard across the highway
two impossible women in red sarees
arrive to sell coconut oil, smiling
coyly at cowboys rushing in wagons
towards Austin and not Mylapore.

Biting into a greasy hamburger
outside Austin, I remember sweet mangos
in Madras. We cousins ate them whole
up on the large, empty roof-terrace,
facing into the evening sea-breeze,
the warm tiles beneath our naked feet
still reminiscing of the afternoon sun.
Juice dripped over our fingers, yellow,
staining our shirts, and cool from the fridge.

The best was not the voluptuous pulp
but sucking at the end on the thick seeds,
so wooden and hairy and sour
with a mango's memory of having been green,
of having once nestled amongst leaves.

6

Shedd Aquarium, Chicago

One fish waits. Another, parti-colored, darts
with seeming ambition, chanting to itself
some soundless refrain. The other fades,
brown against brown of rock, dead eyes glazed
with what some would call ancient watchfulness.
The ambitious one swiftly disappears,
with quick flick of tail, behind a rock,
chasing some invisible importance.
Moments bubble through the indifferent water.
At last the fish reappears, red and blue,
murmuring to itself still. Yet the other waits,
eyes glazed. More moments bubble through the water.

A blonde, staring boy (three feet tall and dreamy eyed)
breaks my meditation on the fish.
I lift my fingers in salute. Yes, I am
a brown man from across the unfathomed seas.
The boy darts away, red-faced, denim-clad,
searching after his father with his shrill voice.
I turn back to my fish and fish thoughts,
to my fishy drama in a watery tank,
but now both the fish are nowhere to be seen.

7

New York, New York

(The old ones finger their sepia memories,
turn the pages of their family albums,
and sadly remember and remember.)

Standing on the boat to Staten Island,
New York proud and monstrous over me,
I focus camera on Manhattan's skyline.
From a black watcher's boom-box behind me,
Jimi Hendrix' guitar gathers itself
in exaltation. I prepare to click
my camera. Unconcerned, the tall twins
of the World Trade Center, standing arm in arm
in the sun, step out of the frame, saying,
"Excuse me while I kiss the sky." I complain
loudly into the wind. Kneel and focus,
the watcher advises. I comply,
obediently. The towers of Manhattan,
unmoved, are not so easily placated.

Later in the week, Nelson Mandela
is to visit New York. Already,
posters in Harlem announce his arrival.
Mayibuye, the posters cry. Come back,
Africa. Come back, Africa. Come back,
to Harlem. Meanwhile, in a shop-window
near Wall Street, a television remembers
recent political events in color.
Long-faced men in grey suits, discussing
the Iran-Contra affair, dissolve
and give close-up way to Ronald Reagan,
who can't remember. I do not remember,

he repeats. I do not remember. Indeed,
I do not remember anything at all.

In the concrete streets of New York, the past
is often the ever-dissolving shadow
of a sax player in Africa Square,
washed and rewashed by the floodwater
of the headlights of passing cars. But elsewhere,
in one of the city's great temples
called MoMA, grave priests in black jackets
jealously stand guard over a fetish
called The Persistence of Memory.

8
Sears Tower, Chicago

The winter breeds inappropriate voices
out of the snow, old voices speaking
a language of remembered things: the fire
circling the god's face, slowly, surely,
in the priest's hand; the metal of the bell
so solemnly repeating itself,
so insistently naming itself.
At the back of my mouth I taste Indian dust.

I am Trishanku, I note atop Sears Tower
to a dear friend. Trishanku? he asks,
blue eyes curious behind glasses. Trishanku, I repeat—
and look down over Chicago,
unquiet city pretending quietness,
silently reaching tentacles upwards,
upwards, ferociously— yes, Trishanku,
desirer of other worlds, defier

of gravity, frozen in his ascent,
by the gods, between fresh earth and old sky.
My friend nods and cautiously fingers glasses.
But aren't we all, always, Trishankus?
he asks with a disarming simplicity
that I jealously want to suspect.
Silently, we turn and look east where,
beyond the veiling mist, the lake must bound
the manifold exertions of Chicago.
Behind us the glittering, white peacefuless
of a vast continent in wintry rest
promises a future beyond history.

Miss Vindaloo

Natasha Singh

I looked at Miss Vindaloo and tried to memorize her round shape. Pulling on the corner of my mother's sari, I dabbed at my eyes. Miss Vindaloo was a short lady. She had long black hair always carefully braided down her back. Her large breasts hung to her waist and were carefully supported by a belly which protruded outwards. Mind you her sari hid most of it. Folds and folds of her sari covered legs gone white at never having seen the sun.

Miss Vindaloo. Her real name was Vinnie. Actually that's not true. She was called "Vinnie" by my mom. Vinnie, (Ma always said) was better than Vivian. And Vivian, well that was not her real name either. Miss Vindaloo had told me her real name had been changed to Vivian when she was a teenager, by an angrezi schoolteacher.

"That's mean," I had exclaimed as Miss Vindaloo regaled me with the story of how her favourite angrezi teacher had come upon her name and had stated, "Why, you can't go through life with this name!"

"Why?" a young Miss Vindaloo had asked.

"Because it's simply not suitable," her teacher had replied. Miss Vindaloo had told me this same story many a time, how she had become the envy of all the schoolgirls at having been renamed by an angrezi. I had never understood why she loved this fact so much—being named by an angrezi.

Yes I am getting sidetracked. You see, Miss Vindaloo was like my auntie, although she told me I must call her "Miss Vindaloo" and never "Auntie." "It's the Canadian way," she had laughed, despite my mother's efforts to have me call her "Auntie." She had been the only other Indian where I lived. Naturally she was the only person my parents had entrusted with my care. In fact, my parents never invited any one else over except her, though we knew everyone in our town of only five thousand.

"Those angrezis," Ma would always say. "They know nothing of how to love their children. They kick them out at eighteen and make them pay for rent and food. They have no souls I tell you, no souls at all."

"Yes. Yes," my father always agreed. So Miss Vindaloo, who was a poor spin-ster, according to my mother, and had no children of her own, spent much of her time looking after me. Though she was like family, I knew secretly that my mother looked down on her for never having married.

"Don't you ever be like Miss Vindaloo," Ma always warned me. "See how unhappy she is without any children, no man to keep her company. Trying to be angrezi. Chee! Shame on her!" Yet strangely enough, when Miss Vindaloo would come over my mother would spend hours with her laughing and gossiping, and complaining about me and Papa.

Mostly when Ma and Miss Vindaloo were together they laughed a lot. Yet one day I remember she came to our house crying. "Reena! Go upstairs!" my mother ordered. So I ran upstairs, making a lot of noise, and then when I heard the tea kettle boiling, I crept back down. They were speaking in Hindi. "Whatever is the matter," Ma was crooning at a sobbing Miss Vindaloo. I inched down from my step. "Here, drink some chai," Ma said, handing Miss Vindaloo a cup as she went back into the kitchen. I rolled my eyes. I knew it. My moth-er was digging in the fridge for cold pakoras to offer Miss Vindaloo. As always, food was a quick remedy to any problem. I peeped around the corner and I saw Miss Vindaloo munching on some pakora. Both of her cheeks were full. It looked like she was eating two fat gulab jamuns. I almost started to giggle, when I heard her trying to speak though her mouth was full.

"That daycare where I work, that's the problem." Ma opened her mouth to speak, yet Miss Vindaloo kept on talking. "That wicked women who is now my boss. That woman came in and told everyone that I had been hired because they felt sorry for me. You know she is just a B I-T-C-H." She spelled it out. I quick-ly memorized it: B-I-T-C-H. *Those stupid grownups, always spelling things out.* I wondered if they knew I was listening. Anyways, Miss Vindaloo continued talk-ing and shoved something under my mother's nose.

"What's this?" my mother asked reaching for her glasses.

"Just read it!" Miss Vindaloo groaned as if in agony. As Ma read Miss Vindaloo kept on shaking her head and popping one pakora after the other into her mouth. Fascinated, I watched as she reached for her sixth one.

"It says here you are more skilled at cleaning up after the kids. Well . . . what is the problem?"

"Read on, read on. Those damned angrezis," said Miss Vindaloo, licking her fingers.

"Oh Bhagwanjee!" my mother exclaimed, slapping her forehead. I peered at my Ma who usually said that when I did something really, really bad. I knew now that whatever must have happened to Miss Vindaloo was awful. I waited impatiently. My mother reached for another pakora. "Those rascals!" she muttered as she dipped her pakora into some chutney. I saw her swirling her pakora in the sweet sauce and wanted to scream.

"Well what are you going to do?" Ma asked finally.

Do? Do about what? I wondered looking at the mysterious paper beneath my mother's nose. I wished it would float up to me, or that I could sneak over and get it. But it wouldn't have mattered, because if there had been big words I wouldn't have been able to read it anyways.

"I don't know," sighed Miss Vindaloo. "They are trying to tell me I shouldn't be teaching, isn't that right? I hate them. Everyday they watch me like spies and yet I am better than any one of them with their Canadian degrees. When they were babies I was a principal in India! I have my pride. I'm not going to go begging to any of them."

"But you've been at that daycare for years. What else are you going to do? Anyways why should you leave? The girl who wrote this report about you is new—she should leave!" Ma exclaimed angrily.

"It's no use. The new woman is here to stay. Everyone thinks she's so wonderful, because she's from Toronto."

"Toronto, shmoronto," my mother said. I wondered why she always rhymed when she was mad. Even this morning, when I had wanted a donut for breakfast instead of toast, I heard her mutter, "Donut, shmonut."

"Vindaloo, shmindaloo," I said to myself and smiled, liking the sound.

Miss Vindaloo continued, "But me, I'm just an Indian. Do you know that I have to clean up after her as well?"

My mother cursed in Hindi. "You never mentioned that you were having a hard time at work."

"Yes, I wanted to tell you, but was too ashamed. Those people treat me like I'm a maid, like I'm not qualified," said Miss Vindaloo, sobbing. "I was so smart.

Now they make me feel like a first-class idiot. What did I ever do to deserve this? I am so kind to everyone and still they treat me like I'm no better than a servant. Why did I ever come here. Why?" She began to shake and make the most awful sounds I had ever heard. I placed my hands over my ears and watched as my mother offered Miss Vindaloo more chai in silence.

I crept back up to my room and lay down on the bed, trying not to hear the crying from downstairs. I wished my Papa would come home soon, but knew that he wouldn't return till late tonight. I must have fallen asleep but when I awoke the crying was still going on. Jumping out of my bed I crept down the stairs quietly. I looked for Miss Vindaloo's round shape but it was no where to be seen. Then I saw that it was my own Ma who was crying. I went running to her. "Ma, what's wrong?" I asked, beginning to whimper myself. I hated to see my mother cry.

"Oh beti, you would never understand," she said smiling through her tears. I forced myself into her lap and snuggled into her bosom. She cried for a while and I stared up her big breasts, wondering if I would ever grow like that. I wrapped a corner of her sari around my finger and dabbed at my eyes.

"Ma," I said after a while, "what's B-I-T-C-H?"

"Oh, Bhagwanjee!" my mother gasped. "Reena . . ." I ran quickly up to my room before she could say anything else.

Now Miss Vindaloo came to our house quite often after that day, but as far as I knew there had been no mention of the crying incident. I had discovered, however, after listening to my parents talking, that Miss Vindaloo had changed jobs. I was lying on their bed one night pretending to be asleep. I had recently discovered that that was the best way to find out what was going on. No one ever told me anything. "I can't believe it," I heard my mother say. Tossing my arm over my head I then peeked out. Ma was carefully unbraiding her hair. "Now she's cleaning other people's rooms. She's a maid." Her bangles jingled as she worked on her hair, and my father lay on the bed immersed in his paper. I wondered if he was even listening. "Do you know how qualified she is? Those angrezis, they think they are better than Indians. She even graduated at the top of her class. She has shown me all of her certificates. Rajan, do you know she was principal of the girls' college in Lucknow?" My father didn't answer. Ma was clearly upset. I could see her tummy straining against her nightie as she leaned forward to straighten out the blanket. "Rajan, do you hear me?" my mother asked.

"Yes. Oh yes. Shameful it is. Really shameful." I wondered how he could read and hear at the same time.

"Really-shmeally shameful. Is that all you can say?" Ma shook her head and I knew that soon she would poke me with her toe, signalling me to go to my own bed. "Do you remember when we first met her and she had told us she was a day care teacher? Later she told me that she had just gotten that job. She had to fight for it. She took new courses and everything to prove her qualifications. Before she was chamber-maiding. Nine years of cleaning rooms before she got this job. Can you imagine, a smart lady like Vinnie chamber-maiding and now . . . Rajan are you listening to me?"

"Yes. Oh yes. Shameful it is. Really shameful."

"Really-shmeally shameful." I pretended to be talking in my sleep. It didn't work and Ma was furiously poking me with her toe to go to my own room.

I'm taking an awful long time, aren't I? You see, I wanted to tell you about what happened to Miss Vindaloo. I don't mean the job stuff either. I mean, she just started acting weird. Well that's not quite true either. It was the funeral thing that started it.

Not too long after Miss Vindaloo changed jobs, a neighbour of hers died. His name was Mr. Ogilvie. I didn't know much about him, except that he was from England. This I knew because he drank lots of tea out on his porch every morning and Ma had always told me that English people drank lots of tea. She said that that was the only thing they had in common with Indians. Well anyways, Miss Vindaloo came over to look after me one afternoon and she was clearly upset. My mother looked at her worriedly and told her she had just made some samosas the day before. So me and Miss Vindaloo were left alone. I eyed her curiously as I always did. She didn't wear a bindi like Ma but she was soft and smelled nice. That's why I liked to snuggle up to her so much. She reminded me of my mother, except Ma was less into cuddling.

"Hello, Reenaaaaa," she said, dragging out the last part of my name.

"Hello, Miss Vindaloooooooooo," I said giggling as I always did. Sometimes she would look at me strangely when I did that. Other times she would smile. Today she did neither. In fact she went right to the fridge.

"What are you looking for?" I asked, though secretly I knew she was probably looking for the samosas my mother had made.

"Aha!" Miss Vindaloo cried, bringing out the samosas along with some fresh chutney. "Reena, do you know how to make chai?"

"No. I'm not allowed to touch the kettle," I replied solemnly. I had been forbidden to touch the kettle after I had plugged one in without any water. It had gone a funny color inside and had to be thrown away.

Miss Vindaloo sighed, and set about making some chai. She busied herself and the house begin to fill with the smells of cloves and cardamom. "Mmmmmm," I said, hoping she would pay some attention to me. She brought out some cups and placed the samosas carefully in a plate. Next she dribbled chutney over its contents. "Mmmmmm," I said again in a louder voice.

Finally she said, "Reena, come and join me." I tried to climb into her lap but she told me to sit in my own chair. Scowling, I sat in my own seat. She sipped her chai and poured me a little as well. I felt quite grown up especially since Ma said I wasn't old enough to drink chai yet.

"Now Miss Vindaloo," I said, "whatever is the matter?" in the best imitation of my mother.

I was astonished when Miss Vindaloo's calm composure broke and she said, "Why Reena, that is so perceptive of you." I looked quickly at her face to see if that meant something good or bad. I think it meant something bad because soon after she started crying.

"Here, have a samosa!" I said, pushing the plate towards her, as I had seen my mother do. Miss Vindaloo popped one into her mouth and soon after tears poured down her cheeks.

"It's terrible, just terrible Reena," she said. "Poor Mr. Ogilvie died. I just came back from his funeral. Truly what a wasted life. So sad." I slurped my chai, giving her my full attention. I knew about funerals from TV. Dead bodies and everything. I hoped to pick up some information to pass onto the kids at school. "He came here from England, hoping for a better life, and his life just passed so quickly. He had no family here. Nothing. Poor, poor man," she sobbed. "Poor man." She shook her head and I tried to cluck my tongue as I had seen my mother do but it came out sounding like a burp instead. So the afternoon passed quickly. I got to eat eight samosas and drink two cups of chai. Miss Vindaloo ate only seven samosas. I hoped my mother wouldn't be mad.

After Miss Vindaloo left, I asked Ma about funerals, hoping to get some thing more interesting out of her, than what Miss Vindaloo had told me. "Why are you asking me a question like that?" my mother asked.

"Miss Vindaloo's friend, Mr. Ogilvie, died." I said, staring down at my feet.

"Why, she hardly knew the man!" my mother exclaimed. "What else did she tell you?"

"Nothing. She just cried."

"Poor dear, it must be killing her inside to be doing the work she's doing at her age."

"Something is trying to kill Miss Vindaloo?" I asked, with wide eyes.

"Don't worry about these things at your age, Reena." I scowled at her as she laughed at me. Miss Vindaloo treated me more like a grownup.

This happened several more times. The funeral talk I mean. Just a week later, Miss Vindaloo came over to look after me. After my mother had left, we sat at the table drinking chai and eating some donuts that she had brought especially for me. Ma had told her not to feed me too many. "Hello, Miss Vindaloooooo!" I giggled, waiting for her to say, "Hello, Reenaaaaaaa." Today she immediately told me about the funeral she had gone to that morning.

"Another funeral!" How many dead people did she know? I wondered.

"Yes. Another funeral. Today it was poor Miss Veronikas. She came here from Greece twenty years ago. I remember she was one of the first people who said "hello" to me. Poor thing. She worked so hard all her life. She was kind to everyone, and now death. Where is the justice in this world, Reena?" I passed her a donut, thinking that talking to grownups really wasn't that hard. Sip some chai, eat some food. I even managed to cluck my tongue, due to practicing hard every night. I had gotten into trouble from Papa who thought I was burping on purpose. "She left her family to escape marriage and came here to this country where she thought she would be treated well. Canada. Canada, shmanada. Reena, these people here have no souls, I tell you, no souls at all. She should have stayed. Oh, she left so much behind." I looked up at Miss Vindaloo who was no longer crying but mad. Maybe this would get to be more fun. I looked out the window, wondering when Ma would arrive. I had eaten most of the donuts but I knew Miss Vindaloo wasn't paying much attention. Her eyes seemed sad again.

Her shoulders were slumped forwards as she sipped her chai and carried on. I heard the door open and knew Ma was home. When Miss Vindaloo turned around I grabbed the last donut and hid it down my pants.

Ma came in, and sat down at the table. Miss Vindaloo got up to give her the remaining chai. "Have you two had fun?" my mother asked. I nodded my head up and down. My Ma began to address Miss Vindaloo and I made a run for it, clutching the lump in my pants. Sighing with relief as I made it to my bedroom, I hid my treasured donut under the pillow.

Later that night my parents came to tuck me in. "I'm worried about Vinnie," my mother said to Papa. "She's working so hard all of the time. Everyday she looks worse and worse. Today she told me she didn't mind being a maid again. Rajan, it's so unlike her. Before this she used to tell me how miserable it was, how hard it was on her back. I just don't understand." Papa came towards my window, making sure to see if it was locked as he always did. He rested his hand on my head as Ma continued. "Poor Vinnie, my heart just goes out to her. Do you know how much she has done for everyone in this angrezi town? She invites people to her home, cooks them our food. Do you think any one of them has ever invited her back? " I clucked my tongue and Ma looked at me sharply. She came towards me to fluff my pillow and my father moved towards the door.

I got up and said, "Goo-night" in my best baby voice.

"Reena!" my mother shouted. In her hand she was holding my donut.

The next week it was the same story. Miss Vindaloo came over from being at yet another funeral. She cried and cried and ate all the pakoras as well. Ma wasn't gone long and when she returned Miss Vindaloo was still crying. "Oh, Vinnie," Ma said, and hugging Miss Vindaloo, she too began to cry. I joined in soon afterwards, forcing myself between both of them. Using their saris I wiped my face. "Reena," my mother finally said, "just go to your room." Sulkily, I climbed the stairs and sat in my room. My eyes felt heavy from crying and I fell asleep and dreamed of sirens. I was awakened later by my father.

"Reena, I have some bad news for you." He looked uncomfortable, shifting from one foot to the other. "Miss Vindaloo had a heart attack earlier and she passed away."

"What does that mean?" I asked.

"It means she died. I'm sorry beti, I know how much she meant to you."

"But we just talked today," I said, beginning to whimper as I heard Ma crying in the other room. I was afraid and threw myself into Papa's arms. Even he could not hold me and I ran to my mother. I lay beside her on the bed and cried like she did. As she wailed, my wailing grew louder. Wrapping a corner of her sari tightly around my finger, I fell into a deep sleep.

The priest looked nervously at us. We sat in the front row. I knew he knew that we had never come to church before. Since there was no temple in town, the church was where we had to come. Ma had been horrified at the thought of this but there was little we could do. My mother dabbed at her eyes as he told us how Miss Vindaloo had been a real community woman. "Yes, she came to many of the funerals I conducted and was a real solid presence." I looked up at my mother who was looking at the priest strangely. How could anyone go to so many funerals, I wondered. I heard the door slam several times behind us. I turned to look, but Ma grabbed my arm telling me to be respectful. "Yes, she worked hard in this town. I know she even looked after my son at the day care before she was, ah, let go." He finished by saying she was really loved. Ma smiled through her tears. I remembered to wait as she had told me to after the priest had finished his sermon.

"Be respectful of Miss Vindaloo, the priest and the people behind us," she had said. "We were her only family here."

The priest's voice droned on. "Now let us pray to our lord Jesus and . . . " My mother and father quickly bent down to pray to lord Vishnu. I heard the door slam again. Quickly I looked behind us to see all the people.

"Ohhhhhh," I gasped. The wind was blowing outside. Puffing up and letting go it danced in and out the doors of the church, causing the doors to slam even as I looked. Poor Miss Vindaloo, I thought. Though the church held a few onlookers, not a soul was there.

emerald's bubble

Aly Remtulla

an exotic fox running through your green pastures
i am trapped inside a bubble which cannot be collapsed
i might be a chasm in the flawless gem
but i know that i enhance your perfection

wearing a dark skin i stand out
as india ink on cream silk
and i notice my melanin

i am your twin
but the spices still smell hot on my breath
as the arabic is thick on my tongue
and the drums are trapped in my cells

Visualizing Three Continents: An Interview with Filmmaker Mira Nair, June 3, 1996

Sunaina Maira and Rajini Srikanth

Editors: Do you consider the U. S. one of your homes, Mira?

M: You know, not any more, but I might have to again. Professionally, I'm very much at home, and I have great friends in New York. And I feel just plugged in. But on a lifestyle level, on a laying-down-your-roots level, I had sort of decided it wasn't, in '91 when I left; having lived and felt at home in East Africa, and, of course, in Delhi, but more in East Africa, because now I've been there longer, it's hard to buy the whole stress-machine-rat-race aspect of this country again. Especially my work, because the cutting edge is here; living in it is not entirely necessary. I've found out a way to live absolutely away from it.

Editors: So you just come here and . . .

M: Exploit it. But unfortunately because of Mahmood's [Nair's husband] being from another field and from another country, from East Africa, New York is probably the most democratic place for both of us to pursue our own work. Because India is much more my situation than his, Africa is much more his than mine, which I have made work, but I've had to travel a lot. With my son at five years old, I just don't want to leave him, it's just a really nice thing to be together. So we're trying, but I don't know what will happen. But there is enormous happiness at home, because we all pursue what we wish to do; neither of us is dampened by the other. So somehow it makes for a very happy home life and Zohran [Nair's son] is certainly blooming for it. But other people just have no idea of how our life works, but it works, you make it work.

Editors: When you came to the U. S. to study at Harvard, did you come with an interest in pursuing film, or was that an interest you developed when you were here?

M: I came as an actress. I was an amateur but very committed actress from Delhi University. And I was very strongly influenced by Peter Brook and Grotowski and had worked with people in India who had worked with them. We did fairly radical work in India. Unfortunately, most of it was in English, which was dissatisfying to me, but I was also fairly involved with the *jatra* tradition, you know the whole mythological folk theater tradition—just as an observer. I was so moved by that kind of theater, and I worked for one summer in Calcutta's political theater, street theater. So I was under the illusion that I was an academic because I liked to learn. And I thought, anyway I've got this full scholarship to come to Harvard.

When I came there, it was the years before Robert Brustein, and there was *Oklahoma* playing on the main stage, hoop skirts! It was completely retro, you know, in my opinion. I did one sort of Puerto Rican version of *Antigone*, in which I played Evita Peron. But it was very disillusioning. So I used to come to New York and spend the summer at La Mama. But when I returned to Harvard University, I was always uninspired. So I took the next best thing—most related thing—which was documentary filmmaking, which seemed to be a place where my interest of working with life and working visually came together. And I really felt lucky, and felt that I had found my vocation, through that. Then after seven years of making documentary films in the very pure cinema verité style which they teach you at Harvard, I began to get tired of waiting for things to happen. I wanted to make them happen, in a controlled way, in a way I wanted—the light, the gesture, the story. So one thing led to another.

Salaam Bombay was a coming around full circle of all these experiences, because basically I used the same techniques of theater workshopping with which I had been involved in the Delhi period, before I had come here, to organize the street kids and work with them. So it was like all these different interests being fused into one piece of work.

Editors: But did you see that as the outcome of a political stance?

M: *Salaam Bombay?*

Editors: Were you trying to make a statement about the street children?

M: I do not have agendas like that. First, I really respect the inexplicability of living, of people's contradictions, the gray areas. And the first thing that attracted me about the street kids, was not that I wanted to expose this terrible thing to the world, because this kind of holier-than-thou approach can just put me to sleep. It was really their absolute lack of pity for their own lives; they had no pity, there was no room or time for it. They want to have a good time, they suffer, too, but they are going to be flamboyant. They are going to be 'fuck you' in your face, or they're going to be full-bodied, right there, in all their multifaceted glory. And I just liked that, that spirit. That's what inspired me initially. Once you respect that, and you go with it, then the humanity is immense and inspiring. It's that really, their resilience. And the lessons that has for people like us who are just cosseted in our little worlds, and who think it's hard, and use words like depression and things like that. It's like a slap in the face—the way they live, are forced to live, and some of them must continue to live, because that's what their community is. That is it, and I think that through that type of a way of entering that world, it becomes political, because it is, warts and all.

Editors: It is a very political film when you see it.

M: But that's how it becomes like that. Not, "Now I feel like a political film." I don't have lists that I go in with. I'm thinking of a film now about identity in India. What makes a Muslim, what makes a Hindu, that type of thing. That, I would say, on an overt level, at this point, is totally political; but I'm sure by the time I finish with the movie it's going to be just another mountain of detail which may or may not be political.

Editors: What process led you from *Salaam Bombay* to *Mississippi Masala*, drew you to making that story?

M: That story was again this idea of trying to explore the hierarchy of color, which was stemming from a very personal experience of being an Indian woman undergraduate in a white university with black people who regarded me as their own, and whom I could regard as close. It was very interesting. I was like a sister, "Third World sister," and black women looking at me like it would be cool for the men to date me. I'm not white, therefore there's no territorial thing. Having these kinds of accessibility to the white and the black, being aware of invisible and sometimes visible lines that were drawn—I was finding out a new social order for myself as the kid from India. I had never been abroad. I remember, there used to be a guy who I used to be in a study group with, my first semester, I used to study with him at Hilles library; and then one day he talked to me about how he can't commit. I looked at him—I wasn't asking for anything, it wasn't even a relationship in my view. He was white, and there were these kinds of new lines, cerebral kind of whacking, a new language. And that always stayed in me, what happens if you transgress and you cross into another, how do you do that. So that kind of principle of hierarchy was in me, and I was seeking a story to tell based on that.

Then it was one of these things in *India Abroad*, and I found out about all these Indian motels all over the South; and I read an article about the Asian expulsion, a non-fiction piece, from Uganda. It just seemed to me that this was the place where both my themes, of the hierarchy of color and the notion of home, met. What happens to an Indian who doesn't know India and regards India as home but is in Africa, and what happens to an African American who regards Africa as home in a mythic way but has never been there, and what happens when one crosses the border to another. Of course that was the intellectual premise, and then it was through working with Soni Taraporewalla, the screen writer—and we worked together on *Salaam*—it was the same process of researching, documentary-style. And it was through months of work of running around Mississippi and then Uganda, Kenya, and England, interviewing exiles and finding out what really was this dream, that the story evolved. The real story, the story of the film.

In the process, of course, I fell in love with Mahmood, who had been expelled from Uganda, and it really fueled the details, which everybody, all East Africans are really amazed by, because it's absolutely right. We filmed in absolutely the same locations all the time. And said the same things. They used to have these African guys singing Indian film songs at that time, 1972, because it was a part of life there. So *"Zindagi ek Safar he Suhana"* and stuff. And I taught the Afrigo, the local pop group, the Indian film song, because they had now [in the 1980s] gone through a generation, they didn't know the song. And we had Afro wigs, bell bottoms, we created the era, and we filmed that in the same night club in which they used to sing, and often with the same guys, extras, just twenty-five years older, in those bell bottoms and flowered shirts and stuff. And *"Zindagi ek Safar he Suhana."* Just the whole idea of black groups singing this Indian song, and now they sing it again, because now it's part of the repertoire. It happened. When Ugandans see it, they freak out.

Editors: We were wondering, too, how you perceive the debate that sprang up at the South Asian Students Association (SASA) conference [at Brown University, in March 1996, where Nair gave a talk and screened clips from *Mississippi Masala* and a short, *"The Day the Mercedes Became a Hat"*] that focused on your representation of Indian Americans, women. What was your observation of that discussion?

M: I felt an enormous sense of affection and a slight bemusement. Precisely because there are so few of us at the moment. There will be many of us in five years making media portrayals of ourselves and our communities. Right now, because I am one of the first, I am looked upon as a kind of Messiah. I mean, that first question [from a student in the audience], "Do you believe in arranged marriage, should I have an arranged marriage?" It was strange, like I'm supposed to tell this boy how he should live his life. And what gives me the right to tell him how to live his life. I find it sort of cute, not cute, but touching— "Come on, grow up a little." But then I understand, because there are so few "leaders" for the young people. But I was very powerfully saying that I refuse to concede to this position you're giving me just because I'm the only one doing movies, because then I'm this self-appointed spokesperson for the community and nothing could be more dreadfully boring than that. So that's one point. I think that there are so few of us out there doing this thing [representing the South Asian community], and it's so good that you're doing this [referring to *Contours*] for instance, because it just gives us all voices. Then there'll be less pressure on people like me, because everybody will do their idiosyncratic versions, which is really what the world needs rather than one ambassador.

Secondly, I do take the point of this emasculation thing [several students in the audience accused Nair of portraying the Indian American male, in *Mississippi Masala*, as emasculated and somewhat of a buffoon]. We were not setting out to do that. I was perfectly honest when I said that it's the irreverence that is born from seeing it from the inside, but it's an irreverence that comes with compassion for sure.

Editors: Essentially, what you're saying then, is that you're expected to be the ambassador for Indian America because you are one of the few visible Indian American filmmakers, probably the only one at this point out there. So you think that some of the criticisms leveled at your representation of the Indian American male will minimize when there are many more of us making films?

M: There will be more room for all shades of us. I can tell, absolutely with hand on the book, that these characters in the film have really been inspired from actual folks we've met, and the sort of ludicrous "Don't touch my car" kind of insanity [a character in *Mississippi Masala* is fiercely protective of his car], and also the passion and familial responsibilities of the patriarch, both things, they exist. And our racism is wild and kicking, out there, it's alive. But the pressure to do this and have the doctor in a Porsche in the same film [the reference is to a comment from a viewer, several years ago, that Nair should also include in her films portraits of the successful Indian American male, such as a doctor in a Porsche], that's my pressure, imposed by such people. But I can't listen to that while I'm making a film. It'll be interesting to see the reaction to *Kama Sutra* [referring to her most recent film], because once again, it has much more power, in an overt way, it is a female film. Not a woman's movie for women, but female- empowering, a female film with two really strong female protagonists.

Editors: We had a paper that was submitted to the anthology [see "Moments of Identity in Film" in the anthology] by someone who was doing an analysis of different films—Srinivas Krishna's *Masala* and *Mississippi Masala*. The writer makes some observations about the depiction of Mina in the film, her sexuality, the "hot and spicy" appeal of Indian women. We were wondering what you feel about that, when people make those kinds of observations about the exoticization of the Indian women on the screen or the portrayal of their sexuality.

M: In *Mississippi Masala*, that she was exoticized?? Cleaning bathrooms in t-shirts?

Editors: The writer's point is that Mina initially starts off wearing K-mart clothes, but then once she and Demetrius develop this passion for one another, she suddenly starts wearing salwar kameez and dupattas.

M: Only at the absolute end of the film, which is a slightly surreal sequence, she wears an Indian skirt. And the only other time, is when her mother makes her wear Indian clothes to the wedding. But otherwise, it's completely K-mart. In fact it broke my heart each time that I had to dress her in K-mart clothes; it was K-mart all the way. Wait till you see this movie [*Kama Sutra*]! Here we go high order of the exoticizing.

Editors: We're interested in your depiction of female sexuality, the Indian woman's sexuality. When you thought about making *Kama Sutra*, was that one of your primary motives? Where did the impetus for the film come from?

M: The impetus to make the film came from the absolute sickness with which I see sexuality and male-female relationships being depicted, depicted in India, on the Indian screen. I just have not seen anything more vulgar and subversive and twisted and sick, and I think it has really skewed our whole consciousness, especially the male consciousness in India. It's astonishing to me that this is the country that really has thought very deeply about love and the philosophy of love and sexuality in the Kama Sutra, which can be interpreted as a male-oriented book. But the film is our own version, a female look, a completely radical look, in the sense that it is matter-of-fact: if you wish to do this, wish to have the skills of love, these are the skills. But if you wish to have the skills of love with a lover, with a true lover, it can be transcendent like the divine love. That kind of pathway of approaching sexuality and love is a deeply philosophical and beautiful one, and we're so far away from it that I wanted to find out, involve myself with the source. After *Kama Sutra* [the book] itself, I read, we read, Kalidas' erotic poetry and Geet Govind and the Ramanujan stuff, all the Sanskrit erotic poems, the Sufis, the kind of emotion of union with the divine, the double entendres with the lover and the divine, and then Moghul and pre-Moghul work, to understand the kind of milieu.

We settled on sixteenth-century India to base this film, for purely pragmatic reasons, because the locales I liked were sixteenth-century—couple of palaces and forts. I didn't have the money and didn't want to create anything from scratch. I had learned that from [a film on] Buddha, which I was earlier going to do and which fell apart, which was eleventh-century. At that time, we went around the whole country looking for appropriate locations. Obviously there was nothing left. I just wanted to be pragmatic while making *Kama Sutra*, and do things my way. So it's an invention, but an invention with an attempt to address the issue of lost ancient knowledge on sexuality and how to bring it back. And I'm sure the reverse [rejection of *Kama Sutra*'s message of sexuality] could happen, where India is not ready for a film that is so natural and explicit and elegant in its sexuality. But who knows, I have to cross that hurdle when I come to it. That's the main inspiration for it.

What I wanted to do was not just to make the love scenes erotic. The whole film is erotic, the whole film is sensual, because it's in India, and it's not some romantic view, it's completely an insider's view of the eccentric things that are erotic for me. Like an older woman bathing on a traffic island, with clothes on, is for me deeply sensual. It's like part of a tapestry. Aesthetically in the film it's very tied in to, very influenced by, Tantric art, Tantric aesthetic, and of course the Tantric belief of the sexuality of the divine. As it happens, we shot in Khajuraho, which is our main location. And there, it's so alive and well: every banyan tree has *lingams* [Shiva represented as a stone penis] and *yonis* [stone representation of the vagina] and fruit, coconut and a lamp; every place is alive with this belief of the meeting of the *lingam* and the *yoni*. Just so happens. In urban India, in our work and in our media there, we've gotten so far from the kind of beauty of that thought. I'm sure the film is going to be turbulent, with people perceiving that I am actually exoticizing Indian sexuality. I'm sure it will happen. Whereas actually, I'm really revealing the source for me, interpreting it in my way. It's there, it's almost totally documentary. And of course, that translates into how I film the love scenes, which is documentary. It's artistic, whatever, but it's not pretense, it's not like panning to the bra and the cigarette. It's beautiful. It's filmed in a time when there was no shame involved with sex; this was a skill to learn, and this was the fact, if you wish to do it. There were schools for it. The character of Rekha [Indian film actress] is a priestess, one who teaches. Rasa Devi is her name. You could go to her to be a courtesan or wife.

Editors: It's interesting that you anticipate that people are going to criticize you for *Kama Sutra* and your depiction of sexuality in it.

M: I'm always being criticized. Thank god I'm not in this academic scene. If I was, I would be so straitjacketed and so worried about who will think what. I just go off into a deep zone when I am working, and I follow my heart. Completely instinct. But of course, instinct based on a kind of education and all kinds of eclectic influences. But I'm not sitting there second-guessing myself at all.

The reason I'm saying this to you is that I had my first screening of ten minutes, but the hottest and the most diabolic ten minutes of *Kama Sutra*, at Columbia [University] in Gayatri Spivak's class. I didn't know her, I'd never met her. She invited me and I went there. She said it was just a small class. There were people hanging from the rafters, it was full. It was electric! It was exciting. It was my first glimpse of this movie in the outside world. Wow! Explosion! It was very interesting, very positive. They couldn't catch their breath; it was unbelievable. I'm in my cocoon here making the film, and that's the way it should be, otherwise I'll always be catering to this one and that one. But I had a feeling for the first time that it's going to be dreams [how she hopes audiences will respond to *Kama Sutra*]. As it is I get papers, people actually writing papers on me, and I can't understand half of them. I just don't speak that language.

It's a completely idiosyncratic view, my view. It's really dramatic, and finally I think it's really spiritual.

Editors: Was there any theme or issue in the film where you had some difficulty or which was a point of struggle, when you look back on it now that you're almost close to finishing? Was there any question that came up that made you really stop and think and reflect on how to play it out, or was it just a very smooth process?

M: Oh, no! I mean, it was not at all smooth, making the film was hugely difficult. There's a scene in the film which was always trouble, right from the writing to whether we should cut it out before shooting it, and then we decided to go ahead and shoot it. It was a scene in a brothel and it was [with] Maya, the protagonist, who has met Jai, the sculptor, and she's not sure of what his intentions are with her, and she asks him whether he's just like any man on the street, sometimes he confuses her. And she asks, "Are you just like them?" And he says, "Come I'll take you somewhere, you can see yourself, how bestial men can be." So this was a scene we wrote to show how bestial men can be and how he is not. But the question of whether we should do that, and how we should do that, and of course, we wrote it fairly . . . pushed the envelope on that, we never filmed it that way.

But at the heart of it is a young virgin who is sold in that scene—all of this is absolutely, definitely what used to happen, even today it happens. But just filming it and it was like somebody did *jadoo* on me, it was *soo* difficult, a normal shot. And this was a fully clothed scene; we had done many nude scenes before that with our principal actors, and love scenes and stuff. But this was one of those few completely clothed—not few!— a big scene that was not delicate on that level. It was just the idea of it, it was hard for me . . . and it was a fairly strongly female set and it was hard for us to have this young girl and present her like that, again [in] clothes, and nothing as such demeaning, everybody was acting, but it was a tough one, tough, tough, tough. And as it happens, it's a scene that's riveting, which is so hard . . . I almost thought I didn't get it, because somehow, even to walk from A to B was difficult.

But there was lots of stuff that was physically much harder. But that was a big question, you know, morally, does this [scene] need to be in? We finally decided ourselves, let's shoot it and see. You'll see it, it's dramatic rather than voyeuristic. It's a point we're making rather than depiction of that point.

Editors: We were wondering when you showed *The Day the Mercedes Became a Hat* [a short film about the assassination of the South African Communist Party's leader, Chris Hani, shown at the SASA conference at Brown in spring 1996], have you been making shorter works alongside or in between these bigger projects, or was that an unusual work?

M: That was unusual, I'd love to [do work like that], I love it.

Editors: What made you make that film?

M: It was an amazing weekend, Chris Hani was assassinated on a weekday and then, South Africa changed, Mandela was being referred to on television as the president, there were no elections. And the ANC had organized, and the Communist Party had organized these incredible mourning marches, all over the country we were marching with them, totally organized, no looting, nothing. And I would come home and then I would see that two shops had been looted, but on television only that would be shown, as like, "Look at what's happening."

We were living in South Africa for five months, and this happened in the fourth month. And we were living in a white area, because we couldn't live anywhere else. We couldn't live in the black area, you know. And everywhere around us, "For Sale" signs just sprung up, within twenty-four hours, people were leaving, New Zealand, Canada, anywhere! And they were just terrified, and I could see the reality that I was participating in was one thing, which was an amazing thing too, because some of these white cities [were] being populated by these waves of black people coming out of those townships, and with such dignity. And then coming back and seeing on televion this whole other picture. But also, just seeing them in that city that I had lived in without seeing them ever before, you know.

So Helena and I—Helena is South African—she and I were writing *Kama Sutra* at the time, and I wanted to do [a film with] this idea of the kids, this nonverbal competition [between two South African boys, one black and the other white], so we just merged the two ideas and made this film. It was for a big project that never happened, and I was really pleased with it, we shot it in four days and it was done. South Africans can't get over it. It's just absolutely South African. The accents, the details, the way they wear those clothes. I knew all those things. I used to go to this gym, and they were all these girls, white girls, who dressed like that. They dressed like that for grocery shopping, almost naked, naked! They put L.A. to shame in South Africa, I'm not joking! And they would have this dyed blond hair, black roots, brown roots, and dyed blond hair that they hadn't touched up. And in the gym, I would see all these girls, naked girls practically, with these roots and dyed blond hair, and I remember this poor actress, who was naturally a blonde, and I made her go and get brown roots. She said, "Why are you doing this to me?"

Editors: We haven't talked about *The Perez Family*. We just wanted to come to that, we remember you saying at the SASA conference at Brown that it was a "studio film." So does that mean you didn't have as much latitude as you normally have?

M: Yes.

Editors: What were some of the ways in which you felt circumscribed by that?

M: Well, I was sent the script, and I liked the script, and I was sent the script at a time when two films I had worked on had not happened, [a film on] Buddha and this South African film. And so I just wanted to make a film, and I liked the script enough. And I must say I got the script to a point which I wanted, I wanted to make a film that hovered between dream and reality, because that is the nature of reality. I think that I had brought the script to that point of the dreams, and making the dreams very real, very much a part of the film, a non-linear kind of thing.

And I made the film because the president of Goldwyn is an old friend, Tommy Rothman, and he pursued me heavily to do this film and I really like him, he's a very bright, eccentric fellow. I got the best crew in the world and it was great, and shooting was just ecstatic, and they were ecstatic about the footage. And then the day we finished shooting, Tommy came up to Miami and took me for a walk on the beach and said, "Guess what? I've been given a chance to set up my own division at Fox, so I'm leaving." And I said, "Yeah, what happens to the film?" He said, "Oh, we're so happy about it that nothing can happen, my being here's just relevant."

But of course, it wasn't like that; he left, and another guy came in, and it was not his project, and the negotiations with Goldwyn, there was nobody to control them. Tommy was really an intelligent person and I was now left . . . and they kept smelling this potential sort of *Four Weddings and a Funeral* kind of hit, you know, like a comedy. And I finished a slightly more—I mean I love comedy and there's a lot of comedy in the film—but it was a slightly more serious, artistic film, it was really hyper-real, it was magical, and it just teetered [between dream and reality], just like I had thought of it.

And it did very well in the marketing, they have these previews. But because it did well, they thought, "Oh, it can do better." They kept second-guessing themselves. So they kept pressuring me to make it more cut and choppy and fast-paced and moving, and I kept fighting that for four months, and I felt like I was winning all those battles, and I really had won a serious amount of battles because they wanted to do all kinds of things that were different, change the ending. . . . All of that I won. But cumulatively, when I step back and think of it—and I haven't seen it really since I finished it—it is not that film that I finished, first gave as my cut. It is twenty percent different. Because they had marketing on their minds all the time, and they don't know any more than you or I. So from a film that was a more serious, artistic film it became a very well-made roman-tic comedy with seriousnesses that flies by, I guess. And they went ahead and absolutely made a hash of the release when they opened it, they didn't support it enough in advertising and they were just ill-equipped and they just fucked it up. And it's no fun to be strategizing, you should be making the film, you shouldn't be doing politics, and there were serious politics for four months.

But the Cubans, who are really fiercely nationalistic people, they just think this film is really about them. They don't know about all these other struggles, they just see it for what it is, they think it's spot-on about Cuban culture, and it's really Cuban. I won the Best Director [award] from the Spanish Film Critics' Association and it won the Best Actor and the Best Actress. . . . But I, just at the moment, have written it out of my consciousness because it's too painful to think of what I went through and too painful to see what they did to the finished film, I mean even the finished film as it is, is a far better film than most films that are out here. And they just ruined it. So I'd rather have it back in my hands again.

Editors: What has been your response to the questions that focus on the issue of casting, from the Latino community?

M: I mean I understand the premise of their objections, but I find it so limited in vision; one, because, a Hispanic person, generic, like a Puerto Rican, I think can be as far as from being Cuban as an Anglo is. And there's no understanding of that. I mean, by that thinking, Rosie Perez who was dying to the film with Marisa's role would have been politically correct, but for me, and for any of us, she's a Brooklyn–Puerto Rican girl. Ask any Cuban who has any head for all this whether Marisa was real "Cubanaza," and they will tell you that she walked like them, danced like them, talked like them, that she's an actress, number one. So, the belief that just a Perez last name can do this, you know, it's just so limited, and I think finally it is an artistic choice.

And I went through four hundred people, it would have been much better for me, I wanted to submit myself anyway to the culture as I did, so it would have been a huge boon to have the actress be [Cuban/Cuban American], you know, but there was not one that got my blood spinning. It's absolutely an artistic decision, intuitive decision, and one has to judge the end, not the last name. But I can understand it, I can really understand it, but I find it a little demeaning also in making Latinos generic. Like a Tamilian can play a Punjabi, you know, without a problem. It's just really different. And the caste system in the Latin American community is alive and well.

Editors: So, Mira, if you had to talk about the ways you've changed as a film-maker, since you started doing *Salaam Bombay*, what most comes to mind?

M: That's a good question. Well, I'm used to having more resources now. It would be very hard for me to give up that international standard of complete excellence and working with the best people, and I'm talking behind the camera. I'm still a guerilla when it comes to casting, you know, Indira's [Varma, from *Kama Sutra*] never been in a movie and she's carrying the whole film. So I still bust my butt with trying new actors, non-actors, all that goes on all the time. But technically I'm used to—because I'm so much of a producer at the same time—not a kind of flagrant "I want a crane and I want it forever," but I don't want to compromise, and I cannot, on the technical support and awareness that I need.

And in *Salaam* we did everything ourselves and we really didn't have that, and

I did everything, I was producer, director, assistant director, co-writer, tea-maker, everything. I don't think I could do that again, that kind of do-or-die—I mean it is [always] do-or-die, even this film was deliver-or-die—but the few other people, not many, but the few other people just carrying it with me, not alone.

Jumbee Curse

Marina Budhos

There's a saying about Indians like my Grandfather who voyaged to the Caribbean in the nineteenth century: gone to Tapu. It means: Gone to the Islands. It also means: disappeared. The folks who gathered their wooden feeding bowls, their rupees and chappals and trudged onto the huge English boats, couldn't think too much of a return. In their world, if you traveled west of the Indus River, you were lost to them, back in India.

Often I think there are other ways to be lost, to fall off the edge. Just by not knowing the people closest to you.

Our family was like a small lit box, surrounded by a deep purple space, a space I always wanted to leap back into. In this space, which circled like a wilderness, were the stories of our shared family past—Guyana, the hot, drowsy sun, tales of madness, all the uncles and aunts and family friends who'd disappeared to Toronto and New York. The older I got, the more I started to ask questions, at dinner, at bed, when I woke up. About my father's six brothers and sisters down in Guyana, whom he and Aunt Inez never visited.

The summer I was ten, a baby sparrow fell from its nest in the chestnut tree. Aunt Inez came running when she heard my shout. We both stared at the broken-necked bird, pale as an eel, smashed on the pavement. "That's bad luck," she whispered. Bending down, she scooped it into her salmon palms. "Its own family bring it down." She nudged my arm. "Meggie, go get Uncle Tom's spade from the shed."

I went inside the shed where I pulled out the spade underneath a bag of peat moss. Aunt Inez was waiting by the steps, the baby bird balanced inside the tent of her apron. Together, we squatted and began to dig. She shook out her apron, so the bird tumbled inside the hole. "A dead baby bird is the same as a lost child," she told me. "If it's not taken care of properly, during a high wind it returns and comes to torment you." She added, "That's what happened with your Uncle Joseph."

A few days later I was sitting on the back steps with my mother shelling peas when I asked her to tell me about Uncle Joseph. "Oh, Meggie," she laughed. "Why do you always want to know about those old stories? It's not nice to talk about your father's family so much."

"But they're my family too," I whined.

My mother considered this, running a fingernail down the bowed seam of a pod. Her green eyes shone, as if lit up from behind. I knew she enjoyed these stories as much as I did, but felt funny because we were living with Uncle Tom and Aunt Inez, who didn't like it when my father talked about the past so much. She set the bowl down. "All right. I'll tell you. Joseph was brilliant. He and your father were the only boys in the whole village to pass their overseas exams. Everyone said Joseph was going to write books and one day be famous. He got a job in the government, pretty high up.

"He did so well, he was offered another job on a government base in Aruba. Only your grandmother wasn't too happy about this. She sent him letters every week. She went to the obeah who made a spell so her son would come home. And sure enough, he did return after six months. Only something was wrong. He complained about a funny noise in his head.

"One day he left the house and put on a suit and tie and went for a walk. He didn't come back for two weeks. When he did, he couldn't say where he'd been. He sat on the veranda and talked about the birds in his head. Soon that was what he came to do all the time. He would stay for a few weeks and then go wandering the countryside. Your aunt calls it the jumbee curse."

"What's that mean?"

My mother shrugged. "They say that every season, when the old folks planted their sugar seeds in the fields, they wept tears of longing for India that mingled in the earth. The sugar cane sprang up fine and glossy as mare's heads. The fields glowed with a copper fire. But it was a dangerous, hard glow. The sugar carried the burnt taste of loss. The rum they made muddled their children's heads and made them slow-footed and melancholy so they could never leave home.

"Everyone says the boys from Letturkenny walk under a jumbee curse that comes from their families. They say they've mixed up too much ambition and history in the boys' heads. That way they don't know if they want to go forward or back." She laughed. "Oh, I hate when your aunt and father talk that way. They're living elsewhere now. It's so ridiculous, so backward. In this day and age!"

I didn't know what to believe about Guyana or my father or the jumbee curse. Whenever I thought of my father and Joseph and those he'd grown up with, I saw these little boys walking along the dirt roads with enormous heads they could not carry on their shoulders. Once I dreamed of sitting in a boat on the ocean with my father, his own head sitting in his lap, huge as a flaming orange pumpkin, as he talked to me about the meaning of light. On and on he went about the crazy, infinite energy of the universe, how he and I could be sitting in a thousand other boats on a thousand other seas. As he talked, the ocean swelled and tilted, tugging our boat toward the equator, which to me was the edge of the world, of my own understanding, where everything fell off.

I often wondered why we didn't spend more time with the men who had taken boats and airplanes and landed in America and England to find work and apparently could carry their heads just fine. When I asked my father about what happened to them, he said, "We all move on, Meggie. We pick up our selves and start new again. We try to become what we can." He patted me on the knee. "Besides, that curiosity of yours going to burn you up one day."

In all the stories, though, I could also hear the other, darker Guyana: how Grandfather Barath threatened to keep his children in the sugar vats if they dared defy him. There were the roads that flooded in the rainy seasons and would not drain, the mud beaches, and broken down plantation houses, and rum house where Grandfather liked to drink and gamble. A lost ambition, a slow going backward. There was his brother Joseph who wandered the dirt roads. My father always spoke of the relatives who stayed behind in sorrowful tones, as if they had buried themselves in the old cane fields.

One day, Sheila Perreira came to stay with us, bringing news of all the people we'd lost touch with. A second cousin of my father and aunt's, Sheila grew up in Georgetown. "She gone Casablanca," the family used to say of her, which meant she was a girl who ran with a fast city crowd and did as she pleased. At nineteen she ran away with a rich Brazilian businessman, though we never saw him.

My aunt called Sheila the Punjabi Princess, sniffing at her tailored tweed suits, pockets hung with loops of chain gold. Her skin was a smooth teak, her waist perfect. I thought Sheila beautiful. I could not take my eyes off of her, as she gave me some idea of what I might look like when I grew up, since I did not resemble my own mother, who had green eyes and pale, freckled arms. I closely watched the mischievous curve of her mouth, the way she tilted her long neck, later mimicking her in my bedroom, hoping that I might imprint every gesture of hers on me.

Sheila brought me a red velvet vest, woven with silk-stitched arabesques and studded with mirrors. The vest was given to her, Sheila told me, by an Air India pilot who occasionally arrived in London to swoop her up and take her to places like Bombay or somewhere on the horn of Africa. He would call at all hours of the night. We never knew his name, exactly, but he always chimed out something like, "Moobie" or "Boomboom here, calling from Dubai, can you put Sheila on?" He said this as if he'd just stopped by from around the corner. It made the glamour of their globe-trotting life seem terribly close, and we would scurry and bump about in the house as we frantically tried to figure out where Sheila was staying now.

Then the pilot's family arranged a bride for him. Sheila and he would not be able to see one another—at least not as easily. The last time he saw Sheila, he bestowed on her this beautiful vest. He told her that each mirrored sequin was for a country he flew over to be with her. By now, though, Sheila felt quite done with her pilot and gave the vest to me. "That woman is downright vulgar," my aunt scoffed, brushing away the shiny scales she found scattered on the rug.

"Leave her alone," my father said. "She come here and give us a taste of all the folk we gone forgot."

Annoyed, my aunt banged into the kitchen to make us supper, fuming, "That's one taste I don't need in my mouth!" She couldn't have been too mad at my father for his homesickness, though, because that night she made us a huge pot of chicken curry. When my father scooped up meat between his fingers, she scolded, "That's uncivilized," tapping her fork on her plate.

Sheila, leaning back in her chair, a small, mirthful smile on her lips, said to my father, "Look here, dear. You really ought to give some of the old boys a ring. You can't lose touch altogether, you know."

The next morning my father picked up the telephone to call some old

Guyanese acquaintances living across town. To my delight, my father had gotten himself invited to a cricket game that afternoon in a nearby park.

"What do you want to do that for?" my aunt asked when he told her his
plans. She and Tom were getting ready to visit a sick friend on the other side of
town. She had dressed up in a mulberry wool dress, Sunday hat pulled down over
her curls. Aunt Inez didn't approve of Guyanese anymore; she thought them lax
and deceitful, and hated how they wore their shirts open, showing black curly
chest hairs. Indian-Indians ranked much higher in her mind. They slipped their
sandals off on the hall mat, didn't eat beef, and impressed her with their moral
purity.

"Warren likes to play cricket," my mother put in. "He'll meet up with some
old friends."

"Old friends," Inez grumbled. "I know all those rum-headed fellows. You
watch, if you invite them over the first thing they do is they going to ask us for
money. Those boys are lazy. They don't know how to get on with their lives."

"Oh, Inez. You are too much sometimes. You forget you were an immigrant
once too."

"Forget!" She opened the door, tugged on her gloves, and pointed to George,
who was going with them. "I made a good life for myself here. I didn't come
here to listen to their stories and moan about the old country. I married a good
man." She patted Tom on the arm. Then she flounced through the gate, shouting over her shoulder, "No visitors!"

The moment Inez and Tom left, the house took on a different, careless air.
Anything was possible. I zig-zagged through the rooms, wearing my velvet vest,
thrilled by the spangles of light that danced off my chest. Instead of folding the
laundry, which lay in crumpled heaps on the chairs in the back parlor, my mother and Sheila snapped open Sheila's suitcase. Inside were stuffed dozens and
dozens of shalwar kamizes and saris bought by the Air India pilot. Out they
poured in a stream of riotous color: pink chiffon duputtas, sea-blue saris flecked
gold. Next to the dusty grays and blues of Aunt Inez's blouses, they looked
tempting as as a meal. I wanted to dive inside, nuzzle my face in the buttery yellows and creamy browns. I grabbed a cotton woodblock kurta with a tassle of
cork buttons, and pressed it to my face, sniffing its mysterious, woody scent.

Giggling, my mother and Sheila were already slipping into outfits and parading for each other on the oval rug. My mother wore a lime-colored shalwar, the deep orange duputta running down her back in an extravagant flame. Sheila put on a slinky silk kurta with matching harem-style pants that gapped open, giving quick glimpses of her slender thighs. Then they lounged in the deckchairs with lemon slices on their eyes and spiked iced tea by their feet. I trailed after them and sat at their feet, my vest's gold brocade rubbing rough and stiff against my bare arms.

A few minutes later, my father came back from the cricket match, bursting through the door in a swell of chatter and laughter. I felt a jiggle of nervousness. I had never seen my father like this. His Caribbean dialect had returned in those few hours away, like a musical record he'd kept locked and unplayed in a closet. "Look it here!" he greeted my mother. "This here Maywa and Charles, they second cousins of mine and now they living over here!"

Charles was golden-skinned, his round bald head shining like an upturned brass pot. Creases etched the corners of his mouth, so he looked as if he was always laughing. As he crossed his arms across his barrel chest, I grew afraid, imagining that his laughter would fill the room and we would never sweep it clean and neat again.

"How was the game?" my mother asked as she hurriedly scooped the bright-colored clothes into a pile on the open suitcase and followed them into the front parlor.

Sheila pushed a wave of hair from her brow, eyes flashing. "You boys play all day and forget about the girls at home, hunh?" Sheila's accent also seemed suddenly thicker, saucy with teasing.

Charles waved a hand. "Now Sheila, how we stay away, knowin' you beautiful women waitin' here?" He turned to the others. "Besides, you think we can play one of those games whole day long? They interminable, man, interminable!"

My father had hurried into a corner of the room, where he was busy pulling out liquor bottles from the cabinet. Now I knew the Guyanese talk would begin. Usually my dad started and the others chimed in, full of challenge and good humor. It was a game, a different kind of storytelling than he did with me. It could go on for hours, their voices a soft and rum-warmed swirl of sound, the rooms filled with a yellow warmth I loved to swim inside.

But I kept remembering Inez's disapproving glare when she'd left in a huff that morning. I chimed in, "We're not supposed to open the liquor cabinet. Aunt Inez said."

"Oh, Megan," my mother laughed. "Stop repeating what adults say."

"Listen to that!" Sheila giggled, tugging on the edge of my vest. "Meggie got a touch of Inez's starch in her!"

"Don't worry, little lady. Just a nip to get the boys going," my father teased, and winked at me. His laughter rumbled loudly in the room. "I cannot believe it! I look over to the other team, and who is there but that old clown, Charles! And Maywa, you used to climb the coconut trees, man, faster than a rat."

"Not anymore," Maywa said, bending over and rubbing one of his kneecaps. "I'm a serious fellow, Warren. Just like you. I going to be a doctor."

I could not stop looking at Maywa, as if he were somebody I already knew. He was rail-thin, trouser hems falling above the bony knobs of his ankles. I watched him pace between the sofa and chairs, never once settling down. He stopped moving only when my father handed him a glass of rum and drank in long, noisy gulps.

"I know Charles since we were babies," my father explained. "Our mothers, they like sisters."

"What you saying, man! Your side of the family so proud, it don't talk to mine!"

Maywa looked up from his glass, grinning. "Charles, you makin' up stories. It my side of the family they pass on the road and turn their heads away. They think we too common and stupid."

"That is the damn blasted truth," Charles laughed.

Sheila pranced around the room like a pretty colt, fist on a hip, while the men watched admiringly. "And why he not pass you on the road!" she teased. "He got better things to do than hang with you slow-movin' boy! I'd pass you on the road too and never come back!"

"Oh, Sheila, you gone passed us long ago," Maywa smiled, and pretended to grab his chest, out of feeling heartsick. Smirking, Sheila flounced out of the room to go help my mother in the kitchen.

More drinks were passed around, and the conversation churned on. I grew dizzy, trying to follow what was being said. Every time someone said something, it was loudly and vehemently contradicted. I had the feeling some kind of joke was being passed between them, but no matter how hard I listened, I couldn't get inside them. Their talk teased and spun on, making me wish I might plunge into their words, like rubbing my face in the smells and bright colors in Sheila's suitcase.

Charles had grown the loudest by now, while Maywa's laughter whipped in the air, his yellow teeth flashing like small, sharp blades against his dark skin. "Come, Meggie, come!" he bellowed. "Talk to Uncle Charles." He made gobbling noises in his throat and swung his arms out in front of his face, waving them like tentacles.

They're making a joke of me, I thought with dismay, and shrank against the wall, glaring at these strange men, who now seemed so foreign to me. Charles waved insistently at me. "You come to Guyana, child, and we drive a jeep, how you like that? We drive a jeep very fast to the jungle and Keiteur Falls. You know we got the tallest falls in the world there?"

"I thought Niagara Falls were," I said and puffed out my chest, stroking the sequins on my vest, which felt like a shiny armor against Charles, who was now rolling back on his seat, slapping his knee as he wheezed with laughter.

Downing the last of his drink, Maywa cocked his head at me. "She half-Indian," he said. "I can tell."

"She look a little like Vivie, don't you think?" Sheila asked. "So pretty."

"She better have more brains then!" Charles put in.

"What she need brains for?" Maywa sneered. He stared at his empty glass. "She a girl!"

My mother reddened and my father twitched in his seat, a furrow showing between his brow. I was sweating in my vest, the stitching rubbing my neck. The velvet pressed thick as hammered metal against my chest, my breaths short with fury. I ran my hand along the collar and a clump of sequins came loose in my palm. I hated Maywa at that moment, and for a brief instant, wanted to fling the sequins at him, wishing they'd cut his sullen face into a thousand pieces.

"Uh-oh, now you've done it," Sheila said, cracking a nervous smile. "You don't know how Warren is raising this little girl. She got us all on our toes."

My father nodded, wagging a finger in my direction. "You watch what you say. My daughter going to tell you the longitude and lagitude of Keiteur Falls and how old a fool you are! This little girl going to pass us all by one day."

With my father's intense gaze upon me, I felt myself glow from the inside. Then everyone roared with laughter, which I thought idiotic, Charles especially. Even though I was glad my father had paraded my smartness before stupid Maywa, I remembered all the things my aunt had said about the Guyanese, how lax and coarse their humor was. I was still glaring in Maywa's direction, but he did not seem to notice. He chewed on one of my sandwiches as if the talk itself had made him hungry. When he finished, he licked his fingers and nodded. "You doing good, man. Your sister's husband own this house here? You must make a good salary. You go Yankee up all right."

"We do fine." My mother's voice was brittle and nervous, though.

"It's hard, man," Maywa went on. "All us Indians leave but we can't take any money out of Guyana."

"You stop your bellyachin' and you go Yankee up too," Sheila sneered.

Charles, my father, and Sheila burst out laughing. Only Maywa didn't seem to enjoy the joke. He hunched over his knees, shoulder blades two jutting wings.

A disgruntled air settled on the room. Everyone quietly sipped their drinks. I suddenly noticed how dark it was getting outside. Pale, melting circles of car headlights bloomed through the curtains, then sank into the evening shadows. My mother sprang up from her stool and walked over to the bay windows, parting the curtains. I knew what she was thinking. Aunt Inez and Uncle Tom had not called. My stomach began to hurt, thinking of the mess in the back parlor, our guests sprawled on the chairs. Even in the few moments that my mother stood by the window, the darkness seemed to come more swiftly, and I wondered how much longer Charles and Maywa could possibly stay.

As my mother returned to her stool and the circle drew inwards again, something was wrong. No one could think of anything to say. A long silence passed. Then we started to notice a low, mumbling noise, like a small animal growling in a bush. I turned my eyes to Maywa. Long legs stretched out on the carpet, Maywa had slid far down in his seat, arms crossed on his chest, muttering inaudible words. The mumbling surged and ebbed, none of it making any sense. My mother exchanged baffled looks with Sheila. Gently Charles nudged my father and they both got up, slipping through the door into the hallway.

"How long are you here for?" my mother asked Maywa in a bright voice.

Maywa's head lolled backwards on his shoulders, and he regarded her with glazed, half-shut eyes. "I study in Georgetown. Medicine. But I not so lucky, like your husband. I come here and work on lorry, now I sell pharmaceuticals." His sentences slipped into a slow, angry rhythm. "I study medicine, but now I work. Sell pharmaceuticals."

My mother jerked out of her seat and Sheila followed, picking up the dirty glasses. I felt badly, being left with Maywa and his strange mumbling, like I was missing out on what was really going on between everyone, why they'd come to visit. A few minutes later, angry voices on the other side of the wall came crashing down the hall. "Just a little favor, man!" I heard Charles yell. "It don't cost anything in the end!"

Maywa sat up, tense and alert. Aunt Inez was right, after all: they just wanted money. But as I stared at Maywa, I couldn't help feeling that she was wrong, too. There was something sad and beautiful in his face, the muscles in his slender neck straining as he tried to hear every word on the other side of the wall. He made me think of a long slim horse, pushing at a wire fence. When a door slammed shut elsewhere in the house, his whole body trembled.

"Are Keiteur Falls really the tallest falls?" I asked, suddenly interested in him. If I could put a finger on the velvety skin on his neck, I thought, I might understand what he truly wanted, and who these people were to us.

Maywa's head slowly rotated in my direction. "You don't believe your Uncle Charles?"

"He's not my uncle."

"Everyone your relative, child," he said softly. "Everyone related."

He made me feel ashamed for being mistrustful, and I would do anything to keep him there, help me understand what was going on. But before I could utter another word, he had jerked towards the door. My mother's voice broke through the barrier of wall. "I heard you there before! You think we're rich just because we live in the States?"

"Not give!" Maywa shouted at the shut door, and flung it open. Maywa was already streaking down the hall, shouting, "You don't have to give anything!"

In the back parlor, Charles, his shiny face now dull with anger, was standing next to the dining table. "It's all very simple and straightforward," he kept saying. What he wanted from my parents didn't seem straightforward at all. He kept running over complicated routes for getting money out of Guyana, so Maywa could go to medical school rather than work selling pharmaceuticals. The plan never got any clearer to any of us. A crucial step in this scheme had something to do with my father's bank account in the States. Every time this was mentioned, my mother's voice rang out, hot and forceful, saying angrily that money was our hard-earned savings, and we certainly weren't going to part with it.

A surge of pride and resentment rose in me too, as if I could see the quarters and dollar bills stacking up in a bright silver box and these awful men snatching them away. But I didn't really understand what my mother was objecting to. Did she or didn't she trust them?

Sheila stood between the two groups, her face stricken. Her silky shalwar top fluttered limply at her hips; I had never seen her look so pale and defenseless. "You all have to stop fighting now!" she pleaded. "You know each other since you children, you can't be carryin' on like this!"

Maywa turned to her, his face swollen with rage. His arms shook, loose and crazy at their sides. "What you sayin' with your fancy clothes and that high look on your face, Casablanca girl? So you marry up! Is all the same!"

Charles shoved Maywa in the arm. "Maywa, you watch what you say. We don't talk like that here."

Shoulders slumped, Maywa dropped to a seat and cut the conversation short. "Forget it, man," he mumbled. "Forget we asked."

My father recapped the rum bottle. He looked relieved. It's over, his face seemed to say, all that bold talk about money. Maybe everyone would leave nice and quiet before Inez and Tom returned and we could go back to our summer the way it had been. I knew he regretted inviting Maywa and Charles in the first place. He announced: "Here you go! One more round to warm you up before you're on your way!" As he pushed the glasses across the tablecloth, I had the sense he was pushing himself away too, making larger the distance between himself and Maywa and Charles.

Before anyone could reach for their drinks, though, Maywa suddenly tore off his cricket sweater, threw it into a heap on the floor, then raised his arms and began flapping them. He circled the room, swooping into furniture like a gangly bird. "Ya—eeeh!" he shouted. I watched his arms flap in the air, listening to the tick of his fingernails as they struck a lampshade, the edge of a picture frame. Is this a jumbee bird, I wondered. One hand caught on a duputta flung across a chair and it went streaking across the room like puff of yellow wind.

"Maywa!" Charles cried. "What you doing now!" Maywa was already at the back door, tugging on the knob. "Work now, sell pharmaceuticals," he chanted and wrenched open the door. "Pharmaceuticals!" he shouted into the night air.

I scrambled after the grown-ups, who had crammed through the narrow doorway and onto the steps to watch Maywa race around the darkened garden, tripping over flower beds, thrusting his skinny arms into the strips of hung wash. "Doctor!" he kept shouting. "I going to be a doctor!" He fought and struggled with the straggling pieces, then, finding his neck wrapped in a cowl of sheets, gave an angry cry, and swerved towards the low shadows of rose bushes.

No one left the steps, terrified that any minute now Inez and Tom would come striding down the path. We watched as Maywa hurtled through the garden. He managed to avoid the bushes. Rocking off on his heels again, he raced towards the rubbish pile which sat in a sloppy heap in the hedge corner. Wet leaves kicked into the air. Over and over, he swerved out of danger just as a new obstacle presented itself; this time, it was a stack of bricks. I heard the sharp crack of his shin bone as he stumbled forward.

Wincing, Charles stepped down from the porch as Maywa came pounding up and halted a few feet away. Sweat was pouring down his face. He began tipping forward. Raising his arms, he suddenly flung himself on the ground, as if hugging the earth to his chest. I heard a dead, moist thump when he landed. Charles made a noise of disgust in this throat.

"Is he all right?"

"He's fine. Just actin' up like the crazy boy he was in Letturkenny."

"Oh, you boys," Sheila sighed, her voice tinged with regret. "We better get him out of here before Inez come back. She on the warpath as it is."

We hurried down the steps and gathered around him, staring at his long, broken shape lying in the grass. When my mother spoke, it sounded like she was crying, though she wasn't.

"I can't help it," she said. "He looks so much like Warren's brother, Joseph."

"Same hard head," Charles agreed. Then he added wistfully: "Same sadness inside."

My father touched his friend's sleeve before speaking. "It all right." His voice sounded like he was talking through the blades of a spinning fan, far-away and wobbly. "Everything going to be all right now."

The air was cool. From the nearby station came the faint clacking of a passing train. It made me feel as if Guyana and all they'd come from were not far away at all. I wondered if everyone was thinking what I was: that maybe Maywa had the jumbee curse, too. The faint odor of diesel seemed mixed with the sadness they all spoke of; it spilled as the dreamy weight of memory, as if it were my memory, swimming into my thoughts. For once, it seemed, I could swim inside these old places and see everything I wanted to know.

When we hurried into the house, the phone was ringing. It was Inez, saying they would be home by nine-thirty, and to please leave the front porch light on since the street was so dark. My mother heated the leftover curry and rice from the night before. We all were suddenly very hungry, but it was more like a craving, an emptiness we had to fill. I had the sense, as Sheila was lighting two candles, that the grown-ups were trying to keep what was fast disappearing, the warm glow of a certain trust between them, before it was broken again.

The room echoed with stories about Guyana and Trinidad and America and England and people I didn't know, their chatter making spaces in the air of so much left unfinished, so many mysteries. I grew annoyed, my stomach squeezed tight into a knot. The hands of the mantle clock edged toward nine-thirty, their conversation veering wild and hilarious as they frantically scooped food into their mouths.

It was my mother who caught the squeak of the front gate. Then we could hear Inez's voice on the front path as she scolded George to hurry up, stop dragging like that, she had a lot to do. Frantic, Sheila began stuffing her bright clothes into her suitcase and tamping down Aunt Inez's wrinkled heap of blouses.

As my mother rose to meet them at the door, I saw Charles tap my father's shoulder and say quickly under his breath in a conspiratorial voice: "Tomorrow, Warren. Tomorrow we work out the details."

I put my fork down. I had missed a signal, something invisible agreed upon between them. The feeling that I was part of their memories, evaporated in the air. Annoyed, I jumped up onto my chair and shouted over the din of voices, "Are you giving Maywa money?"

My mother flashed my father a distressed look. "Warren, you promised—"

But I didn't want them to start fighting between themselves. I wanted to know what was going on. I began shouting again. My father waved at me. "Megan, get down from there."

"Tell me!"

"I'm warning you, young lady! This is no way to behave!"

Aunt Inez's high voice was already sailing through the walls. "Who's here?" she called. "Who's come visiting at this late hour?"

Still in her coat, she pushed through the door. Aunt Inez's eyes widened with shock as she took in the scene. "Charles? What you doing here? I knew it!" Aunt Inez cried. "I can't leave for one day and my house is not my own!"

My knees began to tremble. "Tell me," I began to sob. "Does Maywa have the jumbee curse?"

"Jumbee curse! Is that what kind of talk is going on here!" Her hat bounced angrily on her head as she stamped into the room, and swept an arm over the table, which was littered with capsized bottles and half-filled glasses. "Is this what you do the minute my back's turned!" Seizing the rum bottle, she waved it by its neck. "Talkin' jumbee while my niece jumpin' like a fool bird on the good dining chair! Get down from there, young lady, and take off that ridiculous vest!"

I bent my head, my vest looking suddenly garish and ugly. My aunt glowered at my father. "And you, Warren! What you promisin' now?"

My father cast his eyes downward. "Nothin', Inez," he mumbled. "Really."

"And my clothes! My poor wrinkled blouses! What is all this?" She plunged her hands into a shimmering pink and blue shalwars, tufts of silk and nylon cloth floating in the air.

Charles kept glancing at the kitchen door. I could see scrolled across his mind: Please don't Maywa come in now. But as luck would have it, the ruffled curtains trembled on their rods, the door gave an impertinent bang, and in lurched Maywa, roused from his sleep, hair springing wild, as he lunged forward, groaning, "Where, the loo, man?" Stunned, Inez let the shalwars and blouses slip from her fingers, as if she had seen a ghost.

Maywa and Charles did not come back and visit us. Sheila left a few days later for Paris, much to my aunt's relief. The house fell quiet. The specialness that shone in me rubbed off and I wandered through the rooms, searching for the bits of Guyana I'd glimpsed that night, like the sequins that still glittered in the rugs.

I did hear stories. One day when Maywa was making one of his pharmaceutical deliveries to a public clinic, he sneaked into an empty doctor's office. There he slipped on the doctor's white coat, snapped pens to his pocket. He tapped the old women waiting in the hallway, told them he was the new doctor, helping with the extra cases. Once inside, he smiled and listened to their ailments, feeling for the pulse in their bony wrists. On a prescription pad he scribbled the names of ointments and antibiotics, all learned from the carton labels he delivered on his route. After an hour, the other doctor wondered what had happened to his patients. When he and the nurse opened the door, they found Maywa standing in front of a mirror, taking off the white labcoat, then putting it on again, and taking it off.

The authorities did not put Maywa in jail but sent him "for observation" for two weeks at a psychiatric hospital. Then we began to receive letters from either Maywa or Charles, almost every other day. My father would read them sitting on his bed, mumbling under his breath. Apparently the authorities had forgiven Maywa and said if he could raise the money, he could go to medical school. I would hear arguments behind closed doors. "That doctor talk is nonsense," my aunt told my father. "You know those Guyanese boys. They never tell the truth. They can't help themselves." My mother agreed, but there was a wistfulness in her voice, as if remembering the good time we had that evening, before everything went wrong. "Maybe you should write them back, and say we're thinking about it," she told my father. I often found the shredded letters scattered under his desk.

One evening, after another one of his fights with my aunt, my father shuffled downstairs to make a phone call. From the parlor I could hear his voice through the wall, though I couldn't tell what he was saying. When he returned, he held out both hands, palms up. "Come Meggie," he said. "Come keep your old man company."

I was sad. The father who walked beside me was so tired he could barely hold up his shoulders. "It's hard being who I am," he confided to me. "The people from my past, they want so much. They want more than I can give."

In silence we crossed Greenford Avenue and hiked through the woods. Our feet were slow, kicking through the damp leaves that lay on the ground. The sun had already set and the trees struck long poses against the sky. I thought of the nests sheltered in their branches with baby birds, shrunken legs pulled against their fragile ribs. Frightened, I shivered in my polo shirt and shorts.

"I used to take long walks like this when I was a little boy," my father told me. "In Guyana the land is so beautiful at night. When there's no moon, you can't see anything. And the silence! That quiet can kill, Megan. But if you listen, you can see and hear so much. If you're not afraid, you can understand things. The earth, it can talk to you."

"Aunt Inez told me that you have to bury a dead baby bird in the ground or it will come back to haunt you."

"That's right," he said, slipping his hand into mine. "They say when a high wind come, you have to shout the names of lost children otherwise they going to harm you."

"Were there lots of lost children in Guyana?"

"Some."

"Was my Uncle Joseph lost, Daddy?"

"I tell you, Megan. I loved Joseph. He and I do everything together. Maybe you don't understand this now. But it's not easy, growing up the way we did. The day each one of us children were born, my mother stick a knife in the door so we never leave her house. That's what all the old folk do. But they also send us to school where we learn about a world outside our village. We learn you can be anything if you study hard enough. I believe them so much I used to sleep with a book under my pillow."

I giggled.

"Your Uncle Joseph, he believe this too. He grow up to be a man of high thinking, but he also could not stay away from the sound of my mother's voice. He drink too much of my father's rum and can't think straight so he walk round and round our house, never able to get out. He cannot hold everything inside him and so he become a man with a bitter mouth, sitting on the verandah, talking away his big dreams until he can talk no more."

"I'm scared," I whined. The dark seemed to press in at all sides; the birds would tumble out of their nests. "Uncle Joseph is going to hurt me."

"You mustn't be scared, Megan. You the one that going to carry us higher than we even dream. Why you scared?"

"Uncle Joseph is going to bring me down too."

"Oh no. We can take care of that."

"How?"

"We going to shout your uncle's name."

"Really?"

"You bet."

Together, hands cupped over our mouths, we began to shout into the air, Joseph! Joseph! Our voices soared over the trees, mingling in the air. My lungs seemed to fill with a strong wind that blew the lid of sky open. The tops of the trees shivered, the nests burning like garlands of light until the sky spread into a banner of flames. I felt such strength and fiery power, I hardly noticed that my father was leading us to a small clearing in the woods.

Who should step out from behind a tree, slippery as a mist, but Maywa. He looked thinner than I remembered, bent and old like one of the trees. As he stepped around a stump with an uneven jerk, I noticed dark circles ringing his eyes. From his jacket my father drew out a light blue envelope. Maywa's voice sputtered with gratitude as he stuffed it into his pocket. "You a good man, Warren. You don't forget." He reached for my father's shoulders but my father danced sideway in embarrassment. "That's okay, man. You get yourself settled, you hear?"

Left with his arms in the air, Maywa suddenly swerved around. Before I could step away, he lifted me up. His bristly chin rubbed my cheek as he whispered, "I see you there, little girl. What you watching?"

"You." His hands pressed as if they were going to crush my spine into my ribcage.

"And what you see?"

"I see a man," I choked out.

"Not just any man, child. You see a doctor. You see a doctor who one day going to come back for you and take you to see Keiteur Falls. We going to see the home that still shine so bright in your eyes."

I didn't like this Maywa. From between the spaces of his teeth drifted the yellow scent of rum. I thought about the jumbee curse, and imagined for a moment that his skull was filled with the burning fire of my grandfather's rum, spilling out of his mouth. His eyes were the color of dead leaves that I feared I would lose myself in.

My father stepped forward. "That's enough now," he said. "Leave my girl alone. You must go."

Maywa squeezed me tighter and my chest split with fiery pain. I thought I was going to break apart, fall and die smothered inside the loamy darkness of his eyes.

"Go!" my father barked.

With a jerk, Maywa let go and I dropped down, gasping, as I stumbled backward. A flurry of leaves blew into our faces. A moment later, it seemed as if the ground had parted and Maywa had split into a thousand men, each one stepping inside the spaces between the trees until they had vanished like a thousand ghosts.

My father and I did not leave right away but stood for several minutes, staring into the desolate forest, the shouts of before long gone from our throats. The leaves settled around our feet, smelling of Maywa. My father stroked my head. Not once, but several times, his palm brushing against my hair. It was an odd gesture, as if he were pushing something aside. I could not help feeling that he—maybe all the adults—were waiting for me to reach some place they could not get to themselves.

Sounding the Challenge

Changes

Amitava Kumar

(For Daya Pawar and Ramji Rai)

In a letter from Los Angeles
written by an upper-caste chemist,
the untouchable poet in India
learns that Indians in the United States
are treated like dogs.
This, I imagine, is in the fifties,
before Ravi Shankar played
with the Beatles
or Hollywood had sold Gandhi
with popcorn to millions.
Beside a dusty rose bush near Bombay,
the news being read on the radio nearby,
our poet looks at the long letter.
His joy makes him cry.
That afternoon, he will sit down
to write. He wants to be honest.
I felt so damn good, he will write.
Now, you've had a taste
of what we've suffered in this country
for far too long.

The poet's Indian upper-caste friend
in Los Angeles has a son
in college now, I imagine. I do not know.
But, if this is true, then how
sure would you be that he doesn't call
Mexicans "tonks" because that's

the sound a flashlight makes
on their heads when cops hit them
at the border?
　　　Because I suspect
he has read volumes of computer
manuals but not the poem his father
got in a letter from Bombay, the smart son,
I believe, rails against affirmative action
for Blacks, Asians, and Latinos
whom he calls only by other names.

I don't allow niggers in my cab.
The Pakistani driver looks so small
inside his rearview mirror.
An Indian was stabbed in the neck
in Queens the other day. I don't even
sleep with them. He spits and pulls out
a cigarette. You? I don't smoke, I say.
No, who do you sleep with? I shake
my head, and look out of the window.
The drizzle is very thin by now.
Never sleep with Americans. No sense
of family or respect. I like Germans.
Once I had an Italian girlfriend,
very nice. These words press around me.
I sit still in my corner, more than
voiceless, as if I have lost my identity,
wanting to be back in the movie theater
where I had been only five minutes ago,
my arm thrown around my lover's
　　　American shoulders.

Mehdi Hassan is singing for us
giving the evening sky its color
which is red like the eyes of a rohu fish
pulled fresh out of water. I'm back
in India after three years and my sister
sitting on our roof with the kites
flying above our heads wants to know more
about my divorce. I keep rewinding
the tape to listen to the same ghazal
about the smoke rising in the sad air.
There is so much patience in my sister's voice,
such persistence. We have been talking
for an hour before I say, No, that's true,
touching her hand, but I also don't know
how you'll figure out in this calculus
the outrage of love's imbalance,
or, for that matter, the reasons then
for all that abides which we do call love.
Her remark floats still like a kite.
You are a man, she had begun, and to add to that,
a man living in America.
I don't think we're meeting on equal
terms at all. We withdraw into silence.
In the pale twilight, there's between us the song
about the smoke rising in the sad air.

Felicia

Mahmud Rahman

She saw me eying the empty seat next to her at the back of the bus. As I walked up, she tilted her head back ever so slightly, her eyes narrowed and stared into mine, and while no words came out of her mouth, her face unmistakably said, "Ex-c-u-u-ze me, but I hope you don't think you're sitting next to me!"

For a second I nearly lost my nerve. On most occasions, I confess that the idea of sitting next to an attractive woman intimidates me. But today I was tempted. On this cold December morning, the woman was undoubtedly freezing, but the glow on her dark brown face and her frosty breath took shape in my imagination as inviting as a fresh cup of coffee, poured steaming hot. She was stylishly dressed, though I couldn't really see much of her. Her body was wrapped in a long, red wool coat, and her hair hidden behind a black hat, the kind that had a scarf coming down from inside covering her ears.

I took a deep breath and settled in next to her. When I had first looked around the bus, I thought I had seen something about her that said, go ahead, take a chance. Besides, I was now curious why she had reacted so strongly to me.

"You goin' near or far?" I asked, flashing her a smile to see if that would break up the ice that had formed between us.

"To Akron." She paused. I could almost hear her debating whether to stop the conversation right there. My heart halted for a moment.

But she continued, "And you?

"I'm headed for Detroit. That's where I live. Right now, anyway."

For the next four and a half hours we shared the Greyhound ride to Cleveland. Somewhere along the way I would learn that her name was Felicia. She'd had two weeks off from work, when her factory took its annual shutdown. In Buffalo she had visited an uncle whom she hadn't seen in a while. Though the trip went better than she had anticipated, this had not been her first choice.

"Two of my girlfriends said they'd go with me on a car trip to California. I was really looking forward to that. But at the last minute, they chickened out. Said it was too long a drive."

Pausing for a moment, she added, "They left me stranded." Time off from work was precious and the thought of staying home during Christmas break had nearly crushed Felicia's heart. She decided to take off for Buffalo.

Although she was going home by bus, she had come by Amtrak. The train ride had taken twenty-six hours. Akron and Buffalo are only a few hours apart. If you drive or take the bus. Even less if you fly. But there are no direct trains between the two cities. Felicia had to first go to New York City, lay over for three hours, and then switch to the Chicago-bound train that passes through Buffalo. She opted for that even though it cost more than the air fare between the two cities.

It seemed like quite a roundabout way to get there. I must have looked baffled, because she tried to explain, "I had never been on a train before." She noticed that I still wasn't convinced, but she simply shrugged her shoulders. To me it sounded as if on this Christmas vacation, Felicia had wanted a trip that took a long time to get to wherever she was going.

"You want to know something?" I said, "Buffalo wasn't my first choice either. I'd planned to fly to Kansas, but the air fare was over $400. Then I saw an ad saying I could fly to the island of Fiji for $600. Hey, I thought, why take snowy Kansas when you can get sunshine and ocean for only a couple of hundred more?"

"You didn't do too well, did you? I have no idea where Fiji is. But I see you ended up in Buffalo where we probably had more snow this week than Kansas. So what happened to Fiji?"

"Oh it was just a dream. I might do it someday. I came to see friends here. And you know, on Greyhound the price was right."

"Ain't that the truth."

Felicia wanted me to know that it wasn't unusual for her to do something like leaving home during the holidays. She said she was frequently struck by the "ramblin' blues."

"As often as I can, I like to get away. There's so many places in the world beyond Akron I'd like to experience. Last year I got motivated to go to Myrtle Beach. That was one fun trip. But it doesn't always work out right. Another time I drove down to Cincinnati. I have a sister there, but when I arrived Sis' didn't seem to have any time for me. I hung around downtown by myself and then went home."

"I'm somewhat the same way myself," I ventured, opening up another part of me to her. Her eyes lit up, and the smile that formed on her lips this time came from somewhere deep inside, like she was finally glad that the stranger she'd opened up to was turning out to be a kindred soul.

"Yeah? Tell me some of the places you've been."

I rattled off a few. Oklahoma City. Boston. New York. Chicago. Dallas. Los Angeles.

"W-h-e-e-w," she whistled, "You've sure been around." Then her smile faded away as she said, "But it don't seem like we've ever touched down in any of the same places."

"Sure we have. Just this past week. In Buffalo," I reminded her, "And I've been through Cincinnati a few times. Had a brother living there some years back." I went on to describe an afternoon I'd hung out in Fountain Square, watching black teenagers dance and pretend like they were models on a runway, accompanied by music from a boombox.

Now the worlds we visited in these cities were most likely far apart, but Felicia found it reassuring to know that her seatmate, with whom she'd discovered she shared an adventurous spirit, had been in a few of the same places. Her whole face broke out into a grin while I told the story about downtown Cincinnati. I wondered if she took heart from the fact that for both of us, Fountain Square wasn't just an image from the opening scenes of WKRP in Cincinnati but a place where we had both hung out, taken a walk, seen folks sing and dance.

Felicia already had other trips sketched out in her mind. Some of her friends had brought up the idea of a cruise. She wasn't sure about that, since she preferred solid ground under her feet. Besides, there was only so much that her sense of adventure could handle. The layover in Penn Station had made her nervous. She had wanted to go outside and get a glimpse of New York City, but she only saw escalators going up and out. She couldn't see how she was going to get back.

"I think I know how you felt," I said, "When I first came to this country I landed in Boston. Now I'd never seen a subway system before. I was supposed to change trains at this one station, but when I got there, instead of finding my way to the other train I found myself standing in the middle of the street outside."

"But you know what else?" she continued, "The folks at the train station looked strange. The ladies at the coffee shop looked black. But they weren't. They talked different."

Felicia had never met black people from the Caribbean before.

"Hey, the first time I came across some Indians from Trinidad I didn't know what to make of them either!"

"Where's Trinidad?" she quizzed me.

"If it isn't the same place, it's probably close enough to where those black ladies in the coffee shop were from. The Caribbean."

"You ever been to the Motor City?" I asked. She shook her head. A bus she had once been on had stopped in Detroit. She would have liked to stay over, but she didn't know anyone there.

Then, with her eyes focused on mine, she said real slowly, "But now I know someone." And her mouth widened into a smile suggesting satisfaction as well as a hint of playfulness.

The factory where Felicia worked employed over a thousand workers. They made plastic kitchenware. Because of all the injection molding machines there, the place was always hot. Even in winter the workers wore T-shirts and shorts. She worked the day shift, but frequently stayed for overtime. She also took overtime work during weekends. I did some mental calculations. Felicia must have been working nearly seventy hours a week.

Seeing the puzzled look on my face, she explained, "Oh the work isn't too hard, and I enjoy it. I don't have to do the same thing all the time."

"Do you need the money that much? Or is it 'cause you have your friends there?"

"The money helps. And yeah, my friends are there, but it ain't on account of them that I spend so much time there. I just like keeping busy."

While we talked she pointed to her wrists and hands. They were thin and pretty. A small gold watch adorned her left wrist. I noticed a thin wedding band. A couple of more rings on her right hand. Long red fingernails, with gold glitter on some. "My own," she said proudly. But Felicia wasn't simply asking me to admire her nails.

"My hands hurt. I think I have that carpal tunnel. They did some tests on it last week. Stuck some needles and electricity . . . " She searched for a word.

"An electromyogram?" I suggested.

"Yeah. They don't have the report yet." Then her eyes narrowed and all emotion drained from her face.

"Why, you a doctor or something?"

"Not even something," I replied, bewildered about what could have possibly returned Felicia's face back to that icy glare, even if it had been for an instant.

I went on, "A couple of years ago I went through some of those same tests. One of my wrists hurt awful bad. I think I injured it from too many years on a keyboard."

"So are you all recovered now?" I realized that there was more than curiosity about my wrist in that question. She wanted to have some idea about what her chances were.

"They gave me some cortisone shots. Since then I've managed. The pain only comes back once in a while." I didn't tell her that her pain sounded worse than anything I'd experienced.

Felicia had been at this factory for five years. It was the longest she'd worked in one place.

"Funny thing 'bout it is that I hadn't planned on working there. I took my son in to get hired, but the company gave me the job instead."

"You . . . have a son old enough to work in a plant?" I asked.

"Yeah," she replied, "He's twenty-six now."

"No?! I thought you were in your twenties. You couldn't possibly be. . . . "

"What, forty-three?" she finished my question, relishing the pleasure she'd had in deceiving me with her youthful looks.

I looked at her face again. This time I stared. I swear, the woman didn't even look thirty.

"And what 'bout you?" she asked, "It's your turn."

"Oh, I just turned forty last month," I said, my voice trying to match the cool with which she'd revealed her age.

"Damn, I thought you were my son's age!"

"Hey, it looks like we both thought we were your son's age!"

"And what's your secret? How do you keep yourself looking so young?" she asked.

"Certainly not with seventy hours of factory work, that's for damned sure."

By this point we must have become pretty loud, because the teenagers behind us started to giggle.

The bus stopped in Ashtabula for ten minutes. Some passengers, Felicia and I included, walked out for the break. When we returned to our seats, I thought I'd finally ask her the question that had been rolling around my head.

"When I first got on, did I imagine it, or did you really give me a look that said, 'I hope you don't think you're sitting down next to me'?"

"I did," she replied without hesitation.

"But why?"

"From what I've seen, Indians don't care much for black folk. If you ask me, they seem stuck up and act like we don't exist. Even though y'all are colored, you seem to think you're white."

As she alternated between "they" and "you," her eyes revealed a mixture of anger and hurt. And confusion. She wanted to express her anguish and disapproval about what she had perceived about "my people," but she didn't seem sure where I fit into the picture. Though I knew her charge wasn't directed at me, I was still taken aback. When I had wondered about why she had been so icy toward me as I first approached her, I'd thought it was perhaps because she simply wanted to have the whole seat to herself. It just had not occurred to me that when Felicia first saw me she had judged me on the basis of my ethnic origins.

"If I thought about it I could probably come up with some way to explain it, but it wouldn't satisfy either one of us," I confessed to her.

Her reaction should not have surprised me. To her experiences I could have added dozens of my own. I could recall the wealthy Indian family in suburban Detroit who'd threatened to ship their daughter back to India if she didn't stop hanging with the black students in college. Then there was the Bengali physicist—himself a "revolutionary" in his younger days in Bangladesh—holding forth at a dinner party about how blacks were poor parents, a conclusion he'd drawn from some incident he'd witnessed in a supermarket line. Clearly the man had learned a lot from his scientific training. And how could I forget the distress I'd myself felt when a relative, upon hearing that I was dating a black woman, nervously remarked, "I hope it isn't serious." She'd never said that about any of my white girlfriends.

I threw my hands up in the air and simply offered, "Okay, there are some, perhaps many of us, who act ignorant. But that's still not all of us."

She thought for a moment and nodded, "It wouldn't be fair to say that I've only had bad experiences. When I was getting my GED I had an Indian teacher who was good to me. And she was a great teacher. But then, there are these people in suits, some of the doctors I've come across, some of those in the offices of the factory. . . ."

I sensed that with those "people in suits" Felicia had been a victim of both racial and class prejudices.

"You know, some of those people in suits don't know what to make of me either. And for sure, they look down on our own people who do manual labor for a living. If you don't drive fancy cars or live in expensive suburbs, they don't think you're worth much. Just last month my boss, an Indian engineer, told the secretary at work that he couldn't understand why at forty I'm not 'more successful'."

Felicia replied, "If he's so smart why couldn't he figure that one out? Heck, even I can tell. It must be 'cause you spend your time hangin' with lazy-assed black folks like me."

"So tell me, Felicia, have you lived in Akron all your life? Is that where you got married and stuff?" I asked, feeling that she might now be comfortable enough to venture into more private areas of her life.

"Oh, you noticed my ring."

"Hey, don't all men do that?"

"I s'pose. No, I moved to Akron from a small town in Mississippi when I was seventeen."

"What brought you north?"

"I was pregnant. I wanted to finish high school. You couldn't do that in Mississippi. Not in those days anyway. So I came up to live with my dad who'd moved to Ohio. My mama died when I was small. Never really knew her much. Grandma raised me and my sisters. She worked in the town café. It was a place where black folk had to go in through the back door. You know what I did when I went down there a few years back? I went to the cafe and, like always, I went to the back. Without thinking. But they turned me away. The cook came and told me, 'No, you can't come in this way. You gotta come in through the front door'."

"You hadn't gone back in a long time, had you?" I asked.

She nodded. As she went on, I learned that Felicia hadn't left home just because she was pregnant and wanted to finish school.

"My son's father would beat me. He was only a couple of years older. He'd go with other girls, but when I griped 'bout that, I only got a beating. I wasn't about to stay in a place and get beat all the time."

The move north wasn't easy. It took Felicia three trips to make up her mind about staying in Akron. The differences were unsettling, and she was often homesick. But the move also held out promise for her. The excitement of the late '60s was in the air, and Akron signified freedom to this wide-eyed country girl from Mississippi.

"This may sound crazy, but one of the first things I wanted to do was to hang with a white boy. Never could do that in Mississippi. In Akron I found one with no trouble at all. But he lied to me. Said he was nineteen, when he was only fifteen. I didn't leave beatings in Mississippi to settle for lies in Akron."

"You know, I left home at seventeen too. With me, it was in the middle of a war. In the country we were part of back then, we were the 'niggers'. The people who ruled us were taller, bigger, and lighter-skinned. They called us darkies and black bastards. And when we wanted our freedom, they murdered us like dogs." I tried to give Felicia a picture of what life had been like for Bengalis in Pakistan during the years of revolution and war.

By this time she was no longer surprised to hear of the parallels in our lives. She thought about what I'd said for a moment, then offered, "We also had our war, even if it wasn't your kind."

She reached back into her childhood memories and recalled Mississippi as a place of violence. There were the daily racial humiliations and the periodic terror of the Ku Klux Klansmen. But the violence was even closer. Her dad had gone away to the army, and by the time he returned her mother had given birth to another man's child. Her father couldn't hold back his jealous rage. He stabbed her mother, who lost a lung. She remembered other stabbings as well.

Felicia had seen her share of blood as a child. More than I, I thought to myself. During my war, I had heard the gunfire, seen the flames, heard the cries, and seen some of the bodies. But she had seen more blood close up than I. And of loved ones, no less.

Once she had made a new life in Akron, Felicia eventually found a man she liked well enough to marry. She had now been with him for seventeen years. Two more sons had come along, the youngest now fourteen. But she didn't talk about her children much. With some bitterness, she described her home as empty. She did not mention physical abuse. Not for a moment did I think she would tolerate that anyway. She'd already made it clear to me that she had left that life behind in Mississippi.

"The man doesn't want to go nowhere, do nothing. Every day he just comes home and turns on the TV. It ain't right. He's five years younger than me. I've raised three kids and been through a lot more than he has. How come I still have the energy and he doesn't? Don't get me wrong. He's a better man than many. But somehow he's let his spirit be drained away from him."

When Felicia was home—and she tried her best to stay away as much as she could—she simply slept a lot. Still she always felt restless. She said that she'd like to learn how to play the piano.

"I used to play the guitar once. Back in Mississippi. For a teenager I was good. Learned it from an uncle. You should have heard some of those blues licks coming out of my fingers. But it's been a long time. Sometimes I wake up and feel the music way down inside of me. I'd like to do something with that feeling. I worry about the pain in my wrists but I can't let the pain get in the way of something I need for my soul, can I?"

She confessed that she shopped a lot. Mostly clothes. Always new. "No Salvation Army for me. I had enough of other people's hand-me-downs when I was a kid." She had also bought a computer. She used it to learn typing. And to play games.

"What do you play?"

"Solitaire."

I shouldn't have asked.

Overtime wages paid for shopping and her trips. She had also bought a new car. A Mustang.

"What color?" I asked, already guessing the answer.

"Red."

"Of course. Is there any other color?" I laughed.

"It's either shopping or having an affair," Felicia described how she saw her options. "I'm more comfortable with shopping."

She stopped for a moment, thought about what she'd said, and softly added, "Maybe I haven't yet met a man I'd consider having an affair with." Her eyes met mine, and they lingered there for a while. We both let the conversation pause. And then together we both broke out into self-conscious grins.

The bus came to a stop in Cleveland. We were both getting off, to catch different buses. Felicia only had five minutes to make her connection. As she squeezed past me, we said a hurried goodbye and her lips brushed mine.

"Hey, if you ever want to wander somewhere together, give me a call," I whispered to her. I doubted that would ever come to pass, but I wasn't ready to accept that this stranger with whom I'd so easily become comfortable would simply be in my life for a four-and-a-half hour bus ride.

"Yeah, sure. But the next time you tell me why you get the ramblin' blues." She yelled as she rushed away, flashing me her smile for one last time.

Moments of Identity in Film

Bakirathi Mani

The growth of the South Asian community in North America prompts a radical reconsideration of the position and situation of diasporic communities in the industrialized world. In the attempt to compensate for the popular perception of the South Asian diaspora being a polluting influence on the purity of the hegemonic white American discourse, South Asian immigrant communities have, quite literally, erased themselves from public view. However, from posing as exemplary evidence of the so-called "model minority," the rise of a vocal second generation within the diaspora has quickly dispelled any pretensions of assimilating silently into the convenient categorizations of hegemonic social groups. In the attempt to broaden and redefine the parameters which formerly contained minority communities, the second generation of the South Asian diaspora has collectively gone through an "identity crisis" of sorts. In the aftermath of the crisis, a new diasporic space has evolved on the interstices of the parameters of containment; however, it is a space which still remains latent and underutilized, hidden from the eyes of mainstream North American society.

It is in response to this invisibility that a number of films have sought to identify and legitimize the presence of the South Asian diaspora, in movies that have been written, directed, and produced by South Asian Americans/Canadians. There is a certain self-consciousness about these cinematic texts: they disregard conventional narrative structures, bring out the figures on the sidelines, and articulate, through their characters, the opinions of the directors themselves. The films of the diaspora are also a unique ground for the construction of public and private identity: they are a visual projection of the "identity crisis," capturing several different perspectives on the issue in a single frame. In *Mississippi Masala* (1991), directed and produced by Mira Nair, and *Masala* (1991), written, directed, and produced by Srinivas Krishna, the first and second generations of the South Asian diaspora come to the forefront through their representation of the existence of a hybrid space within a seemingly homogeneous society. While the films emphasize the process of constructing identity in the second generation, they are influenced by the earlier conclusions on the necessity for adaptation and assimilation that have been reached by the first generation. Hence the films debate the relevance of "authenticity" and the necessity of fixed geographical/personal identities, while legitimizing—and indeed celebrating— the so-called "bastard existence" of diasporic communities that has been denigrated by societies that prize cultural "authenticity" over hybridity. Moreover, Nair and Krishna illustrate the conflicting tensions in the South Asian diaspora among generations of immigrants, religious groups, and different social classes, particularly in their attitude towards the requisite degree of assimilation into the adopted society. Such tensions are embodied in the actions of the protagonists: in the process of constructing an independent personal identity, the second-generation characters of the films find themselves split between personal loyalties, ethnic ties, and cultural histories, seeking to reconcile parts of themselves through a search for a temporarily satisfying identity.

Both *Mississippi Masala* and *Masala* illustrate in detail the necessity of confronting stereotypical images of ethnic identity imposed by the hegemonic (in this case white North American) society. Such stereotypes range from the popular "model minority" myth to a variety of set character-types: for example the stingy, overworked motel owner or the calculator-carrying science nerd, and include the thickly-accented buffoon as well as the demurely feminine South Asian female. The acceptance of such images offers an easy method for members of the South Asian diaspora to situate themselves in pre-carved niches in their adopted society: they are marginalized, but at least they have included themselves within the cultural parameters of the dominant discourse. However, the result of posing in set character types is silence: an erasure of personal identity and the negation of a collective socio-political voice. The alternative is to name oneself: to explicitly reject the stereotype and carve out a space for the expression of multiple individual identities. The process of articulating one's own voice is an act of rebellion against the dominant cultural discourse as well as against the enclosed diasporic community. It threatens to sabotage the process of peaceful assimilation that was begun by first-generation immigrants, and denies national integration programs based on such myths as the "melting pot" theory. It follows, therefore, that any affirmation of a stereotype cannot be viewed as a legitimate conclusion to the process of constructing identity, because it implies the acceptance of a (false) pre-given niche that serves to retard the growth of a truly diasporic space in society. Thus, it is through confrontation with South Asian ethnic stereotypes that the individual characters of the films surveyed come to terms with the process of constructing a personal diasporic identity.

One of the earliest films on the South Asian diaspora is Mira Nair's *Mississippi Masala*. The film provides an inter-generational comparison of the questions raised by the construction of identity, taking as its subject a family—Jai, his wife Kinu, and their daughter Mina—who are part of the "double diaspora," born and raised in Africa and now relocated in the United States via Britain. Their Indian cultural and religious heritage persists through these territorial shifts in context, and yet no one in the family has ever been to India itself. The result is that Jai, on a slight tangent from the trajectory of the prototypical first-generation Indian immigrant, struggles with creating a personal and political identity founded on Uganda (as opposed to India), while Mina seeks to create an identity for herself within American society. The result of Nair's directive efforts, however, is a movie projecting a romanticized vision of diasporic identity, catering to the tastes of a mainstream (white) American audience. Despite this major drawback, Nair suceeds in illustrating, through Jai and Mina, the possibilities for an alternative mode of diasporic existence in a homogeneous social structure, and publicly introduces one version of the "identity crisis" of the South Asian diaspora in North America.

Like any other first-generation immigrant, Jai is a vehicle for nativism: he intends to locate his roots by attempting to return to an imagined, unsullied past. In doing so, however, Jai realizes that the attempt to discover a permanent identity in Uganda is a futile task, for he is viewed more in terms of his race and economic class rather than in terms of his personal cultural identity. In a conversation with his Ugandan best friend Okelo, Jai exclaims, "But this is my home, Okelo! I've always been an African first and an Indian second." To which Okelo replies, "Not anymore, Jai. Africa is for Africans. Black Africans." The shock of being classified according to superfluous racial qualifications prompts Jai to break away from Uganda and begin a process of self-evaluation. Haunting him is his stagnant religious and cultural heritage, an entity virtually untouched and only periodically invoked during the family's trans-continental travels.

The process of self-evaluation for Jai, as for Mina, consists of several points where different components of one's personal identity seem to collapse into a single crystallized form: points which may be called "moments of identity," a collection of pauses in a life otherwise led in fast-forward mode. The process of recognizing these moments of identity begins with Jai's expulsion from Uganda, when, on the way to the airport, Kinu is forced to empty the contents of their luggage. Out spills a tape recorder, which wails in Hindi:

> O, my shoes are Japanese
> These trousers English, if you please,
> On my head, red Russian hat
> My heart's Indian for all that.

The song is a reminder of what Jai and Kinu should be—loyal members of the Indian diaspora, 'dislocated' abroad strictly for the purpose of making money without integrating into the local community.

Jai and Kinu face a dilemma which is common to most first-generation South Asian immigrants worldwide. The attempt to reconcile the conflict between cultural and commercial homelands often results in bipolarized identities, where the immigrant either completely assimilates him/herself within the hegemonic culture, or retreats into a walled ethnic community, characterized and stereotyped by a ghetto mentality and insularism. The obsession of the first-generation South Asian with an unsullied ethnic identity, or at least the appearance of one, is highlighted in *Mississippi Masala*. Historical links to the Indian subcontinent, however distant, are to be kept intact. Kanti Napkin, a local businessman, declares, "Even though we are 10,000 miles away from India, we should not forget our roots, our culture, our tradition, and our gods"—all categories which need to be placed in double quotation marks. Simultaneously, if assimilation into the adopted society by an immigrant extends beyond financial involvement, s/he is accused of a loss of moral purity. As Jammubhai, proprietor of the Motel Monte Carlo states sadly, "Anil, you have become American." To which Anil promptly replies, "So what? I live here. If you don't like it, go back to India"— the irony being, of course, that there is no India for the immigrant to return to. Paradoxically, the recognition of this loss of "home," which is a tragic loss as far as the first generation is concerned, becomes the springboard for the process of constructing identity in the second generation. In *Mississippi Masala*, the off-spring of Indian immigrants laugh at the attempt to retain a pure ethnic identity. Mina and her gaggle of teenage friends snigger behind Kanti Napkin as he launches into a patriotic religious song following his drunken speech.

Jai remains ambivalent about the apparent choice between assimilating into white American society or closeting himself within the insular Indian community. He tends towards the latter, but his Ugandan origins prevent him from fully assimilating into the mentality of the Indian community in Mississippi. At the same time, Jai fails to take the opportunity to create an individual space for himself as a double immigrant within the Indian diaspora; instead he remains pre-occupied with his need to re-establish a material, commercial, and thereby an emotional basis in Uganda. His lawsuit against the Ugandan government is symbolic of a nativist desire to reclaim what is lost; the reality, as General Idi Amin demonstrates, is that Jai's claims to his birthplace were the product of his own illusions, and were in fact rejected by the indigenous Ugandan community from the beginning.

A watershed in Jai's conception of a geographical and emotional location of identity occurs during the final scenes of the film. Upon a long-awaited return to Uganda to attend a hearing on his law suit, the diasporic inability to establish permanent bases of identity becomes clearly apparent. Uganda, devoid of family and friends, provides no source of emotional stability for Jai; it is instead an impetus for him to realize that he cannot seek in a fixed geographical location a sense of public legitimacy and authenticity. In the final scenes of the film, Jai writes a letter to his wife from Uganda in which he says, "Home is where the heart is, Kinu, and my heart is with you." The desire to return to an imaginary homeland has evaporated, because in effect there is no homeland to return to. Jai's attempt to locate a stable locus of identity for himself finally results in the realization that his present self can only exist as it is in the present context, wrapped around the lives of his wife and daughter. Thus, the sustainment of family ties, primarily of his love for Kinu, becomes a basis upon which Jai can finally construct a space where he can accept and legitimize his permanently geographically dispossessed self.

Mira Nair's projection of Mina's attempt to construct identity, however, seems to emphasize more strongly the need to be rooted, both physically and theoretically, within the bounds of the hegemonic social discourse. Mina is a classic example of the commercialization of the South Asian diasporic image; she is the epitome of exoticization, a picturesque combination of the Oriental and the Occidental. Throughout her travels across continents with her family, Mina accepts the transient, mobile nature of her self—and yet it is while living in the backwaters of Mississippi that she finds the need to anchor the previously unexamined and fluid components of her identity. In part this may be a reflection of the particularly acute nature of the "identity crisis" in the late adolescence of the second generation, when young women and men are poised to leave the sheltered family nest and enter the outside world. It is a time of decision-making and of identity formation, when it becomes necessary to present oneself as an individual to society at large. Hence Mina's self-absorption; her ensuing search for a temporarily satisfying locus of identity revolves primarily around her geographical location in the deep South, as well as around her position within the sexual and racial 'underclass' of the dominant society.

It is interesting to observe that Mina begins her process of constructing identity by readily describing herself as "Indian," assuming that the mere possession of racial and religious characteristics allows her to subscribe to the national identity of a homeland that she has never even seen. At the same time, Mina is consciously aware of her non-"Indian-ness," and it is this which she exploits to project an exotic image of herself. Thus, while introducing herself to Demetrius, her future African American lover, Mina says, "I . . . I'm a mix, masala." To which Demetrius responds, "Hot and spicy, huh?"

The conversation sets the stage for the rapid progression (degradation?) of Mina into the stereotypical image of the South Asian diasporic female. From wearing K-mart clothes in the initial scenes of the movie, Mina clambers into cotton kurtas on the beaches of Mississippi, mirror-embroidered scarves with shorts, swathing herself in clothes which package her into a saleable commodity for the white male gaze. Mina's physical difference and racial desirability is emphasized further when she and Demetrius have sex, where the camera work focuses solely upon the colors of their bodies. Simultaneously, however—in a reading that may not have been intended by Nair—the prominence given to this combination of a South Asian female and African American male, both characterized by their virility and sensuality, may be taken as an attempt to subvert the ruling hegemony of the primarily white audience. Mina and Demetrius, constructs of the seductive "other," do not pander to the desires of the audience, but instead take pleasure in their own and each other's bodies. The viewer is left on the sidelines as the voyeur; and the marginalized individuals take center stage as they assert their sexual, and thereby their political rights.

Although Mina's "hot and spicy" image—which is a calculated effort of her own making—may be palatable for the mainstream audience, other facets of her image are constantly criticized by the immigrant Indian community. As a South Asian in the United States, Mina rejects the stereotype of many of her fellow migrants. She is not college educated, revels in the beauty of her dark skin, and cleans toilet bowls in a motel while her mother runs a liquor store. As a result, in the marginalized Indian community of Mississippi, Mina is sidelined: for as one woman comments on Mina's apparent "catch" of the local eligible bachelor, "You can be dark and have money, or you can be fair and have no money, but you can't be dark and have no money and expect to get Harry Patel!"

The culmination of Mina's construction of identity away from the norms imposed on her by the immigrant community—and the point at which Nair asks the audience to observe Mina's supposedly radical independence—comes in the form of her relationship with Demetrius. Not only is Demetrius a foreigner, alien to the cultural and ethnic ties of the Indian community, but he is also African American. Demetrius is used as a public service announcement of the latent and continously denied existence of racism between the South Asian immigrant and African American communities; as Demetrius remarks to Jai, "Soon as you get here you start acting white and treating us like we your doormats. I know you and your daughter ain't but a few shades away from this right here!" At the same time, there is an attempt to pull the past into the present context, as Jai's antagonism towards Demetrius seems to stem more from Jai's memory and hurt over his rejection by Okelo, emphasizing the complexity of the identity crisis which confronts both generations of the South Asian diaspora.

Mina's relationship with Demetrius is intended to be symbolic of her rebellion against the consolidation of tradition that is found in many of the first-generation immigrants, and yet at the same time the director stokes the Asian female fetish of white male audiences. The "Asian female," stereotypically over-endowed with sensuality, "femininity," and the need for dependence, translates into Mina, gorgeously feminine and fully dependent on Demetrius to support her newly-found identity. Through her relationship with Demetrius, Mina attempts to place herself within the (non-existent) melting pot. By eloping with him, she intends to remove herself from the physical confines of the Indian community in Mississippi so as to explore the possible points of identification available to her as a woman independent of ethnic, racial, religious, and historical ties. What Mina fails to realize, however, is that she is still caught within the parameters of sexual and racial stereotypes, and has not developed a truly alternative space for herself. Consequently, Mina and Demetrius fade into the new model diaspora, becoming an invisible part of Mira Nair's vision of a rainbow coalition of the underclass.

Mississippi Masala concludes with a storybook ending; it is stained with Nair's romanticism and apparent naiveté. Both Jai and Mina have reached seemingly finite conclusions on their individual processes of constructing identity. Jai has anchored himself with Kinu, while Mina has created a world that revolves around herself and Demetrius. The closing shots of the film depict Mina and Demetrius, the progenitors of the new multi-diasporic community, embracing in a field of cornflowers: Mina wears a salwaar kameez while Demetrius is swathed in kente cloth. It is a whirl of colors and fragrances, of re-hashed masala washed over by the fragrance of American wild flowers. Mina's masala identity becomes stale, rather than an innovative presentation of the second-generation diasporic context; it is integrated into the parameters of the white gaze and contributes to the extension of stereotypes, thereby self-defeating the alleged purpose of its construction. While Mira Nair's deliberation on the doubly-displaced immigrant identity of Jai is thought-provoking, her portrayal of Mina's creation of identity is one that only scratches the surface of the plethora of issues that are raised. The result is a movie which plays on shallow images, which cannot remove itself from the mass-market basis of its audience, and which consequently produces a commercialized image of the South Asian diaspora.

Any such romanticization of the South Asian diaspora is quickly dispelled in Srinivas Krishna's *Masala*. Like *Mississippi Masala*, this is a film which seeks to describe the forces that motivate the construction of identity across the generational divide of the diaspora. In contrast to Mira Nair, however, Krishna makes the fluidity of diasporic identity the primary focus of his movie. He does not lock projections of identity within a single freeze-frame, but instead allows multiple identities to spill over throughout the film and recontextualize themselves like the objects falling out of the bombed airplane in the opening scene. The continuous refrain of *Masala* is the metaphor of flight. Several references to 'flying' symbolize the desire for movement in second-generation South Asian Americans/Canadians. The film itself is an illusion of the diasporic identity. It intervenes at strategic points with reality, but it is largely an exercise in escapist fantasy from the constraints of the present. Reality in the South Asian community of present-day Canada manifests itself in Lallubhai Solanki, supposed patron saint of Krishna's family, who, entrenched in the glamour of upper-class white Canadian society, realizes that his ties to the 'mother country' have been reduced to commercial profit lines; it is manifest in Anil, the model child of the diaspora, who makes a poor attempt at being a role model for his peers; finally, it is manifest in the racist gangs which lump all South Asians under the derogatory label of "Paki." The process of constructing identity—including the perception of the need to construct an independent identity—varies widely among all the characters concerned. For illustrative purposes, the viewer can focus on the construction of identity as interpreted by Lallubhai and the central protagonist, Krishna.

Lallubhai Solanki's construction of a first-generation South Asian diasporic identity in *Masala* is path-breaking, in comparison to the situation of other film and real-life characters of his generation. Lallubhai's character is a conglomeration of surface images, for, as he so frankly states, "Indians make a living selling images." His only remaining connection with the Indian subcontinent is his sari shop, and yet unlike other first generation immigrants, the shop itself does not symbolize an institutionalized nostalgia. Instead, it is pragmatically viewed by Lallubhai as a modern business enterprise motivated solely by mercenary and personal ambitions. It is a motivation that becomes clear when Lallubhai lets out the basement of his shop for a pro-Khalistan Sikh movement, not in some twisted proclamation of his patriotic sentiments, but in exchange for $500,000 and total control of the future Khalistan sari trade. "Give up this crazy dream!" he tells the Sikh cab driver when informed of the latter's plans to rebuild his ethnic community in India, "Look at what you have in this country!" The subcontinent may be brimming with fond memories, but an actual relocation back to India is never given serious consideration.

Yet Lallubhai persists in transferring the ideal of an unsullied ethnic identity to his progeny in the form of an arranged marriage for his son, Anil; he fails only—as demonstrated by his choice of Saraswati as bride-to-be—because such ideals are not even marginally relevant to the lifestyle of the second generation. The insistence on the arranged marriage proposal also demonstrates that there are, perhaps, some cultural forces that are too powerful to be overcome. Such packages of tradition, however, should be reconstituted and revitalized with relevance to the present context rather than being allowed to degenerate into absurdity; otherwise they become fantasies caught in a time warp that exist only in the wet dreams of Anil.

For the most part, Lallubhai avoids sinking into self-indulgent nostalgia. He manipulates and adapts himself to white Canadian reality on his own terms, backed by his considerable financial wealth. He is, in the eyes of the Canadian community, the ideal negotiator. As a government representative comments, Lallubhai "plays by the rules" and believes in a "spirit of compromise" between the dominant and subjected communities—not realizing that Lallubhai can do so only because he is socio-economically privileged. Lallubhai does not insist on movement or stagnation in the process of constructing identity, his persona is one that is continuously refined through his irrespressible desire for capital accumulation. Financial aggrandizement is thus not only a means but a mode of existence for Lallubhai—it is an alternative to the conventional nativist bases of identity of first-generation South Asian immigrants.

Krishna's self-definition of identity is also one that defies conventional stereotypes of the second-generation South Asian diaspora. In his punk clothes, asymmetrical haircut, drug-infused lifestyle, and permanent unemployment, Krishna has created, like Mina, a rebel character type who challenges the perception that all South Asian Americans are a model minority. By spurning the charity of his aunt and uncle, Krishna deprives himself of a conventional launching pad for the formation of an independent identity. What proves to be more intriguing, however, is Krishna's questioning of the efficacy and satisfaction of his self-destructive lifestyle; it is in response to this that Krishna the god appears, saying, "This boy yearns to come home. We must provide the way."

Thus 'home' for Krishna becomes a space beyond his immediate territorial realm, an imaginary space fed by the religious mythology of his ethnic history; it is a home to which Krishna the god attempts to manipulate fate to guide his earthly namesake. The fantasy lies in envisioning pre-configured spaces of diasporic identity, which need not be articulated by the second generation themselves, satisfying both their own requirements and the demands of their parents. The reality, of course, is that the South Asian youth— Krishna, Rita, Shashi, and Anil—find themselves fumbling for a means to resolve the conflicting emotional and cultural needs of their generation and that of their predecessors, awkwardly carving out a space for both, creating individual histories upon which they can legitimize themselves. Such a hybrid space verges on being liminal, circling the boundaries of the South Asian immigrant community, and silently infiltrating the larger discourse of hegemonic social groups; it is left up to the second generation to articulate the space and thereby validate their existence.

Images of flight and various metaphors of movement come together in the persistent desire to leave one's immediate geographical surrounding and abandon the accompanying emotional baggage, for the task of trying to carve out a hybrid space often proves to be too difficult. This need to move out and away can be interpreted as a kind of nativist search by the second generation for a "homeland," if not in the Indian subcontinent then at least in an escapist mental construct. The perception of the need to extricate oneself from the immediate context and create an independent diasporic space arises at various points in *Masala*, particularly when Krishna asks Rita, tongue in cheek, if she intends to start a revolution. To his question Rita replies, "No! I'm starting flying lessons!" In effect, both amount to the same thing—flying lessons constitute a rebellion against Rita's father's plans for his daughter's future occupation, and satisfy her own exploratory desires in an environment where the repayment of parental sacrifice is often seen as being the primary objective. Even the idealized offspring of the South Asian diaspora, such as Anil, voice their frustration with the confined parameters of first-generation stereotyped ethnic identity, whining, "I don't wanna go to med. school. I wanna learn how to fly!" Like the model airplane which flies of its own accord in the travel agency office, a push of mental horizons or an actual geographic shift can provide the second generation with a will and identity of its own.

Simultaneously, the images of flight—and the fantastical nature of *Masala* itself—are an act of escapism from the reality of the present context. A movement away from the current environment is sometimes necessary for the redefinition and recontextualization of identity. Yet simply flying off with eyes closed cannot by itself help in achieving independence. To subvert the confining parameters imposed on the creation of a self-defined identity, it is necessary to return to the original location of the second generation and attempt to create a sociopolitical space there that will accept the fluidity of diasporic identity. Metaphors of flight cannot, therefore, be uni-directional but rather round-trip. The fruits of travel outside of the original geographical location should inspire alternative forms of identity that can be implemented in reality.

At times when the central characters in *Masala* are given the opportunity of flying and do move out, however, their attempts are thwarted. The plane carrying Krishna's family to India explodes in a moment of hesitation while the protagonist chooses between a Western breakfast and an Indian one, symbolizing the dual-generation diasporic dilemma of living in limbo in the unarticulated space between two cultures. Moments of identity are created around instances of choice between movement and non-movement; and sometimes when the characters want to move outwards, they are deprived of the tools for doing so. Krishna, for example, finds a source of temporary stabilization in his relationship with Rita, but the relationship per se does not provide an emotional anchor for the formation of his own identity. Individuals like Krishna, who can exist only in a state of so-called 'hypermobility,' are the test cases of post-modern theories of identity. They live in areas of ambivalence, on the margins of the marginalized community, but are scattered to such an extent that they cannot command the resources to make their combined presence known. It is people like Krishna who denote the beginnings of a new South Asian diasporic identity. For in response to a question posed by his aunt,"What kind of an Indian are you?" Krishna prefers to remain silent, exploring the possibilities of a reply as well as the validity of the question in the silence of his answer. In direct contrast to the superficially "finished" structures of identity in *Mississippi Masala*, the process of constructing identity in *Masala* is left mid-way to remain deliberately ambiguous.

The irony of *Masala* is that the reality of the South Asian diaspora in North America is conducted within the realm of fantasy. There are lengthy song-and-dance sequences mimicking Hindi films at key junctures of the movie. *Masala* mocks the attempts of both the first and second generations of the diaspora to retain direct links to India, revealing the futility of locating vestiges of tradition within imports from the subcontinent. Even Rita's devout grandmother, for example, has been corrupted by her fascination with the latest electronic gadgets, and the god Krishna is reduced to a flicker on the TV screen. However, the failure of fantasy to continue, signaled by Krisha's death, is a depiction of the continuing pessimism of reality. The construction of an independent identity for the second generation cannot be easily resolved, especially because of its constantly mobile state; but it is not a process that can be easily abandoned either, because its articulation at every stage is vital to the legitimization of the presence of the South Asian diaspora worldwide.

What is important to note in both films, however, is the complicit participation of Mira Nair and Srinivas Krishna in the construction of a monolithic South Asian cultural history. In the choice of ethnic communities within which to situate their rendition of diasporic identity, both Nair and Krishna have chosen to negate their own ethnic identities and have situated their films in a community that is more familiar to mainstream society. Consequently, their films take place within what are largely Gujarati and Sindhi communities, respectively. The choice of these two communities only serves to reinforce their stereotypical public image in North American society; it also indicates the mis-perceived necessity of constructing a single source of South Asian cultural history. Although there are a plethora of regional South Asian cultural associations in North America, they are usually seen as social gatherings, rather than as more politically-oriented assertions of regional cultural and ethnic identities. Consequently, the second generation is often uneducated as to the immensely varied cultural and social histories of specific ethnic groups on the Indian subcontinent. It is vital that this multicultural aspect of the South Asian diaspora be articulated both within the immigrant community as well as outside of it, since a knowledge of personal family histories may prove to be a useful initial basis of self-identification for successive generations of diasporic South Asians. What also forms a matter for viewer awareness is the ease with which visual techniques tend to gloss over the fragility of temporally constructed identities in both films; the disadvantage being that without a script, it is sometimes easy to dismiss the pain and struggle with which any diasporic identity, however unsuccessful, commercially driven or stereotypical it may ultimately prove to be, is formed.

Mississippi Masala and *Masala* mark the rise of the supposedly polluting Third World within the sterile First World: the alternative South Asian diasporic discourses that they present challenge decaying constructs of geographically bounded communities and static cultural identities. In bringing heretofore invisible and marginalized ethnic communities into mainstream commercial cinema, Nair and Krishna have represented the importance of the diasporic presence in what were imagined to be homogeneous societies. Within the boundaries imposed by mainstream audience reactions to the film, and the reception of the movie by South Asian communities in North America, both directors have managed to clarify a number of ways in which the protagonists of each film attempt to construct an independent identity. Concurrently, the films have opened up other socio-cultural issues of relevance which are important in themselves in relation to the construction of a South Asian diasporic identity. These include the construction of gender within the diaspora; the existence of alternative sexual identities and their acceptance by the immigrant community; the construction of diasporic "histories of identity," and appropriate techniques for its accurate representation; and the necessity and means for the widespread political participation of immigrant communities in the assertion of individual identities. By participating in the act of constructing and articulating alternative diasporic identities, both Nair and Krishna have taken the initiative to exist in an unnamed space on the interstices of society, neither entrenched within the immigrant community nor in the dominant cultural discourse. It is through like-minded efforts that members of the South Asian diaspora can begin to create a language through which to assert their historical, social, sexual, and political identities and validate their presence in their adopted societies. Thus, by inserting the South Asian diaspora into the public consciousness of mainstream society, *Mississippi Masala* and *Masala* mark the beginning of the creation of a post-present, non-hegemonic, social, cultural, and artistic discourse of diaspora.

The Moon and My Mother

Himani Bannerji

The moon is dangerously close to the earth tonight. Over the city plunged in a grey light from roads and high rises, trees in dark clumps standing in the pit of the park, outlines of buildings rubbed into the sky, the moon hangs low, global, filled with pock marks. A leaden pale form, it hangs there shorn of its glory. Trying to light my cigarette against the wind, I am struck by its irrelevance. But once it was not so. Not for my mother certainly, not at least for a long time, well into her middle age. Surrounding the moon, which is controlled by a male, not a female deity, is spread out the mysterious, galactic universe of our ancestors. The glow that emanates from the moon received much of its light from their heavenly aura—as from the consumptive god with his rabbit companions. In the hollows, hills and dales of the moon, they dallied, meditated, reasoned, these ancestors—and waited for their once-a-year propitiation, of remembrance by their eldest male progenies. "Here is water, drink it and be satisfied," "here is food, eat it and be satisfied," "here is flower and cloth, sesame seeds and basil leaves"—on and on the litany went. Sonorous voiced men, with the sacred thread between their index fingers and thumbs, announced and supplicated. Those were the days when the moon was powerful, populated, sat in the middle of our earthly affairs, the passing of generations, giving the flight of souls from the body a destination, an eternal and blissful refuge.

But one day it all ended. The crystalline cosmology shattered like my mother's essence bottle when the sparrows fought on the shelf over a space to nest. The moon, and my mother, fell from grace and plummeted down a dark, empty, cold, and scientific sky. The moon hit the ground, fractured into dead porcelain pieces, and was patched together by television, newspapers, text books, and science fiction. My mother was not so lucky. No one picked up her pieces or shone a new light on her, gave her moon creatures and lores of reason. My mother continued her flight down into this darkness, bouncing off onto the hard ground of fear, of an absolute eternal dissolution—a galactic refugee of a soul with no glowing ancestral haven. I remember it well—I was with her when her fall began, and also at the end.

That year I got married, in a manner of speaking. There was a harvest moon that night—light glinted off the coconut palms, their long branches swaying in the wind. Clouds were piled up on the eastern end of the sky, shaped like elephants. I was leaning against the cold iron bars of the balcony, suffering the first loneliness of a marriage. My mind was not on the moon. But even as I stood there, unheeding of the natural world around me, and my groom lay groaning in bed with what appeared to be a bout of malaria, the earth was moving closer to the moon. Americans were planning, executing the first steps of their conquest of space in heaven and on earth. Peasants that year did not have a good harvest, a drought was forecast, three planets of particularly inauspicious nature had crossed each other's path and Shibu, our cleaner of coconut fronds, gleaner of the fruits, shimmying up a coconut tree with ankles joined with a loop of rope, had seen strange insects on the trunk. These insects, he claimed, have iron drills for their jaws, they bore holes into the trunk and eat into the pith, the life of the tree. I saw him and my mother standing near the gate deep in conversation. There was much discussion about this strange appearance. My mother came upstairs, and later in the afternoon while we drank tea, she asked me what I thought of all the omens which were claimed to be appearing as a result of this inauspicious planetary conjuncture. I assured her that this was rank superstition, and that her coconut trees were in no real danger. My mother retired to her bed with the Bengali newspaper, and lying on her side, propped up against pillows, and her bifocal glasses pulled down her nose, busied herself with learning about the world, as she called it. Having been a little more than unalphabetical for a long time, my mother taught herself how to read better with much daily diligence since my father's death. With the guava tree peeping into the room, with the ties for mosquito nets dangling from the window bars, framed against a lime-washed wall, lying sideways in a soft heap of clothes and limbs, she read every afternoon, especially the newspaper. From the title of the paper to "printed and published by," taking in the advertisements as well. What news she was particularly attending to I did not know or care to ask. But I discovered that was soon after my marriage and it had to do with Americans, machines, and moons.

Unheeded by me, but noticed by cameras and newsmen, there were steel locusts, giant cicadas climbing up the vertical inside of the hollow lid of our universe. Reflecting a bluish glint, deflecting the rising arms of gravity which sanely pulls back all things to the earth, simulating the motions of a bullet fired by some celestial cowboy, the capsule rose moving every second closer to the moon. And my mother waited every day for the news of its landing, for findings that would add to or subtract from her cosmology. And finally it happened. Again I was unmindful, preoccupied as I was with problems at my workplace, marking exams, and securing extra income for my impoverished new family. In fact the crowd of people standing under the arch in front of the United States Information Service remained peripheral to my vision. They had put a few television sets on the other side of the glass, and some men—unemployed or during their office breaks, vendors with their boxes of yellow, orange, and green drinks and ice sticks— formed an obstruction on the sidewalk. I had to get onto the street to skirt them and went my way.

It was a long day for me. After the classes at the University I went to give private tuition to a very young woman struggling with the distant literature of Britain. I stopped by the coffee house for a quick coffee and dry sandwiches and shopped for fruits to take home. After this when I reached home, made the trek between the bus stop and my mother's house, accompanied on a stretch of abandoned land by a few barking mangy dogs, I was exhausted. As there were no electric lights except in the houses, I noticed that the moon was very bright. The swamp full of water hyacinths, with their purple flowers and poisonous green by daylight, looked magical. The wind was fresh and cooled my sweaty body, and the humped silence of buffaloes standing darkly in the pen of the milkman was calm and reassuring. There was a light left on at the entrance of the house, and the purple flowers of bougainvillaea stood out in it. I went up the steps, into my room quietly so as not to disturb my mother, who generally went to bed early. But tonight she was up. She was sitting in an easy chair in my room reading the paper. There was food in small brass bowls covered with a brass plate on my table, in the usual place, and a glass of water. Not until I washed myself and sat down to eat did she break her silence. Then it was preceded by a physical unease, a set of uneven movements until her full body turned around to face me. She seemed deeply perturbed.

"Do you know that they didn't find anything?" She asked.

It was not clear to me what she meant. Who "they" were and what was to be "found" were elusive.

"Who?" I asked. "What should they find?"

"The Americans," said my mother, "the ones that went to the moon. They landed, came out of their aeroplane and walked on the moon, And they didn't find anything."

"And what should they find?" I replied utterly unmindful of any lunar lores. My mother frowned, looked at me strangely.

"*Pitrilok*," she said. The world of our fathers. Surrounding the moon, in that aura, our ancestors reside in their incandescent bodies. But no one was there, they saw nothing. Just darkness, and on the moon too there was nobody—just a hard ground with grey volcanic ashes, craters. It is an abandoned wasteland. There is nothing there.

She repeated the last sentence twice, and the bitterness in her voice stopped me from laughing or coming out with a quick rejoinder. I could not tell her that scientists with telescope eyes had predicted this anyway or that I did not care whether they saw anything or not.

"They lied to us," she said.

"Who?" I asked cautiously, infected by her seriousness.

"All those holy books I read. Mahabharata, Ramayana—they told us of three worlds. The inferno under the earth, the earth itself, and heaven with the celestial sphere of the ancestors, where we all go after death, to await rebirth, not to come back at all if we have released ourselves or to come back as enjoined by the deeds of our previous life.

As I was going to respond humorously by saying, "Maybe the ancestors were scared of the Americans, they hid themselves," my mother raised herself painfully from the chair. Before she left the room she looked at me with a face full of sadness, her eyes held an expression for which I have no words.

"Just darkness. Nothing. After death nobody goes anywhere. There is nothing there after death. You know, I should have studied science instead of these story books about souls, hells, and heavens."

With that sentence my mother left the room. I sat there for a while, the chill of rationalism slowly rising through my body. I heard her move heavily, slowly in her room, prepare for bed. The light under her door went out. The wooden bed creaked a few times. I too turned out the light in my room. Through the huge windows which formed the two sides of my room a tide of moonlight rushed in. The moon was wild and exuberant that night over the coconut trees. A pale star stood dimly apart. I suddenly felt a strong spurt of anger against the Americans, against the scientists, against locusts of steel that landed on the moon and ate into our ancestors' world, and my mother's heart and faith. That was the hour of the fall, when my mother and the moon fell together.

II

I could say that I don't remember that evening and night very well, or that I can never forget it. A parenthesis of forgetting and remembering has bracketed that time for me for so long and so effectively that when little whispers are overheard in my ordinary day and night, when a clock ticks away beneath my time here and now, they have the feel of another's memory, and a mythic reported time. Yet they are my memories, in my time—and only I can recall them.

I knew she was dying. I knew I would never see her again, and I also knew that I had to leave. Where I was going and why, that is now unimportant. But the important thing is that I sat under the tree in the front of the house, facing the driveway, the hedge that fences us from the street, the lopsided green wooden gate, sat for the longest time holding back my cries, tears, spiralling pains, guilt, remorse, and longing to see her whole and walking again, speaking with unclouded eyes and mind, and bit by bit let go of her. Once a mother she had to free herself from the clutches of my clinging limbs, now I unwound myself from her and renounced my possessive pronouns, transformed her into a common noun—"mother." So I sat in that hot and dusty June afternoon, my suitcases packed, facing an emptying out of time. Light began to die, clumps of green foliage surrounding me began to absorb a bluish grey from the darkening sky. The weeping heads of the white lilies, the crushed fragrance of the jasmines battered by the day's heat rose in the breeze, someone turned on the light in the living room and I sat transfixed in my cane chair caught between history and nothingness.

Someone came out of the living room, stood by the columns near the steps. It was the maid. She said, "Your mother is calling for you." I rose and went in.

This is how I remember it, or recreate it perhaps. It was an evening without definition or boundaries and yet frozen in and as time. I have never entered this time fully, no mortal can, nor have I left it. A little part of me sits still in that gathering darkness where street lamps are lit by invisible hands, and voices of vendors, bird calls, passing cars, bicycle bells fall in confusion on the threshold of time. Death lingers by the door, and his shadow engulfing my mother, partly engulfs me. It is then that I discovered my mother again in that cold dead lunar landscape, in the full flush of her fear whose intimations I received on that night when men in machines invaded the moon and sucked up my mother's faith, her certainties.

My mother lay hidden under a pile of blankets. It was difficult to discover her, so small and shrunken had she become, a little cipher of a body, hollow reeds, a voice of bones, from her former round confidence in taking space. The little head with a bobbed haircut, her bun of long hair gone forever, her face looking young and small like a child's with the skin stretched on it in a pallor. Death had already rubbed into her face an embalming wax that had a luminous quality. Only her eyes, dark, endless pools of light, looked up at me—human, thoughtful, enquiring, and called forth the infinite tenderness that the still alive feel for those who are dying—so common till now, to become rarer than a miracle soon. The room was small, the walls a pale ochre and a small electric light bulb did not make for much visibility. Outside, in the branches of an acacia tree, light thickened, the sky faded and birds made chirping noises. Surrounded by her small belongings, a humble and rusting tin trunk with her few clothes, a silver box of betel leaves and condiments, a wooden shrine of her now forgotten gods and goddesses, she lay there mostly in silence, drifting in and out of a sleep, whose enchantment daily grew stronger on her. From the wall above her bed my father looked on—a touched-up enlargement from the days of before his illness, and I realized how young my father was when I saw him ancient with authority. I sat down and moved a few strands of hair from her forehead. The forehead was damp and cool—a coolness that shades off into the end of any inner heat or light. She lifted a hand, her fingers now shrunk to bird claws, and with the feathery touch of a sparrow took my hand into hers.

With a voice uncannily firm coming from that frail body, she said, "I will not see you again."

Fearing that admitting this would begin a turmoil that would hurl the whole world into madness and shrieks of despair and impossible wishes, I resorted to banalities. "That is not true, I said. I will be back in two months. You will still be here. It isn't long."

"No," she insisted, "no." She would not be here. She was forcing me to live in the very ultimate, on the border of life and death. I was speaking to her, only momentarily, on this side of the other side.

"So be it," I said to myself. So be it. I will not lie to her, or trivialize her being at the beginning of dissolution. Holding my hand in her partially numb left hand, she signalled me to move a little closer. Her voice was the sound of little waters in the crevices of rocks lapping in secrecy. She had something important to tell me.

"What is it, mother?" I said bending closer, our faces almost touching.

Becoming smaller than a pupil shrunk by a strong flash of light, she said, with the simplicity of a child wanting to urinate at night and afraid of the dark, "I am afraid."

She snuggled closer to me and repeated, with those dark glistening eyes of little creatures, uttering the words on her tongue, "I am afraid."

Dear, small creature, who had become all living things, a child and a crone, an animal in a trap struggling to be free, I could have scooped her up in my arms and leapt across mountains and gulfs to free her of this fear.

"Mother," I said, "mother. Have faith. Remember all that you believed— they are all there on the other side, as you used to say. My father, your mother, my grandmother, my eldest brother whom you lost a long time ago."

She shook her head. A moan rose from her indicating the futility of my reminders. But a stronger and colder voice came from her in a little while.

"You don't believe in what you say, do you?" she asked. Then I did not lie to her. Though my mother, she was invested with the sacred authority of a dying human.

"No, I don't," I said sadly, with my heart contracting. I searched every part of me for a tiny flake of faith. But I could not give her the certainty, the last moment of what could be a sacrament. Her eyes closed and faint creases showed around her tired eyes. Without opening her eyes, she asked, "What is on the other side? What will I encounter? What will happen to me?"

Watching her disappearing body, I could have said, mother you will be a spirit, a soul on its chiaroscuro twilight of birth and rebirths. But I could not. Not a word escaped my mouth. It is she who spoke, with a bleakness that human voice can rarely attain, with the voice of an abandoned wasteland where lepers and dogs wander driven away from habitations, she said, "I know what there is on the other side. An immense, great darkness. All of what we read, were told were just stories. There is nothing there. No ancestors, nobody."

And I her atheist daughter, cried out to her, "And God? Isn't there God, on the other side? Will it not be to us as we believe? And if we believe . . . "

Silencing me with a vehemence I had not seen her in in a long time, she said to me, "No, my daughter, there is nothing on the other side of death. On this side there is life, that's where we lived, and on the other side, there is nothing. On the other side of death, there is death."

My mother's wisdom blew a chill wind through me, I remembered one other conversation we had about being, time, and our place in life and death. My mother had become like the dead moon, lit by a false glow of a sun about to withhold its light from her.

That was the last time I saw my mother. We left each other without any consolation, and she blessed me with her active left hand from the pinnacle of her bleak realization, drank a glass of water, turned around to the wall and seemed to drift into her private darkness and nothingness. Two weeks after that, as I heard in a grey dawn, she died. And for those two weeks she had spoken to nobody.

III

What a bleak wisdom! What a negative, horrible destructive vision she left me with, I thought as I sat there looking at a moon thousands of miles away from where she lived and died. The moon was now even lower, closer to me. The wind was stronger. Little bits of noise drifted up from the park below and somewhere a dog barked. And by a strange trick of a car passing by I heard my own name, the last syllable of it elongatedly pronounced. The moon seemed to be looking at me as well. It spoke to me of my mother, of a time long ago, of when I was a young woman, when my mother was active and alive. But most of all it had become one with my mother, a very private and personal moon, populated with memories of hope and horror, with a parable of faith and its loss. It was not empty, that moon, I thought. The Americans were wrong.

—20th October, 1992

Convention Fairy Tale

Anjalee Deshpande

Once upon a singles night
bar scene littered with fakesmilesclinkingicecubes
reflectionsofmybreastsindroolingeyes
the word "loathe" took on new meaning.
"yes, I speak Marathi." lousy shit toad
watch out "I'm in Health Care" boy
your ego's showing out between the
gaps.
HELLOPERSONALSPACEPLEASE
"Yes I know who Margaret Thatcher is,"
we theatre majors occasionally possess intellect as well as a nice
ASKMENOMOREQUESTIONSTELLMENOMORELIES
why am i here
why the Fuck Am i Here

and then you

you
with your longhairsidestepaloofpersona
you, with your talk of uniting of the Marathi community,
quoting Kalidasa
leaving the country on a whim
to help people

You rubbed my lamp baby,
you rubbed my lamp.

and I stopped short

like a puff of blue smoke

cause there you were
just like that
like a snapblinksneezeachooGodblessyou
you
everypreteenmasturbationnamelessfacelessshimmering
knight

and me
bewitched, bewildered and completely
seduced

simply by your smile

VeryColgateWinter-Freshchimeintheairsolitarysparkle
betweenyourtoprightincisors
you

yea

you rubbed my lamp baby
you rubbed my lamp

and I could see through your eyes right through to the back of your head
gloriousglimmeringshimmeringsilverbluebraintissue swelling up
bursting at the juicy seams
Alive!

with possibility

and 72 hours later
you said good-bye and told me
"It Can."

And there was glittersparklemagik in the air there baby
Cracklin' in the air

2 years later
you're looking in the mirror
wondering what ever happened to your beatnik babe

"An Actress! An Actress!
PICK UP ONE OF YOUR OWN!
Impress Your Friends! Shock Your Mom!
Maybe Even Date The Cover Of A Rolling Stone!"

ExpressoDrinkinCloveSmokinBlackDresswithaBeret "Arteest"
with a capital A

that you threw back
when the novelty wore off

yea
two years later
guess where I am
bar scene singlesnight
toads
drool

fear

I 'm down here at the bottom of the ocean baby
the bottom of the ocean

I'm doubledoverfetalcurledupinside these beat up brassy walls of mine
that seem a lot thicker

than they used to

I'm here
at the bottom of the ocean

remembering when

it could

Divided Consciousness Amidst a New Orientalism: South Asian American Identity Formation on Campus

Sucheta J. Doshi

Preface: I understand the problematic connotations of the terms Eastern, Western, and South Asian in their tendency to categorize diverse peoples into neat little boxes, sometimes with very negative images. For the purposes of this essay, I use West in reference to its usage to describe the educational experience of the nationalists during the Indian independence movement. While I realize that the phrase South Asian is often used interchangeably with the word Indian, I use the term only to relate to all South Asians. When I am describing the Indian independence movement, a personal experience or an experience that I have only known other Indians to have, I use the word Indian. At the same time, I also understand that by placing this essay in the context of college education, I describe experiences of privileged South Asians. If this essay emphasizes the educated Indian-American experience, it is only because I speak from my own personal experiences.

"The Orient was almost a European invention," states Edward Said in Orientalism. Those nations east of Europe represented the image of the Other, images that encompassed Europe's cultural contestant as well as the source of its civilizations and languages.[1] In order to justify their rule in India, the British created various constructions about India and the Indian character which combined to suggest that the Indians were incapable of governing themselves. The Indian nationalist movement arose in part as a reaction to these constructions and was initiated by those educated in institutions embracing the British template of learning. Their struggle to create a counter definition for themselves and their emerging nation shaped the identity of the Western-educated Indian middle class while it also terminated British rule in India. The impact of British culture and the influence of the West on the ideas and lives of Indian intellectuals such as Mohandas K. Gandhi created the consequent struggle to assimilate Western education and technology with Indian traditions; a theme that continues to illustrate the lives of South Asians growing up and being educated in America.

Such issues of identity are consequences of cultural collisions, falsely assumed to be rigid and unyielding. As a second generation Indian-American struggling to come to terms with my identity, I have always felt an intense connection to the struggles of the Indians educated in a Western system of education during the British Raj in India. They were intellectuals caught between two worlds, intellectuals with a divided consciousness stemming from their Western education. Second-generation South Asian Americans are experiencing a similar struggle in America, trying to integrate the cultures and traditions of our parents with our uniquely American experiences; we too possess a divided consciousness that lies at the heart of efforts to build coalitions toward an emerging pan-Asian identity.

The "Invisible" Asians

While I was a student at Wellesley College between 1990 and 1994, I was constantly frustrated by the minimal representation of issues pertinent to South Asian students in various areas of the college such as the curricula, student governing bodies, or college committees. The only three courses related to South Asia were an art course, a religion course, and a literature course on Indian writers.[2] These classes were rarely offered and nowhere in any of the other departments was there any mention of courses addressing the history, politics, or economics of all our countries. Along with other second-generation South Asian American students, I had eagerly sought courses that would enable me to learn about the history and politics of my people, in South Asia and especially in the diaspora. While constantly pressuring the "multicultural" student body to claim their cultures, the administration refused to fund programs that would enhance the curriculum. At the same time, the President of the College embarked on an extended trip to Asia, but chose not to visit any of the South Asian countries. Her actions are representative of a larger phenomenon in America that continues to impact the growing and constantly changing identity formation of South Asian Americans.

The tendency for most people in the United States to envision Asia and Asians as exclusively from East Asia is one that affects the ongoing identity strug-

gles of South Asians all over the country. It is an especially important compo-
nent of the struggles faced by South Asian youth during college and one that
influences coalition building. During my years as an undergraduate at Wellesley
College, I rarely ever saw South Asian representation either within the Asian
Student Association or during events celebrating Asian or Asian American her-
itages. Always, there was an emphasis that exclusively highlighted the experiences of East Asians living in America. Once during an art exhibition celebrating Asian American experiences, after failing to find any art work representative
of the South Asian American experience, many of my fellow South Asian sisters
and myself had to ask ourselves, "Who are we and where do we fit in?" Many
of us had always believed ourselves to be Asians or Asian Americans and now all
of a sudden, that identity was called into question. Nowhere in this exhibit were
our struggles as South Asians living in America mentioned. Were we Asians or
weren't we?

During college, I saw the formation of many different Asian student groups,
created out of universal dissatisfaction with the homogeneous Asian Association
(AA). It was not that South Asians had not tried to become involved with AA.
A few women had initially gone to the meetings and felt very uncomfortable; one
South Asian student was told that she wasn't really "Asian." While President of
the South Asian Student Association (SASA) at Wellesley,[3] I had often argued
that we needed to become more active within AA in order to change the organization, only to be reminded by my other sisters that women before us had made
the effort and no one had the right to judge whether this effort was strong
enough or not. My frustration with the political apathy among South Asian students was met with various defenses from my constituents. One woman pointed
out that just as India is composed of various loyalties, languages, and traditions,
so is Asia. Do various loyalties, however, mean that we can not even work together? Yes, our cultures are different, but an Asian American Studies program
should involve all Asians, not just East Asians. Until we stand up and voice our
opinions, we will continue to be the "invisible Asians." When the message has
been sent that Asia does not include South Asia, however, we begin to suspect
the universality of such a program. We feel that emerging Asian American
Studies programs in universities across the nation will not include South Asian
experiences; therefore, we have lost the will to become involved.

Constant exclusion has a damaging impact on our own identities as well as our involvement in the growing Asian American political movement. Wellesley's admissions application asks the applicant to define herself as a minority, with the usual African-American, Hispanic, and Asian American being among the choices. Many South Asians mark "other" instead of Asian American as a consequence of constantly being told that we are not Asian. Even in the United States Census, those South Asians who are not Asian Indian are classified under "Other Asians." [4]

The politics of college campuses and the rest of the nation are such that the minority group is given the task of educating the rest of the society. Why should it be our responsibility to educate others about South Asian culture? What happens at a college where there are no South Asians? Will there be no classes taught on South Asian American and South Asian issues because there is no 'target group to pacify'? While it is true that historically cultural studies departments have arisen from pressure from the cultural communities, as was the case with African American Studies departments and the Civil Rights movement in the sixties, continuing such a tradition will never lead to enhanced curricula. At colleges without concentrated vocal minority groups, the student body will not learn about cultures and world issues that developed outside of European roots. College and university administrations need to realize the importance of teaching these issues for the sake of knowledge and as a way to work toward ending racism, imperialism, or anti-Asian violence, rather than as a way to satisfy the needs of a 'special interest group.'

SASAs across the country have begun to network with each other. Every year, there is an annual SASA conference on the East Coast where second-generation South Asians discuss issues relevant to our experiences in America. But no conference is considered complete unless it has the requisite fashion show and dance party; in the past the workshop and lecture components have always been sparsely attended as most second-generation, heterosexual South Asians attended these conferences to scope out members of the opposite sex. For the first time, in 1996, the annual SASA conference addressed our political identities and the many different South Asian experiences that differ from the "norm." At the same time, however, the annual East Coast Asian Student Union Conference did not have a strong South Asian participation once again, despite great effort from Asian

Associations to recruit a South Asian presence at the conferences. I find this lack of South Asian involvement in Asian American political alliances frustrating. While awareness must come from all sides, South Asians should take an initiative in making their voice heard in the Asian American community as well as in the United States in general. The lack of a South Asian participation in the Asian Association is not a Wellesley phenomenon; even at Harvard, at the annual Asian American Association Conference in 1994, none of the panelists were South Asian.[5] How are Asian Americans to fight for rights and earn political recognition if we can't even unite ourselves?

Discrimination from Within

The result of segregation is the creation of particular characteristics by the South Asian community to define one another's South Asianess. When one identity is destroyed, another is established to replace it; this new one sets standards for everyone, leading to the feeling among many who do not fit each standard that we are not as South Asian as others. Separated from South Asia, the greater South Asian community in America has tried to recreate the religious, cultural, and social traditions left behind in South Asia. For those of us who are Indian American, while our uncles and aunts in India have progressed with time, our parents continue to hold on to the old mentality that existed in India when they migrated. As second-generation South Asian Americans, we face pressure from our families to follow the path they followed, to marry the appropriate man or woman from the same country, region, religion, and culture who speaks the same language. The isolation from South Asia has led to a tendency to judge and condemn everyone who does not fit the "elite, educated, heterosexual and wealthy" South Asian standard; a divorced woman is ostracized from South Asian American society and poor families are ignored by those who believe that poverty and welfare, like domestic violence, are not problems for the South Asians in America. Gay, lesbian, bisexual, and transgendered youth are forced into closets through internalized homophobia and shunned, sent to psychiatrists, or cast off by the community if they have the courage to come out.

Growing up in America, in trying to fight the multicultural mantra of reclaiming our culture and resisting the pressures from the South Asian community to hold on to cultural traditions that no longer address our experiences, we retaliate by refusing to have anything to do with South Asia or South Asians. Many gay and lesbian South Asians do not join South Asian organizations out of fear of homophobia and ostracism; yet at the same time, because joining confers a sense of being South Asian, these youth also grow tired of being South Asian and refuse to deal with their South Asian identities in all aspects, trying to meld in with white gay society as much as possible. Being told that they are not South Asian because they are gay, they believe it and try to become "white," refusing to date other South Asians, and creating another form of racism within the queer South Asian communities. At the same time, gay South Asians face marginalization from a white gay society that will not accept minorities who do not mimic the white way of being gay.[6]

The heterosexist attitudes of the greater South Asian community and the tendency to ostracize any who are "different" have been replicated among the wealthy South Asian students on college campuses. This is partly due to the emphasis most SASA organizations have always placed on the social as opposed to the political agenda. When I first entered Wellesley, all the Asian organizations suffered from reputations that labeled them "party" organizations. Trying to cast off these labels, the Asian Association soon became more politically motivated and began to lobby for more Asian languages, for more Asian representation in the college government, and for more Asian involvement in the political process. The leaders of SASA during that time continued to concentrate on their party focus. At that time, I was alone in lobbying for South Asian representation on college government, and I alone had the desire to be the senator representing the South Asian voice on college government. The executive board of SASA refused to do anything political; the top item on their agenda was when to hold the next party. Rather than also focusing on the issues that faced us on campus and the world beyond, they focused exclusively on networking only with the social chairs of the other South Asian organizations at MIT and Boston University, and then only to hold a joint dance party. I was already a controversial member because I was "too" political. When I became President and fiercely advocated more lectures, more education, and more political alliances with the other groups on campus, I was told that I was a "controversial" president because I was too vocal and actually had an agenda that also focused on something other than social activities with other South Asian organizations which had only furthered our isolation in the past.

Fear of ostracism forced many of my fellow lesbian and bisexual South Asian sisters into the closet while at Wellesley, despite their desire to be out and proud among their lesbian sisters at a women's college. Worse, many could not even come out to themselves because of the pressures of fitting a "South Asian" or "Muslim" or "Hindu" standard. One was either a lesbian or South Asian, one could not be both because established South Asian society standards deemed it so. If it had been difficult to convince SASA to work with other Asian groups, it was impossible to even suggest an alliance with the lesbian and bisexual student group on campus, because homosexuality was "not a South Asian issue." Many women I have known have experienced the feeling of being judged and being victims of established South Asian social norms; we have all at times had a similar desire to "prove" (to ourselves or others) that we are just as South Asian or just as American as anyone. Those who can not stand the thought of being judged refuse to join South Asian organizations and then are labeled "ABCD's" [7] by the South Asian American socialites in these organizations.

While at Wellesley, my own identities shifted daily. Most South Asian students are sent to Wellesley by parents who believe their daughters will remain sheltered and "proper" at a "girl's school." Eventually they will find a good husband at nearby Harvard and settle down. Few South Asian parents realize that this is only a reality for very few women at women's colleges. Rather, for me, I found my home amidst the powerful ideas of feminism and the close friendships I developed with other women, ties that I know will last a lifetime. At the same time, I fought the 'ABCD' label passionately because I most surely was not one. After all, I spoke both Hindi and Gujarati fluently. I knew the history and politics of India better than my cousins who lived there. My senior thesis was on the Indian independence movement. But all this disappeared when people learned the simple fact that I was born and raised in America. Despite my knowledge of Indian languages, history and culture, I was not "Indian" enough because I was "American." To many of the more socially oriented South Asian students at Wellesley, I was too enmeshed in political issues like "those radically militant African Americans" to be a "cool" South Asian. Why was I a feminist? Why couldn't I just go to parties and look for cute South Asian boys like the rest of them? If I didn't like to party all the time, there had to be something wrong with me.

None of my friends could understand why I remained in the group. I remained out of a perverse belief that I could change the organization, that I could change the political apathy, that I could make the women in the group more open-minded and tolerant of differences. It was only during my junior year at Wellesley that the older women who had led SASA in the past moved on to allow the younger classes to bring in fresh ideas.

SASA politics seem to run in cycles both at Wellesley and at other college campuses. After I graduated from Wellesley, the organization returned to a social agenda but this time, the new group of first-years was larger, more vocal and strong willed than my class had been. They forced the new leaders to look at political issues and created a major turnover in the executive board for the next year by winning in elections against the incumbent leaders. The tide will no doubt turn again the following year toward a more social agenda, but I believe that slowly more South Asian students are becoming politically aware and will focus on issues such as hiring more South Asian faculty, adding more courses on South Asia and forging alliances with other groups on campus to further the awareness of a political South Asian presence on campus and beyond.

The New Wave of Orientalism: Multiculturalism

As members of the second generation, we ourselves are divided about our experiences. Hence, those of us who do differ from the "norm" try to reject our South Asian identity in search of a new identity that speaks to our personal realities, only to be confronted with racism and prejudice from the "Western" societies. We are victimized for being different among South Asians and victimized simply for looking different among other Americans. And in a multicultural society embracing oppression, we are martyred; consequently, at Wellesley, I saw many white women who became lesbians or claimed to have minority blood, only because they felt a need to be oppressed since the "oppressed minorities" were being given such "wonderful" special treatment. I only felt anger at such hypocrisy and condescension. Why would anyone wish to have our existence? Why would anyone choose to be hated, discriminated against, and ridiculed, just for being "different?" Amidst the happiness I found at being at a college reputed for feminism and the joy I experienced at developing a confidence I never had before, I was constantly frustrated by the subtle undercurrents of patronizing racism.

We are constantly facing Western constructions about how minorities in America should bond together and enjoy our communities. If we are seeking relationships, we are told by the white majority that we should stick to "our own kind" and find ourselves a nice South Asian boy or girl; interracial relationships are again becoming taboo in the new multicultural American society as they have always been in South Asian and even some South Asian American communities. We are too American by South Asian standards and too South Asian by white American standards. We are a part of two worlds, but belong to neither; yet, we are forced to choose a world when we shouldn't have to. Our consciousness, like that of the Western educated Indian nationalists, is also divided.

In spite of efforts to explore the intersections of race, ethnicity, and gender in more complex ways, multiculturalism is still accompanied by white guilt, a guilt which continues to manifest itself in hideous forms that seek to apologize for past imperialisms with a neocolonialist attitude. Many white feminists still argue about trying to bring feminism to "third world" countries, believing that women in South Asia are so oppressed that they need white women to teach them how to "liberate" themselves from patriarchal institutions in their own cultures. One South Asian woman's reality is magnified to represent the realities of all South Asian women. Hence, many white feminists bemoan the fate of "the Islamic woman, suffocating under her veil," without sufficiently understanding the subjectivities and strategies of diverse populations of Muslim women. This is a feminism completely disregarding cultural ramifications; rather than being liberating, it is oppressive. The very presumption that it is liberating reeks of imperialist attitudes that "we know what is better for developing nations than the people of those nations do themselves."

Not being given the opportunity to learn our various histories, the most damaging consequence is that we as a group have bought into western projections of our identity so much that our parents pressure us to uphold the model minority image, we believe what white feminists say about oppression in India, and we nod as society bemoans "the poverty in Calcutta" and waxes poetic about Gandhi's non-violence movement and the "passivity of Indians." We write short stories that depict the oppression of women in India without stopping to remember the matriarchies that once ruled kingdoms all over India, that South Asian countries have had strong female Prime Ministers while the United States cannot even cope with an intelligent, politically conscious First Lady. Once again, we are victims of Orientalist constructs, allowing one reality to supplant all others. I remember my tremendous frustration at a Gandhi Conference held at Wellesley College where everyone seemed to believe that non-violence could solve all the problems in the world because that was how "the passive Indians had cast off British rule." The irony was that while Wellesley praised a great figure in Indian history, nowhere in the curriculum was there a course on his philosophy. Had Wellesley offered courses on South Asian history and philosophy, the people at the conference would have understood that the independence movement did not win on the sheer force of non-violence alone. The Quit India movement which finally gained independence from the British was far from being a passive movement; even Gandhi had admitted at that time that India was not ready for non-violence.[8] His original movement was itself inspired by Henry David Thoreau's treatise on Civil Disobedience. Nevertheless, I noticed that my fellow South Asian sisters, never having had the opportunity to learn the truth, agreed with the white majority and believed that Indians had given this passive legacy to the world.

Fighting Essentialism and Labels

As second-generation South Asian Americans, fleshing out our identities becomes a rite of passage because of everything we have to prove. We have to be "Americanized," or else we are not cool enough for the other members of our generation who are always out at bars and clubs and refuse to learn their South Asian languages because it "just isn't cool." We have to be "proper South Asians" for our parents. We have to prove that we are American when asked ignorant questions from white society such as "where did you learn to speak English so well?" When I travel to India, I can't help but notice the many problems that do exist such as corruption, gender discrimination and violence; yet, while in America, I am forced to be an ambassador from India, forced to represent all the cultures, views, and images of all South Asia, forced to deify them and hide the bad in the face of a largely ignorant white society that seeks to denigrate the "third world."

I'm tired of fighting. I'm tired of educating both the outside world and the South Asian American community. I am tired of being thought of as an "other," as a "special interest," and yes, even as a "person of color." The connotations of these terms are demeaning to our self-images, as if specifically invoked by "white" society to mark an essential difference. Not only does the second generation have to fight prejudice outside of our cultures but then we also have to fight prejudice within our communities, fight to make the South Asian communities accept and tolerate differences within the community on one hand and fight to make it more politically aware on the other. We have to fight the 'ABCD' label, and then the multicultural labels that tokenize and subject us in the greater society. I am tired of being told what I have to be, and I am tired of defending who I am. If I choose to be "Western," I shouldn't be told by some politically correct advocate to claim my culture. If I choose to be interested in Indian history and politics and learn classical Indian dance, I shouldn't be told by an Indian American that I am allowing my parents to lead my life or be patronized by other Americans for being "so in touch with my culture." No one has the right or authority to judge how "South Asian" someone is; after all, what is an authentic South Asian? Who defines what is authentic and what isn't?

Separation from South Asia and segregation from the Asian American communities has led to isolation, self-doubt, and conflict within the diaspora about identity and its definition. Our identities have naturally become so much more hybridized than those of our parents because of our particular American experiences. As an Indian American whose parents are from two different religious communities, when asked who I am, I struggle to answer the question. Am I American? Indian-American? Indian? South Asian? Gujarati? Hindu? Jain? For many, the added dimension of sexuality can negate all the other identities if we allow the conservative older generation to claim the right to define who is South Asian and who isn't. The labeling can continue forever, if we allow it. As we develop as second-generation South Asians, these questions of identity and essentialism become the key elements which will ignite questions, conflicts, debates, and arguments for our peoples. We are the ones who will be able to resist falling into the myths of model minorityhood that our parents did. In doing so, the process will either become more volatile, if we let it, as many more questions of identity are being confronted, or it can bring an added dimension of harmony if we learn to listen to one another, work together as a group, network with other Asian and minority organizations and tolerate each other's opinions and ideas. Most of all, we need to learn to understand that we do not need to be defined or have to define ourselves.

Notes

[1] Edward Said, *Orientalism*, (New York: Pantheon Books, 1978), p. 1.

[2] South Asian diversity is often ignored in the courses that are taught on college campuses. As most courses focus on issues prior to 1947, the cultures of Pakistan, Bangladesh, Sri Lanka, Nepal and other South Asian countries are lumped together in courses that refer to only India. Responding to the diversity of our people, many college organizations have changed their names from Indian Subcontinent Association to include the South Asian reference. The titles of these specific courses also represent the popular misconception that South Asia's important contributions to the world are limited to art and religion.

[3] Wellesley's South Asian student association is entitled Wellesley Association for South Asian Cultures. As this essay refers to the general politics of student organizations at colleges and universities, I refer to Wellesley's organization as SASA for the sake of simplicity.

[4] Discussion on the term South Asia and the hegemonic implications of the term India or Indian are raised in Naheed Islam's "In the belly of the multicultural beast I am named South Asian," *Our Feet Walk the Sky: Women of the South Asian Diaspora*, ed. The Women of South Asian Descent Collective (San Francisco: Aunt Lute Books, 1993), pp. 242-245.

[5] With more students becoming politically active on college campuses, there has been a concentrated outreach effort over the past two years to encourage pan-Asian alliances. The 1996 Harvard AAA Conference will include South Asian participation; my essay, however, relates conditions as they existed during the time I was at Wellesley. Nevertheless, there are still many instances where South Asians remain left out of Asian-American alliances beyond the university walls, sometimes despite efforts from South Asians to join such alliances.

[6] The development of organizations such as SALGA, MASALA, and TRIKONE aid in providing a network of support and a sense of identity for gay, lesbian, bisexual and transgendered South Asians going through any part of the coming out process. In addition, the recent publication of *A Lotus of Another Color: An Unfolding of the South Asian Gay and Lesbian Experience* (Boston: Alyson Publication, 1993) bears witness to the presence of a strong and vibrant queer South Asian community in the United States, South Asia and the rest of the world.

[7] 'ABCD' refers to the phrase "American Born Confused Desi," a term used in a derogatory manner to describe second-generation South Asian Americans who are thought to be ignorant of the South Asian cultures and traditions.

[8] *In The Intimate Enemy: Loss and Recovery of Self under Colonialism* (Delhi: Oxford University Press, 1983), Ashish Nandy analyzes Gandhi's nonviolence philosophy by considering the British theory of racial superiority that painted Indians as passive, childlike and effeminate, while the English were aggressive, mature and masculine. He argues that Indian nationalism arose as many pre-Gandhian protest movements sought to "redeem the Indians' masculinity by defeating the British (9)." Gandhi, himself, believed that by buying into the stereotypes, England was emotionally and spiritually mutilating herself (*Indian Home Rule*, Bombay: Young India, 1921, pp. 26-35). Nevertheless, by embracing passive resistance as an intrinsic part of Indian spirituality and tradition, he supported the British conception of Indians as passive, weak beings. The emphasis Gandhi placed on India's natural affiliation with nonviolence is representative of his internal conflict between his Western and Indian selves as he embraced a distinctly Indian philosophy by accepting a Western construction of Indians. This is pointed out by Nandy who uses Nirad Chaudhuri's observations about Hindu traditions to show the extent to which Gandhi created an Indian image that

never existed before: "The current belief is that the Hindus are a peace-loving and non-violent people, and this belief has been fortified by Gandhism. In reality few communities have been more warlike and fond of bloodshed . . . there is not one word of non-violence in the theory and practice of statecraft by the Hindus (50)." In *Imagining India* (Cambridge: Basil Blackwell, 1990), Ronald Inden also points out that "Gandhi's concept of non-violence played the central part it did in Indian nationalism because it had been singled out long ago as a defining trait of the Hindu character [via Orientalism] (38)."

The Lakshman Rekha

A Fable

S. Bari

In the Indian epic, The Ramayan, the hero Ram entrusts his brother Lakshman with the care of Ram's wife, Sita. When Lakshman is nonetheless forced to leave her alone, he draws a circle on the ground around their forest home, within the confines of which nothing can harm her. He warns her not to step beyond it. Sita steps out to serve a wandering holy man, and is abducted. The line she crossed is known as the lakshman rekha.

In the North there are two Twin Cities. They sit cheek-to-cheek on the banks of the Mississippi river. In the smaller sister, you will find a neighborhood of quiet lawn-mufflered streets with dainty white houses hanging on the fringes of the green. Old people live here. They labor out the door in the morning to pick up the newspaper at the end of the path, through the geraniums and pansies that spot their front lawns. Sunday mornings the sidewalks spill over with white heads on their way to church, a slow halting procession to the faith and neighborhood gossip.

There lived in this old neighborhood a family who did not go to church on Sundays. In the afternoon, if you found yourself in this house, you would hear (around five o' clock) a reedy voice rising in song, a compelling voice. You would follow it to the living room, padding across the thick carpet, and find it emanating from the mantelpiece that jutted over the spotless, never-used fireplace. The voice would rise to a pitch at the end of each line and then drop back to the starting note. You would discover that it sang forth from a tiny golden clock in the shape of a mosque, with shining minarets and a green face. Five times a day the clock would sing that melancholy call to prayer.

Atique Rahman lived in that house with his two daughters and his scientist wife and a collection of Bengali poetry books of which he was very proud. Nazia worked at the Institute for Nuclear Safety, where she wore thin gloves in her airless lab, and Atique drove the Lexus to his job at 3M. Their lawn was cropped close, because old Mrs. Murphy's grandson mowed for the Rahmans whenever he came visiting. Narmeen and Sharmeen brought him lemonade sometimes, and they all stood out on the front lawn chatting till Nazia called them in to finish their homework.

It was in the summer of '89 that Narmeen and Sharmeen graduated from high school. They wore sarees that day. The house resounded with the clicks and round vowels of Bengali, of cousins and aunts and uncles, flown in from Montreal, Austin, and San Jose. Kamran Uncle thought the girls should go to UC Berkeley, and Zareen Auntie argued that they should go to Princeton. Nazia, who was preparing the *biryani*, shouted her daughters would stay right here and go to the U of M. It was just as good as any school on the coasts, and why should she send her children so far away? Wiping the onion tears from her eyes, Sharmeen laughed and told her aunt Ma would never let her go away unless it was with a wedding veil on her head. Zareen, who had never married, turned silently to the stove. Zareen lived alone and worked. She had her own investments and went wherever she liked on vacation. She was like a white woman.

Narmeen followed her father around as he went from brother to cousin to uncle. But, Abba, she repeated tirelessly, we won't be out long. Atique took the glasses of orange juice, apple juice, Coke, and Sprite from the tray in her hands and passed them out with resigned smiles. He wanted to remind her of the distance her relatives had come, and of the evenings her mother and he had leaned over math problems with her on the kitchen table. When a boy had come to the door, when the American world had come knocking with its venereal diseases and its homeless, he had protected his girls.

In the afternoon the carpets were obscured by prayer mats. The clock man keened out his song, and heads touched the ground. Sharmeen and Narmeen sat a while longer to repeat their thanks to Allah, hands cupped in front of them. Sharmeen wanted to see if the lines in the upper part of her palm formed a V or a U. The sharper the curve, the happier she would be in love. But hers were a fairly flat, unlovely U.

After their graduation, the sisters were sent to an aunt in Saudi Arabia. For a semester, they stirred curries in her kitchen and learnt the Quran from a haughty Saudi woman. Sharmeen, always brilliant in Islamic school back home, was the woman's pet. Narmeen never memorized her *suras* properly and disappointed both her aunt and her teacher. When the Northern winter gripped the Twin Cities and sheathed them in snow, Atique and Nazia arrived in the sun-toasted town of Jeddah. They took the girls to the black and gold center of the faith, kissed the stone and ran exultant up and down the air-conditioned paths with the other pilgrims.

· · ·

In the end, the sisters attended the University of Minnesota. Atique chose microbiology for Sharmeen and Nazia chose computer sciences for Narmeen. She was allowed to register for some anthropology classes as well. It could do no harm, Nazia believed, as long as her profession was a respectable one. When the grade reports for the first semester arrived, Atique was proud enough to make a trip to the motor mile and return with the shining keys to new matching Honda Accords. Narmeen's was blue and Sharmeen's was green. They were the envy of classmates, who lived on five hundred dollars a month and ate canned food.

Narmeen had always known this. Her mother had told her stories of parents who left their children to their own devices, of their sad unloved lives. By the time she was in middle school, Narmeen, like her sister, wore thick tights so her legs would not lead boys into temptation. She knew what temptation was from sex ed class (she and Sharmeen agreed not to talk to Ma about that class; it fell within the circumscribed area of their lives outside). She knew the fear her parents held in their hearts.

Once, on vacation in New York, her father crossed the street because a black man with a shopping cart stopped and looked at them. Holding her father's hand, ten-year old Narmeen recognized the jerk of cold, unrelenting fear. When his friends from work went out to drink, Atique called on his heritage to bale him out. Atique's religion wouldn't allow him to drink, they all knew, and Atique breathed easier.

Narmeen wished she could cocoon herself in her beliefs like that, wrap them comfortingly and familiarly around her. But somehow her self spilled over the boundaries, into other allusions of language and body that were not of her parents' making. When she told the girls at school she couldn't date, they nodded without interest. She tried to draw finality into her voice, the way her mother could when she said, "It is not our culture to date." After they turned fourteen, friends stopped asking the sisters to sleepovers. Sharmeen was not ashamed by this as Narmeen was.

Nothing rent Sharmeen's self-containment. In her drawer, you would find only thick tights. If you opened Narmeen's, you would be surprised at the coils of Hanes and L'Eggs tucked in the back, thin and shiny. At night, Narmeen slipped her arms into the silkiness of the black tights and wondered how a man felt to touch.

The cars, like the Barbie townhouses and the ten-speed bikes and the two-hundred dollar dresses that had come before, consoled Narmeen and reconciled her to the thick tights, for a time. Reconciled her to the outline of the life her parents had drawn for her. But, even if you slipped into Atique and Nazia's bedroom one evening, you would never hear them discussing the layout of these boundaries, hear them utter the words.

If we give them cars and tuition, they will remain with us, they will take care of us in our old age, and follow our rules. In bedrooms around the world, parents make this bargain in the unspoken heart of their instincts, not in crude verbal form.

In the mornings, their mother followed Sharmeen and Narmeen as they drove to campus. Her car stayed behind them till they crossed University Avenue and pulled into the parking lot. Atique drove into the lot after six, and found them waiting inside the glass doors of the Italian cafe. When their friends asked, Sharmeen smiled and said their parents worried excessively about car accidents. If you watched carefully, you could discern Narmeen's slightly knitted brows at this excuse.

What was it, you may wonder, that fueled the shepherding instincts of Nazia and Atique? In their pride and their fear they had drawn what some would call a lakshman rekha around the goings and comings that constituted their lives. If they stepped outside of that circle, no one could assure their safety. Narmeen understood that when her parents crossed the ocean and found a home by the Mississippi, they had overstepped. Frightened by the bare new country, they got out their chalk and drew the protective line around their home and their minds. America was exiled to beyond.

That was where Sharmeen and Narmeen ventured out every day, where the rest of their selves existed, beyond the iron-clad certainty of their parents. They circumscribed this life outside carefully, so that their parents would never bump into and hurt themselves on these other daughters. These daughters skipped their prayers and played hooky from class; Narmeen wore thin stockings and went to movies that fell short of the family's approval; and Sharmeen fell in love. Somewhere over the years of careful chaperoned existence, confused with the incessant translation of self between home and beyond, Sharmeen lost her self-containment.

• • •

Now that both had finals and study groups that met at odd hours ("Because so many of our friends work, Abba"), the girls could drive without the cortege of parental watchfulness. Narmeen met Abdul Nathan in Advanced Calculus class, where his black face was the closest to her brown one in the whitewashed class-room. But it was Sharmeen whose pupils dilated at the sight of him, and whose virgin thighs tightened in involuntary anticipation. At night, she got out the student directory and studied the tiny black letters, Abdul Nathan Rashad, major: electrical engineering. And then an address. A good address. Her parents would like that address, they would like that name and the circumcised man. After class, between study groups and over lunch, Sharmeen and Nathan drew their new couplehood, delineated their own faithfulness. On her own, she determined the address, the acceptability, and felt deluded, reassured.

Envelopes, though, were arriving on the desk in the study of Atique and Nazia Rahman. The envelopes were loaded with pictures and bio-data, the minutiae of height and profession and grandfather's residence that could be encapsulated, if you so wished, into a young man's plea for companionship. Proposals, the word shot out of Atique's mouth at dinner one night when Sharmeen asked for money to take the GRE so she could attend grad school. I have always understood, Atique told his daughters, an education does not only equip you for work but for marriage. I am proud that such good proposals are coming for you. Engineers, doctors, MBAs, professors (in the technical fields), green card holders, citizens. Families that knew the value of an educated woman. The earnest (Narmeen thought it was posturing) young men peered out of the pictures hopefully.

Nazia vetted the list of hopefuls. Boys from Bangladesh will not be considered, she informed the family, because who knows if they are marrying our girls only for the citizenship? No, someone like my daughters, born-and-brought-up or at least a green card holder.

In Sharmeen's bedroom you could eavesdrop on the sisters. Why Sharmeen did not speak up about Nathan, who was after all a Muslim, so that was one less thing to worry about: this was Narmeen's daily question. Sharmeen opened the top drawer of her dresser every night and reached behind the tights to a velvet box, and you would see the glint of the ring as she showed it to her sister. Narmeen sat sternly, disappointed, and berated the new fiancée for her cowardice and her deceit. We know now that Sharmeen's parents would not have forced her into a marriage, tied her down and made her repeat, I do.

This is what would have happened, had Sharmeen continued in her delusion of acceptability and told her parents she wished to marry a black man. Nazia would have cried and Atique would have run his fingers through his hair. The boy mowing the lawn would hear lamenting voices, which he would not understand. It would be the parents' voices, remembering and reminding, that their children were the center of their lives, the sun around which they traveled in their own limited orbits. Sharmeen would be sent to her aunt in Saudi Arabia, to take her away from that boy's influence and see if they really loved each other. There, she would be introduced to some suitable Bengali boys, and surely Sharmeen would realize the greater value of this choice and marry happily.

But Sharmeen could not comprehend that her parents were bound by the same circle that contained her life. She could not see the lakshman rekha that ordered their lives just as definitely as it ordered hers. She saw only the magic beyond the boundaries of their home. One winter night before she graduated from college, Sharmeen came into her sister's room with a shoebox full of nailpolish bottles.

Narmeen applied base, color, and topcoat, and left Sharmeen to dry while she searched the wardrobe where they kept their Indian clothes. They packed the saree and the jewelry in Sharmeen's backpack. In four large garbage bags, they stuffed more of Sharmeen's clothes. This was all she would take when she crossed the line. The girls went down to dinner in the silence of guilt.

On this street with its row of white houses, a note was left on a desk that was covered in proposals. Four garbage bags were carried at night to a car trunk and taken out in the parking lot of the concrete apartment block where Nathan lived. In the municipal court house, a daughter stood in a red saree that a mother had bought. Atique Rahman's house with its dome of snow woke to what had never been seen on this street.

Sharmeen's pictures, in frames on the dining room sideboard, the refrigerator, the coffee table, and the mantelpiece, even on Nazia's dresser, were never touched. She was there, next to Narmeen, or with her arms around her father, smiling, or graduation-gowned. But if you looked carefully, you would almost think this was a trick of your eyes. In the spot where you saw her face, there would appear a hole, singed around the edges. In this house, a gaping hole with crinkled burnt edges.

In conversation, Nazia spoke of her daughter, one. Atique signed all the New Year's greetings cards with, Nazia, Narmeen, and Atique. They got out their blackboard erasers, to redraw that lakshman rekha, tighter and closer to home. Blackboard erasers cannot obliterate burn marks.

When the clock called to prayer in the black morning hour of the winter, Nazia rose shivering to sit on her prayer mat brought back from Saudi Arabia (which made it purer in her mind, closer to the holy beginning). She tried to pray with her whole attention, picturing every word clearly in her thoughts, and still Sharmeen seeped in like water marks. At the Christmas break, when Zareen came to visit, she wanted Atique and Nazia to call Sharmeen, to talk to her. Tell her how you feel, and then tell her you love her, was how Zareen put it. Are we American parents, Nazia asked angrily, that we have to constantly remind our children we love them? Is that not obvious? Every day since they were born all I have done has been for them.

The Egyptian preacher at the Islamic center called Atique one morning. Brother, he began delicately, I wish you to know that I married your daughter today. Her husband is a good one. Outside, the snow was blotting the street. Atique sat with the receiver in his hands, the blood in his head deafening the persistent beeping of the unhung phone. His daughter with her shy eyes had worn her veil and spoken her words of agreement to the marriage contract, and he had not heard them.

Whenever Sharmeen telephoned, Atique called Narmeen to the phone. He watched her face to read any signs of her sister's distress, was she all right, did she need money, what was she eating? He felt he no longer had the right to ask. Sharmeen had walked away, not looking behind at the home he had built for her, and his care did not extend beyond his orbital path. He could not extend it.

Before the spring loosened the icicles and slushed the white sidewalks, the hopefuls began visiting Atique Rahman's house. Of a watery afternoon, you would find Narmeen in the living room entertaining her present suitor dispassionately. Nazia and Atique sitting on the couch approvingly: tea and biscuits, and if the boy was a promising candidate, dinner. Narmeen became a skillful weaver of excuses; her evenings, between writing papers and finishing lab work, spent weighing and discarding reasons for rejection, of which she had a store. In her inventory, she found different tastes in music, haughtiness of manner, risible dress sense, lack of study or job opportunities in the area where the suitor lived. Sharmeen would supply her with fresh ones when she visited the concrete apartment block.

Narmeen found her sister had a courage she had kept hidden under those thick tights. Sharmeen fearlessly shopped at Goodwill and ate meat only once a week. Second-hand furniture sat unwelcomingly in her cramped apartment, where she bravely decorated with flowers and plants. Hobbled by fear and inculcation, she had slunk out of her parents' home only to confront poverty chest thrust out. Narmeen drove over from the lawn-lined street, from the home where no one had ever checked grocery prices, and helped her sister select Value Pak beef and generic toilet paper. And found a fear within herself, a fear of this grubby existence of scratchy paper and closed quarters.

Narmeen never saw, never had the eyes to see, through that concrete block when Sharmeen and Nathan smiled and made love. She could not have noticed they had no memory of the patched couch or the creaking table. They perceived only the new spring blossoming through the windows, in that sudden overnight way of the north. Of that gray, worn building, Sharmeen had made her circle of love.

Though the man in the clock sang out five times a day, Narmeen heard, or rather listened, at most twice. When the evening job at the lab opened up, she informed her parents she would be home late every night. In front of her blue screen at the lab, she would sit mesmerized, her fingers tapping at the letters.

She created worlds, for-loops that mapped and logic gates that opened a domain of her own making. She had only to key in the demarcations in the simple satisfying language of the machine, and the world unfolded before her the way she drew it.

She had discovered her parents' desperation, their knitted brows when she asked for something previously proscribed: not daring to say no. You may feel some sympathy for Atique and Nazia, adrift now. Narmeen held the chalk in her hands, and they became tired keeping up with her redefinitions: holding the piece of chalk makes tyrants of us all. Narmeen lived in her blue screen, the prayer mat of her days, and grew quite separate from her family. To walk by herself, she felt at ease, gliding by, only the color of her skin and the sway of her hips drawing any attention, and then always flattering. But she did not like to walk with her family, with Zareen Auntie or her mother, or the cousins who came to visit from Bangladesh that spring. They drew curiosity, drew the quickly averted stare at the covered heads, or the tights, or the flocking movements of immigrant women, always grouping together. With them, she felt different, singled out, herded on to a label.

•   •   •

The sisters graduated that summer of '94 with honors. Narmeen insisted on a dress, and Nazia, thinking she must hold on to this daughter, agreed. They went shopping at the Mall of America together. Narmeen drove, and looked sideways at her mother. "Amma," she finally said, "I don't think I'm ready to be married." The excuses had run out, and the hopefuls had stopped coming, so Nazia was not surprised. Would Narmeen be like Zareen Auntie then, alone with no man to care for her? Narmeen smiled indulgently at her mother and patted her hand with a feigned reassurance..

Atique, preparing for the graduation ceremony, asked his wife whether none of the hopefuls had pleased Narmeen. In their bedroom, Nazia peered at herself in the mirror. Carefully plucking out a single hair that had strayed from the groomed arch of her brow, she lied to him. None of the men were really of Narmeen's calibre, were they? You saw their GPAs, not a single one was better than hers. We will have to look harder. Atique's eyes would have told you he knew his wife was misleading him. Why was he accepting, you wonder? Because he knew she was leading somewhere, albeit on a (surely necessarily) circuitous route. After she had pinned her long hair into its managed coils and tucked the top of her saree in, he helped her straighten the folds of the fabric. She had heard (Narmeen had harped on it) that Nathan was a good student, and he helped at the Islamic center. Atique picked up the cue: he had seen Nathan at Friday prayers. Kept discreetly away, too, Atique remarked; didn't force his presence on me.

If you had eavesdropped with any regularity, you would have known this was not the first time Mr. and Mrs. Rahman had thrown lines to each other about their invisible son-in-law. Narmeen usually initiated the exchanges at the dining table, and the words with their newborn thoughts tiptoed up the stairs into the hushed bedroom.

The picture of Sharmeen in her shabby but happy married apartment block was painted stroke by stroke on to Nazia and Atique's hearts that they tried so hard to wipe clean. When Ramadan started, Nazia had sent some dates with Narmeen (Because your aunt has sent them from Saudi Arabia especially for Sharmeen, and how could I tell her no?).

Nathan and Sharmeen prepared with less talk and more nervousness. He wore a kurta, encasing his tall body in the correct look; she wore a saree, one that had escaped in the plastic bags. At the ceremony, the sisters (last names still the same, but different colleges) sat in separate sections, and waved to each other as the classes stood to accept their degrees. To the measures of the music, they walked out.

It was then that Nazia saw the fall of the saree under the gown and remembered: that day they had stopped for soft drinks in a stall before they entered the market. The men had leered at Sharmeen, her foreign way of walking with her head held up and looking people in the eye. The last time the girls had been to Dhaka—maybe five years ago? They had wrinkled their noses at the musty smell of the shop. Sharmeen's preference for green, the gold embroidery as it spilled on to her fingers; Nazia wanted to stretch out her arm and touch it now. Spectators who cared to look at the middle-aged Asian couple would see parents with proud tears in their eyes as they watched the graduates march out. The woman, distinguished and petite, maybe a doctor, would seem to be crying rather a lot, holding her husband's arm as he covered his eyes with his hand. Asian parents were not usually so demonstrative, the spectator would remark. He would watch them as they left early, the wife still leaning on the husband's arm.

Outside, under the melting summer sky, the children waited.

· · · · · ·

In the house on the orderly street, you could see once more the pictures of the twins, miraculously repaired. Try as you might, you could not find the fine dust of burnt paper around the edges. Mrs. Murphy's son came around no longer: Nathan could be found raking the fall carpet off the lawn; Sharmeen could be found inside, helping her sister pack, in suitcases, for her move to Silicon Valley, where she was to work and live alone. When Narmeen left, Atique and Nazia stood on the lawn, still bronze with unswept leaves, and waved.

Big respect and thanks to Kartar Dhillon for her warm words of encouragement and her fiery spirit of Ghadr & to Ved Prakash Vatuk who preserves the Ghadr heritage.

Desh: The Contradictions of 'Homeland'

Vijay Prashad

The broken pots of antiquity, from which the past can sometimes, but always provisionally, be reconstructed, are exciting to discover, even if they are pieces of the most quotidian objects.

—Salman Rushdie, 1982[1]

Ever since the Indian government invented the notion of the Non-Resident Indian (NRI), corporations have tried to use that idea to their benefit. Indian banks try to attract the NRI's savings to India by offering them fabulous interest rates (and the ability to retain their money in Indian banks in 'hard currency'). Indo-American businesses try to entice the NRI to buy goods and services related to Indian 'culture' with their petty cash. Enterprising telephone companies try to attract the NRI to their phone companies by introducing Indian Americans and pop-Hindi phrases into their advertisements. Travel agencies try to sell India to the NRI who wants to go 'home' for a vacation. "Embrace the land your ancestors ploughed," says The Royal Orient, a company which arranges short train tours of "India's most culturally fascinating states."[2] In search of "memories of a lost world," the NRI will travel in a train "modeled on the grand coaches of the Maharajas" in order to "get to the land," the land ploughed by the NRI's peasant ancestors. The romance of the advertisement is almost overwhelming: "touch it, feel it," we are told, touch the land, feel the land, the homeland. The romance of the homeland is evoked through orientalized metaphors: Maharajas, peasants, the soil, the culture, the wildlife, and the wonderful phrase "India's people" which might as well be rendered as "India's colorful people." To go to India, for the NRI, is to embrace the land, to feel the soil and touch the roots of one's 'culture.' India, in this representation, is a place of nostalgia and of syrupy sentimentality.

But India is so much more than that. The NRI became an important figure for the Indian government in the mid-1980s because the Indian economy desperately needed foreign capital to finance its increasingly expensive imports. The NRIs, the government hoped, would remit part of their accumulated wealth to the homeland that gave them their childhood, but that lost their working lives. The economic crisis that made the NRI so very important also drew the vast mass of the Indian people into the vortex of economic uncertainty. Inflation rates in India are no longer a viable indication of the misfortunes of those families that now rely upon underemployed kin and that must buy hoarded goods on the open-market at dollarized prices (rather than subsidized goods in government shops for their rupee wages). One underrepresented response to the deteriorating conditions of life is the intensified struggle by sections of the Indian population for justice and for liberty from the clutches of an economic destiny that cannot be of their own making.[3] The world stage has silenced the voice of the millions of active and militant Indians. We hear only of those consumers who are happy to buy the vast array of goods that have currently become available in certain metropolitan markets. These are the consumers whose faces grace the magazine covers which celebrate the new 'liberalization' of the Indian economy. The NRI's middle-class relatives 'back home' constantly reiterate the need for exaltation of the new policies of the Indian government; the NRI repeatedly informs the relatives 'back home' of the success of 'supply-side economics' and the need for less governmental intervention. A conversation across oceans erases the social costs of these politico-economic policies: nobody invites the working poor into the discussion.[4]

The India of struggle and of protest cannot be sold in the overdeveloped world as easily as the orientalized India of Maharajas. For the affluent NRIs, the image of the homeland as the post-colonial battlefield between the wealthy and the impoverished is an embarrassment in their bourgeois American context. The

NRI prefers an India of exotic culture and of conservative tradition for these provide the basis for the NRI's claim to being a special 'minority' in the U. S. as well as for the NRIs to stand apart from the complex problems of late imperial America. This essay will provide a critique of this notion of 'homeland' by juxtaposing it with other contradictory dreams of 'India,' as a land of struggle for freedom. The 'homeland' of inspiration for social change will enable me to argue that the tide of struggle is our only hope in an increasingly unfriendly world.

Actions of Nostalgia/Cultures of Sentimentality

Hum to hai pardes mein,
Des mein nikala hoga chand.

Rahi Masoom Raza, famous literary figure, famous for his astounding novel *Aadha Gaon* (1966), for *Katra Bi Arzu* (1978) and for the screenplay of the *Mahabharata* (1990), wrote an intriguing song for the movie *Ae Mere Dil*. The song, sung by light ghazal artistes Jagjit and Chitra Singh, was made even more famous by their album recorded live at Wembley Stadium in London and circulated internationally. *"Hum to hai pardes mein"* is familiar to most people who have even a passing familiarity with the light classical genre. "We are overseas," the singers intone, "in our homeland the moon must have emerged." The symbol of the moon indicates that the song is about a particularly common North Indian-caste Hindu festival, Karwa Chauth or Karka Chaturthi. On the fourth day of the month of Kartik (the eighth month of the Vedic Lunar calendar), many married women present sugar pots (*karvas*) filled with rice and other offerings (*baya*) to their parents-in-law and they pray for the well-being of their husbands. During the day, the women fast to demonstrate their devotion to their husbands as well as to renew their own purity. Women retell the myth that drives this social practice as they await the appearance of the moon at which time they break their fast. The myth opens with the young Virvati fasting for her princely husband. Worried about their sister's health, her brothers fabricate a moon; seeing the false moon, she breaks her fast. The divinities punish her husband who is stricken with needles and goes into a coma. In order to revive him, Virvati is enjoined to pull out the needles, one each year at the time of the festival. When one needle remains, Virvati's maid-servant out of curiosity pulls it out and the prince wakes up. Since the maid pulls the needle out, the prince thinks that she is his wife; Virvati has neglected her duties again. The moral of the tale is that wives should offer their complete attention to their husbands.

In Rahi Masoom Raza's song, the NRI remembers the Karwa Chauth festival with longing. The woman in the song wonders how the moon is doing in India without her attentions (mera bina kis haal mein hoga, kaisa hoga chand). The practice which stands in for 'Indian culture' is Karwa Chauth. Indian 'culture' is here reduced to Punjabi Hindu culture, which is itself fed by a homogenized notion of the Hindu religion. This depiction of 'culture' reduces it to a homogenous thing with neither complexity nor the ability for change. The creative contradictions that fueled the debates over the ideas and practices of a people over centuries do not appear in such an understanding of culture. All the creativity of the past is removed by the idea that India's history provided it with no resources for progressive social change. Such a static idea of Indian 'culture' treats India as conservatism in excelsis. The roots of this idea take us back to colonial Britain, which ruled over India with a self-given mandate. To institute an illusion of permanence, the British sought to subjugate any internal processes of change. A picture of squalor, poverty, dirt, and oppressed women and untouchables was put forth at the same time as the only viable liberators were seen to be European. This tradition has a hold on Anglo-American common sense, where it is only Mother Theresa, Amnesty International, and PepsiCo who are doing anything to bring change to misbegotten India.

When the Indian people struggle, colonial thought says that they are being short-sighted and old-fashioned. Colonial thought in particular, and tenets of modernization in general, point out that the forces of history lead us to productivity and growth with necessary 'social costs': that some people suffer is treated as a tragic, but inevitable consequence of unfettered economic progress. That the masses never share in prosperity is not entertained as an indicator that 'progress' inevitably works in the service of capital. Given all this talk of inevitability, the bureaucrats of 'progress' inevitably deride the struggle of the Indian peasants and workers as a quixotic hindrance. These struggles, however, are neither worthless nor anachronistic, for these are the only means for the people to demonstrate their correct instinct that the 'forces of history' work against them at each turn. Struggle, in sum, is a crucial category for the lives of the working masses. When 'struggle' as a category disappears from the representation of India, then the colonial descriptions of India (poor, backward, cultural) are seen as verities that stand outside history.

Dominant NRI culture follows neo-colonial thought to validate two images of 'India' that have one element in common—both images are static: (a) India is economically impoverished and (b) India is culturally superior. If anyone challenges these verities, they are seen as anti-Indian. Hence, an attack on misogynist institutions (such as dowry) is seen by the global Indian bourgeoisie as anti-Indian rather than as anti-patriarchal. This bourgeois Indian attitude towards things deemed Indian has an ancestry going back to colonial days when the anti-colonial Indian bourgeoisie responded to the colonialism's denigration of Indian things by their championship of those very things. If the British said something cultural was 'bad,' the bourgeois nationalist said it was 'good.' At one level, this normative inversion allowed the Indian bourgeoisie to assert itself against a colonial cultural project whose goal was to smother things Indian. From that perspective, the inversion was an advance on a simple acceptance of colonial norms. However, the inversion functioned to create an unsavory internal intolerance. That certain cultural artifacts chosen by the British for criticism were not generally present amongst the population was not the question. All internal criticisms of the chosen practices were denied legitimacy by a bourgeoisie intent upon upholding its fallen dignity. Any criticism was equated with colonialism itself. This ostrich mentality continues today both in India and among the NRIs. For the NRI, inversion functions as the easiet way to assert oneself in the heart of whiteness. Normative inversion, however, is hardly the way to combat racism.[5]

When one is divorced from the subcontinent's geography and history, one cannot simply hope to replicate the totality of Indian culture with its many resplendent contradictions. Of course, the migrant might try: temples can be built, geological formations can be identified with mythical figures (as a rock formation in Fiji was with the image of Naga), shops can be opened in the manner of an Indian city. Nevertheless, even these attempts to import culture are selective. Rather than worry about importing Indian culture tout court, we must worry about which aspects of Indian culture to select. We need to imaginatively account for the origins of our various 'cultural' resources and draw from them with care to solve our contemporary problems. Should we seek to reproduce the conservative Brahmanical customs whose provenance is itself not very ancient?[6] Should we, on the other hand, introduce the elements of social fellowship that saturate Indian culture, the traditions of Buddha, of Kabir, of Meerabai, of Bulle Shah, of Gandhi, of Ambedkar, of Telengana, of the 1974 Railway Strike? In 1993, some South Asian American students came to our flat in Rhode Island; they were startled to see some secular and democratic posters I had on my walls from SAHMAT (Safdar Hashmi Memorial Trust). The posters reproduced the best of modern Indian art, from Vivan Sundaram to M. F. Husain to Akbar Padamsee to Arpita Singh, as well as the wisdom of Guru Amardas, Kabirdas, Bulle Shah, and Namdev. The students were amazed to see modern Indian art; they were even more puzzled by early modern Indian literature, modern political struggle, and modern social visions. The NRI has, so far, succeeded, in making Indian culture seem ancient and conservative. Certainly the NRI view of 'culture' is inadequate.

Take the longing for Karwa Chauth. The song does not suggest any criticisms of the festival, although these are aplenty within Indian folklore; for example, in a Punjabi song (boliyan), a woman implicitly criticizes the oppression of women: kankan lammian, dhian kiyon jammian ni maye, she sings, "the ears of corn are tall, why are daughters ever born, mother?" We must also import the folkloric traditions of the subcontinent that undermine the comfortable oppressions of most of our dominant traditions. To appreciate the complexity of this critique, alongside Karwa Chauth we must keep in mind groups such as Stri Sangharsh, Mahila Dakshata, Janwadi Mahila Samiti, and Nari Raksha Samiti who are aggressively opposed to oppressive social practices (such as the commercialization of marriage and the subordination of girls). The NRI must not be allowed to construct a vision of the homeland as the place of conservative culture where children obey their parents without question, where women bow down before their men, where girls help their mothers in the kitchen while boys are chained to their desks brushing up on their mathematics.

There are other visions of the homeland (and consequentially of Indian culture). We need not go very far to see this vision, for it is available in the United States amongst the few thousand Punjabi men who traveled here during the previous fin de siècle: their leitmotif was patriotism that has only now reverted to its lonely status as a noun worthy of cynical derision. In those days, patriotic struggle was a cherished value. People struggled to make a better world and for that they turned to their 'homeland' for inspiration. Rather than making them chauvinistic, their turn to the 'homeland' was geared towards making them all the more concerned about social and political justice globally.

Actions of Struggle/Cultures of Solidarity

> Let the rascal tyrant cut my hands
> Let him deprive me of pen and ink
> Let him sew my mouth with stitches
> Let my tongue not work to utter my
>   sentences
> Even then I will send the
>   thundering waves of my heart in every direction
> Saying, 'I am a servant of my
>   country
> I will die for her'

(*Deshbhakti ke Geet*, 1916)[7]

In 1913, on the west coast of North America, radical Punjabi migrants founded the Ghadr Party. Ghadr means revolt or rebellion and draws inspiration from the sipahi and peasant rebellion of 1857 in the subcontinent. The radical Punjabi men used this name as a means to renew the spirit of rebellion, of Ghadr. They founded a paper called Ghadr that was first published on 1 November, 1913. The inaugural issue explained the purpose of the party: "Today in a foreign country, but in the language of our own country, we start a war against the British Raj. What is our name? Ghadr. What is our work? Ghadr. Where will Ghadr break out? In India. The time will come when rifles and blood will take the place of pen and ink." An important figure in the Ghadr Party as well as in the Indian communist movement was Baba Sohan Singh Bhakna (1870-1968). In 1904, when Sohan Singh arrived in Seattle, an immigration officer asked him about polygamy and polyandry in the Punjab. Sohan Singh did not deny the existence of both sorts of marital practices. When the officer pointedly asked him how he could say that he was against this sort of thing if it happened in his village, Sohan Singh replied: "Everyone has the right to reject a particular tradition or custom which he does not like."[8] This statement tells us much about the notion of 'home' operating among the Ghadrites of the west coast.

Migration allows communities to selectively appropriate traditions and customs. The weight of previous generations continues to weigh heavily on the minds and practices of the migrants, but territorial separation makes some customs impossible in and others inadequate to the new location. Given that the Punjabi community in the north America was almost entirely male, the men could not put much stock in their various endogamous marriage traditions; most married Mexican women. Without access to the sacred geography of their childhood (the host of shrines to pirs, to saints, to preceptors such as Sakhi Sarvar, Baba Farid, Nanakdas, and Ghulam Mohammad), the Punjabi men began to turn to the Gurdwara at Stockton which functioned as a social, political, and theological center. Customs were negotiated within the new landscape. When Sohan Singh met the immigration officer his encounters with progressive movements in Punjab had already taught him to judge cultural practices and choose from them. In America, the act of choosing was a necessity. Of course, as Kartar Dhillon points out in her autobiographical fragment, migration does not necessarily produce a more progressive society: her elder brother insisted that she return to India to marry the 'right person.' She, however, had met a Punjabi man who had impressed her "by his fiery speeches at meetings of the Gadar Party."[9] Kartar Dhillon's younger brother, Bud, went to the Soviet Union in his teens to struggle against injustice and to free India; he, Kartar says, was her main ally in her struggle for personal and human freedom.[10] At the Desh Pardesh festival in May 1995, Kartar emphasized the difference between her two brothers: the elder brother was wedded to what he considered was traditional (which meant the subordination of women to the men in the family) and the younger brother was wedded to an alternative tradition (which meant the freedom of women to struggle for more power in the family and society). These two brothers looked back to India with different eyes: the former sought a place to gain strength for his own insecurities in a racist land, while the latter wanted to win liberty for the homeland to create the possibilities for justice everywhere. Bud and Kartar embody the values of Ghadr: patriotism, fellowship, sacrifice, and a strong instinct against global injustice.

Of course, actions of struggle themselves are no guarantee of progressive politics. The image of India was the 'Mother' who had to be saved by her bold and noble sons:

> My darling sons, come to the
> battlefield
> Carrying the power of knowledge in
> one hand and a sword in the other
>
> Extinguish the fires of
> selfishness
> By pouring over it the waters of
> patriotism
>
> (*Deshbhakti ke Geet*, 1916)[11]

Her daughters, however, were not to be called to her service until Gandhi took leadership of the freedom movement. To gender a colonized nation female is to do two contradictory things: (1) to replicate the patriarchal notion that a community's men need to protect their women from foreigners and (2) to produce an image of a fiery and militant woman ('Mother India') who exhorts her sons to battle (but in other songs, 'friends' are called upon to save the 'Mother').[12] The 'Mother' image opened up space for activism by women: if the nation was to be saved, women were needed as much as men. Different parts of the nationalist project called upon women in their own characteristic manner: the bourgeois faction called women to ensure the spiritual and political health of the next generation of boys; the Gandhian faction called women to purify the non-violent movement by what Gandhi saw as their necessarily non-violent participation; the militant faction called women to act as Durga for the community and as Kali against the British (keep in mind Shanti Ghosh, Suniti Chaudhary, Bina Das, Preetilata Wadedar, and Kamala Dasgupta whose 'terrorism' in the early 1930s awaits its memorial). The doors to active political work opened via the image of 'Mother,' but that image came at a price for women, who not only participated in the struggles, but carried the burden of national tradition and honor as well.

Further, the image of 'Mother' reinforced the notion that women, like the nation, must be protected from the will of the colonizer. At its best, the Janus-faced image of 'Mother' allowed for contradictory usage, while the one-dimensional NRI image of the submissive woman as the protector of a conservative tradition allows for only grief and resentment. If Indian 'culture' is to be relevant in the United States, we must entertain the contradictory notions embedded in Indian history to ground our own struggles in the heart of whiteness. We must pick up pieces of the broken pots and make of them crockery useful to our own context.

Groundings

In North India, there is an odd phrase that does the rounds: *ghar ser per uthana*. Idiomatically, the phrase suggests a more common expression of burden (*bojh ser pe uthana*). Furthermore, this odd phrase has a meaningless literal translation: to lift the home onto the head. Its meaning, however, is appropriate to this essay: to raise hell. I want to conclude these meandering observations with a plea for us to understand the home (*ghar*) as a place we can put on top of our heads in order to gain inspiration for struggle in the name of social justice.

Struggle is seen in NRI terms as anti-Indian. Don't get involved in radical activities, we are often told, for those are not in keeping with our traditions. Our traditions are imagined as dedicated hard work and cultural conservatism. The ideas of social justice are rarely considered: the global Indian bourgeoisie has put Gandhi, the icon of struggle, in moth-balls and retired his antics to another time, another place. Conservative thought is wedded to the idea that history has ended and that now we must get on with the job of making a living and ensuring a similar future for our children. For the first generation to be born in America, the 'homeland' is a place of dread and of awe. Their parents, lost in the welter of America, enforce a rigid notion of 'culture' in order to get the children in line. On occasional trips back to the subcontinent, naturally jealous middle-class cousins taunt them about their 'incomplete Indianness.' Then there are the new migrants who use the ponderous and overused 'ABCD' acronym to emphasize to the accidental Americans that they are 'confused.' The 'homeland' is wielded by all these people over the next generation, which is forced to feel culturally inadequate and unfinished. In search of their culture, these young people turn to those aspects which are proffered by orientalist educational institutions, by their untutored parents, and by rapacious groups such as the Vishwa Hindu Parishad and the Hindu Students' Council. These various agencies are unable to introduce the next generation to the complexity of their situation, to the difficulties inherent in their pastiche cultural location.

There is a need to go in search of other traditions: histories of struggle allow us to tend to our current contradictions rather than those histories of 'culture' which force us to slither into inappropriate molds. The latter tradition dovetails with the politics of identity whose only tactic appears to be a false search for coherence. Rather than fall prey to the culturalist notion that all 'races' must take their place on the American spectrum of high cultures, we must fight to forge complex cultures of solidarity. Rather than turn to 'India' for the pure tradition, we must be able to turn to the complexity of 'India' in order to take elements of the tradition which are meaningful solutions to our own local questions. Rather than graft on cultural components which make no sense in our New World, it would be far better to take those things Indian which we can place on our heads in order for us to raise hell globally.

Notes

[1] Salman Rushdie, "Imaginary Homelands." *Imaginary Homelands*. London: Granta, 1991: 12.

[2] *India Abroad*. 15 December 1995.

[3] Jeremy Seabrook, *Notes from Another India*. London: Pluto Press, 1995.

[4] This process is captured in Sadhu Binning's poem 'Chameleons' in his Punjabi/English collection, "*Watan Dur Nahi/No More Watno Dur*." Toronto: TSAR, 1994: 40-43.

[5] For more on this, see Gita Sahgal, "Fundamentalism and the Multiculturalist Fallacy." *Against the Grain*. Ed. Southall Black Sisters. Southall: Southall Black Sisters, 1990.

[6] For example, the dominant image of the devoted wife (*Sati/Savitri*) under close scrutiny is seen to be rather modern. See Uma Chakravarti, "Whatever Happened to the Vedic Dasi?" *Recasting Women: Essay in Colonial History*. Ed. Kumkum Sangari and Sudesh Vaid. New Delhi: Kali for Women, 1989.

[7] Ved and Sylvia Vatuk, "Protest Songs of East Indians on the West Coast, U. S. A." *Thieves in my House*. Varanasi: Viswavidyalaya Prakashan, 1969: 75.

[8] Sohan Singh Josh, *Baba Sohan Singh Bhakna*. New Delhi: Peoples' Publishing House, 1970: 12.

[9] Kartar Dhillon, "The Parrot's Beak." *Making Waves: An Anthology of Writings by and about Asian American*

Women. Ed. Asian Women United of California. Boston: Beacon Press, 1989: 217.

[10]Letter from Kartar Dhillon, 20 November 1995.

[11]Vatuk, 76.

[12]These contradictions emerge in the lyrical spoken-song by Fun^da^mental entitled 'Mother India' on their 1995 CD *Seize the Time* (Beggars Banquet 92421-1).

A Sketch from the Campaign in the North

Vijay Seshadri

Just before dawn the women are washing
skirts and blouses, slacks from Hong Kong,
scrubbing their cotton on pockmarked boulders,
cleaning their limbs with mud and lemons
along the turbid river.
At the end of the jungle, in surplus tents,
the men are talking without weakness or strength
of the recent change in the government.
On the other bank the soldiers are waiting
for the sun to rise from the hills beyond them,
not smoking, not talking, in place and umoving
as the leaves above them waver.
The day unfolds as if kept on a folder
on a desk in the capital.
The sun rises and blinds the river
the soldiers line up and fire from its cover
the air is gravid with sulfur
the river takes blood without changing color
a siren signals the end of the hour
and later in the capital
word is leaked to the foreign papers—
not even their souls climbed free to safety.
There are no handholds up that wall of light.

Lifeline

Vijay Seshadri

As soon as he realized he was lost, that
in kicking around his new job in his head,
the new people he'd met, and how
he could manage a week in Seaside,
he'd stumbled past the muddy fork of road
that slithered down in switchbacks
to Highway 20, and now couldn't tell,
through rainclouds coarse as pig iron,
and about as cold, which languished
over each of the sacred mountaintops,
where west was, or east, or north,
or feel the sun's direction,
he stopped, as he knew he should,
and doubled back. An hour at the worst
would bring him to the International
inert in a ditch with its radiator
punctured, its axle broken, and blood
from his temple on the steering wheel.
He wished he'd never set eyes on that truck . . .
here he was, trudging like an idiot
through a thousand-square-mile dead spot
of Douglas fir, soaked to the bone
and hungry, with his head throbbing.
He wasn't up to this, he said to himself,
staring disconsolately outward
to the numberless ridges and valleys, singed
with the bitter green of the firs.
But why hadn't he reached the truck yet,

or at least somewhere familiar,
where he could get his bearings again?
He didn't recognize the ridge he was on.
He'd never seen this particular patch—
glinting with wild crocus prongs—
of clear-cut ground, touched and scarified.
Should he keep going, or return again?
There and then he made his third mistake.
Hearing, or thinking he heard,
deep in the valley below him plunged
in mist, a chain saw start and sputter,
he made off down toward the sound.
It would be a gypo logger, scrounging
deadfall cedar for shake-bolt cords,
or a civilian with a twenty-dollar permit
to cut firewood for sale at a roadside stand.
Either way, he could get directions
and hitch home by dark. Hours later,
night found him in a hollow, shouting
until he was hoarse for someone, anyone.
The weekend was almost here, and no one
at work would miss him before Monday . . .
he lived alone, idiot, he lived alone
and couldn't count on a single person
to send out an alarm. Those first hours
he spent shivering under a lip of rock,
wide awake, startling at each furtive,
night-hunting animal sound, each flap
of the raptors in the brances overhead.
On the second day he lost his glasses.
It happened like this: As he struggled
over the cryptic terrain all morning—
terrain that would seem, if he looked at
from high above, from a helicopter

or a plane flying low enough to pierce
the dense, lazy foliage of clouds,
created, finessed, meticulously contrived
to amaze, like a marvellous relief map
of papier-mâché, revealing its artifice only
in the improbable drama of its contours,
its extravagant, unlikely colors—
he had what amounted to a real insight.
All this was the brainchild of water.
Stretching back beyond the Pleistocene—
how many millions of years?
imperial rain had traced without pity,
over and over again, its counterimage
on the newborn, jagged mountains
until the length of the coast had been
disciplined to a system designed
to irrigate and to nourish the soil.
He decided he'd follow the water down.
He'd use each widening tributary
like the rung of a ladder, to climb down
from his awful predicament, and soon
work his way to the ocean—though, of course,
long before that he'd run across people.
With this in mind, he came to a stream
heavy and brown with the spring runoff,
its embankment on his side steep
to the point of perpendicularity, thick
with brush, though on the other side
a crown of ferns tumbled gently down
to the next watershed. It seemed like
a good idea to cross, and farther on
he found a logged fir with a choker cable
still attached (it must have snapped
when they tried to yard the falled tree

to the road high above) straddling
the stream. A little more than halfway over
he slipped on the treacherous wood
and would have gone in but for the cable,
which he lunged at just in time.
That was his lifeline, though flailing
to save himself, he knocked the glasses
from his head. Now they'd reach the sea
long before him, if he ever would.
He knelt down in the ferns, exhausted,
by fits growing determined never
to leave that spot. They'd find his bones
fifty years from now, clothes and ID
rotted away, a trillium poking through
his ribcage, a cucumber vine trellised
by the seven sockets in his skull.
The play of the thin, unending drizzle
on the overlapping leaves he sank below,
on the bark of the impassive trees
looming around him, grew indistinguishable
from the pulse turning loud in his head.
The bruise on his forehead throbbed.
There were rents and gashes everywhere
down the length of his rain gear, which
let the mist and the dampness in.
Beyond a scant dozen inches, the world
looked blurry, smeared bright, unattainable.
Nothing in his life, up until then
(and if this had been pointed out to him
he would have acknowledged pride in it),
suggested that anything resembling
a speculative turn of mind cannibalized
the adequate, rhythmic, progressive
movements of his thoughts and feelings.

But, still, as almost everyone does,
he'd occasionally had inklings, stirrings,
promptings, and strange intuitions
about something just beyond the radius
of his life—not divine, necessarily,
but what people meant when they referred
to such things—which gave to the least
of his actions its dream of complicity.
Now he recognized, with a shock
almost physical, that those inklings
were just the returning, reanimated echo
(on a different scale but similar
to the echo we sometimes hear in our skulls,
which leads us to the uncanny feeling
that an experience we're having is one
we've had before, at some other time—
but does anything ever repeat itself?)
of the vibrations his life made
bouncing off the things around him
sunk deep in their own being;
and that life, his life, blossoming now
in this daisy chain of accident and error,
was nothing more or less than what there was.
There was nothing hidden underneath this,
but it was small, so small, as the life
of his family was, his people, his species
among the other species—firs, owls,
plants whose names he didn't know—
all of them minute, and the earth itself,
its four billion plus years of life
just the faint, phosphorescent track
of a minute sea creature on an ocean
for the annihilating dimensions of which
words such as "infinite" and "eternal"

were ridiculous in their inadequacy.
He lay on his back inside the ferns
and listened to the rain's clepsydral ticking.
He tried to grasp—what was it?—
but it clattered away, that slight change
in the pressure binding thing to thing,
as when an upright sleeper shifts
just a little, imparting to his dreams
an entirely different train of meaning.
Beyond those clouds, the blue was there
which shaded to blackness, and beyond
that blackness the uncounted, terrifying
celestial entities hung suspended only
by the influence they had on one another.
And all of this was just a seed
inside a seed inside a seed. . . .
So that when, finally, late the next morning
he half-crawled out of the woods, and came
in time to a wire fence in a clearing,
less than two feet high and decorated
with gleaming ceramic insulators,
which indicated that a mild current,
five volts at the most, ran through it
to keep the foraging animals off
the newly sown vegetable garden
enclosed inside its perimeter, and saw
beyond it the sprawl of the lawn,
the 4-by-4 parked in the driveway,
the Stars and Stripes on the flagpole,
and the house, he stopped, paralyzed.
The wind was blowing northwest, the clouds
were breaking up under its steady persuasion,
but, try as he did, he couldn't will
himself to step lightly over that wire,

and cross the garden's sweet geometry,
and go up to the door and ask to be
fed and made warm and taken home.
By that small fence, he sat down and wept.

Nupu Chaudhuri—from the film *Kama Sutra*

Inventing Territories

For Sylvia: Two Poems

Abraham Verghese

Empty Spaces

My love, your waist is so small my
                    little finger can encircle it.

Last night, as we lay pressed
            against each other—after making love once then once more
You sucked in your belly
        where it pressed against mine
                and I felt our flesh unstick.

An hourglass-shaped window opened up
        between our two bodies,
Hot air rushed up carrying your juices and mine
            air that I would bottle
                and keep for the centuries

"I felt you suck your belly in!" I said
        and you laughed that beautiful, guilty laugh
                that, like a bell pealing in the dark prairie,
Shakes me from my solitude and reminds me
        how I can no longer stand to be alone.

And you said, pleading, "But my love, I'm too fat."

Tonight, when you are away from me,
        our parting hard and bitter,
                I lie next to that space where
                        our bellies   lay separated
I lie imagining our chests and lips still together
        our legs intertwined.

I think if we should part,
        then my room, my house, my life
           would be full of

                          empty spaces,
As though someone had taken
an eraser and wiped out all the places
where you had walked, and sat, and talked.
In that scratched out universe, I would stand alone again
A figure cut out from a magazine with child's scissors

Love of my life, reason for my living,
        you are not too fat,
                nor too thin, you are   just right,
And your flesh
        and your face and
          your laugh
fill my universe so completely that
when we are together again
There will be no empty spaces.

Untitled

You and I were flying in coach,
snuggled together, the arm rest up,
honey-roasted peanuts rolling around on our tray,
       heading back to El Paso after
visiting my kid brother in Idaho.

We were talking about him:
how he was more like you than me:
       born in America.

He came to the world thirteen years after me, growing up
in Jersey, never knowing the India
or the Africa I left behind.

He had briefly flirted with
an "arranged" rendezvous with an Indian girl
also raised in America,
and when that didn't work out
(the seriousness of this get-to-know-each-other-movie-and-lunch
not apparent to him until he dropped her home and
saw the overanxious-nail-biting-parents on the sofa)
he had gone back to dating girls
with names like Amber and Kimberley
in Boise.

"Why, after growing up in America" you asked,
"would he want an Indian girl?"
And from your tone, I knew you were testing me,
asking me why I wanted you,
why I wanted a Hispanic woman after
having been through an arranged marriage
to an Indian girl, a marriage that,

for all the things we had in common
(our Syrian-Christianess,
our Madras-college-days-mutual-friends cousins-relatives) didn't
work out.

"But sweetheart," I said, "the men you were
engaged to—three of them—and then the man
you finally married,
were all Hispanic!"
        You said, as though seeing it
        for the first time,
            "That's true, huh?"

And so, 30,000 feet above sea level,
we arrived together at a point in time,
flying over the desert southwest,
where all our Indianess and Hispanicness
and all the other "-nesses" of our till now separate
but American lives
had come together in this inexplicable union.

I have drunk from the waters of your arroyo, been entwined by
your desert roots, your growing up in El Paso,
your cheerleading days at high school, your wonderful family,
your work, your

            marriage to him
        (such pain to even write it)

And, in turn, I have carried you
into my past, my rootlessness, my children,
my search for a place to call my own country
my marriage

to her.

And as we put the tray up,
and bring the seat back forward,
tighten our seatbelts to descend over the Franklin Mountains
preparing to land in El Paso, your home,
my home for five years,
it comes to me, my love, that from now on
      my own country is simply
      wherever you are

        nothing else survives.

Lahore in the Sky

Sunaina Maira

My grandmother once told me that when she fled to Simla with my mother and her two brothers, she had so little money that they could only eat two chapatis and some yogurt for dinner every day. Then my grandfather joined her and they moved around, staying with different relatives in houses already overflowing with refugees, until they were able to rent a house in a small town some miles outside of Delhi. She said that their home in Lahore was a sprawling, elegant bungalow, and they had a horse carriage and even a car, in those days a great luxury. While my grandmother was telling me this story, my mother's face began to cloud over and she asked her why she'd never really told her how difficult it had been during those days of partition. Nani replied, "Well, actually, you never asked, and for years I wanted to forget about it. Now I want her to remember." She pointed at me, and I felt a little chill, like the damp shadow of rain, that sometimes crept up on me when the older folks got that nostalgic look on their faces. I didn't want to have to hold someone else's memories of a lost home.

It was summer when nani-ma first came to live with us two years ago; I know, because I had just finished tenth grade. I remember the feeling of sun on my bare legs as I lay by the river on late afternoons, naming cloud-countries wafting in blue oceans of atmosphere. I would get off my bike on my way home from school, and fling myself down on the grass, which was luminescent and heavy green and a little prickly beneath my thin cotton tank top. Nani-ma had two major problems with me that year: my clothes were too skimpy, and I was far too tanned. Both these issues were related, of course. She'd bought me long-sleeved cotton kurtas from Delhi and she constantly showed me magazine photographs of Indian models with chemically pale faces and hennaed hair who were trailing chiffon dupattas. I was not amused. In fact, I was outraged. "They want to look white, nani. Don't you have a problem with that?" Nani would wordlessly turn the page to an advertisement for skin cream that proclaimed that regular use of the product would ensure a husband-winning complexion and a shining wedding.

She did not understand, however, that Salim liked my skin just fine. Salim liked my tanned legs and he liked my firm arms, he didn't even mind the dark silky hair on them. If I ever talked about shaving, he'd say, "Nah, forget about it. Why should you? It's there for a purpose." Salim was really into having a purpose. In school, at home, in life. He and I were going to start a rock band. I met Salim for the first time at the Newbury Comics music store, in the world music section. He was looking at the album covers and laughing. "What's so funny," I had asked, half-annoyed and partly curious. "It's these Indian and Pakistani dudes! They're all dressed up in this fake shit, as if they wore this stuff everyday at home. Just because Americans want to see them look all foreign!"

I could have fallen down and embraced his brown, scarred knees. I followed him around the store, picking out album covers and laughing at the things I had always found strange or absurd but no one else seemed to think so. Not in my family at least. Dad would nod indulgently, "Yes, beta, yes!" Mom would give me a piercing, quizzical glance from behind her owlish eyeglasses, but she was actually wondering what on earth I was talking about.

Salim understood. His parents were Pakistani but he had lived in Malaysia till he was seven, so unlike me, he knew a country other than the United States. I looked at Malaysia for a long time on the world map in my room, imagining the hills and houses nestled in that chili-like peninsula. Salim said that he loved Kuala Lumpur, but he was happy to be here. I didn't understand how anyone could want to leave a city with gold-domed mosques studding hills that were green year-round because it rained everyday, afternoons broken by tropical thunderclaps and steamy showers. So different from Boston, old red brick and a short summer that was nothing more than a dream. Salim snorted in disgust everytime I melted into reveries over his photographs. "You're the same as the others, Pips, when you say things about domes and minarets. You sound just like an American tourist. When you live in a city, it's just home."

I knew what he meant. I felt the same way when boys, and men, whistled at Sarita. She was just my sister. What was all the hype about? Maybe it was the way she tossed her Kashmiri shawl around her shoulders, black embroidery matching the sultry kohl carefully outlining her eyes. I once tried wrapping Sarita's shawl around my T-shirt, just the way she did, over jeans and loafers, but Salim' snort was enough to wake up even nani from her sleep.

"What do you mean, it isn't *me?*" I think I knew I was angry not at Salim, but at those whistling men, yet I needed someone to yell at. The words bubbled out of my mouth in a furious cascade. *"Just* because I wear shorts and listen to rock music, doesn't mean I can't play the Indian femme fatale!" Salim retreated behind Rolling Stone magazine and let my words stream out till they were dripping down the windowpanes, like afternoon rain. Then he got up and stood next to me, gently lifted the shawl off my shaking shoulders and patted my hair awkwardly.

"You are going to be the greatest Indian American female rock star ever. You are going to cross over big time, and it isn't just going to be bhangra or world music, Pips!" The words, and my misery, dried on the windowpanes and the afternoon light gleamed gently on Salim's head as he folded the shawl and put it away.

It would have seemed to Salim—and to others—that nani should have loved Sarita's fondness for dangling silver earrings and embroidered vests, but I often noticed that she watched Sarita with an edge of suspicion. I suspect nani, for all her talk about turmeric cream and fair skin, was a bit of a firebrand herself in her younger days and found Sarita too aloof. Maybe its because of the way nani would stride down the sidewalk for her morning walk, her still-fit legs pushing impatiently against the chiffon folds, her eyes darting over the neatly mowed suburban lawns.

In fact, I think nani takes those walks for more than just fresh air. One evening when we were sitting on her bed, poring over the sepia-colored photographs in her cloth-bound album, she paused for a long time at a picture of her taken in Lahore with her two younger sisters. "Jasmine and Nalini were always the pretty ones. But you know, I had the nicest legs." I stared at her, hardly believing the words. Legs? Did nani really think about her body? As if to offer empirical truth, she lifted the hem of her cotton sari and I glanced, almost surreptitiously, at her supple calves, smooth as if from years of waxing and paler than her dry, tanned arms. She said quietly, with a wisp of wistfulness lacing her words, "Of course no one could ever have known." Always hidden beneath the demure salwars, veiled by layers of Kashmiri silk and Rajasthani cotton.

"You do have great legs, nani." I said. "Much better than many grandmas I see in shorts and skirts."

I've even caught her watching MTV sometimes, and I see her smile slyly when she catches a double entendre she thinks I shouldn't understand. I think, and Salim would never believe me, that she secretly gets a kick out of the fact that I'm going to be the lead singer of the Orange Pips. My hunch was confirmed a couple of months ago, when my parents announced to me over dinner that I couldn't go to the Orpheum to hear Echobelly. I had told them I was going on my own, it's not like I had a date, for crying out loud. I sobbed into my pulao and spluttered that Sonia Arora-Madan was *even* Punjabi, and she was coming *all* the way from England, and she was my heroine, and I couldn't *believe* that my parents wouldn't let me go to the show just because it began at eleven.

Mom wandered off into the kitchen, trilling loudly that the food was getting cold. Out of the corner of my eye, I noticed nani smile and wipe her mouth with a napkin. "Pramod, it's funny, every time you say the word curfew, it makes me think about the partition, or the riots in Delhi after the Golden Temple massacre. Now those were dangerous times. What are you afraid of now?" Dad's morsel-bearing hand froze in mid-air. I winked at nani. The battle had been won for me. There was no way dad could argue with history, not if nani put it like that.

After that standoff, there were few tense negotiations over the dining table, and in fact, once Sarita went away to college dad stopped taking Isabgol after dinner every night. He said his digestion had finally improved, just in time for my post-pubescent turbulence. My backlash never happpened, however. I think they were enormously relieved and quite surprised. Other Indian parents had warned them about The Rebellion, cautioning them to save Cultural Values from being shredded by their children, telling them not to be content with scraps of tradition flaunted in the name of new identities. My parents had been armed with critiques of American freedom and individualism, but Sarita had been too clever and I had been too quiet, they said, my waywardness taking unexpected forms.

For example, they pondered, why did they never hear rumors that I was dating any boys? I think they might even have welcomed boyfriends in the name of normalcy, their ammunition and very foothold having been torn from them with the discovery that, in her junior year, Sarita was going out with a woman. The word femme took on a new meaning for me, one that I finally welcomed as it punctured the high school hysteria over male attention. Perhaps nani had always understood something about Sarita's mysterious femininity that none of us ever had, but she also simply refused to acknowledge that her granddaughter did not want to be courted by a man. Mom had high blood pressure ever since, and put Sarita's shawls and kohl sticks into the dumpster. Dad's ulcer reappeared and proved incurable, so he turned to transcendental meditation.

"Do you er, like, any boys in your class, Priti?" Dad would ask after looking at my report card every term, and I would always fail this biannual test.

After Sarita's family-shattering phone call, I tried to placate him by answering, "Sure I like boys. Salim is great, and so are . . . others." Dad would nod benevolently as he stirred his Isabgol in his warm milk and gulp it down with relief. Yet Dad wasn't particularly anxious to meet Salim, nor any of the other boys in school, especially after Sarita's proclamation; he was simply glad to hear that my fantasies were the lesser of two evils. Mom was, as usual, a little more persistent and wanted to know why Salim and I never wanted to meet outside of school. I had learned from my Indian friends that parents generally preferred their daughters lie about boys, so I told her I was simply too busy with work and college applications, and besides Salim and I were just friends.

My parents even encouraged me to go to the prom. Their friend, Professor Banerjee, had told them this event was an important rite of passage which, if handled inappropriately, could be drenched in disappointment and bitterness that would stain my memories forever. So mom bought me a dress and dad loaded his camera with film. Their anticipation was exceeded only by their confusion. First I told them I didn't really want to go; the music was not my type and was sure to be terrible. They said they didn't want me to feel left out, and suggested I go with Salim. As mom began to reminiscence about all-girl parties at her convent school and the always hoped for dream of dancing with a boy, she began to get that soft, drippy, far-away look on her face. So I told them I'd acquiesce to Salim's invitation.

Then they got terribly upset because I told them Salim couldn't pick me up but was going to be at the prom, waiting for me. Their suspicion waned somewhat when I lied again and told them he had to be at work, so they drove me to school themselves. Mom indulgently patted my hair, finally tamed by mousse, and nani took one last envious glance at my sheer black tights. She said she'd come back with dad to pick me up after the dance, and she flashed a conspiratorial smile, as if assuring support should there be any parental disagreement.

When nani found me four hours later, I was still sitting by the swimming pool, listening to my Walkman and watching the notes bounce off the calm, chlorinated water. "What's this, have you been here long? Where are your friends? Didn't Salim wait with you?"

I don't know why I told nani then, perhaps I was too tired of the stories, too tired of sitting here alone pretending to be on a date. "No. He never came."

"He stood you in?" Nani's terminology wasn't accurate but her anger was enough to make the water sizzle. I opened my mouth and words spilled out into half the truth.

"He didn't stand me up. He's not really my friend. I mean, I don't really hang out with him anymore. He moved away some time ago. Back to Malaysia. But I just couldn't forget about him and not talk about him, you know." I grasped at the lure of memory. "Like your stories, you know, about Lahore. It still exists for you, doesn't it?"

Nani sat down by the water's edge, absentmindedly lifting her sari, letting her feet brush the water. "But, so, do you write to him? Do you have any pictures of him?"

Nani's calves were almost half-immersed in the blue-green ripples, her words penetrating deeper into my bottomless story. I stared at the black tiles undulating at the bottom of the swimming pool. My words seem to rise as if from below twelve feet of pressing, airless water, "Nani, Salim doesn't exist."

The shell-tipped toes clenched the blue surface, as if trying to hold on to something solid. Nani stared at me, her face looking gray like her tightly coiled hair, her eyes black and uncomprehending. Her mouth tightened, and the air suddenly began to feel steamy and heavy. I concentrated on my breathing, on inhaling and exhaling this dark, long summer night. I had never had to articulate the truth, to myself or to anyone else, to find words to explain what had seemed a natural thing to do for the past two years. But was it really untrue? All those conversations I had imagined that had kept me from feeling like a total misfit, were they simply irrelevant? I began to feel dizzy, until suddenly I remembered Lahore.

"Nani, it's like what you said."

"What is it, huh beta?" Her face softened suddenly, as if she had seen cream-skinned coy faces rippling in the water instead of our reflections. "You mean you made it up because you wanted to have a boyfriend like the others?"

I shook my head. "No. No."

She looked at me hard, her eyes still dark in the shadows, only her silver hair gleaming. She waited.

The night breathed into me more gently. "You told me your story so that you wouldn't forget who you were. Well, it's the same way with me. Except your story happened to you. I had to make mine up." I peeled off my black tights, crumpled them into a ball, and threw them into the water. They unfurled and sank slowly, a pair of translucent black legs falling, sliding gently over the backs of well-groomed horses, pirouetting above blue minarets and sun-baked forts, wafting over hills that always looked green, no matter what color they really were.

Nisma Zaman

Ethnic Ambiguity was a series of color photographs created for the centennial senior photography exhibit at Ithaca College. The images are of my sister, Hanan, dressing up in different identities. As children of a mixed heritage raised in the U.S. (our mother is American with ancestry from Great Britain, and our father is from Bangladesh, with Middle Eastern ancestry), we can pass for a number of different cultures, and the project was designed to reflect upon our own cultural heritage and identity and those cultures which people think we belong to.

—*Nisma Ziman*

Nisma Zaman

Excerpts from *Funny Boy*

Shyam Selvadurai

Of all our varied and fascinating games, bride-bride was my favorite. In it I was able to combine many elements of the other games I loved, and with time bride-bride, which had taken a few hours to play initially, became an event that spread out over the whole day and was planned for weeks in advance. For me the culmination of this game, and my ultimate moment of joy, was when I put on the clothes of the bride. In the late afternoon, usually after tea, I, along with the older girl cousins, would enter Janaki's room. From my sling-bag, I would bring out my most prized possession, an old white sari, slightly yellow with age, its border torn and missing most of its sequins. The dressing of the bride would now begin, and then, by the transfiguration I saw taking place in Janaki's cracked full-length mirror—by the sari being wrapped around my body, the veil being pinned to my head, the rouge put on my cheeks, lipstick on my lips, kohl around my eyes—I was able to leave the constrains of my self and ascend into another, more brilliant, more beautiful self, a self to whom this day was dedicated, and around whom the world, represented by my cousins putting flowers in my hair, draping the palu, seemed to revolve. It was a self magnified, like the goddesses of the Sinhalese and Tamil cinema, larger than life; and like them, like the Malini Fonsekas and the Geetha Kumarasinghes, I was an icon, a graceful, benevolent, perfect being upon whom the adoring eyes of the world rested.

Those spend-the-days, the remembered innocence of childhood, are now coloured in the hues of the twilight sky. It is a picture made even more senti-mental by the loss of all that was associated with them. By all of us having to leave Sri Lanka years later because of communal violence and forge a new home for ourselves in Canada.

Yet those Sundays, when I was seven, marked the beginning of my exile from the world I loved. Like a ship that leaves a port for the vast expanse of sea, those much-looked-forward-to days took me away from the safe harbor of childhood towards the precarious waters of adult life.

The visits at my grandparents began to change with the return from abroad of Kanthi Aunty, Cyril Uncle, and their daughter, Tanuja, whom we quickly renamed "Her Fatness," in that cruelly direct way children have.

At first we had no difficulty with the newcomer in our midst. In fact we found her quite willing to accept that, by reason of her recent arrival, she must necessarily begin at the bottom . . .

In the hierarchy of bride-bride, the person with the least importance, less even than the priest and the pageboys, was the groom. It was a role we considered stiff and boring, that held no attraction for any of us. Indeed, if we could have dispensed with that role altogether we would have, but alas it was an unfortunate feature of the marriage ceremony. My younger sister, Sonali, with her patient good nature, but also sensing that I might have a mutiny on my hands if I asked anyone else to play that role, always donned the long pants and tattered jacket, borrowed from my grandfather's clothes chest. It was now deemed fitting that Her Fatness should take over the role and thus leave Sonali free to wrap a bedsheet around her body, in the manner of a sari, and wear araliya flowers in her hair like the other bridesmaids.

For two spend-the-days, Her Fatness accepted her role without a murmur and played it with all the skilled unobtrusiveness of a bit player. The third spend-the-day, however, everything changed. That day turned out to be my grandmother's birthday. Instead of dropping the children off and driving away as usual, the aunts and uncles stayed on for lunch, a slight note of peevish displeasure in their voices.

We had been late, because etiquette (or rather my father) demanded that Amma wear a sari for the grand occasion of her mother-in-law's sixtieth birthday. Amma's tardiness and her insistence on getting her palu to fall exactly above her knees drove us all to distraction (especially Diggy, who quite rightly feared that in his absence Meena would try to persuade the better members of his team to defect to her side). Even I, who usually loved the ritual of watching Amma get dressed, stood in her doorway with the others and fretfully asked if she was ever going to be ready.

When we finally did arrive at Ramanaygam Road, everyone else had been there almost an hour. We were ushered into the drawing room by Amma to kiss

Ammachi and present her with her gift, the three of us clutching the present. All the uncles and aunts were seated. Her Fatness stood in between Kanthi Aunty's knees, next to Ammachi. When she saw us, she gave me an accusing, hostile look and pressed farther between her mother's legs. Kanthi Aunty turned away from her discussion with Mala Aunty, and, seeing me, she smiled and said in a tone that was as heavily sweetened as undiluted rose syrup, "So, what is this I hear, aah? Nobody will play with my little daughter."

I looked at her and then at Her Fatness, shocked by the lie. All my senses were alert.

Kanthi Aunty wagged her finger at me and said in a playful, chiding tone, "Now, now, Arjie, you must be nice to my little daughter. After all, she's just come from abroad and everything." Fortunately, I was prevented from having to answer. It was my turn to present my check to Ammachi, and, for the first time, I did so willingly, preferring the prick of her diamond mukkuthi to Kanthi Aunty's honeyed admonition.

Kanthi Aunty was the fourth oldest in my father's family. First there was my father, then Ravi Uncle, Mala Aunty, Kanthi Aunty, Babu Uncle, Sedan Uncle, and finally Radha Aunty, who was much younger than the others and was away, studying in America. Kanthi Aunty was tall and bony, and we liked her the least, in spite of the fact that she would pat our heads affectionately whenever we walked past or greeted her. We sensed that beneath her benevolence lurked a seething anger, tempered by guile, that could have deadly consequences if unleashed in our direction. I had heard Amma say to her sister, Neliya Aunty, that Poor Kanthi was bitter because of the humiliation she had suffered abroad. "After all, darling, what a thing, forced to work as a servant in a whitey's house to make ends meet."

Once Ammachi had opened the present, a large silver serving tray, and thanked us for it (and insisted on kissing us once again), my brother, my sister, and I were finally allowed to leave the room. Her Fatness had already disappeared. I hurried out the front door and ran around the side of the house.

When I reached the back garden I found the girl cousins squatting on the porch in a circle. They were so absorbed in what was happening in the center that none of them even heard my greeting. Lakshmi finally became aware of my presence and beckoned me over excitedly. I reached the circle, and the cause of her excitement became clear. In the middle, in front of Her Fatness, sat a long-legged doll with shiny gold hair. Her dress was like that of a fairy queen, the gauze skirt sprinkled with tiny silver stars. Next to her sat her male counterpart, dressed in a pale-blue suit. I stared in wonder at the marvelous dolls. For us cousins, who had grown up under a government that strictly limited all foreign imports, such toys were unimaginable. Her Fatness turned to the other cousins and asked them if they wanted to hold the dolls for a moment. They nodded eagerly, and the dolls passed from hand to hand. I moved closer to get a better look. My gaze involuntarily rested on Her Fatness, and she gave me a smug look. Immediately her scheme became evident to me. It was with these dolls that my cousin from abroad hoped to seduce the other cousins away from me.

Unfortunately for her, she had underestimated the power of bride-bride. When the other cousins had all looked at the dolls, they bestirred themselves and, without so much as a backward glance, hurried down the steps to prepare for the marriage ceremony. As I followed them, I looked triumphantly at Her Fatness, who sat on the porch, clasping her beautiful dolls to her chest.

◆ ◆ ◆

The referendum took place a few weeks after Jegan's departure. It was a disturbing day. My parents went to the polling booth near us, but they never got a chance to vote. A member of Parliament arrived with his thugs, held the voting officials at gunpoint, and then proceeded to stuff the ballot boxes with false ballots.

That evening, we watched the results begin to come in on television, and it was soon clear that the government had won. They would remain in power for another six years.

My father got up and went out into the garden, where Anula had set up his usual cocktail. Only Amma and I followed.

"Chelva . . ." Amma began. "We need to open our eyes. We need to think about our future."

My father shook his head. "Never. I will never leave this country," he said.

Amma tried to persuade him to change his mind and apply to Canada or Australia, but he would not hear of it. Angry and frustrated, she stood up and went back into the house. I stayed behind to keep my father company, and sat on the swing, sharing his silence. The sun was declining and a dark blot seeped across the sky, obliterating shades of red and yellow. I looked at the expression on his face, and I felt I understood what was in his heart.

My father did not come inside for dinner that evening. Instead, he sat on the lawn and drank until long after the sun had set.

◆ ◆ ◆

August 25

Today I received my passport. As I looked at it, I finally realized that we are really leaving Sri Lanka; that in two days we will be in a strange country. I thought about how, when we were young, Diggy, Sonali, and I would sometimes imagine what foreign countries were like. All those Famous Five books, and then *Little Women* and the Hardy Boys. We would often discuss what fun it would be to go abroad, make snowmen, have snowball fights, and eat scones and blueberry jam. I don't think that we ever imagined we would go abroad under these circumstances, as penniless refugees. We are going, not with the idea that something delightful awaits us, but rather with the knowledge that great difficulties lie ahead. First, Appa won't be coming for a while. He has to settle many things over here. The thought of not having Appa around is frightening. Amma didn't want to go without him, but he said that it was too dangerous for us to stay here, because we don't know when the next riot will break out. Second, we will have to live with Lakshman Uncle. This news makes me want to stay behind. It is bad enough living off Chithra Aunty and Sena Uncle, whom we know so well. But to be in a foreign country, living off the charity of somebody I hardly know, is terrible. Appa can't take his money out of the country because of government regulations. We are only allowed five hundred pounds each. The thought of being this poor scares me.

Today I watched a beggar woman running from car to car at the traffic lights, her hand held out, and I wondered if this would be our plight in Canada.

Tea-time

Kavita Sharma

This Saturday morning, my father reads my poem,
dedicated to his sister. Handing him the paper,
thinking report card, I explain
that it's not ready. I pour him tea,
cloud it with milk. He holds up his hand.
Stop. Enough. Too much? I can't decide.
I crunch noisily on a piece of toast. Fresh
marmalade drops on my skirt. I jump,
knock down his tea-cup. *The New York Times*,
lead smudged in front of me, reflects his response.
He wipes up the mess and hands me
my tea-flecked poem, saying nothing.

We the Indian Women in America

Chitra Banerjee Divarkaruni

We the Indian women in America
have come from many places
Calcutta Jodhpur Trichy Bhopal
small seashore villages in Goa or maybe
hill settlements with names like Ghum
and Pahalgaon. We come from Fiji
and Uganda, from Lagos and London. And
from right here in California,
our skins matching the color
of its goldbrown hills.

We Indian women in America
wear *saris* and *salwaar kameezes*, yes,
we have kept our culture well. On
Navaratri nights we put on *chania
cholis* and dance the Garba. In Gurdwaras
we veil our heads with shimmery *dupattas*. But see
us also jogging the morning pavement
in Memorial Park in sweatpants, our fluorescent
Nike shoes. In our jeans at the Safeway
checkout. In streamlined suits
and silkpearl blouses, our heels clicking
as we enter conference rooms.

We Indian women are faced with many questions.
From children: Mom, not *dal-chawal*
again! Can't we eat

at McDonald's tonight? and *Why*
can't I go on dates when all
my friends are? From parents:
Hai, are you truly never going
to come back home to India? From
husbands: Where's my favorite tie, my matching socks, my
clean underwear? and, What d'you mean we're eating
at McDonald's tonight? At work: Did you
de-bug that program yet? Or, Why are the sales
so low this month? Or, Doctor, is he
going to be OK? From strangers: What's that dot
on your forehead? Do you people really eat
monkey brains? What's a good Indian
restaurant? Do you believe in
fetal sex selection?
And sometimes, Why don't you go back
where you came from.

It is not always easy for us, Indian women in
America. We came with dreams of instant riches,
Hollywood or millionaire husbands, not knowing
how much we'd miss the paint-peeled houses filled
with grandmothers and aunts, the old *ayahs*
who loved and scolded us. Weddings
and *namkarans* when we made big beds on the floor
and slept, all us cousins together. Not knowing
there would be no way back. But slowly we learned
being alone is not all bad. We learned,
in this country, to stand straighter,
speak up for what we want.

And what we want is this: for us and our daughters,
India *and* America,
the best of both together. If you tell us we cannot have
it, we refuse to believe you (for we have learned
to say no). Refuse to choose. We laugh
(for we have learned to laugh also,
loudly and in your face). We know
we can have it all, and are ready
to fight for it. We the Indian women in America:
watch us hold the world
like a great goldbrown *gulabjamun*
juicy and sweet as a promise in our hand—
and bite in.

Harderson Park Days

Jaykumar Menon

I locked the car door, then stepped back to check myself out in the side window. I looked wide, like a kid in a fun house mirror, except my deltoids were bigger. My time in the weight room was paying off. Red mesh jersey and basic black shorts, a classic combination. Had to look good, you know, since this was my first time on their turf—Harderson Park, near Diwan Street, on the North Side of Chicago. I tucked the back of my jersey into my shorts and let the front of it hang loose. The tube socks rode tastefully low, just a few inches above my leather Converse hightops. My friend Edwin, who makes extra cash by playing two on two basketball for money, says that the quickest way to spot a chump was to see if he had his socks pulled all the way up. "Elastic on the calves," he always tells me, "means dollars in your pocket." But my socks were pushed down, just enough for the three horizontal stripes to merge into a single thick blue one. I left the car. First impressions count when you're playing hoop.

I went down the path that led to the courts, making my steps extra bow-leggedy. I had only met these guys once before, at one of those conventions in a hotel past the airport. Another guy of Indian descent was coming towards me. I looked at him and gave him the Nod, which is what I give to folks from the subcontinent, whether I know them or not. But instead of giving the Nod back, he dropped his head down and to the left and skulked by. What an asshole.

Around the bend were some tennis courts. This was a pretty nice park. Three Koreans and a desi were playing doubles and they were good. I watched them for a few shots, but left when they had to chase the ball after an overhead smash. I looked up in time to catch a svelte young woman with silky red hair approaching me on the path. I liked the way she walked, firm strides, confident in herself. Our glances rubbed together, and we half-smiled for each other. After she passed I swear I almost grabbed my crotch and yelled "Anyday, anytime." I've been watching too much damn MTV. The park opened up into a huge field. There were lots of people: kids as high as my knee playing kickball with a ball that came up to their waist; middle-age guys with big lovehandles playing soccer in their undershirts; ten year old girls and boys in polyester shorts teaching themselves how to play volleyball; mothers with braided hair lunging at badminton birdies; young guys in sweatsuits and swaggers and gold chains doing nothing more than being cool. Two hundred folks, at play in the city. And about ninety percent of them were South Asian. I couldn't believe it. They weren't there for any conference or festival or any organized function at all. I'd never seen that many Indians at one time, at least not in this country. It was interesting.

I rolled over to the basketball court just in time to see Phil, this Christian guy I knew, steal the ball and take it in for a layup. He ran back with his fist in the air, hooting "Yobabyobaby yo!" Then this little girl on a tricycle somehow ended up in the middle of the court, proclaimed "Aiyo!" in Malayalam and scooted off. The guys saw me and came over. They buried me in a mountain of hand and back slaps like I was an old friend. . . . It was time to play ball.

It seemed like people were watching me after I dribbled behind my back a couple of times. Maybe they were impressed by the moves I learned in six years of basketball camp. But maybe they were just looking at my clothes. Big shorts and air-soled leather high-tops were scarce on the block. Most of the people seemed stuck in that Indian polyester time warp. But the guys were still good players, really good considering most of them had grown up playing soccer and table tennis, if anything. Hoops were as new to them as they were to America. The one exception was the guy who I was guarding. He was an older guy, Phil's uncle I think, who had played ball in his college days. It must have been quite a while ago, though, because he kept taking these running, lunge-at-the-basket-with-one-knee raised shots from way out at the top of the key. He looked like a big brown hood ornament. I came very close to busting out into a belly laugh the first time he did it, even before the ball clanged hard off the backboard. The second time he got the ball I jumped up in his face and went for the block. A blocked shot, when done well, you know, is more than just a deflection. It's a message, a here-and-now message of "I am here and this is my turf." But while I was delivering this message his right knee caught me full in the stomach and the shot went clean over my bent body. I pretended I was all right. After all the man was at least forty-five years old. But afterwards I let him shoot that goofy shot all he wanted to. I just hoped the ball wouldn't break the backboard.

The game ended when a guy called Choopaloo made a crazy move through the dark to get completely free right next to the basket and then missed the shot so badly that we all fell down and started laughing like crazies. After the concrete stopped feeling comfortable we dragged ourselves over to the grass by the side of the court where women in saris or pantsuits were sitting and chatting. It was eight-thirty on a warm summer Sunday night. A little kid scooted up and asked his mother something in Tamil and then ran back to his friends yelling, "I can play! I can play!"

We sat back on the grass like long lost friends, letting the sweat on our necks turn cold and evaporate. The older man, whose knee imprint was still fresh on my stomach, sat to my right. He looked out across the field contentedly in his sweaty, V-necked undershirt. His name was Bala.

"You play quite nicely," he said to me. "But your footwork is no good. When you shoot you are standing too still. You should get your feet moving, so they are taking you toward the basket. You can get good power in your shot that way, especially with your knee up. And besides, once you learn how to move your feet, you can use that for any sport."

I smiled. Then I propped my head on my other arm, so I faced away from Bala. I stayed like that, watching the little kids play kickball. The ball came up to their waists.

"So Phil tells me your people are from Ponnani," Bala said from behind me. I looked back over my shoulder.

"Yes."

"I too know people there. Some classmates of my father's, you must be knowing them?"

"I wouldn't, but my father probably does," I replied, still facing the kids playing kickball.

Bala patted his almost venerable belly. "You know, your grandfather, he was a highly respected man. He built many roads, the first metalled roads to go by many villages."

"I know," I said.

Bala continued. "People used to come to him for advice, and they took his word for law. Even in Trivandrum we had heard of him."

"Really?" I rolled onto my other elbow. Now I was facing him.

"Sure, sure. Everyone knew that if you had a problem or a dispute you could bring it before him. He was almost like a judge. Actually, a cousin-brother of mine had a dealing with him. It happened during the middle of monsoon. I do not know if you have ever seen a monsoon, but . . ."

"I have."

"But this year it was tremendous. Have you noticed that the shower that starts from the clear sky is the most powerful one? This monsoon season had nothing but that shower. All of the red mud from the hills was sliding down into the road, so you could not drive. And because of that it was almost impossible to get bookings on the train. They said you needed to book at least one month in advance. So my cousin-brother went to your grandfather to see if he could, you know, arrange, some bookings for next week. Of course, he could not simply speak to him directly, even though he had known your grandfather for ten years. He had to try and impress your grandmother, the intermediary. That's the way it worked in those days.

"My cousin-brother, he had a way with words, so he managed to get the audience. The next day he was summoned into the drawing room where your grandfather was sitting in his arm chair. 'Uncle', he said—in Malayalam, of course.

"Yes," said your grandfather.

"I was wondering if I could ask you for a favor?"

"What is it?"

"I was wondering if you could get a booking on the Mangalore Mail to Quilon?"

"Who needs to go?" asked your grandfather.

"Me."

"You? What for?"

"Well, I promised my friend that I would go visit him, and he is going from there after this week."

"Now you can just imagine what your grandfather had to say," said Bala. "He fired my . . ."

"He what?" I said.

"He reprimanded my cousin-brother and told him that he would not make special arrangements in times like these for such a purpose. He very calmly told him to think of all the people who had much more urgent reasons to travel, and what reason was he having for presuming to displace them."

"Was your relative angry?" I asked.

"Oh, very much so. He right away turned his back, he walked out, he went home and fumed, he swore never to talk to him again." Bala waved his arms from left to right with each phrase.

"Did they ever make up?"

"Your grandfather was not the one who was angry," said Bala.

"You know what I mean. Did your cousin-brother ever forgive him?"

"Well, not until the end of the monsoon. You see, the mud slides ruined the rice field transplantations, so he and his whole valley lost half of their crop."

I made my best sympathetic noise.

"But your grandfather, now this was unasked for, mind you, quietly got a State subsidy passed to aid the entire affected area."

I watched the sandstone and brick butcher and shops through the tall swaying hedge that surrounded the park. The dopplering wake of a Cutlass cruising by, broadcasting the latest house mix into the neighborhood as its driver leaned so far back that he ended up in the rear seat; a guy named Manu sitting on the curb griping about his job at the water faucet assembly; a woman standing on the sidewalk giving a public lecture as to why she should be allowed to return the tape player—the street chatter sifted through the bushes and on into the park. I said nothing, but just looked at Bala.

"The key to basketball," he said after a while, leaning forward as much as his belly allowed him, "is in the footwork."

I nodded in agreement.

A Better Life

Diane Mehta

Driving on midsummer's deserted roadways
past the forts and empires, temple idols
praised like liberty, the abandoned tires
in your expression.

How the evenings spread like a rooftop fire
in the heat of winter; Diwali sparklers
making citizens in the sky, your gilded
gardens with fences.

Countries have no sympathy; only praises
amplified like distances for the newer
land: the housing gauntlets we had to enter,
stripped but with freedom!

Standards change like faith in a foreign country:
how the slurs ignited like gas; remember
when he lit the match, then the flame was dancing,
swaying like cobras.

Don't you miss the rains in July, your mother's
hair in wet braids, sandalwood-scented, spices
shaped like cones on plates and the servants laughing,
chewing on peppers?

Did you pledge allegiance to lawns and fences,
better lives for us; the best western education?
Neighbors take the place of extended families,
freedom expires

like your father dying in Bombay, hardly
sixty when he leaned into whiteness. Packaged
smoke unfurled and pulled him with yellow fingers
past all the rooftops.

Now you drive on highways to work and homeward.
Winter cuts the windshield with blistered fingers,
feeds you flashes: corn in the husk on street-grills,
red with paprika.

Excerpts from

Once Upon An Elephant—a down to earth tale of Ganesh and what happens when worlds collide

Ashok Mathur

Parvati

Men never listen. Or when they listen they don't get it. So you tell one man you want a child and he laughs at you, goes off dancing with godknows how many bimboes, figuring you can want all you want but without him there will be no baby. Like you need him for that. So you tell another man, look boy, I want to have a bath in privacy so just stand outside and don't let anyone in, a simple request you would think, and he goes and loses his head over it. And then you confront the wouldbe/wannabe-father of your child that it's up to him to make reparations, and what does he go and do? Goes on a killing spree, that's what he does, and then has the audacity to say it's your fault. Men never listen. Or when they listen they fuck up.

Vighnesvara

I swear I'd forget my head sometimes if it wasn't screwed on ha ha ha. Now now, shouldn't make fun of myself, tusk tusk. Hoo-boy. I'm the one. It's all my fault. I'm the one who makes history. I write it down word by word by word until the story's done. Ain't nuthin gonna stand in mah way. See, it was like this, I was just standing there, just standing there, when this dude comes along and tells me to move aside. Move aside, I say, not hardly likely, though if truth be known I wasn't sure what I was standing there in the first place for. But step aside, remove the obstacle, never. So this dude pulls a Little John tactic, 'cept in that story the hardware was a staff and in this story, my story, we're talking sceptre. But I'll get back to that later. Do you have any idea how hard it is to interrupt your own story and write it down as you're doing so? Talk about obstacles.

Man. But let me tell you this. Around the world they're feeding me milk. Cow milk, goat milk, mother's milk. One per cent, two per cent, homogenized, unpasteurized, half and half, soy, rice. Milk milk milk. You name it, they're feeding it to me. Mostly I take it because it's time, but occasionally even I've had my fill. But back to that story later. Right now all you need to know is my robinhood was no match for his littlejohn. I know I shouldn't say this, because that's not how it's written and all, but since I'm doing the writing, I'm going to say it anyway, which is I should have stepped aside. But, no sense crying over spilled milk.

. . .

"All rise."

Everyone rises.

Judge McEchern walks in, robed in black, sighs as he negotiates the three steps up to his judge table, sets himself down, squints out at the courtroom.

Another dreary day, he thinks. Stupid caseload. He squints harder at the courtroom, tries to identify any troublemakers he might be able to cite for contempt. He likes citing spectators for contempt. He's proud that he's cited more spectators for contempt than any other judge on the Queen's Bench. He doesn't put up with any guff from spectators. No fooling around in his courtroom. He squints. Tawdry looking bunch. A few foreigners. He doesn't say things like this aloud any more because of those pesky young lawyers who keep sniffing around, looking for any excuse to prove he's gone off the deep end, senile maybe, or at least some sort of monstrous xenophobe. That's what the editorial columnist for the *Star* called him. Xenophobe. Just because he speaks his mind, doesn't put up with any guff from anyone, whether they're coloured or normal. No guff. He squints.

He squints even harder just in case he's mistaken.

He looks around cautiously to see if anyone else has noticed. His mind is as sharp as ever, but he has to admit his eyesight is getting a bit dim. But, no, he's sure, even if no-one else has noticed.

"Ahem. "

The Crown Prosecutor looks up at him nervously. The legal aid lawyer looks up at him nervously. The clerk looks up at him nervously.

"Ahem. Could someone please tell me if this is a courtroom or a Hallow'een party?"

Eyes shuffle nervously. The question is rhetorical, but everyone knows the pattern of the court. Judge McEchern will repeat the question until someone tries to answer, then he'll interrupt and answer his own question. That's how it always goes.

"Hello? Will someone please tell me if this is a courtroom or a Hallow'een party?"

A count of three and the Crown rises. She adjusts her collar. She begins to speak. "If it please the court . . . "

"It would certainly please the court," Judge McEchern interrupts, "if members of the gallery treated this court with a minute amount of respect and did not appear dressed up like damned football mascots."

He pauses for effect. He likes to pause for effect. Gives people some time to stew. Then he can hit 'em with contempt if they speak out of turn. He was up to thirty-six contempt charges this year but it was already November. In 1986 he had charged forty-nine insolent bastards with contempt and he was determined to break that record this year.

"I think we all know whom I'm addressing." He squints even harder now so that his eyes close completely and he has to open them a titch so he can see people's reactions and he hopes no one notices his eyes were completely closed because then people would start to talk like they did about Judge Hargood who actually used to wake himself up by snoring too loud in the courtroom, at least before they put him on medication. Judge McEchern wonders how ol' Harry Hargood is doing and makes a mental note to look him up, although he always promptly forgets any mental notes he makes which is why he has to write things down these days.

The Crown speaks again, still tugging at her collar. "Your worship, if it please the court, I believe there exists a minor misunderstanding, perfectly explicable of course, and which has the effect of creating some confusion; however, if it please the court . . . "

"Misz Block," interrupts Judge McEchern, intentionally elongating and accentuating the honorific so it sounds simultaneously redundant and offensive, dressed up like a bloody jungle animal!"

"He's not dressed up," the Crown retorts, almost petulantly. "That's the way he is."

"That . . . that thing, that head? You're telling me that this. . . this person in my courtroom has an elephant head?"

The Crown smiles and nods.

Judge McEchern is silent. He is confused. There is an elephant in his courtroom, a gallery full of foreigners, a woman Crown prosecutor, and he hasn't the slightest idea what to do.

"Court will recess for lunch," he says, fully aware of the multiple sets of eyes which glance clockward and note that it is ten minutes past ten in the morning. For emphasis, Judge McEchern decides to rap his gavel like they do on TV. He reaches out for his gavel and grasps for it. It is not until his hand begins to close that he notices the clerk has failed to put his gavel in its place. Then Judge McEchern remembers that Court of Queen's Bench judges don't actually have gavels. That's only on American TV. Judge McEchern feels foolish. He opens his hand and bangs on his bench two times, hard, with his palm. He thinks he must look like those goofy MPs when they're making noises of approval on that House of Commons cable channel. Judge McEchern is very glad they don't let television cameras into Canadian courtrooms.

Ganapati

But Your Honour, I stand before you, living proof that this homicide is not one.

If the son was murdered in a fit of jealous rage, a sort of reverse-Oedipal thing if you will, then the son would be dead and the father, indeed, guilty of homicide, sonicide, most particularly, me-icide.

But Your Honour, I stand before you.

I speak to you, somewhat nasally perhaps (but wouldn't you if you had to talk through this enormous snout?)

All right, I grant you, he did take off my head, and there is that minor matter of the dead elephant, but he did ask permission before beheading the beast, and permission was duly granted. Granted, too, it took the entire volunteer fire department and then some to get his elephantine body from the river, but they did so in due course before decompositional elements could pollute the holy river, and I should add both my father and I feel deeply for Fireman Ephram Paglia and we hope he makes a hasty recovery from that nasty inguinal hernia. However. Homicide?

I submit to you that, being as I stand before you hale and hearty, albeit a mite uglier and somewhat more smelly than before, the only crime my dear father is guilty of is the unlawful disposal of a dead animal. I further submit the charges of murder, debasement of a body, and cruelty to animals be dropped and the sentence on the new charge be set at time served.

Let us be done with it.

Let's go have some milk.

The Fat Man Sings: Reflections On The Music Of Nusrat Fateh Ali Khan

Somini Sengupta

I call him Trickster, this Sufi giant of the gap-toothed grin. He has seduced us all, appearing like a specter in a dream, each time in different garb. How many Nusrats, I want to ask him, rest under the folds of his considerable chin? How many incarnations will spring from his belly? How many guises will he spawn, to capture how many jaded, faithless hearts like mine?

• • •

Qawwali—the Urdu word for "utterance"—is the ancient Sufi Muslim tradition of devotional song. According to Sufi belief, the act of listening to qawwali can elevate the pious to a state of intense devotion and, ultimately, enable them to touch the divine.

Nusrat Fateh Ali Khan is qawwali's largest living legend, but he doesn't sing for Sufi ears alone. A crossover superstar, Nusrat draws listeners who understand not a word of his Urdu poetry, nor the Sufi mysticism behind it. The fans at his last New York City concert, for instance, included Susan Sarandon and Tim Robbins. Grunge-rock giant Eddie Vedder and jazzman Henry Threadgill were also there: both are collaborating with him musically. I was there too, along with throngs of my Urdu-illiterate compatriots, South Asians raised on these shores.

Each of us turn to Nusrat to massage our vastly different, and sometimes conflicting desires, and Nusrat, I suspect, whispers something different into each of our ears.

There are, for instance, his expat South Asian fans, for whom a line of his Urdu poetry stirs up nostalgia, or for whom qawwali serves as a religious rite.

There are his ethno-chic, generally white, middle-class listeners, who turn to

Nusrat when they want to be lifted into that mystical, Eastern other-world. For them—my friends—Peter Gabriel's RealWorld Records has released several art-fully-packaged, accessible Nusrat albums.

And then, there are my peers, the children of the subcontinentals, for whom British bhangra deejay Bally Sagoo has laced Nusrat's signature siren with sounds familiar to our transplanted ears: a dub bass, a throbbing house mix, a bumping concoction that offers our thirsty generation a quick fix of desi pride. Nusrat is our Bruce Lee, if you will, our icon of Cool. But he is our roots-man too, shut-tling us back to the musical traditions of the so-called Motherland.

Surprisingly, Nusrat's artful metamorphoses have managed to steer clear of controversy and conflict. At a time when artists like Cheb Khaled have come under fire for corrupting traditional culture, Nusrat has avoided any serious back-lash from conservative critics at home or abroad, even as he has encouraged club-goers all over the world to shake their booty to hymns dedicated to Ali, the Sufi master believed to be the Prophet's son-in-law.

I think of my cousin Mo's report on the last Nusrat concert in Los Angeles. Mo chuckled on the phone as she recalled the spectacle. Two female Deadheads were twirling around in front of the stage in the middle of an overwhelmingly South Asian crowd, "doing the noodle dance," she said. The Deadheads twirled and twirled until one of them became so excited that she got dizzy and fell. "It was as if," Mo said, "they had discovered a new Jerry Garcia."

We laughed. She and I had attended many a fashionable party, where Nusrat's signature song, 'Mustt Mustt' was all the rage. We knew that ever since the Maharishi mumbo-jumbo of the 1960s, white Americans—though not exclusively—had been dipping into the Indian well to quench their thirst for exotic spiritual upliftment.

We called them culture vultures. Righteous in each other's company, we hated them for sticking their grubby, greedy fingers into what we figured was ours. We mocked their sinewy moves on the dance floor, and we gave them dirty looks. But for all our public taunts, our private truths were a bit more compli-cated. Mo and I had both loved noodle-dancers. And neither of us understood Nusrat's lyrics anyway. We were erstwhile Hindus, Bengali-Californians who ultimately had as little natural claim to Nusrat as our "firengi" friends, the for-eigners. In the end, wasn't their craving for Nusrat just as much of a highway robbery—and an embrace—as my craving for the Southern black church music of the Rev. Al Green?

Still, when I listen to my desi peers listen to Nusrat, it is clear that they hunger for another kind of upliftment. Just as the firengi have discovered in Nusrat a new icon of the East, second-generation South Asians on both sides of the Atlantic see in Nusrat a consciously hybrid reflection of their own mixture. Theirs is the Nusrat manufactured by Bally Sagoo, the bhangra mix-master from Birmingham, England. Reminiscent of tinny Bollywood numbers, Bally's collaborations are clumsy, musically, replacing the subtle filigree of tabla, harmonium and voice with a wall of pounding house beats and a frenetic drum machine. But it is this stuff—particularly Nusrat's contribution to Bally's definitive 1989 bhangra compilation 'Star Crazy' and in 1990, 'Magic Touch,'—that exposed qawwali to a generation of South Asian youth. Because, as my friend, DJ Rekha once said, "we would never be caught dead buying a world music album."

• • •

"I sing to be able to walk in the footsteps of my elders," said a quiet voice on the phone, long distance on the phone, "and to bring out the Sufi message."

Nusrat Fateh Ali Khan was born in the year after Pakistani independence into a long line of qawwals. His father, a famous and accomplished singer, wanted him to be a doctor, because as Nusrat recalled laughingly, he wasn't sure the child had a qawwal's strength. But music chose Nusrat. From an early age, he trained with his father and uncle, first mastering tabla, then the North Indian classical repertoire.

Today, his central mission is to bring new recuits to the qawwali tent, and ultimately, to its classical heart. This is the raison d'être for what he called "my little experiments" with Peter Gabriel and Bally Sagoo. "That was for our kids who grew up here, so they could know about Indian and Pakistani culture," he told me. "I simply borrowed their instruments. I did that especially for the younger generation. It's not for the mature people or the fans of qawwali."

Qawwali, he insisted, can never be modernized. But to effectively convey its central message, qawwali can adjust to the demands of different audiences, incorporating new instruments, embracing the musical styles of the day, changing tempo or absorbing new languages. "If the younger generation listens to and appreciates my voice and they come to the real thing," he said, "then I will have performed a great service."

I know that Nusrat has fulfilled his mission with at least one young Pakistani-American in Queens. Five years ago, when Tariq Subhani was head-banging to Def Lepard and Pat Benatar, a family friend brought him a copy of Magic Touch. At the time, Tariq regarded qawwali as the boring, classical stuff that his father favored. But this bhangracized Nusrat of 'Magic Touch' turned his head. Tariq began exploring and his head filled up with Nusrat.

Now, at age twenty-six, Tariq is a father himself. His shelves are stacked with 105 Nusrat albums. These days, he says he bristles when he watches his peers get down on the dance floor to a rousing rendition of the hymn, Allah-Hoo. Tariq is drawn to the classical Nusrat; for him, the music is a return to roots.

"I was getting consumed by American culture," he told me. I thought he sounded like a caricature out of a Hanif Kureishi novel, but I didn't say anything. "Nusrat has brought me closer to my religion, to my culture, to my language. I can't thank him enough."

• • •

Nusrat, I feel guilty when I hear Tariq speak of you like that. I don't want qawwali's magic carpet to take me back to the Motherland. And I'm not really comfortable dancing around you like a maypole of ethnic pride, the way some of my desi peers do.

My devotion is cut of another cloth. I am drawn to the protean spirit of qawwali. Ever since it was invented in the 10th century as an amalgam of Persian and Indian classical forms, qawwali has recruited new converts to Sufism by stealing their hearts, musically, by giving the people what they want.

I don't always love what you churn out, or the fans who hover around you. But I am enchanted, Nusrat, by the many guises you have spawned—the classical, the ambient dub, the acid jazz, the bhangra. Qawwali's constant mutations, its ability to be so many musical creatures at the same time mirror my own everyday rituals.

"When you have two civilizations meet, new paths are forged," you told me, and it sounded like a warning. "But there is a limit to that too. As long as the color of where you come from is reflected in what you're doing, it's good."

Now I want to warn you, Nusrat: manipulating tradition can be risky business. At your New Jersey concert last summer, I stood in the back of the dilapidated old theatre in downtown Elizabeth and watched an old rite reinvented. Your fans, following tradition, had scrambled up on stage to dance and throw money at your feet. Inside a shrine, that would be considered a religious offering.

Here, the beefy bouncers who had been installed at the foot of the stage to ward away the fans had given up their posts by the middle of the show. By the time you started up "Mustt Mustt" the stage had become a sea of adoring fans, gyrating and tossing dollar bills. Then, a posse of young desi men jumped into the fray and began pocketing all the loose cash they could.

I know you witnessed all this. But you didn't see them outside, peeling out of the parking lot and howling up at the night sky. An older man standing next to me furrowed his brows and sucked his teeth. "Bad luck," was all he said.

And I wondered, Nusrat, do you visit their dreams too?

Returning to Camp

Beyond the Walls, Amreeka

Tahira Naqvi

Sakina Bano was afraid. Afraid not of the fact that she was on an airplane larger than her house for the first time in her life, nor of travelling alone, companionless, on a twenty-two hour journey with four stops in cities she had not heard of before with names she could not pronounce correctly, although this was something that would surely crowd fear into the heart and mind of any sixty-nine year old widow. No, it was not the journey that troubled her. Why, when the plane lifted itself from the ground and the noise and vibration rattled her skull, she felt not fear but an exhilaration, as if she were being pulled toward the sky by some unseen force. No, her fear had little to do with such concerns.

"Son, I can't come," she had written to Asad. "I'm old, I want to take my last breath in my own country, and be buried among my own people. If I die there, what will happen to me?"

First Asad admonished her in his letters, telling her in frank, unshielded words that she was being stubborn and childish. Sakina Bano was amused when he scolded her. How ridiculous to be drowned in a storm of anxiety over something like this, he chided her. Ridiculous? What did he, a young man whose whole life lay ahead of him like a stretch of fertile fields, know of such things? Letter after letter fell into the tinny silence of her letterbox on 73 Sabir Street, Gujranwala. Finally Asad gave her an ultimatum: he told her he would not come to Pakistan to visit until she first visited him in America. She smiled to think that is what she often did: give him ultimatums. Now it was his turn.

She relented. Dragging her fear along with her, she boarded the plane and thought, 'He'll never come back and live on 73 Sabir Street. I must now see where his new home will be.'

A clinking, clattering noise interrupted her reverie. Within minutes the air was redolent with the smell of richly spiced food, laced heavily with garam masala, like wedding fare. We're going to eat, Sakina Bano told herself nervously. She wasn't really hungry, having eaten dinner at Iffat's house an hour before her departure from Lahore. "Who knows what you'll get on the plane," her daughter had remarked, carefully depositing another helping of rice and peas pulao on her mother's plate.

The trolleys began to crowd the aisles. Sakina Bano had been warned about the possible presence of pork, and meat that was not halal, in airline food and elsewhere. And there was alcohol too. She could smell it, like urine left overnight in the open drain along a street wall. What she had to do was ask. She could lose nothing by asking.

But that proved to be an arduous undertaking. Food trays were being passed with such rapidity that she found it impossible to hold the stewardess' attention long enough for a question. Also, she felt awkward, overcome by a diffidence she could not account for since she was not a woman reluctant to speak her mind. Her tray remained untouched. She did not even try to slip her finger under the silvery wrapping and lift just one corner to see what she was about to eat. Then, when coffee and tea arrived, she swiftly laid a restraining hand on the stewardess' arm. Her reserve disguised with a smile, she asked, "This is all halal meat, isn't it?" She held the young woman's gaze boldly.

"We serve only halal meat, Ammaji." The woman's tone was devoid of emotion, but she returned Sakina Bano's smile, her eyes, drowsy-looking from the weight of mascara and layers of green and blue makeup, meeting hers openly.

Rid of her dilemma, Sakina Bano turned to the food before her. She removed the silver foil on the tray and looked down on biryani and korma. Not to get up to walk and stroll after this rich food—why, wouldn't it make one, well, uncomfortable? Some of the buttery brown rice slipped onto her kurta front as she neatly rounded off small portions with her fingers. After the first morsel had been chewed and swallowed, she realized she was hungry after all. The food was well-cooked, spicy, and although she would have preferred a whole wheat chappati and some daal of maash, this was something to talk about when she returned to Sabir Street.

Afterward, she wiped her hands with a white paper napkin. What a waste, she pondered. She could just have easily walked to the bathroom and washed her hands. Where was the bathroom, could she easily walk to it? she asked herself in sudden consternation. 'There will be many new things, Amma," Asad had written. "Just watch what the others are doing." Well, no one was running to the bathrooms to wash hands.

On her left sat a dour-looking man, in his late sixties perhaps, or maybe older, with a stomach flabby like risen dough and a gray-haired beard, and she wasn't about to learn anything from watching him. He was probably as much a novice as she; he had dropped cutlery at least twice and his paper napkin was lying forlornly on the floor while he used his handkerchief to wipe his hands. But now the young girl on her right, in the window seat, who had told Sakina Bano earlier that her name was Abida and she was going back to college, now *she* seemed like a person who had made this trip more than once. She had handled the paper napkin deftly, making no fumbling moves with the cutlery that came wrapped in a narrow plastic bag. Sakina Bano briefly fidgeted with the bag in the hopes of getting a spoon out, but she soon discovered she would have to wrestle with it before she gained access to what was buried inside. Why, who needed the spoon, anyway? And, she was not going to flounder clumsily with a fork and knife and make herself look foolish. She had enough sense not to reveal her shortcomings. So she ate as she had always done, with her fingers. The pretty young girl, with big, almond-shaped eyes and long hair that fell on her shoulders like strands of silk, was Pakistani and therefore no stranger to old customs. However, what was all this compared to the cacophonous noise that clamored in her head, threatening to drown out all other sounds?

Suppose she suffered a heart attack just this instant and died? Why, people often died quietly and without a fuss, didn't they? Would the airline transport her back to Pakistan? What if the plane had to make a landing in the country they were flying over when she died, and her body abandoned there, among strangers? She knew Cairo was their first stop, but were they near Cairo? She couldn't be certain. But the thought that Egypt might be the place where she was left for burial provided some comfort. At least she would be among Muslims. Sakina Bano leaned back in her seat, her hand firmly wrapped around the hot cup of tea in front of her. She sighed. For the moment the fear was put to rest.

Cairo was a hurried stop. The passengers were not allowed to get off, something about terrorism, she heard one of the passengers say. After Cairo she lost track of time. Day and night seemed to cross over so rapidly she didn't know whether to sleep or remain awake. When the plane came down at Frankfurt, it was nearly morning, she saw. Below her, when the plane descended in sudden swoops as if it were about to fall, were dark smoky whorls streaked with orange and red and fringed with gold.

The airport looked isolated, the only passengers in sight wandering about like mindless creatures, their faces ashen from exhaustion and lack of sleep, bodies slouched with fatigue, their steps dragging. In the transit lounge, some were stretched out on shiny, slippery benches to snatch whatever fitful sleep they could. Airport officials, usually crisp and alert, also wore crestfallen looks, moving about in a slow and unhurried manner. The clock on a white wall above a red sign she couldn't read said three.

No sooner did she deposit her fatigued, aching body into one of the chairs that lined a large glass wall than a tiny spurt of anxiety crawled out of her thoughts like a worm, and seemed to edge its way into her blood, spreading like a chilling current under her skin. "What if?" The possibility was too frightful for her to weigh. Sakina Bano stiffened in her chair. She must not fall asleep. Her eyes strayed to the clock, she looked for the second hand. But the hand was stationary, it seemed, stilled. A German clock keeping German time; what could it mean to her? Turning away, she looked about her anxiously and observed Abida, her young companion from the plane, slumped in a seat not too far from her. Her thin arms crossed over a large canvas bag in her lap, the girl slept soundly. How Sakina Bano envied the untroubled and tranquil expression on her face. How happy her dreams must be, unencumbered and free.

Later, back on the plane, before the food trolleys came clattering down the aisles again, Sakina Bano decided she would talk to Abida. The two women reminisced about places they knew; Anarkali Bazaar in Lahore, Bano Bazaar, Mcleod Road where all the cinema houses were, and the shrine of Data Darbar where you made a vow and prayers were answered.

"Is this your first visit, Ammaji?" the girl asked, placing the book she had been reading face down on her lap.

"Yes," Sakina Bano said, sighing. "My son has been asking me for a long time, but it's not easy you know. Iffat, my daughter, was having her first baby, and then the house had to be whitewashed before the rains. Asad, my son, lives

in Dan-bury, Con-necti-cut." She emphasized each syllable as Iffat had instructed her. Such difficult names. "And where are you going?"

"I live in New York City," Abida replied, looking at the older woman's face
for a glimmer of recognition, "a place called Manhattan. It's not too far from
Danbury, your son will know where it is. Your son's married?"

"No, but Iffat and I have found a girl for him. If he likes her we will have
the wedding next year." She rubbed her forehead and hung her head. "If I'm
still alive then."

The girl's eyes widened in alarm. "You're not sick Ammaji, are you?"

"No, no, I'm not sick, except for the pain in the legs, in my back, the cataracts
that keep growing too fast. No, but old age is a kind of sickness too, isn't it,
child? I only pray my maker allows me to die in my own country." Sakina Bano
was overcome with a feeling of relief after this confession.

"You shouldn't talk like this, Ammaji. In America men and women in their
seventies get married and start new lives." Abida spoke with a smile.

"Ai hai, child, what nonsense is this? And when do they prepare for death?
Or is it that they think they will live forever? New attachments, new pain, who
wants it all over again?"

Abida laughed and Sakina Bano wondered if the young girl could help.
"Child," she whispered with her hand gently on Abida's arm, "what happens if
someone dies? I mean how do they bring the body back?" She was intent on
knowing the truth, all of it, however ugly.

"What?" Abida turned to her in surprise. Then, realizing her companion was
serious, she said, "Ammaji, I don't know too much about these things, but I'm
sure arrangements can be made to transport the body. Actually I think four airline tickets have to be bought. It's expensive, I've heard. But you know Ammaji,"
she looked at Sakina Bano solicitously, "nowadays there are burials right there in
special cemeteries that have been allotted by Muslim communities."

This piece of information proved unnerving. There was little solace in what
the girl said. Asad could never afford four tickets, and then she'd have to be
buried in . . . Dan-bury! Sakina Bano collapsed in her seat, her spirits fallen, her
desire to continue the conversation waned.

Perhaps he can get a loan, she mused over her next cup of tea. Surely it would
be a burden, but he could have all of her savings, nearly fifty thousand rupees,

and all the other property would be his anyway. She will not mind, although her husband's soul would be agitated, it's been in the family for nearly sixty years, but Asad could sell the house on 73 Sabir Street and invest the money. There was also some agricultural land that had belonged to Asad's grandfather. The picture began to look a little less bleak. She arranged a pillow behind her head and settling into a comfortable position, shut her eyes.

"At the airport, keep your wits about you," Asad had shouted into the phone. Although he had described the airport to her in detail, she was still like a child lost among strangers in a crowded bazaar at JFK airport. Her son's instructions were explicit: "Have your passport in your hand when you're in line at Immigration, stay close to people from your flight, if you're in doubt ask someone, ask Amma, don't be afraid to ask. At Customs, open your suitcases quickly if told to, but don't volunteer, tell the officer what you're carrying if he inquires, and please, Amma, don't bring mangoes. Carrying fruit is not permitted." She was on her own, she realized, instructions or no instructions.

At customs a tall, thin man with a deeply lined, ashen-white face, thin red nose, and probing eyes asked her if she had any mangoes. She knew the English word. She shook her head, wondering if he would question her further. Deep inside her suitcase, carefully wrapped in a plastic bag were two bottles of pickled mangoes that she had prepared with her own hands, the small, dark green, tart mangoes taken down from her own tree growing in the front garden. No, he didn't want to know more. Anyway, snug in those bottles was not fruit, just tiny pickled raw mangoes that Asad liked so much.

Afterward, a dark, stocky man, distinguishable from the others by a uniform he wore, silently piled her two cases along with Abida's on a large trolley, and signalling them, began pushing their luggage toward gray double doors that seemed to dominate a whole wall.

Beyond the walls Amreeka began. Never before had Sakina Bano seen so many people in one place, not even on Eid shopping days in the market. So different from each other, they milled about restlessly, speaking languages that seemed like noise to her. Some of the people looked familiar, men, women and children from either India or Pakistan, but there were others who must be from countries she was aware existed on a map, but knew nothing about.

She and Abida followed the dark man in the uniform, and as she lifted a hand to adjust the slipping dupatta from her head, she felt dizzy. If she hadn't caught on to the railing on her left she might have stumbled and fallen. Where is Asad? she wondered, gnawed by anxiety And suddenly she spotted him. He rushed toward her, his face clouded by anxiety, as if she were a child who had gone away and was returning.

Outside, Abida said goodbye and got into a car with a young man who couldn't be much older than she. Her brother? Her husband? Maybe just a friend. Sakina Bano waved, saddened by the thought that she would probably never see her again.

It was cool, the sky was a dark blue, and she saw stars. In the midst of all the strangeness the sky seemed to afford a sense of comfort. Was it not the same sky she saw every night in Gujranwala, now thousands of miles away? Her fear receded as she trudged alongside her son.

• • •

Asad's apartment was small. Just one bedroom barely affording enough space for a low, three-drawer bureau and a bed that had no headboard and shook as if it had a loose bottom when you sat on it; the kitchen, tiny and doorless, was the size of a bathroom in her house, and the area between the bedroom and the kitchen her son had set up as the drawing room with one upholstered sofa not very clean, a low table scratched and marked with circular cup stains, and two chairs on which the paint was peeling untidily. Is this what he had come to Amreeka for? He had left the long, circular veranda of 73 Sabir Street, the spacious rooms with elevated ceilings and windows everywhere, the wide, open red-brick courtyard with the large mulberry tree where the winter sun warmed you and where you slept under dark blue starry skies on hot summer nights, for this? There must be something she could not see as yet, something that eluded her because she was old and because her mind was clogged with uneasy thoughts.

On a Friday, nearly a week after her arrival in Danbury, Sakina Bano accompanied her son to what he informed her was the local Islamic Center. Having envisioned, if not a mosque, at least a place which had some trappings of the Islamic, she was stupefied at what she saw.

"This is the Salvation Army Church," Asad whispered in her ear as the two of them entered a long passage where she was greeted by dark-haired children shrieking playfully, many of them running, chasing the others. As she drew her dupatta about her, a girl no older than seven or eight, her plaits ribboned, her eyes wide with excitement, ran into her and almost fell. Sakina Bano stooped quickly to hold her, buffing the girl's fall with her arm. The girl looked up at her, stiffened and moved away awkwardly.

A church, she wondered in amazement. Muhammad and Issa in the same place! What would her husband say if he were alive? She saw a few women, some wearing shalwar and kameez, three others in long robes with scarves covering their hair. Who are these women? Sakina Bano wondered, Egyptian, Saudi, maybe Iranian? A group of men stood in the narrow passage, removed from the women, many young like her son, a few older and gray-haired with somber and wearied faces, they talked in low voices.

Not used to being in the company of strange men, unless she was in the bazaar or on a train or the bus stop, Sakina Bano felt uncomfortable when Asad introduced her to the people in the passage. Of course he wants them to know his mother has come to visit him, she thought, trying to placate herself.

"Walekumsalaam, walekumsalaam," she mumbled with her head lowered as she made her way behind Asad. He led her to a room where more women sat, most of them tending infants.

Asad introduced her. A woman who reminded her of Abida because she had a boyish figure, long hair open to her shoulders, and was younger than all the rest, came forward quickly to greet her. Soon all of them engulfed her as if she were a special guest.

"Do you like *Amreeka*?" a plump, attractive woman with a chubby baby on her arm, asked genially. She was rocking back and forth while the baby drooled on the sparkling gold bangles on her wrist.

"Yes, yes, I like it, what is there not to like?" Sakina Bano wondered if any of them knew anything about transporting bodies by air.

"You must come and visit us soon," the plump woman said, smiling again, and before Sakina Bano could respond to her invitation, the child began to whimper and the young woman walked away, patting the infant and cooing softly.

Her name, Sakina Bano soon discovered, was Husna, while the one who resembled Abida was Sabiha. They were all eager, these women, eager to be friendly, and as they talked their solemn enthusiasm lighted up their faces, imbuing their voices with energy so that the most trivial topics of conversation seemed to assume undue importance. One day Asad's wife will be here, among them, first alone and then with a child on her arm, while on Sabir Street, Sakina Bano will wait out her days by herself, expecting the postman's rattle at the letterbox, running out for letters, for photographs charting the progress of her daughter-in-law, her new grandchild.

The children assembled for class. One of the men, fair-skinned, with a beard that was black like the overused surface of a tawa, a short, chubby man no more than thirty-five or thirty-six, came in and started talking to the children. Why, Arabic is his mother tongue, Sakina Bano realized in pleasant surprise, and when he began reciting from the Koran, how buoyantly the words of the ayaats fell from him, like unhurried rain from the heavens.

"He's from Egypt," Asad told her later. Class was being held in a section of the large hall in which everyone was congregated, and separated from the place where the women sat by a movable partition. The women in the long dresses and scarves had come in too, and Sabiha chatted energetically with them in English. Asad and the other men had moved in behind the partition as well, perhaps on the other side of another movable wall.

Her attention was suddenly snagged by the drop of a word that wiggled its way into her consciousness and was suspended there, like a kite trapped precariously in the branches of a tree. Because she had been deeply engrossed in the melodic recitation, she missed the first part of the conversation, but the word 'buried' didn't elude her. She turned to a slightly older woman, closer to her in age perhaps, her hair thickly patched with gray, large glasses hiding nearly all of her diminutive nose, who was now talking.

". . . she had cancer so her family knew she didn't have too long to live, and her son didn't take her back to Pakistan when she passed away. It was a Sunday, and all the stores were closed. Do you know, they couldn't even buy white cotton for her shroud? Isn't it just terrible?" She shook her head gravely and rubbed her hands.

"What did they do?" It was Husna, the baby now asleep on her shoulder.

Sakina Bano's heart convulsed. The ground seemed to slip from under her feet. She held her breath and stared at the older woman.

"What can I say, it was just dreadful. May Allah save us from such a fate. All the friends of the family donated whatever new white bedsheets they had, and the women made a kaffan. She was buried in the town cemetery. Thank God there was a Turkish maulvi who could say the burial prayers."

Sakina Bano's mouth became dry. She felt sweat rise like tiny thorns on her skin. It was as if a thousand little invisible insects had set down their furry legs upon her person and begun to move, slowly. Bedsheets! What an unfortunate woman. And what guarantee they were all cotton? Wash and wear is what they are making these days. And to be buried among strangers—such isolation. Poor woman, to be so far from home and die, to be wrapped in bedsheets which said, on small tags somewhere, 'Made in Amreeka.' Will the angels condescend to enter a grave where a body lay draped in a shroud made by Christians? Sakina Bano shuddered at the possibility of being abandoned by God's messengers at the hour of reckoning.

Conversation veered off to other subjects, but Sakina Bano remained entangled in a web of irreversible anxiety. Later that night, agitated and unsolaced, she tossed and turned on her bed as if she was on live coals. Sleep evaded her. Finally she decided to pray. For a long time she sat on the janamaz with her prayer beads.

"Ya Allah," she entreated with outstretched hands, "I ask you only this. Let me return to my home, and then my life is yours to do what you want with it. I have no fear of death. I ask not to live forever. But there is great fear in my heart of dying here. In your infinite mercy grant me this one wish and I will never want anything for myself again."

She didn't know when she dozed off, the words still forming in her head, gathering thick on her tongue like molasses. When she fell forward on the sajdahgah, she woke up startled and realized she was still on the prayer mat. Extending both arms out, she slowly brought the edge of the mat toward her, folding the rest of it as she rose to her feet slowly. It was time to sleep.

• • •

The day was warm, but nothing like a warm day in Gujranwala. There the temperature must have already climbed to a humid, pasty hundred-and-two degrees, while here, it was pleasant. With the car windows down, a small breeze quietly fanned her face, making her drowsy.

She could not pronounce the name of the place Asad was taking her to. They were on their way to visit her niece Fatima, her husband's cousin's daughter, a dear girl who always visited her in Gujranwala even though it was an out-of-the-way town, always brought gifts. Sakina Bano was taking her a hand-blocked brick-red tablecloth and a set of matching napkins. She knew what Fatima liked. And for Fatima's husband she had brought a vest that all the young men were wearing these days, for the year-old baby an embroidered cotton kurta and pajama.

Sakina Bano would soon be asleep, except that the greenery astounded and startled her and she had to constantly move her head to see it all. Never had she seen such density of foliage, of such variety. No two trees seemed alike. Like walls, the greenery rose on either side of the road until the sky, when she gazed up, was only a narrow strip of sharp, clear blue.

Something seemed to grasp at her attention when Asad stopped the car at one of the traffic lights. She glanced to her right and gazed in open-eyed wonder at the image before her. A hill, sloping lazily upward from the edge of the road, carpeted with grass so finely clipped it was like a velvet mantle, greener than any green she had ever known. Fresh, washed color interlaced with a trellis of sunlight filtered through tall trees lining the hill's highest borders. And little clusters of the brightest, sharpest red flowers, and each cluster was attended by a small, squat slab of gray stone. Sakina Bano gasped at the beauty she had stumbled on.

The question was squelched as soon as it raised its head in her thoughts. She knew the place. The perfect little slabs of stone had a voice that fell clearly into her ears. The car was moving again, and Sakina Bano fell against her seat as if she had travelled a great distance on foot and must rest now to catch her breath.

Her eyes closed, she journeyed to another dwelling, a portion of land where her husband and so many of her relatives were resting. Dismal, overgrown with weeds and wildly tangled shrubbery, the only color was brought into the place by those who came to visit the graves. A red tinge from a dupatta here, a green kurta, a dab of purple chador, a brightly-white cotton shirt, spotless like a new shroud. The earth here was dry, caky and cracking, gashed where the pressure from the countless heavy stone mounds had dragged it open. The ocher of the earth presented no other hue. The trees that bent over the crumbling graves in postures of despair, were thin and untended, their spindly branches forever bare and shriveled. Spring seemed not to touch them, even lightly. It was like a place forgotten. By time, by nature, by life. The tall brick wall that enclaved the cemetery and which half-stood and half-fell, as everything else did there, seemed to shut out nature's benevolence just as it shut out the living world.

Sakina Bano moved restlessly in her seat and let out a long sigh.

"Amma, are you all right?" Asad glanced at her anxiously.

"Yes, yes I'm all right," she lied. She wished she would be as fortunate as her husband. She longed to be buried like him in the cemetery where earth had lost color. Her father was also there and her mother, her uncles and also her grandparents. There, she would not be alone.

She was assailed by fear again. Words in your head are like dreams, no one knows of them except you, the dreamer. She must let her son hear the words that milled through her thoughts like a winter dust storm, thick, suffocating, cleaving through what stood in its path. She made up her mind.

"Asad?" she said casually, as if she were going to ask him about Fatima's husband, whether he had decided to go back to Pakistan after he finished his training, or whether the baby had begun teething.

"Yes Amma?"

"Listen, now don't get upset . . ."

"What is it? Are you feeling all right?" Asad slowed down and she thought he might stop. So much traffic around them, he might get into an accident. What a burden she was, and she wasn't even dead as yet.

"I said I'm fine, I just want to discuss something, now don't get worried." She patted his arm. "If something were to happen . . ." she increased the pressure on his arm as he opened his mouth to protest. "If, if something should happen, I want you to send me back to Pakistan." There. The words were now shaped, ponderous, no longer erasable.

"Amma, what kind of silly talk is this? Are you still carrying that absurd notion in your head? By God's grace you're healthy and there's no reason to suppose anything will happen." His tone was brusque. He was angry at her stubbornness.

"Don't get upset, son, you must understand, you can't get upset. I'm serious."
She pleaded tearfully.

He shook his head and chuckled. "Amma, Amma, what's the matter with
you? All right, I promise, I promise. Are you satisfied?" His eyes pinned on the
road, he continued to smile.

"I think you will have to buy two tickets."

"What?" He turned to her in amazement.

She continued. "Keep your eyes on the road. You might have to get a loan
because you need forty thousand rupees to send a body back to Pakistan, but
don't worry, I've got fifty saved in my account in Pakistan, and it's all yours."

Asad started to laugh, catching himself when she sniffled and tugged
at his sleeve.

"I said I am serious. Why are you laughing? Promise you won't bury me
in—what's the place called—Dan-bury." With a corner of her dupatta she wiped
the tears on her cheeks.

"I promise, Amma," Asad said in an apologetic tone.

"Promise you will take me home." She clutched her son's arm.

"Yes, I will," her son said earnestly, "I promise."

Sakina Bano blew her nose with her handkerchief and leaned back in her seat.
The strip of blue sky seemed to have vanished. The branches of trees formed a
crested canopy, hiding the sky from her. Feeling weightless, as if a cumbersome
burden she had been carrying all this time had suddenly dislodged itself, she shut
her eyes. Her thoughts, which only moments ago held her down like a chain of
steel, became amorphous and flew inside her head like a kite cut off from its
restraining cord, free.

Language

Sharmili Majumdar

Mother, you sing a song and I
understand it. Do you know
what that means?
I understand it, not
in translation, not having
to reformulate from your smooth
lilted Gujurati into my inflected
English and then back again
so you can grasp my words with
your small worn hands, can push aside
the vines of this foreign language
and understand me, the bark beneath.
You sing a song that I love,
that floats in my memory like the scent
of jasmine that you adore, like
the warm, rich, maroon fragrance
that is you. How often I grapple
with language, tangle myself
within the bramble of words
that catch, tear, won't let me
near you. How often. I still don't
know why I understand this song
without that thick, usually vital
process. You must have sung it
when I was young.

Kismet

Sanjay Kumar Nigam

Sometimes it isn't necessary to invent a story. Or even to spice it up. Take what happened to Hari Ram Shukla.

Hari had just finished complaining to his wife, Sarita, that Arizonan Mexican food was tastier than the appetizers they were munching on at an inexpensive restaurant in Mexico—a doubly foreign land, since they were green-carded Indians living in America vacationing at the as yet undeveloped Pacific coastal town of Mazatlan (where the locals thought them Mexican, which was sort of nice at first, except when one of the beachside vendors whom Sarita brushed off shouted back that he didn't believe they couldn't speak Spanish, that they too had once been like him before they became traitors and swam to the American side of the Rio Grande)—when Hari bit into the main course, trout, and made a nasty face at his wife.

To clarify, Hari made a nasty face at Sarita, right after he bit the trout.

"The food isn't that bad, is it?" asked Sarita.

"No, no, stupid, my tooth—I think I chipped it on a fishbone."

"Waiter!" called Sarita.

But the waiter was in the kitchen, sweating and panting, flat on his back atop the cutting table, bearing the weight of the owner's daughter, who was relishing his deflowering.

"Ah, here it is," said Hari. "No, not a bone at all. It's metallic. If the thing wasn't so lopsided, it could be a ring."

"Hari, it's gold!"

"Hmm, could be. Wait . . . It says something. FEVER YOU SIT."

"Must be Spanish. Put your glasses on, Hari. There are no pretty girls here. Better yet, give the thing to me."

Hari passed the object to his wife. Then he probed his teeth with his index finger. His tooth was slightly chipped, but it didn't hurt and he quickly forgot about it.

"Let's see," said Sarita, examining the object. 'Fever you' . . . what a nice piece of gold. 'Fever you' . . . Hari, you idiot!"

"What?"

"Hari, the words aren't FEVER YOU. They are FOREVER YOURS . . . Oh, my God, this can't be!"

"What? What? Sarita, what's wrong?"

"FOREVER YOURS, SARITA."

It is impossible to do justice to the expressions of disbelief that followed, which lasted long after the waiter, whose pants remained unzipped, delivered the bill and retreated with an enormous tip, thinking that nothing could possibly top off this day, the most incredible of his life—until he found the owner's daughter still lying naked on the cutting table in the kitchen, displaying her charms.

Unfortunately for the waiter, the girl's father returned earlier than expected, and the waiter was caught in flagrante delicto. But this episode became part of a very different story that had nothing to do with Hari and Sarita.

Twenty years before, while playing in the surf at the Indian beach resort of Goa, Hari's wedding ring slipped off.

He and Sarita were on their honeymoon, and that was the end of it.

For the rest of their married life, Sarita accused him of losing the ring on purpose. At parties, she jokingly referred to it as a Freudian slip.

Sarita had a sense of humor.

At parties.

As Hari moved well into middle age and beyond, he often reflected, especially on occasions of mild inebriation, that the lost ring was the first link in a sad concatenation of events that had made his life what it was.

This is not certain. Even less certain is what actually happened to the ring over the next twenty years, until that evening when it chipped Hari's upper right second molar.

Still, such a coincidence warrants speculation.

When it fell to the floor of the Arabian Sea, the ring might have slipped around a strand of seaweed. That strand might then have been eaten by a foolish fish that forgot to spit the ring out. The foolish fish might in turn have been eaten by a bigger, possibly not so foolish (just hungry) fish. And so on.

The food chain, relentless.

And yet it couldn't have just been fish eating fish. Currents must have been involved. And other aquatic mechanisms which moved fish from one current to the next, so as to translocate the ring from the Indian end of the Pacific to the Mexican; if they hadn't been in Mazatlan, but on the Atlantic side of the peninsula, say Cancun, it might be necessary to postulate fish capable of navigating the Panama Canal. Or a tropical storm with hundred mile an hour winds, capable of picking up fish on the Pacific side of Mexico and dropping them off on the Atlantic side.

On the other hand, a lone fish theory can explain almost everything—in principle. Imagine an adventurous marlin intent on exploring the world—the Magellan of marlins. Or a bohemian barracuda that kept switching currents just for the heck of it.

Highly unlikely.

Whatever happened, the ring eventually found its way into a fish befitting the man from whose ring finger it had once escaped.

A trout.

To get back to the couple, who were now in their oceanview hotel room, silent and still incredulous.

A pleasant breeze blew through their open window. Moonlight bouncing off the waves reflected in a mirror on the dresser. As usual, Hari and Sarita lay in separate beds. They listened to the midnight surf pound the beach, each fondly recalling the early days of their honeymoon—before Hari lost the ring.

Around one o'clock, Hari slipped under Sarita's sheets. They made love for the first time in years and slept in the same bed.

Hari dreamt of a mermaid.

She looked like Nargis, the Hindi film actress, all of whose films Hari had seen back in India. The mermaid had swum all the way from India only to make love to him. He was undoing his swimming trunks—while she splashed him playfully with her fins—when she noticed his ring.

"Stop!" said the mermaid. "If I knowingly make love to a married man, I will turn into a shark."

Hari swiftly stepped back and retied his swimming trunks.

And the mermaid swam back to India.

Upon waking just before dawn, Hari was cranky, suffering from the depression which comes from making love too intensely. Without showering, or even brushing his teeth, he went for a walk on the beach.

The sun was starting to rise behind the quiet city. But for a few homeless dogs, the beach was vacant. Fishing boats criss-crossed the horizon. The cool moist sand felt good on his bare feet. Hari sat upon a rock and gazed at the water.

He reflected upon a life of transpositions, an immigrant-melts-in-melting-pot story. And this particular story, though peppered by a few interesting moments, was otherwise fairly standard. The details of what Hari thought—the free-associative caroming of his mind through the past in search of some encapsulation which might constitute meaning—are really not worth delving into, except possibly for the repeated intrusion of fantasies involving a newly hired data processor at his office. She was at most twenty-three, conventionally attractive, with lots of spunk.

By eleven, the meaning of life still hadn't yielded to a headlong assault. Feeling uplifted nonetheless, Hari returned to the hotel.

In the afternoon, he and Sarita went to the old city, where they found a jeweler who hammered the ring back into its original shape and polished it. The ring looked better than it had twenty years before.

While she was getting ready to snap a photo of Hari sipping coconut water against the backdrop of a busy Mazatlan intersection near the jeweler's, Sarita suggested they make this their second honeymoon.

Hari thought for a moment, then said, "What the hell," in a neutral sort of way that could have been interpreted as "Sure, let's do it!" or alternatively, "You've got to be joking!"

Sarita took it to mean the former.

The photo, a Polaroid, came out fine.

It was the day before they were to leave Mazatlan. Hari, who had a passion for snorkeling—he listed it as his sole outside interest on his resume—persuaded Sarita they should hire a boat to an island off the coast, despite reports that the snorkeling there wasn't very good.

Recalling an experience in the Caribbean—where it was possible to see through fifty feet of water—Hari hoped to spy schools of bright green minnows, zebra fish, huge burnt-red corals, floppy violet jelly-fish. So, while Sarita sunned herself on the island's beach, Hari explored the water in full snorkel gear.

But the water off this tiny isle was very dirty. And instead of zebra fish and corals, Hari found nameless fish and rocks. They were grey and, like undershirts, came in three sizes: small, medium and large.

More adventurous than usual, Hari swam away from the shore. Here, the water was a bit clearer. But the fish and rocks were the same.

He had just started back when he spotted a jelly-fish, a giant convulsing polyp, a Portuguese man-of-war.

The creature was so beautiful he stopped to watch.

The jelly-fish stung him, twice, a tentacle whipping each leg.

The stings began to hurt. And now he saw three more jelly-fish approaching. He was trapped in a boot camp of Man-of-Wars!

Fear became panic. Hari swam full-speed toward shore. Halfway there, he felt the jelly-fish venom as it crawled into his groin, the unbearable pain. He curled up, desperately gasping for breath in the unruly ocean water.

He thrashed crazily, snorted a little water. He thought he was going to drown. Yet he was too breathless to cry out.

His life, which had already passed before him that morning while he sat on the rock, refused to make a rerun. He shut his eyes and silently uttered, "Om," as the family priest in India had once taught him to say in times of danger. On opening his eyes, he thought he saw the mermaid of last night's dream, but she vanished with his next gasp.

With a very Indian acceptance of kismet, Hari Ram Shukla was preparing to die when he suddenly realized that the pain in his groin had subsided. He had a mild cramp in his calf but was otherwise all right.

He composed himself, sighted shore and swam back.

He fell on the beach, exhausted, relieved.

Sarita ran up to him.

"What happened?" she asked. "Hari, are you all right? You're breathing so hard!"

Still gasping, he pointed to the red welts on both legs.

As soon as he caught his breath, he related his story. With his hands he described the size of the jelly-fish, exaggerating roughly three-fold. "And there were half a dozen of them!" he added.

But Sarita had apparently stopped listening. Hari was irritated, though he didn't make an issue of it. After all, they were on their second honeymoon, and he was fine now, and tomorrow they'd be heading back to the dry heat of Paradise Valley, Arizona. He had rediscovered the woman he married and, with a few minor qualifications, he loved her. And even though he was still a bit shaken, it was a wonderful afternoon, the air vaguely smelling of seaweed, sunlight dancing on the ruffled ocean for as far as he could see. Even further—perhaps all the way back to India.

"Hari?" asked Sarita in a voice so sweet he knew something was terribly wrong.

"What?"

He looked at Sarita's face. Her gaze was fixed on his left hand. Without glancing at his fingers, Hari rubbed his thumb against his fourth finger but did not feel the metal object he hoped was there. He was then seized by a visceral anxiety, worse than any he had experienced before. Suddenly the sun seemed to be burning holes through his retinas. Hari closed his eyes and had some complex thoughts—about fate and the pointlessness of it all—which eventually turned into a simple prayer.

Under the Gravity of Some Thirty Odd Years

Darius Cooper

The worst choice is always yourself
when poetry tempts you into
an enterprise of nostalgia and bile,
now that you have passed thirty
and are
a thousand miles away.

Searching
in a different land
for people
hidden
under the same subcontinent skin,
I am compelled to reinvent
my own silence.
These people seem determined
to ghazni everything Indian.

Short-pants and braces
were not the only icons
of my growing-up years
in the Saiyadri shadows
of a small town
balanced between
Peshwa and Cantonment.
The goddess of memory
has more than one arm
from which I accept
once again

circulating libraries and flowers,
picked up before they choked
in the oily hairs
of giggling schoolgirls;
baked breads
from Kyani Bakery
eaten slowly over weekends
when I went take my bisected self
and make it whole
before an empty cinema-screen.

A tall city:
the dowried improvisation
of fish goddess and Portuguese princess
came afterwards,
its frenzied turnstile crowds
pushing me
all over a defunct queen's
thirteen railway-platforms
where I tried to bait
the imaginary smiles
of all those sadfaced women
hurrying past me;
in yards and yards
—a colorful Draupadi blur—
of self-immolated sarees.

Reeling from the wrecks
strewn all over the metropolis,
I stumbled, often,
into the white absolute
of naked screens,
letting cinema's healing vocabulary
comfort my deranged soul.

And then suddenly the friends came
stepping out of the same film-frames.
Freeing our souls
from their academic wet-dreams
we chatted,
hanging every thought and image
on a projected beam of light
that slowly expelled the darkness.
Masters of our own mise-en-scène,
we developed our passions,
editing and framing our intimacies
through montage and dissolve.

Now I am separated by an ocean, and silence.

Ignorant
of my own land's
mud,
like a fish I had swum
all these years,
confused
at where the aquarium began
and the ocean ended.
Now,
standing on a pavement
of cleverly buried pieces of glass,
I rise,
straddle alien concrete,
and piss
on this whitewashed wall
defying cops,
defying fear,
content only

to define my proper place
under the gravity
of some thirty odd years.

Excerpt from

An Archive of Myself—
Dichotomized Between Three
Oppositions

Darius Cooper

1.
I was born between
a sea and a mountain-range.

From the sea I absorbed many stories
of white invaders who came
wet behind their ears
to our silent shores
of sun and vocal squabbles,
and enjoying for a time
the friendly latitudes
of an untutored generosity,
they plundered
city and village,
farm and forest,
room and closet,
to establish progressively
the hegemony of what
they called 'civilization.'

2.

My own voice hesitatingly emerged
between the rhythms of rock n' roll
and the bhakti beat of abhangas.
Posed like that calendar baby
near by uncle's Multitone Murphy radio
whose short-wave knobs
had to be constantly adjusted
by the skill of a
carefully placed rubber-band,
I listened late into the night
for the steady immigration
of shakes, rattles, and rolls,
all the way from Radio Ceylon.
Weekends found us static
on the waves and hums
of borrowed musical transfusions:
Wasn't Mohammed Rafi's "Meri Deena"
more original
than Paul Anka's "Diana"
now that Las Vegas had corrupted him?
Elvis only sang "Margarita" to Ursula Andress
when the bulls slept at Acapulco.
Our Rajendra Kumar's ditty to "Priya"
literally shook the whole asmaan.
Talat Mahamud's
"don't shower me with so much love
for I am like a cloud just a vagabond"
had Salil Choudary's Sa-related cyclic
thrashing the opening bars
of the giggling Amadeus's 40th in G Minor.
And when Dada Burman
borrowed Tennessee Ernie Ford's "Sixteen Tons"
and gave it to Kishore Kumar

to tinker with it in a garage
as he repaired Madubala's stalled car
that had stalled in the rain,
raindrops
no longer fell
on my head.
Elated I turned to the emaciated Dylan
and from his coffee-house pilgrimages
in Greenwich Village
he laid bare for me
suddenly at a babyblue sixteen
the lonesome death of my own mother
every ten days of the month
when the menses in her blood
transformed her into a "pollution,"
a pawn for her pious mother-in-law's
religious games
which banished her to the margins.
And, as I screamed:
"It's all right grandma, she's only bleeding,"
the old witch went on cleaning
her prized possessions of deities
with a zend-avesta enthusiasm.
Years later when she died
clutching the strangled neck
of the cockatoo
Susan Alexander Kane left behind
for Charlie at Xanadu,
my mother had to bathe
her stinking Haversham corpse
for the protesting dasturjees outside.
Then Leonard Cohen
stepped into my lonely room
and sat quietly in the corner

stitching his women's desires
to the roar of his own blood clots.
I welcomed him like a drunk
from yesterday's midnight choir,
and like a bird balanced on a wire
I was poised to take off
for the country of my dreams,
but when I landed on a hot humid day
in Philip Marlow's Los Angeles,
a third rate Hollywood actor
took over a first rate country
and turned it into a cheap commercial.

Immediately I lost my voice.
But not for long.
Dylan's steel harmonica
was now replaced by a pumpkin tambura,
and Tuka, Mira, and Kabir
dancing wildly on their bare feet
entered my devastated temple
and made a defiant God hurriedly leave
his appropriate place on the shrine
and sleep under my troubled breaths.
I could sit down and wrestle
with this tonguetied God,
and occasionally when God cheated
and no letters came from home,
and Indian grocery stores got torched or looted,
I would chastise this God and sulk.
And it was then that the Goddess emerged,
not from my God's repeatedly broken ribs,
but as an independent presence,
extending her glowing image towards me
through veils in which I sometimes

glimpsed a Marlene, a Diva, and a Durga.
Numbed by ambulance sirens and LAPD helicopters
searching for stolen cars at three in the morning
under a powerful searchlight
that exploded in my tiny room like a million artees,
I woke to Bhimsen, Kumar, and Kishori,
their hymns tinkling like anklets,
around the lost voices of last night's nightmares.
Tuka's ahanghas in Bhimsen's transparent swaras,
Mira's pranaams in Kishori's pure vessel of throat,
Kabir's dohas in Kumar's onelunged ulatbamsi awaaz,
broke the back of many a racial slur
that dripped down in venomous paint
from the wall opposite my tiny apartment.

And years later,
when my own Krishna's bloody head
emerged from my Mira's bleeding vrindavan wound,
a churchbell mysteriously rang out
from the red Jewish synagogue
thousands of miles away
in the cantonement town of Poona.
And then when the telephone rang
from the Christmas ward of Santa Monica,
one aged parent rushed to the balcony
towards that bell pealing for a star
while the other glued to the urgent
rings of a reach out reach out and touch
someone instrument of AT&T.
And in the halting voice
of their own son
who had emptied their courtyards
and dried up their garden
they saw the vocal formation
of their family's first grandson.

The Smells of Home

Sandip Roy

When she was seven years old Savitri's aunt visited from England. She brought her boxes of delicious chocolates filled with strawberries and hazelnuts and lots of pretty dresses. But what Savitri loved best was to bury her head in her aunt's suitcase and breathe in the fragrance of her clothes and cosmetics.

"Lavender, lilac, rosemary," she would whisper to herself making a daisy-chain of flowers she had never seen.

It was a scorchingly hot summer even by Delhi standards. In the afternoons her aunt would draw the blinds and take a nap. Savitri would tiptoe into the dark room and carefully open the suitcase. Then she would bury her head in the soft cottons and smooth silks and breathe deeply and surreptitiously. It was like a little corner of England trapped in there. She would feel herself falling through it and leaving the hot parched Delhi streets and the cruel blue Indian skies far behind. It smelled cool and fresh—so unlike the ripe kitchen smells that clung to her mother's sari—turmeric and sweat and stale talcum powder.

"Foxglove, primrose, daffodil."

She was now walking down a little cobbled street past houses like the picture on her tin of chocolates. She was going home to have scones and strawberries and cream. Her house had a pointed tiled roof and a chimney. And ivy on the walls or was it honeysuckle?

"Honeysuckle, bluebells, forget-me-not."

Crouched near the suitcase, like a little mouse, Savitri wished she could pack herself in with the soft nighties and synthetic saris. She imagined waking up and finding she was in England.

"Savi," her mother's shrill voice could be heard from downstairs. "Where is that girl? Savi, you haven't finished your rice. Come now or the cat will eat it up."

Savitri decided that when she grew up she would go to England.

Avinash was not quite from England. He was from New York. Well, not

New York, New York but some small university town in the northern part of the state where he was just finishing his Ph. D. in Economics or something like that. It all sounded very difficult to Savitri. She liked to read Wordsworth and Keats. Not even Byron—there was something too hot and sunny about Byron, something sinewy and dangerous seemed to lurk beneath his poetry. For her Keats and Wordsworth had a watercolor feel about them which she found very soothing. Their colors were more muted. Savitri had never liked bright harsh colors—pinks and oranges and yellows.

"Look at that girl," her mother would say. "Only seventeen and dresses like a widow."

Avinash seemed the perfect match for her. Serious, academic and sober—he didn't wear hot pinks and sunny yellows either.

"My son," said his mother to Savitri's mother over a cup of tea, "has always been the top boy in his class. 'A model student' his principal called him. Never one to wander the streets like these other roadside Romeos. That was why I never had the slightest fear sending him to America. You know Mrs. Dutt, it's all about upbringing and family. If you bring him up right, then why you should fear?"

Savitri's mother nodded wisely.

"Everyone told me," continued his mother, "See one day he'll call and announce he wants to marry some American girl. But I said 'I trust my Avi. He would not break his mother's heart.' Arre, he is my only son. He knows his duty. Ever since his poor father died I have brought him up by myself. It was not easy on a schoolteacher's salary. But I had faith and see him now. Do you know he has had papers published in important journals. Why, my friend Sulata said to me 'Look Bani, mark my words if your Avi does not get the Nobel Prize one day.' "

In the pause that ensued as all assembled digested this piece of information, Savitri's aunt jumped in.

"So how old is Avinash exactly?"

"Well," said his mother defensively, "he's thirty-three. But what's age in a man? My husband was eleven years older than me. I don't believe in all this same-age marriages that go on these days. You need some difference in age to maintain balance in the household. And tell me, how can you respect your husband if you are the same age as him?"

"I've been telling him for so long now—get married, get married. But he keeps saying, 'First I must finish my Master's.' Then it was, 'Oh I must complete my Ph.D. and get a job, Ma. How will I have a family on a student's income?' So responsible, no? The day he got his professorship I said 'Enough Avi. Now I have to see you settled down with a good girl. Then only can I shut my eyes in peace.' He said 'But I don't have tenure yet' and I said *'Bas.* I will not listen anymore to your excuses.' We are not running after looks in my family," she said glancing at Savitri who was a little plain. "Good family and education is what we value. Avi's father was a renowned professor you know—he wrote three books. And I hear your Savitri has an M.A. in English Literature."

Avinash took Savitri out for dinner once. He was a thin quiet man with thinning hair and owlish glasses. He smelt faintly of some lemony aftershave. They did not have much in common. She knew nothing about Economics, he had long forgotten his Wordsworth. They concentrated instead on the food and discussed the merits of the Tandoori chicken. When they exhausted that topic, they ate in silence listening to the ebb and flow of conversation at the tables around them.

"What was he like?" asked her mother.

"All right, I suppose," she answered. Though she had not found much in common with him she had not found anything objectionable either. At least he did not wear those loud colorful shirts with big flowers that she had seen American tourists wear.

Only once she said, almost wistfully, "You know I really wanted to go to England."

Her father laughed and said, "Savi, Wordsworth's England is long dead. In your grandfather's time people would go to England for then England still had power and glory. Now it is truly a nation of shopkeepers. And most of the shopkeepers are Indian anyway. You are lucky, you are going to the richest country in the world."

"And such a brilliant husband," added her mother.

"And so courteous and well-mannered," added her aunt "I hope my daughter is as lucky as you."

"Heather, daisy, larkspur," Savitri said under her breath, playing with the words as if they were prayer beads.

Savitri was amazed at how easily she left India behind. As the airplane left Delhi airport she looked out of the window at the lights of Delhi growing smaller and smaller. She had a sense of her past, her ties, her home all falling away behind her like an unraveling sari. "Perhaps," she thought sipping her Coca-Cola, "I was not meant to be Indian at all." She glanced over at Avinash, seated next to her, absorbed in the latest issue of *Time*. He glanced up at her and finding himself caught in her gaze looked away guiltily. Then he said quietly "How do you imagine America?"

"America—I don't know," she said wonderingly. "Big buildings, fast cars, movies."

"Washing machines," she added as an afterthought. "Lawnmowers, microwaves."

"You never thought of America as freedom?"

"Freedom?" she said perplexed "No, not really." Then she smiled slightly and said, "Maybe it was for you when you went there as a student. But I am going there as your wife."

"That's true," he replied.

"Are you afraid that now I am going with you, you will lose your freedom?" she asked half-teasingly.

"Who is really free anyway?" he answered without looking at her and returned to the magazine. She opened her mouth to speak but he seemed to have drawn curtains around himself.

Savitri hated America from the moment she stepped off that plane. The accents jarred her—they had none of the clean crispness of the BBC World Service programs she so loved and listened to on her father's prized short-wave radio. The freeways with their whizzing cars and many lanes terrified her. She could not imagine ever being able to drive on them. Yet Avinash had told her that if you did not know how to drive here you were a prisoner. She was confused by all the machines she needed to handle and all the buttons she had to press whether to get money from the bank or buy a roll of stamps. She got so confused once she ran away without taking the stamps. But most of all she missed having people to talk to.

Avinash spent long hours at school sometimes coming home after she had gone to bed. She would lie in the dark hearing the purr of the microwave as he warmed his dinner. Her mother always waited for her father to come home before she had dinner. But Savitri invariably got a headache if she let herself go hungry too long. She would leave his dinner on the table in front of the jar of Priya mango pickles. She would lie in bed and try and figure out what he was eating.

"He must be finished with the dal, he is probably on the chicken now." She would hear him open the refrigerator as he got some Coke. They needed to get more Coke and detergent and something else. She knitted her brows and tried to remember what. Soon she knew she would hear the tap running as he rinsed the dishes and then the clank of the dishes being loaded into the dishwasher. That was when she closed her eyes and turned on her side, away from his side of the bed. It was her way of punishing him for being late again. But he did not seem to mind. She would feel the bed sag as he climbed onto it. Then the sharp minty smell of toothpaste. In a little while she would hear his gentle easy breathing and she would lie awake angry, making grocery lists in her head.

Everyday she would run downstairs at two o'clock to check the mail. She had even come to know the postman. He always said, "Hi, how's it going?" But no one ever wrote to her. All she got were catalogs from department stores. She would spend the afternoon reading about furniture sales and installment plans to buy home entertainment systems. Apart from that all they seemed to get were bills and coupons from pizza-joints. She had written two letters home but had not gotten anything from India. Mail from India could take twenty days Avinash told her. Once she found a personal letter from India. In her excitement at seeing an Indian stamp she tore it open before she realized the letter was for Avinash. Though she did not read it he was very annoyed.

"I am your wife. We share the same bank account," she said.

"You don't understand," he replied, "letters are different. It could be, could be anything."

Savitri remembered the day she got her first letter. It had been raining all day—a fine dispiriting drizzle. She had wanted to walk down to the library but was stuck indoors since Avinash for some reason had left the umbrella in his office. Frustrated she had spent the whole day rearranging her spices. She had poured them into individual little spice-jars and then labeled the jars in her best handwriting. For a while she debated whether to write the Hindi names or the English ones—haldi, jeera, and dhania or turmeric, cumin, coriander? She finally decided on "Turmeric," "Cumin," "Coriander." But she did not know the word for methi so she left it blank. She smelt her hands—and suddenly remembered her mother cooking and then wiping her hands on her sari. Her old saris always had turmeric stains.

She wiped her hands on a paper towel and ran downstairs to get the mail. And there it was, a neat little envelope with Mrs. Mitra written on it in an almost childish uneven handwriting. She turned it over but there was no sender's name or address. The postmark was local. Puzzled she climbed up the stairs slowly trying to figure out who it was.

She put Avinash's mail on the dining table and pulled out the Kashmiri letter-cutter her friend Leena had given her and slit open the envelope. There was just one sheet in there—a yellow ruled sheet torn from a writing pad.

Dear Mrs. Mitra, (it said)

You don't know me but I have been dreading your arrival for months now. I have been your husband's lover for over two years now. I always knew I would have to keep it a secret but I didn't expect this. Avi says he is merely doing his duty and his mother would kill herself otherwise. Maybe that is so. I don't know too much about Indians. Avi never introduced me to his friends. I am no longer his lover. I couldn't bear the hypocrisy and I did not want to share. He thought we could carry on just as before except it would have to be at my place now. He can't understand why I would make such a fuss. After all, it had always been a secret from everyone else. Now we'd just keep it a secret from you too. Avi said, "It's not as if I promised to marry you or something." That's true, so why am I writing you this? Especially since I have broken up with him? I'd like to think I want to warn you and save you. But I think it's just my own vindictiveness and selfishness. I wanted to make him understand what he is doing to you and me. I wanted to hurt Avinash and the only way I knew how was through you. Forgive me if you can.

Sincerely,

John Elwood

She tore the letter up with shaking hands. Then she sat and put the pieces back together as if she could rearrange the words to say something else. Four times she lifted the receiver to call Avinash. Four times she put it down. She sat and stared at the neatly arranged spices and tried to remember the English for methi. Maybe she should just write methi. She wondered what would happen to her now. How much did a one-way fare to India cost? She sat and watched one television program after another letting the images drip meaninglessly in front of her. When Avinash came home she was already in bed.

"It's only nine o'clock," he said, "are you all right?"

She lay curled up on her side, her fists clenched in her mouth to prevent herself from screaming. She buried her face in the pillow and tried to summon up the old familiar smells of home.

"Turmeric, coriander, cumin," she whispered fiercely as if in exorcism.

But all she could smell was the happy lemon-lime spring-fresh smell of freshly laundered sheets. She buried her face deeper trying desperately to go home.

She felt him approaching the bed.

Mustard, poppyseed, methi. She was drawing a ring of spices to protect her.

She felt his hand on her forehead—cold and clammy. She shrank away from his touch.

Turmeric, coriander, methi.

Flies buzzing round her head.

Turmeric, coriander, methi.

Falling, falling, falling . . .

Her mother in the kitchen . . .

Her father reading the newspaper . . .

Old Sushila chopping the fish . . .

Haldi, dhania, methi

Haldi, dhania, methi . . .

Pitaji's Flute

Reena Sharma

After dinner on Tuesdays and Thursdays Pitaji plays the flute. His flute is made out of thin gold metal and the tip where he blows is red. It looks like a long tube of "Red Rose" pharmacy store lipstick.

Pitaji always plays crooked sounds at first. He tests the sounds, tooting high, tooting low, like a child learning to play for the first time. But when he finds the sound he likes, he sits up straight, holds his head at an angle, and his fingers fly over the holes that look like watermelon seeds. Then the most beautiful music comes out. It is the kind of music you might hear in a forest when the sun hides behind trees, when the cows rest under a shady mango tree, when the hibiscus bloom pink and red.

When I hear Pitaji's flute, I think of Krishna, the boy blue god. I think Pitaji must have been like Krishna when he was a boy, before he grew up, before he came to America and found a factory job cutting shelf boards with two breaks and a half-hour lunch. Pitaji must have teased the village girls with his music, and made them believe in love and fairies and sweet milk with ghee.

Sanju and I sit on the floor with folded legs. Our fingers rest against our chins as we gaze up at Pitaji with love-filled eyes and pretend that he is our boy-god Krishna. In our pretending, we forget that he is our father with the sand-paper-rough fingers and hairy arms. We forget the melon-smooth bald spot on the top of his head. We forget that he has to get up at six o'clock in the morning and wait for Singh to pick him up on the main road by the dented stop sign. All we see is the sunlit hibiscus forest growing in our living room and a boy loving his flute with his fingers.

When Pitaji finishes a song, we squeal with laughter. "Play the one about the woman who was too tall for her husband and so he used her as a ladder to fix the holes in the roof!" Sanju cries out. Pitaji laughs and begins again. We slap our knees and bob our heads in rhythm to his flute. The house is filled with music.

Amma is in the kitchen. Every once in a while she looks out and reminds us that it is getting late.

At ten o'clock, the flute goes back into the cupboard next to the Corn Flakes. Amma has finished packing the next day's lunch. Sanju finishes braiding her hair. And I still have two long division problems I don't understand.

We tiptoe to our rooms and slide into bed.

The house is quiet without Pitaji's flute.

Mother in Iowa, 1969

Minal Hajratwala

She sleeps, one foot beyond the covers, as if she could step off sleep, and run. But the cold is a demon that tugs at her toes, that pulls on her temples like forceps at a birth, steel slipping over blood.

She buys soups that taste like the cans they come from: vegetable lentil, split pea with ham, chicken noodle, smooth creamy tomato. Even adding tabasco and parsley, it is the cheapest meal. 40 cents a can condensed, no beef broth.

The groceries grow heavy as she crosses the bridge. New blue boots rise to her knees, thermal windbreaker material with serious soles of rubber tread like tires. It is icy, she is paying attention to her feet and their capacity for friction against the glaze. She can feel the sharp white beauty of the creek, frozen months now, and the white fields from which the married-student barracks rise, aluminum and gleaming, icicles hanging from their sheaves like knives, which she must call home.

Stirring, she thinks, at least it is not the train. The kitchen car served only beef bouillon. She forced it down and it forced itself back up, her Hindu body raging at the sacrilege. She ate potato chips, then learned they were fried in lard. It was three days to the interior, the heartland of snow and corn and ruddy smiling women who look as if they've sprung from Betty Crocker's cookbook.

She pastes contact paper to empty Crisco cans and knows she is learning the lessons left out by the Methodists, who teach young island girls to set tables and sew baby dresses, men's pants and fauxsilk ties. There are many lies of omission. She has grown two inches since her wedding day and is taller than him now.

He says it's the homogenized D-fortified milk of this country that makes the bones strong and long. But she knows it is the rush of hormones and homesickness that overtake her in the night, afterward, as she tries to match her breaths to his snores. It is the longest winter in memory, everyone says. The store clerks shake their cheeks and grin, the co-workers at the hospital complain as they stomp their boots at coarse mats just inside glass doors. And she writes letters home in missionary script, "It is the coldest winter in memory, everyone says. I am improving my English. We send our love."

As if love were a thing to be packaged and shipped off, she thinks. Wrapped in brown paper and trussed with yellow nylon rope, to the opposite side of the globe, to a land of snow queens and wolverines, footballs and sausages, the rank smell of beef everywhere. If she has questions, she does not write them. She will have children here, and teach them everything she knows.

Counting the Ways

Sejal Shah

The way her arm shoots out
when she is driving
and has braked too quickly
and too hard;
placing her self between me
and the world hurtling by
outside the windshield.

The way we share long hands,
the same strong, ivory nails and
two years of painful piano lessons.
Her knuckles purpled from having
held things together—from having
held me; her knuckles are knotted
knobby, swollen and purple
from scraping the bottoms of pots.

The way my change purse has grown
to look like hers—a broken handle
torn receipts, loose change
a rusty barrette, always open;
catching in my fingers when I search
for a pen or for a quarter.

The way we both have grey hair
but you cannot see it:
hers hidden under a thin layer
of Loving Care, mine approaching

in single, silver wires.
The way she will not accept my
disapproval or my reclamation
of her surname as hers.
They were both Shahs
before their marriage;
I want my name to be
the equal convergence of two
lives. She tells me she would
have changed her name if there
were anything to change it to.

The way she will not fall asleep
waiting up for me to return,
one hand clutched at her throat
smelling of cocoa butter cream.
And her cat eye-glasses,
they have slipped to one side
leaving an imprint around
her red eyes. The book she is
reading lies open, but it is written
in a language I cannot read.

Burning Turtles

Hema N. Nair

Asha Rao swung into the shopping center, sneaking a glance at the curve of road leading up to the drive-in bank. A blue Dodge van was pulling out of the empty second lane. If I move fast, she thought, pressing the gas pedal, I can get there before they close. A few seconds later, she pulled up, rolled down the window and reached for the red box wedged between the slot. Was the teller gesticulating at her?

"We are now closed. Sorry."

The words were squawked into the evening in a sharp, irritated voice. Closed? The clock on the dashboard blinked 5:58. Closed with two minutes left? Shaking her head in vexation, Asha thrust her checks into her pocketbook and drove off. I shouldn't have spent those fifteen minutes discussing the kidney case with Saunders, she thought ruefully. Why can't I be more methodical? Here I am on a Friday evening, with a nice drive to Connecticut on Saturday facing me. Why didn't I go out at lunch-time to finish all my regular weekend chores? Now she would have to leave extra-early on Monday morning, which meant asking Annette if she could come in early and take Mira to school . . . Repressing a sigh, Asha switched on her lights, and pushed in the Subbalakshmi tape.

The slow rhythm of the slokas snaked their way to the back of her mind. Amma had sent her the tape a year ago with instructions to play it at sandhya, when the lights were turned on in the house. "Do you play it every evening?" She would enquire unfailingly during their weekly phone conversation. "It will bring auspicious happenings into your life. I know you are blind to such things but nowadays even your highly educated Americans have begun to believe in the power of mantras and things." Asha, who was rarely home before seven, when all the lights in her three-bedroomed townhouse were blazing, had taken to playing the tape in her car, driving home from work. That way she wouldn't be lying to her mother. The car was a home, she reasoned, waiting for a gap in the traffic to merge into the smooth-running river of red lights, a caravan of leather and chrome with windows that revealed the world as it carried them between destinations. Some nights, driving in the dark with nothing visible except the length of road illuminated by the headlights, Asha was grateful for the silent companionship of others moving alongside. She was not just a pair of hands steering towards an invisible future. The flicker of signals as cars switched lanes were cheerful winks of recognition.

"Shall we take your car or mine on Saturday?" Manoj had asked as they were eating dinner at Mughal Palace on Sunday, and then looked puzzled at the smile that began to widen across her face. "What did I say? Was that so funny?"

"It just struck me," she had explained, laughter bubbling up, "that your question is a new variation of the line your place or mine."

"Well, Asha, if you find my most ordinary queries so full of humor," he had countered, signalling to their waiter for the bill, "I predict a brilliant future for us."

It had been his first declaration of a common goal. His words had stayed with her, till she dropped off to sleep, like the unconscious humming of a catchy jingle.

Manoj Kapoor. A well-built, fairish Punjabi with a genial laugh and sharp eyes behind round-rimmed spectacles. His habit of stroking his thick moustache with one hand, in between sentences, gave his words a nice air of judicious authority, she had decided at their first meeting two months ago at the Aggarwal's annual summer barbecue. Over chilled beer for him and iced tea for her, they had chatted. It was the usual kind of small talk between strangers at such gatherings. How long had they been in the U.S., what did they do? How did they know the Aggarwals? The normal route to discovering the subtext behind the casual queries: the other's social and economic status. The length of time in the U.S. meant that you either had a greencard/citizenship or were working towards one. The kind of job showed the quality of lifestyle you could afford, and intimacy with the Aggarwals revealed whether you belonged to their exclusive circle of friends or was just a one-time visitor, invited as a favor for some service or the other. In their North New Jersey circle, the Aggarwals, with their millions invested in every type of business from Indian restaurants to television shows to computers, were the desi Rockefellers.

Asha had been amused at Manoj's expert handling of each question so that, instead of being the pointblank inquest it usually was, it came out as a warm desire to getting to know her. Mira had run up to her in the middle of their conversation to demand breathlessly if she could go with the others into the swimming pool, please, please. "Yes, but remember darling, only at the shallow end," Asha had cautioned, pulling out the swimsuit she had brought along for Mira. Claudine, the Aggarwals' quiet, efficient French nanny, had come up to collect Mira and assured Asha in her precise, delightful accent that she would be there to keep an eye on her daughter.

"Daughter?" Manoj's eyebrows had climbed up almost to his slightly receding hairline. "I didn't even think you were married."

"I'm not," Asha could not resist replying with the dismal lack of tact that her sister Lata said prevented her remarrying. But Manoj had not reacted with the usual expression of frozen shock displayed by Indian men, followed by a calculating survey of her body with a lingering glance at her bust. Manoj, his smile easy and friendly, had waited with the expectant look that said he was ready for the punchline.

"I'm divorced," she had admitted a little lamely, aware of her first flicker of genuine interest in this man.

"That makes two of us." He had shrugged, with a chuckle, and taken out his wallet to show a picture of his twelve-year-old son. His ex-wife and son lived with her parents in England, he told Asha. No mannerless pressing for details of her marriage, no curiosity whatsoever about her former husband's whereabouts, no follow-up questions about how she managed with a small daughter alone in the world. The long sigh that she expelled seemed to loosen the knot that had gathered inside her stomach one July afternoon, three years ago, when her lawyer, supportive, avuncular, Mr. Ghosh, with a wife and three adult children, had turned to her and said, "Well, the divorce is final and you're free of that man. Now how about some tea? And, as a single lady, you can turn to me for any kind of manly advice, you know. I am always free to drop in during the evenings . . ."

There had been no mistaking the leer in his eyes. Asha had stood there thinking of his pretty, placid wife, cozy and decorative as a colorful quilt, and his two brown, wholesome daughters. Did they ever glimpse the aging satyr behind the paunchy, affable husband-father?

"Thank you, Mr. Ghosh." She had forced a smile, a pleasant tilt of lips that ignored anything unpleasant in his tone or look. "I'll be okay. I have Mira to prevent me from feeling lonely." It had become her standard response to any man who offered, in veiled and not so veiled terms, to fulfill her sexual starvation.

But Manoj had stepped neatly across that barrier by not acknowledging it at all. He called her up, a few days after the barbecue, punctiliously telling her that Mrs. Aggarwal had given him her phone number, and asked her out for coffee on Friday night. "If you don't have a reliable babysitter," he had forestalled, "maybe we could meet Saturday afternoon?"

Saturday she was going to Lata's house for lunch, Asha had hesitantly begun to say and Manoj promptly invited himself, "If your sister doesn't mind, of course. I'm very good at washing dishes."

Lata had unabashasedly approved of him. Late at night she telephoned Asha for one of their week-end marathon talk-with-coffee-sessions. "So mature, so confident, so reliable," she had exclaimed. "Did you see the way he was so patient with Mira?"

"Don't make him out to be such a paragon," Asha had giggled, lighted-headed with the late hour and the amount of caffeine she had drunk. "For all you know, he's probably a secret drinker."

But Lata had not been amused, had not joined in with another outrageous suggestion. "Now Asha, don't take that negative tone. Manoj is that rare find— a good, kind man, and eligible. If you encourage him . . . who knows?"

They had met again the following weekend. Manoj took her out to lunch. Mira had gone for a birthday party and had to be picked up at four, giving them plenty of time to have a leisurely feast at the week-end brunch offered by The Blue Peacock, an Indian restaurant offering rich, spicy Punjabi cuisine. Manoj had sat back with a replete sigh, savoring the steam from the cup of masala chai in front of him.

"They really make good food here—delicious and tasting exactly like my grandmother used to make," he commented. "I love coming here," Asha agreed. "In fact, I've got people at work hooked onto Indian food by bringing them here."

"How's work? Are you happy?"

"Oh yes," Asha smiled. "I love it. After years of doing nursing, it's fun to tackle problems from an administrative point of view."

"Do you miss seeing patients? Talking to them?"

"Sometimes," Asha admitted. "But I don't feel I've lost touch entirely. It's just that now I work behind the scenes to see to their comfort."

"Well, as a vice-president, that's quite a responsibility," he had laughed.

It still could cause a tremor to run through her. She, a vice-president. The enormous raise in salary she had got used to very quickly. There was something about the security of having money that lulled you into forgetting how one lived and feared with a thin bank balance. But the title outside her door in elegant brass still surprised even after a year, still made her feel she was an interloper, as she let herself into the office.

"I haven't got used to it," she had replied. "By the time I have, it'll probably be time to retire."

"Or be promoted to president," he had added promptly, at which Asha had to clap her hand over her mouth to stop spraying the coffee all over the table.

"Manoj," she had gasped, "thanks for almost choking me."

"Why? Do you think it's so impossible? Your company will never raise a woman, that too an Indian, to that position?"

"I don't think my being Indian will come into it," she had said hesitantly. "I've . . ."

"Never encountered racism? The glass ceiling?" His eyebrows had done their now familiar arch.

"Not never . . . I mean, the company is quite open to non-whites in senior management positions. I am the first Asian-Indian woman to get a middle-management post and I don't know about the future." She frowned into her coffee abstractedly and then looked up with a firm nod. "But outside, I have. Racist remarks and behavior, I mean. Not overtly you know? Like, when I used to exercise in the gym at the YWCA, people always talked to me slowly, with a lot of hand gestures at first. The white people, I mean," she explained, thinking of the day she had pulled out *The New York Times Book Review* section as she used the bike and the sudden cessation of that annoying talking-to-a-Third-World-illiterate behavior.

"That sort of thing happens all the time," Manoj shrugged. "No, I meant because of who you are, at the workplace. Have you never encountered the slight put down, the calm correcting of a word, that you haven't pronounced American-style like pronouncing SUNY as sunny, instead of soony?"

Asha thought for a second, her eyes crinkling with the effort to remember, "No. I can't really remember. Anyway, I decided long ago that I would stick to my accent and pronunciation and continue to say herb tea instead of erb," she laughed. "And to keep my name and not Anglicize it to Amy or something. If I can learn how to say Herman Schmidt, they can learn how to say Asha Rao."

"Herman Schmidt . . . an old boy friend?" Manoj had enquired with mock suspicion.

"My car mechanic," Asha had replied demurely.

The memory of of how Manoj had thrown back his head and laughed still brought a smile to her lips. Reaching up to activate the remote, Asha slowed down and watched the garage door slowly rise up. Mira must have heard the car. Asha could hear the excited shrieks of Mummy, Mummy, punctuated with hysterical barks from Candy, the six-month-old golden retriever.

"Mummy I made pay dough, green pay dough."

"Did you? What a clever girl!" Asha gathered up her daughter and snuggled her nose under the warm, soft neck. "Hmmmm . . . somebody smells good."

"Canny too, Canny too," giggled Mira, pointing down at the streak of golden and white fur still furiously circling them. So Asha bent down and picked up the dog with the other hand and stood there with an armful of child and dog wriggling energetically in their efforts to kiss and lick her. Putting them down finally, she turned to smile at Annette, already buttoned into her jacket with pocketbook slung over her shoulder. She rarely stayed beyond a few minutes once Asha was home.

"Good evening, Annette."

"Hello Asha," she nodded pleasantly. "We've had a good day. Mira did coloring and watched *Charlotte's Web*. After her nap we all went off for a walk with Candy. Then we came back and made play dough. Goodnight little one, be good." Bending down to give Mira a quick hug, Annette left.

Other people seemed to be good friends with their babysitter, thought Asha with a sigh, as she locked the front door. But Annette had resisted every friendly overture with a noncommittal smile or word. She was very good to Mira though, and was genuinely fond of her, judging by the way her daughter raced to hug Annette every morning.

"Come on, sweetie, time to have dinner and a bath," Asha bent down to lift her daughter from the floor where she was strenuously combing Candy with the brush she had taken out of her pocketbook. "Ugh, dog hair again?" Grimacing with exaggerated disgust, Asha cleaned the brush and pretended to spank Mira's bottom with it. Mira shrieked and ran around the house, with a delighted Candy charging behind. Asha began to chase after them, growling in mock anger. By the time she had managed to persuade her daughter to eat the standard Friday dinner of a slice of spinach pizza and french fries, given her a bath and read "Goodnight Moon" five times and "The Very Hungry Caterpillar" three times, Asha could barely walk into her bedroom. Washing her face carelessly, she reached for the cotton nightgown hanging on the bathroom door and dropped into bed. 'Do parents ever manage to watch TV or read?' she thought for the nth time, switching off her lamp.

The sparkling splash of morning sun in her eyes woke Asha up as usual and she stretched with delicious ease. A wonderful, unhurried Saturday ahead, she thought with a sleepy smile and then sat bolt upright. This was the Saturday Manoj and she were going to drive up to Connecticut for that barbeque party the Mehras were giving to celebrate the opening of their New York restaurant! And she had to get Mira ready to be dropped off at Lata's for a picnic. Panic-stricken, Asha jumped out of bed and ran into the bathroom. Half-an-hour later, dressed in jeans and a green velour tunic with her damp hair wrapped up in a old, fraying towel, she was coaxing Mira to eat her breakfast and chopping the lettuce for the sandwiches she had promised to send along for the picnic.

"I want pancake," her daughter's round black eyes stared at her mother's back accusingly. "No egg."

"Not today, honey. Tomorrow I'll make them. Promise." Asha turned to give Mira a conciliatory smile which quickly dissolved into a sigh as she encountered her daughter's unsmiling face. Oh god, please don't let her get into one of those sulky moods, she prayed. I don't want Manoj to walk in and see her like this. What did it matter, Asha chided herself. What if Manoj did see her with that cross expression? What difference did it make? But it did, a voice in her mind reminded. You want Manoj to like her. You want him to love her . . . Hurriedly, pushing away the insistent, urgent thought, Asha reached up to get hold of the cocoa tin. "Guess what? Mummy is going to make you hot chocolate with marshmallows!" Asha held up the tin triumphantly. A grudging smile began in her daughter's eyes. Hot chocolate with marshmallows was a treat she got very seldom.

The melodious peal of the doorbell rang through the house and Asha ran to open the front door. It was Manoj, beaming in a freshly-ironed blue T-shirt and khaki chinos. "Good morning! Ready for the fall-appreciation day?"

"Oh, hello Manoj, we are almost ready. Mira's got to finish her breakfast. I was just about to make some hot chocolate for her," Asha breathlessly held up the tin and then feeling foolish, put it down quickly. He must think her an unorganized, unpunctual idiot.

"Why don't I do that? And you can go and dry your hair," he neatly took the tin from Asha and flicked a finger at her towel-turbaned head. She had forgotten about that! Blushing, Asha followed him into the kitchen.

"Mira's a little cranky this morning," she whispered, tugging open the towel from her damp hair. "I was just making the chocolate as a treat."

"Cranky children are my specialty," he announced solemnly. "Now let me see, where did I put my smile medicine?" Patting his pockets with increasing anxiety, he stood in front of Mira, pulling out a wallet, a white handerkerchief and a set of keys and staring at them with mingled anger and bewilderment. Seeing her daughter burst into giggles and Candy bark encouragingly, Asha relinquished her family to Manoj and raced up the stairs to the bathroom. Through the whine of her dryer, Asha could hear the sound of laughter coming from the kitchen below and smiled at her reflection in the mirror. Everything was going to be all right. Brushing her now dry, gleaming hair into its customary, shoulder-length bob, Asha wondered if she should wear any make-up. A touch of pink lipstick and a thin eyeliner, she decided, and leant forward to rummage through her dressing table. Where was that Clinique lipstick that went with practically anything she wore? Turning to see if it was on the bedside table, she caught a glimpse of the time on the clock. Oh no, it was nearly nine. Manoj had wanted to start by 8:30 and they still had to drop off Mira. Forget the make-up. She grabbed a pair of sneakers from the closet and knelt down to tie them. Was that Candy making that squealing sound?

"Asha, we're all done," Manoj called. Asha switched off the lights, unplugged the dryer and ran down the stairs.

"I'm all done too," she smiled. Manoj and Mira were standing in the hall, hand in hand. There was a faint brown stain around Mira's lips but Asha decided to ignore that.

"Hi honey! Finished your milk?"

"She had all of it," Manoj replied. "Didn't you, beta?" He's calling her beta, Asha's heart thumped suddenly, as if she had run down a few flights of stairs instead of a few steps.

"Hot, Mama. Hot choc. . . . Canny too," said Mira, looking up at her mother with the confused look her face wore when the giraffe puzzle would not fit into the zebra-shaped hole.

"Did Candy want a lick too, sweetheart? So how did she like her first taste of chocolate?" asked Asha, sweeping up her daughter and reaching for the foil-wrapped sandwiches. "Where's my pocketbook?" she muttered.

"Behind the sofa," Manoj pointed out. He reached for it and together they walked out.

"Bye Candy!" Asha looked around for the dog. Normally, she would have been running around their legs, trying to slip past the door and into the car. She adored sitting on the back seat with Mira and going for rides.

"Canny, hide, Mama." Mira told her, chuckling."Canny, hide."

"Really? Is she playing peekaboo?" Asha slipped her into the childseat and remembered the diaper bag, bulging with training pants, juicepacks, toys and a change of clothes. "I'll be back in a sec," she told Manoj and rushed back into the house. The bag was on the counter. Swinging it on her shoulder, she quickly checked the kitchen. Coffee maker and toaster unplugged and the sink clean with all the cups and plates draining on the rack. He's neat too, she told herself approvingly and headed for the door.

"Bye, Candy!" she called out again, hoping the crazy puppy would realize that the hide-and-seek game was over.

In the car, Manoj was sitting on the driver's seat and regaling Mira by hanging his head, sticking his tongue out and panting loudly. Mira was laughing, head thrown back, with the front row of little teeth enchantingly white against the rosy lips. "What's the game?" Asha asked.

"Oh, it's called drink your chocolate," Manoj answered, turning around and starting the car. "You don't mind if I drive?"

She was the only one who had ever driven that car, but Asha nodded. After all, he knew the way to Connecticut and the house they were going to, she told herself. They barely had time to deposit Mira into Lata's car, tell her they would be back by nine latest, give Mira a last hug and then speed towards the Garden State Parkway.

"Lovely morning, Manoj commented. "Crisp and fresh like mint chutney."

Asha nodded, her mouth salivating at the thought of biting into a sandwich spread with butter and green, cool mint chutney. "I should have made us some sandwiches too," she said apologetically. "I'm sorry about this morning—everything was so rushed. You must think me very unorga-"

"Don't be silly, Asha." He turned to give her a quick smile. "I think you are wonderful. It can't be easy being a career woman and a mother and to run a house, all by yourself. Lata told me how you never got any help from Pra- Mira's father." So Lata and he had talked and her sister had not even told her. Asha tried to ignore the spurt of anger that rose. The silence lengthened and Asha began to feel uneasy. Was her resentment obvious? Was it going to spoil the day, their friendship, everything?

"Do you want to talk about it?" His voice was quiet, almost absent-minded. But Asha had no doubt as to the meaning behind his query. It had come. The question that Asha knew she would have to answer some day. Manoj had never raised it, had always behaved as if he never even thought about her former marriage or her ex-husband. His silence, his calm acceptance that the present alone was important had lulled Asha into forgetting that such relevations were required, were part of any new relationship that were being created. Her security was also compounded by the fact that she had had no curiosity at all about Manoj's former marriage and had resisted every urge on Lata's part to find out about it. That's his past, she had told Lata stubbornly, why should I know about it? It was enough that they met frequently, ate out together, took Mira to the park, to the bookshop, to visit Lata and enjoyed each other's company in a relaxed, non-threatening, companionable way. What had she expected? That one day they would stand before the registrar and then drive off into the sunset with Mira and Candy? Starting anew on a clean slate without reading the lessons that had already been imprinted? Before the past got ruthlessly rubbed out, it had to be understood first. Well, the past was now being unearthed, like a coffin slowly arising from the depths of its dark, lumpy nest.

"There is very little really," she began in a small voice. "It was an arranged marriage. Prasad seemed pleasant and mild-mannered. Our horoscopes matched and so I agreed to my parents' wishes and married him. It was only when I came to join him in the U.S. that I discovered his temper. And his violence when his anger was aroused. I had a broken elbow, and several cuts on my head in the one year that we stayed together. When I was pregnant with Mira, one night he kicked and pushed me outside our apartment. It was in 30-degree December weather, and I was only wearing a thin cotton nightgown. That night I left him." Asha's fingers curled tightly as she remembered the freezing misery of that decision. "I called Susan from a pay phone and she picked me up. She was an Australian nurse who worked with me, and she agreed to let me stay till I found a place to rent," Asha said softly. "Susan also called the police who arrested Prasad and kept him under lock-up for a night. Prasad was so incensed that I had humiliated him by letting the neighbors see him being led out in handcuffs that he initiated divorce proceedings. Asha let out a long sigh and turned to look at Manoj. "I've never seen him again. I heard he had migrated to England. "

"Lata and her husband migrated here a few months later," she continued after a pause. "They had been planning to come for months and it was a real godsend. I lived with them until Mira was born," Asha said softly. "By then, I had saved up for the down payment for this house and could afford a baby-sitter for Mira."

"Gosh, Asha I never knew . . ." Manoj's voice dwindled away. "What you must have gone through. And Prasad never asked you to return, to see Mira?"

"No. Never." Asha turned to him. "Can we talk of something else now?"

"Sure. Sure." Manoj turned to smile understandingly at her. "We should be there in two hours. Do you want to go to the restroom or something?"

Asha shook her head and forced herself to look at the handwritten paper that Manoj was handing her. "Here are the directions. As soon as we exit from the Mass turnpike, could you navigate? There are some tricky turns then."

And so they drove swiftly on, the map fluttering in her hand to the accompaniment of Ravi Shankar's *Megh Malar* playing on the tape deck.

They found the street easily enough and came to a slow halt at the last house on the street. A long line of cars were parked around the curving edge of road which rose in a smooth, green carpet of grass to a white stucco house.

"This is it," Asha pointed. "17 Maple Avenue."

"Wow, the Mehras are really doing it big," Manoj whistled, edging their car to a neat stop behind a blue Toyota Camry. "There must be at least twenty cars here."

"And more on the driveway," Asha observed. "This must be some business venture."

"The Mehras have the money," Manoj shrugged. "His computer company alone netted almost seven million last year, I heard."

Inside, the crowd of people spread out over the house and the swimming pool outside made Asha think she was attending a traditional wedding in India. The men were dressed for the most part in brand name jeans and Lacoste T-shirts. But many of the women had indeed dressed up as if for a wedding. Standing in the foyer, watching them flit by in their shining salwar kurtas and saris like bright butterflies, Asha felt embarrassingly conspicuous in her jeans. Why hadn't she realized that this would be a formal party?

"Hello, Manoj. And Asha. Welcome!" Their hostess, shimmering in a silvery white silk kurta and carrying a tray piled with crystal glasses, walked up to them with a wide smile. Her eyes slid over Asha and still kept the smile. "How cool and fresh you look, my dear," she cooed, her shocking pink lipsticked lips stretching wider.

Asha could only smile back lamely. Hours later, she felt as if the smile had been stitched to her face like threads tautly held between a loom. Almost all the people here were strangers. Most of them were accountants, like Manoj, or business people. Their world was starting companies in India, investing in sheep farms in Australia or buying onyx tables to decorate their marbled houses. The women were friendly in a polite, dismissive way, as if some inner radar had signalled that Asha was worth only an empty smile and a lifeless hello. Bored, struggling with her desire to go home, she sprang up gratefully when Manoj asked her if she would like to go for a walk. They stepped out onto the patio to an air rich with the scent of hearted charcoal grills and searing meat.

"Hmmm. That makes me feel hungry," Manoj said, sniffing the aroma appreciatively. "Wonder when they'll serve lunch."

"Probably in an hour," Asha responded. "Should we just walk around?"

"Let's go see the lake the Mehras are always boasting about," Manoj suggested.

"They have a lake on their property?" Asha was impressed.

"Well, they don't own all of it. Just the bit that skirts their land. All the houses on this street back onto it, I believe. Ah, there it is." Manoj stretched out an arm towards a gleam of blue peeking at the bottom of the lawn. They walked along the smooth expanse of green, their footsteps leaving soft, brief imprints before the grass sprang up again.

"How do you know the Mehras?" Asha asked curiously.

"I knew them in Delhi when I went to college with Anil Mehra. They are nice people. Filthy rich of course, but not snobbish about it."

You evidently didn't get the head-to-toe X-ray from Mrs. Mehra, thought Asha with an amused smile. They had reached the edge of lawn which descended in a steep slope to meet the silvery blue waves lapping gently in the sun. "Beautiful." Asha breathed deeply. "Imagine waking up to this every morning."

"It is very nice," Manoj agreed. "The water must be too cold now. In the summer its great to go in for a swim."

"Let's go down and wet our toes anyway." Asha began to climb down. "It'll be fun."

"Okay. But not from here, Asha. There are steps leading down to a small sandy shore, beyond that clump of trees. We can sit on the sand and be comfortable." But on reaching the beach, they found a group of people there, huddled over something near the water. Crumpled paper plates and empty beer bottles were strewn around.

"Hello, Art!" Manoj called. A teenage boy with purple hair and a single earring dangling like a silver streak of lightning turned and came forward with a grin.

"Hi! Manoj. The adult party got too boring, huh?"

"We just came down to see the lake, son." Manoj put an affectionate arm around him and turned to Asha. "This is Arjun, Asha. He is the Mehra's elder son and has renamed himself Art."

Asha resolutely kept her eyes from the hair and smiled warmly. "Hello! I hope we're not intruding on your party? We just came to dip our toes in the water."

"You're welcome to do so. Just have to wait your turn, I guess," Art said with a laugh. He gestured to his group of friends still absorbed over something on the sand.

"What are they looking at? Crabs?" Manoj asked.

"Not crabs, turtles," a slim girl wearing a long black and white striped T-shirt called out. "There are a pair of cute turtles here."

Asha strode forward to bend down and stare in fascination at the two lumbering brown, oval-shaped creatures moving clumsily towards the water. Their short front feet could barely push the sand. "Poor things." Asha said sympathetically turning to Art. "I hope they aren't scared by all of us looming over them."

"Not these guys," Art shrugged. "I've seen 'em for years now."

"Watch out! That one's heading in your direction, Art," a girl in pink shorts giggled. "I think he's coming over for a nibble."

"Turtles don't have teeth," Art replied carelessly. "These are box turtles. Watch, guys. This is their disappearing act." Scooping some sand he poured it in front of one of the turtles. Immediately it withdrew its head and limbs into its shell and was immobile.

"Oooh! That was terrific," the girls clutched each other and laughed. " Like a magic trick."

"Let's see the other one do it too," a tall thin boy in a blue T-shirt poured two handfuls of sand in front of the second turtle. After a second's hesitation, it too slowly crept under its shell.

"Wow! That was great." The girl in the black and white T-shirt turned to Asha, shaking with laughter. Asha simply smiled back. She couldn't see what was so hysterically funny about two turtles retreating into their shells. But remembering the number of beer bottles lying around, Asha made allowance for the group's excessive merriment. She walked away and sat on the sand and Manoj followed. He stretched out, cushioning his head in his palms and squinted at the sky.

"Aren't those creatures funny?" he laughed. "As a child, I've played for hours with turtles in my grandparents' village." Art and his friends still circled the turtles, telling each other to wait till the next century for them to reappear. "Having fun, Asha?"

"It's lovely here," she responded truthfully. "There is something so very peaceful about sitting on the banks of a river or lake."

"Hmmm." Manoj lay watching a cottony speck of cloud drifting in the sky. He looked peaceful and content. A sudden rush of hope gripped Asha. Maybe it would be all right. Maybe you were allowed second chances. Maybe both of them could . . .

"Hey, when are those two going to make themselves visible?" the disgruntled tone of the girl in pink shorts rang through the air.

"Takes hours sometimes," Art shrugged. "Once they go in, man, they don't want to leave."

"What a bore. I was waiting to see then swim into the lake."

"Do you want to see them swim?" Manoj looked across at her indulgently.

"We'd love to. Can you make 'em?" she asked eagerly.

Watching him clear a space around the turtles, Asha hugged her knees and lazily wondered what he was going to do. Lift them and coax them out?

Manoj groped in his pockets and bent over the turtles. The girl in pink shorts jumped back with a startled gasp and Manoj patted her arm reassuringly. What was he doing? From where she was sitting, Manoj was obscuring her view. Asha craned her neck down, trying to peer between the forest of feet. The next second she was on her feet and running through the sand, her face twisted in shock.

"Stop it . . . Manoj!" she gasped. "Please, stop it!"

"Hey, hey, calm down, Asha." Manoj drew her back. "It's all right. I've done it hundreds of times as a child. Believe me. There is nothing to fear."

The brown shells were burning with orange flames.

"It'll kill them, Manoj." Asha's voice rang sharply. "You're hurting them!"

"Don't be silly, Asha. Their shell is tough. All they are feeling is uncomfortably hot. Watch now!"

One feeble, questing head slowly emerged from the shell, looked around stupidly and began moving torturously towards the water.

"Isn't that funny?" Manoj cried. "They're moving towards the water as fast as they can. They know it will make them cool!" Art and his friends had been standing still, their eyes hypnotized by the enflamed turtles. But at Manoj's shout, they began to jump about happily, cheering the appearance of the turtles. Pointing to the slow-motion walk of the burning turtles, Manoj began to follow them, his shoulders shaking with laughter.

Asha remained on the sand, one hand pressed against her face, as if shielding a painful blow. Her eyes stared at the cheerleading group unbelievingly. Gleeful faces blinked and faded against the glimmering sun. Eyes rolled upward and tongues were jutting out in exaggerated pantomime.

"Hot! Give me water!" Art was gasping. His tongue hung out comically. In an instant a grey blur descended upon Asha's vision. Candy. Candy squealing and disappearing. Manoj in the car panting with his tongue out. Oh my god, the hot chocolate. Mira told me too, poor bewildered thing. How much did the hot chocolate hurt the delicate tongue of a puppy? The tears still falling, Asha turned and ran up the steps, through the velvet grass, past the house and down the driveway without pausing until she reached her car. Breathlessly, she turned the ignition and began pulling out. The thought of the little, trusting bundle of fur nursing its pain under the bed wrenched her stomach.

At the end of the lane, it occurred to Asha that she had no clue about how to get back home. The handwritten paper had disappeared. For a second she debated about going back and asking someone. Then she squared her shoulders and continued. She would navigate herself home.

Redrawing the Contours

Baby-Photo Inc. vs Michael Egerton Crusz

Rienzi Crusz

Five days old
and Baby-Photo Inc. got you
in color, three sizes, and ten copies.
Your father and mother helped
to truss you up in blue 'Angel Wear,'
blessed the final shots
with a cheque for $18.50 cents.

But like a small avenging god,
you grew a sudden fungus
on the YASHICA's eye,
bawled your way
to shivering the tripod's thin legs,
bent the picture
to a mere grimace of fists.

How without choice
of time or place,
they plucked you out
of the flamboyant dream:
how cradled in your mother's arms,
you watched the Temple Elephant
swaying in purple brocade and flame,
carry the sacred Buddha's tooth,
as lean bodies with drums in their heads
jerked between swirling torches,
the evening crowd hot
with the blood-beat of Perahera.

And your father
laying you down on that sandy beach
he called Wellawatte,
where once he chased the sand-crabs
to their graves,
built castles like some royal architect,
only to have the horizon
collect monsoon darkness like a magnet
and strike.

Without the genetic dream,
Perahera, sand-crab, castle,
the drum-beat of your mongrel blood,
of history made, undone,
in some far green island home,
you are no more exotic
than Vancouver crow.

All we have here
is counterfeit:
infant bones without marrow,
a rhetoric thin as skin,
the cold eye of incorporated men,

without blood, without history.

A Door Ajar

Rienzi Crusz

Everything is green, and the wash
of blue down here, the coral alone
white, twisting its thin warm arms
round my skin.
Air bubbles, globes that burst
to feed my heaving lungs,
have their skins in nothing but gossamer blue.

But I must come up
for air—leave the sharks
curving like lightning in their dance,
their teeth sucking water after
the red ambush of hunger.

Everything is good down here
but we flail our arms
for the blue kingdom of air,
our heads electric
for the sun's nostalgia, the photograph,
the pappadan and ice-cream man,

the green land we left
our childhood faces in.

Just After "Just Between Indians"

Ginu Kamani

In the months following the release of *Junglee Girl*, several editors of erotica have contacted me asking for unpublished work. I have sold many pieces through these inquiries, except in one case, where the rejection proved highly instructive. This particular editor looked at two different pieces, one old and one new, which I provided to her on the assumption that my *Junglee Girl* stories were desirable prototypes. Though she was very enthusiastic about the writing, she finally made it clear that my work doesn't follow the well-defined erotic formula of seduction-climax-denouement. She also hinted strongly that there were too many family members crowding my stories, and that I'd do better concentrating on the lovers alone.

In American culture, individual sexuality has now evolved to a place where, more often than not, the desirable ideal of sexuality is opposed to pleasure-less repression. But in other cultures, including South Asian, individual sexuality is still rigorously opposed to family control, and pleasure/repression are tertiary topics at best. The (overt or covert) group ownership of any given woman's sexuality is still the most pressing subject for a large number of Indian women, including in the diaspora. Given this situation, and given my personal need to write stories exploring sexual transactions in the midst of a variety of restrictions, it is no surprise to me that my work doesn't fit the expected formula of western erotica.

In some ways, however, "Just Between Indians" does fit another kind of erotic formula, where individual expressions of sexuality are still considered one of the worst betrayals to one's parents and elders, and have to be conducted in secret and often in "loaded" circumstances. Every Indian I know of my generation has engaged in individually selected sexual contact, but yet for many, sexual choices as determined by the larger group continue to be comforting, and sexual compatibility is blithely subsumed into economic, class, and cultural compatibilities.

In my experience with some ardent amateur matchmakers, the vicarious thrill in arranging the sexual union of often inexperienced individuals is replete with erotic charge for the go-betweens, who may themselves be trapped in unfulfilling relationships. It never ceases to astound me how little information is passed down between generations in preparation for such major life changes as initiating sexual contact. It continues to amaze me how many unempowered/disempowered women are available in the marriage market, and how Indian men who have engaged in sexual relationships, including long-term ones, routinely request these inexperienced women when it comes time to "settle down."

Part of my passage to adulthood involved coming to terms with women's anger. Both my grandmothers were extremely angry women, and, as a child, I had formed the very solid opinion that these women were mean and nasty and had to be avoided at all costs. As I grew older, I came to know the life stories of both these bad-tempered women, and struggled to comprehend the unimaginable powerlessness that both had experienced. With no permission to confront those who engineered life-long pain, humiliation, and betrayal (the father in one case and, I assume, parents and husband in the other), my grandmothers fumed at everyone else who crossed their path. My experience with the display of anger, especially in Indian women, is that their pain has usually taken a long and complicated route before the women "snap" and start exhibiting distortions of their internal discomfort.

I wanted to work with the character of an angry Indian woman, even though such an individual can be unappealing. At some level, perhaps all of us are better equipped to deal with women resigned to their misery, ensconced in silent suffering, rather than those who show their anger without remorse. Community-oriented cultures have rigid taboos against the expression of anger, which particularly limit the resentful communications of women directed towards parents, husbands, in-laws, and community elders, who manipulate socially sanctioned avenues to abuse and exploit women. My preference, for myself as well as my characters, is to engage in a dialogue to find our way out of resentments, fears, and anger. I hoped in this story to show that certain situations and certain people dismiss dialogue, which then leads to less appealing ways of operating.

On a different note, the most poignant confirmation I got of this story striking a nerve was with an Indian gentleman in his sixties who attended one of my book signings, where I read aloud sections of "Just Between Indians." This man asked me very earnestly during the question-and-answer session to please assure him that the character of Rohit Uncle was merely a caricature. I was struck by the nature of his question, which appeared to me to be an indirect revelation of some personal pain that I could not explore in detail in a public space, but which was nonetheless very moving. I responded that much to my regret the character of Rohit is based on a flesh-and-blood person I know, someone who has had partial success arranging the marriages of his nephews and nieces, but whose own children married as far from their father's sphere of influence as they possibly could. His vicarious, barely concealed lust in matchmaking was blatantly obvious to me. The sublimation of unfulfilled expectations in his own marriage had turned him into a cold, calculating hawk, unwilling to admit to being poorly qualified at best for arranging the sexual unions of others. The privilege of being the oldest male in his family was the only permission he needed. For me, the plight of people like Rohit Uncle is far more depressing than that of "unappealing" fighters like Daya. The fact that the mask of a well-to-do, self-confident Indian immigrant "slipped" enough to reveal his vulnerability made the publishing of the story wonderfully worthwhile for me, especially since I despaired more than once of it surviving the most extensive editing and re-writing of any of the stories in the book.

Just Between Indians

"I wouldn't go in there if I were you," Sahil warned softly. He was dressed in white linen pants and a dark silk shirt, comfortably sprawled on the couch of green and yellow brocade. His eyes sloped down at the corners, adding to his relaxed look. Daya was instantly irritated by his tone. She stopped by the closed kitchen door and looked around the room as though searching out the person he might be addressing. She then turned to look at him.

"Are you talking to me?" she asked with mock surprise. "I just wanted something to drink."

"My father's on the phone with your parents. We could be part of the same family soon. You wouldn't want to jeopardize it." Sahil's eyes were twinkling. Daya looked at him as though seeing him for the first time. He was about five foot, seven in his early-to-mid-twenties. He looked quite at ease and wore a studied expression of amusement.

"Could you stop smirking long enough to explain yourself?"

Sahil sat up and smiled cheerfully.

"There's nothing to explain, really. My brother took one look at you and decided you'd do. He's looking for a wife."

Daya had arrived on the airport shuttle over an hour earlier. She was on spring break from a hard junior year in college, and had come to New York to explore the city. It was her fist visit as an adult to the home of her father's old friend Rohit Patel. Rohit Uncle had insisted that Daya stay at his house when he found out that she was coming East. She would have preferred any place other than the home of conservative Indian immigrants, but her parents had pressured her, saying that Rohit owed them a favor, and in any case, she didn't have the money for a hotel.

When she'd arrived, her fears were confirmed. Rohit greeted Daya in his megaphone voice and thumped her painfully on the shoulder, rubbing his palm up and down her back until she shrugged him off. Daya asked if Veena, Rohit's wife, was still at work. Rohit informed her, "No, Daya, Auntie Veena is away in India for a few more days." Daya's heart sank. She couldn't believe her bad luck. Veena, a big boisterous woman, was as full of humor and affection as her husband was full of bullying censure. Daya had been hoping for Veena's laughing presence; instead, Rohit was playing host to some relatives from London: his widowed brother Subhash, and Subhash's two grown sons, Ranjan and Sahil.

Daya stood in the front room of the house paralyzed with dismay. One by one the men came up to her. Sahil shook her hand firmly and regarded her with interest. Ranjan offered an awkward wave and stepped back hastily. Subhash patted her on the head like a child. Rohit beamed through the introductions, his hand once again vigorously massaging Daya's back. Finally he let go and Daya rushed up the stairs to her assigned room. Rohit's voice boomed behind her.

"The last time I saw you, you were an ugly duckling! Lucky for you, you've changed."

Daya cursed herself for listening to her parents. She was incensed at the prospect of spending a whole week with this gang of Indian men. *I might as well get back on the plane for home.* She emptied her duffel bag onto the bed and tossed her clothes into the chest of drawers. She kicked the bag under the bed and threw herself onto the mattress. With a wry smile she remembered her mother's goodbye at the airport.

"Learn to relax around people. You get so bad-tempered sometimes. What will Rohit Uncle think if you're badly behaved? Just smile, be friendly and make the most of it. It's not asking a lot; after all, this is just between Indians."

In high school, Daya had denounced her ties to Indian men. She resolved to stay away from them completely. Growing up, she had idolized her two older brothers. As children, the three of them had been inseparable. But as the boys entered high school, one behind the other, they turned against their adoring sister, labeling her "just a stupid girl." The summer she turned fourteen, she begged her brothers to let her join them on a camping trip with four of their Indian friends. After much tearful pleading on her part, they finally agreed, and Daya was elated. They would be going far into the woods, miles away from anywhere. Daya imagined a real adventure in the wild.

The camping trip turned out to be a nightmare. For four of the longest days of her young life, Daya was teased mercilessly. The boys were obsessed with flicking up her dress and shouting "Peep show! Peep show!" To add to the fun, Kishore would hold his sister tightly against him and tickle her, while Krishna reached down her back to snap her bra. Daya returned home, humiliated. She refused to speak to anyone about what happened. Her brothers tried to joke with her and cheer her up when they saw how withdrawn she had become, but Daya refused to be comforted, and smoldered behind a wall of silence. The following week, the parents of her brothers' friends sent inquiries about Daya's future availability for marriage. Daya was horrified. She went wild with rage. Her parents tried to calm her with assurances that, naturally, marriage was out of the question until Daya reached eighteen. But it was clear to Daya that her mother's assurances only thinly disguised her delight at having received these early proposals.

From then on, in her own house, Daya felt afraid. She knew it was only a matter of time before she would be betrayed.

Sahil stood up as Daya flushed with anger.

"So your dad's on the phone with my parents. Does he think I'm for sale?" she demanded. "We've never even met before!"

She turned toward the kitchen.

"Wait!" He darted after her, but it was too late. Daya jerked open the kitchen door and marched in. She looked around. The phone was resting in its cradle. Ranjan and Subhash were seated at a sunny table at the far corner of the spacious kitchen, eating sandwiches. Father and son looked up and smiled as Daya cautiously crossed the length of the kitchen.

"Can we offer you a snack?" asked Ranjan in his soft English accent. He held up a plate of sandwiches for her inspection. "Dinner won't be served until much later."

"Uh . . . no. Actually, I . . . I wanted something to drink," stammered Daya, and wrenched open the refrigerator door. She stood there gasping, the waves of cold air chilling her to the bone. Her mind raced furiously, trying to make sense of the situation.

She slammed shut the refrigerator door and walked over to the table.

Ranjan pulled out a chair for her at the table and grimaced. "I know, there's nothing worth drinking in the fridge. I've told Uncle to buy juice or something . . ."

Daya sat down, pulled her chair forward and leaned her elbows on the table. "Did I hear you talking to my parents a little while ago?"

Ranjan blushed and cleared his throat.

"I didn't realize we were speaking that loudly . . . ," he began.

"Well, thanks for taking the initiative and informing them that I've arrived safely." She paused, waiting for Ranjan's reply. Ranjan nibbled at his sandwich and said nothing. Subhash gently pushed his chair back, excused himself and went to wash his plate in the sink.

"I mean, that is what you told them, right?" Daya continued. She rubbed her sweating palms against her thighs. "You were making sure that my parents wouldn't worry about me, *right*?"

Ranjan winced at her loud voice and nodded vigorously. "Oh yes, of course. Absolutely! And . . . and . . . they send all their love, and they'll call you later tonight when the rates are lower."

"And did they pass on any messages from my *boyfriend?*" she barked.

Ranjan shook his head. "Oh no. Not at all. Perhaps later, when they talk to you in person?" He grabbed another sandwich and sank his teeth into it. The kitchen door swung shut as Subhash exited.

Daya exhaled loudly, feeling the blood pounding in her throat. She looked out over the garden to steady herself a little. The neat lawn reminded her of her parents' yard. Her family was all together for the week; all, that is, except Daya. Right at that moment, they were probably lounging around in deck chairs, playing endless rounds of cards. Her brothers would be mercilessly teasing their pretty new wives and her parents would be attempting to join in the fun.

Daya had disliked her sisters-in-law on sight. They resembled human sponges, ready to absorb all their husbands' demands as well as the commands of their mother-in-law. The weddings were agony for Daya, as she was continually scrutinized and remarked on as an "eligible girl." And immediately after marriage, her new sisters-in-law turned their attention to rectifying the unmarried plight of their dear Daya.

Within months, Daya had cut off all contact with her brothers and made sure her visits home never coincided with theirs.

Ranjan darted uneasy glances at her. She turned to him in exasperation. He had a high forehead and curly black hair, high cheekbones and a straight nose. He looked anywhere from twenty-five to thirty years old.

"Your brother tells me you want to marry. Why?" demanded Daya. "Why don't you just pay a prostitute?"

Ranjan stared unhappily at his empty plate.

"That's cruel," he replied softly. "I was actually engaged for quite a while. I loved her. But . . . she changed her mind. Terrible mess, actually. So I'm . . . I'm forced to look again."

Ranjan gave a quick pained smile, then once again pushed the plate of sandwiches toward Daya. "Won't you have one? They're quite good."

Daya picked up a sandwich and lifted the top slice of bread. There were slices of cucumber and tomato and a thick layer of butter. *Uptight vegetarians.* "What are you guys doing here in New York?"

"Dad's thinking of moving to New York, so we've all come for a look-see."

Daya gave a short laugh. "You men go everywhere together?"

Ranjan smiled. "You've heard of a two-in-one? Well, we're a . . . a *three*-in-one." Ranjan waited for Daya to smile at his joke, but she just stared at him.

"It's a joke. . . ," he offered lamely.

Daya grimaced and wiped her mouth. "I have just one thing to say. I won't have you doing things behind my back, okay? If you have anything to say to my parents, you better tell me first. Got that?"

She stood up to leave but Ranjan lifted his hand to stop her.

"So . . . so . . . are you here on holiday?" he stuttered. "Because I am too. Maybe we could go do . . . see . . . eat something together? My treat of course!" Ranjan ended in a rush.

Daya giggled at the thought of going out to dinner with Ranjan. Ranjan took her laughter as assent and relaxed somewhat. He quickly wiped the sweat from his forehead.

"I know you eat meat and fish," he continued quickly, "and I don't mind. We could go to the Victoria Palace. Have you been there? It's very fancy, you'll be impressed . . . er . . . I mean, you'll really like it. I hope you don't mind terribly but I've already booked us a table there for lunch tomorrow since reservations are so hard to come by . . ."

"You what!" Daya gasped. "How dare you, you . . . ," she stopped herself and stood up, then backed away, with one final warning. "Keep your distance, okay, and we'll get along fine."

"So my brother's incompetent with women. So what's new? Come to think of it, most men are." Sahil philosophized in his best BBC accent. He was reclining on the couch once more. Daya was on her way back upstairs, but she stopped, turned, took a deep breath and approached the couch.

"Well since you seem to know so much, professor, why don't you try to educate him a bit?"

Sahil spread his hands. "I'm here, aren't I? I'm watching out for him. What more can a brother do?" he laughed. "Ranjan really does believe that Dad can get him any woman he wants. And the trouble is, Dad believes it too!" He grinned from ear to ear and snapped his fingers. "It's a ma-ma-ma-ma man's world out there!"

Daya felt a smile trying to escape her lips. "That's not funny. I would never have come here had I known that this house was a pick-up joint for Indian men. This is supposed to be my vacation. I should get out of here."

Yet even as she voiced her desire, Daya knew she couldn't leave. Her parents would be furious and certainly refuse to pay a hotel bill.

"If you'd rather stay somewhere else," offered Sahil, "I have many friends in New York. Women. I'm sure they would understand the situation perfectly. None of them are *Indian*, as you might guess."

Daya couldn't help smiling at this last comment.

"Ah," said Sahil with delight, "You're beginning to trust me. Your face really lights up when you smile. I can read you like a book."

Daya clenched her fists in renewed irritation. "Would you please quit with the personal comments? It's really insulting to be checked out like a slab of meat."

"Oh please! Now you're confusing me with my sexually repressed brother! You'll know jolly well when I'm checking you out." Sahil bounced off the couch and turned to face the French windows that overlooked the garden.

Daya was astonished at his outburst. What a joke! Each Patel with a bigger ego than the other.

Sahil turned to Daya with a sheepish smile. "I'm sorry, that was out of turn. I'm being insensitive and making a bigger mess of all of this..."

"It's a friggin' circus," Daya jeered.

Sahil nodded solemnly and launched into another apology. "I'm sorry, it appears that everyone here is rather worked up. All it takes is for one attractive Indian woman to walk in the door and the next thing you know . . ."

Ranjan peered around the kitchen door, then stepped cautiously into the living room. Daya moved away in disgust. Sahil quickly stepped in front of her and motioned for his brother to back off. Ranjan's face crumpled in confusion.

"Let's get out of here," Daya whispered loudly to Sahil, "before Romeo whips out the engagement ring."

Sahil tried to keep up with Daya as she walked furiously around the block.

"So, you and your brother have nothing in common."

"Not a thing."

"You have the same parents, you've lived together all your lives and yet you're utterly unconnected."

"Exactly. Those who know us well wonder what in god's name we're doing in the same family."

"Well?"

"Frankly, I've learned a lot by hanging around with my graceless brother. He makes the mistakes and I clean up after him. It works out well."

Daya puzzled over Sahil's words. *He's pulling my leg.*

"You think I'm joking," Sahil said, "Ranjan really is my lucky charm. In cleaning up after him, I've done my most interesting work and met the most interesting people. Like you."

"Oh I get it!" she cried. "You and your brother do a Jekyll and Hyde routine where he humiliates women and you step in to comfort the poor victims. Right?"

"You've got quite the talent for sarcasm."

"Why did you tell me, anyway? This whole business of your brother looking for a wife. He's such a klutz that I might never have found out, never have gotten insulted, and enjoyed my spring break after all."

"Well, frankly, I like you and couldn't bear to see my brother treat you like some senseless object."

Daya slowed her pace to take in his unexpected words.

"You're *not* by any chance interested in him, are you?" Sahil asked cautiously.

She looked at him in horror. "Are you kidding? No way! Your brother is petrified; I can barely see his face under all that angst. He hates himself. He'd be terrible in bed. I could never be attracted to a man like that."

"I see," Sahil nodded solemnly. "So you are as experienced as you look."

"Yes, and not with *Indian* men, either. They could drive a woman to her grave."

Sahil frowned at Daya's words, struggling with some remembered pain. "I . . . uh . . . I wouldn't *exactly* call myself 'Indian.' We were raised everywhere: Africa, Australia, Singapore, Canada, England. . . I've set foot on every continent."

"I'd rather be dead than involve myself with an Indian man!" Daya continued as though she hadn't heard him.

Sahil frowned again and walked in silence for a while. He resumed in an uncertain tone. "Funny you should mention graves, or perhaps you already knew? It's my mother's death anniversary tomorrow. That's probably why

Ranjan is acting like such an arsehole. It's the same thing every year; he turns into a complete wreck."

Daya flushed with shock and came to a stop, "No, of course I didn't know. How could I know? I don't know anything about your family. We've never even met before. And tomorrow's her. . . oh god! Is that why your brother wants me to go for . . . ?" Daya stopped herself from finishing the question.

"What?" asked Sahil.

"No, nothing. Never mind."

They walked around the block once again, past the sprawling suburban mansions. Daya looked at Sahil from the corner of her eye. He was just taller than her. His body was stocky, and from what she could see, his chest was covered with curly black hair. He walked gracefully and confidently with his shoulders thrown back. Daya suddenly realized that the Indian men she knew walked very differently, with stiff jerky strides, slouched over or with their chests and stomachs bouncing. He turned to her and smiled.

"You keep looking at me. Do I remind you of someone?" he asked.

Daya shook her head vigorously and exclaimed, "No, I would say definitely not!"

Amused, he looked at her with a warm expression. He looked directly into her eyes and she found herself imagining that she could forget he was Indian.

"Is your boyfriend American?"

"Am I required to answer that?"

Sahil walked in silence for a moment, then sighed. "I was just wondering. I can frequently predict all sorts of things about Indian women. I've sort of, been observing them all my life. It's a sort of . . . *hobby* of mine, a bit like solving complex puzzles."

"So *you* must have an Indian girlfriend."

"No, actually. Never have," he replied matter-of-factly. "But there's always hope, don't you think?"

Daya stared at Sahil, stared right through him. *Never had one. He's like me.* She felt a sudden tightness in her chest and closed her eyes. She reached back and pressed her neck. Immediately Sahil moved behind her and she felt his warm fingers on her shoulder, pressing down on the knots of tension.

"What's wrong?" he asked gently. "Are you tired? Would you like to sit down?" Sahil walked around to face her, and Daya opened her eyes. Daya noticed

Sahil's eyes clearly for the first time. They were amber, like cats' eyes, covered by thick curled lashes. His gaze was steady, quizzical, concerned.

She shivered. Her teeth were suddenly chattering in the cool evening breeze. She stepped back and hugged herself. "You can't disguise the way you look," she laughed. "You're definitely Indian."

Sahil inclined his head and gave a low bow. "I will take that as a challenge. I shall do my very best to prove you wrong."

"Daya, what can I offer you? We have Coke and other soft drinks in the fridge, or perhaps you'll take tea or coffee?"

Rohit was playing the genial host, bounding around the kitchen, setting out the Tandoori restaurant food he had brought home. Daya and Sahil sat next to each other at the table, with Ranjan across from them. Subhash sat at the foot of the table, and Rohit's place was, of course, at the head.

"Uh . . . actually, I'd like a drink please. Gin and tonic, if you have it."

Rohit opened his eyes wide in mock alarm and wagged his finger at Daya.

"You naughty girl! You're lucky that Auntie Veena is away because she would be very angry right now. A proper young lady like you shouldn't drink. Lucky for you, I am broad-minded. But keep in mind that liquor is expensive."

Rohit opened the liquor cabinet and pulled out the bottle of gin. Daya silently mimicked Rohit's wagging finger and shook it around the table. Ranjan blushed and looked down at his plate. Subhash cleared his throat loudly and adjusted the napkin in his lap. Sahil looked pointedly at the ceiling. Rohit placed the gin and tonic in front of Daya. All the men were drinking water.

"So tell me," Rohit snickered as he sat down, "does alcohol make you tipsy?" Rohit turned to Ranjan with a broad smile and winked at him.

Daya felt the anger rising in her throat, and was just opening her mouth for a quick retort when she felt Sahil's cautioning hand on her elbow. She exhaled slowly and pressed her lips shut.

Rohit leaned forward with a leer. "Drink up, drink up!" he boomed. "We are all waiting for you!"

"Shall we get started?" Sahil interrupted politely. He lifted the pan of curried peas and potatoes and ladled some onto his plate and Daya's. Subhash took the pan next and looked at Daya as she sipped her drink.

"So, young lady, are you thinking about marriage? I'm sure your parents have received many offers."

Rohit grunted with pleasure as he chewed a mouthful of chapati. "It's essential for our boys to meet girls from good families." Rohit wagged his finger again. "It will help them get sensible sooner. When I heard you were coming to New York, I told Subhash to bring his boys right away."

Daya coughed in surprise. She glared at Subhash and Rohit in turn, then set her glass down firmly. Sahil cautioned her again by shaking his head. "I will marry if and when I want to," she said deliberately, "and my parents will have no say in it. I don't need Indians meddling in my private life."

"Ah," Subhash nodded. "A modern girl. And how do you propose to find a man on your own?"

Daya narrowed her eyes and sneered, "By kidnapping and raping him, how else?" She cut into her samosa with an exaggerated swing of the knife, then licked the blade clean.

Sahil burst out laughing. Ranjan pushed the food around his plate in embarrassment and the two older men shook their heads grimly. "My god!" cried Rohit. "Quite a sense of humor you have there, young lady!"

Daya gulped down her drink and looked questioningly at Sahil. *Do something*! Her eyes challenged him. Sahil shook his head in disbelief and looked away. His foot tapped nervously.

"American-style romance is not for you, my dear," Subhash continued. "You won't like it. These Americans get you undressed, then drop you like *that*!" Subhash snapped his fingers. "Once an Indian's girl's reputation is destroyed, that's the end of her."

"And this kissing thing!" bellowed Rohit. "My god, I hope you're not one of these junglees who likes spit and slobber and stuffing someone's dirty tongue in your mouth. *Chheee*!"

"And then, too, you have to put dangerous chemicals in your body so you don't get pregnant or diseased while you're fooling around. Naturally all of that harms the unborn babies."

"And you, young lady," Rohit pointed vigorously at Daya, "you definitely need to have a baby to round out your sharp edges."

Daya's dropped fork clattered loudly on her plate. She slumped forward in her chair. She felt her throat tightening with rage. *Enjoy yourself . . . smile . . . it's just between Indians.* Her mother's parting words echoed deafeningly in her ears.

"Perhaps you shouldn't talk about her like she's not in the room," Sahil cautioned the older men.

Rohit waved aside Sahil's comment. "What's the problem?" he demanded. "In my day, the women used to eat in a separate room. We could talk about whatever we wanted. If she's such a modern girl, let her deal with it. She's too proud to be one of us!"

"So, tell me again what you're doing hanging around with this family?"

Dinner was finally over. Rohit, Subhash and Ranjan had hurried down to the basement to watch sports on the giant screen TV, leaving Daya and Sahil to clear the table.

"On days like this," Sahil replied bitterly, "I really don't know. All three of them should be shot, or castrated, or both."

They stood side by side at the sink. Daya rinsed the plates and handed them to Sahil to place in the dishwasher.

"They're completely fucked up," she said gloomily. "It's really depressing." She pushed the hair out of her eyes. She couldn't handle another meal like this one. She wanted to talk to her parents, but as per their warning, she had to wait for them to call her. Long-distance phone bills were a touchy subject with her parents and their friends.

Sahil wiped his hands on his pants and turned Daya toward him.

"They really hurt you, didn't they? I'm so sorry. I felt like an utter fool sitting there, politely attempting to steer the conversation away."

She shrugged nonchalantly, but her grim face betrayed the pain she felt. "It's only normal. Indian men are like that."

He gently touched her arm. "Don't take it in," he murmured. "Don't let it get to you."

Daya turned back to the dishes in the sink. "I don't need your pity! I'm sure you've never been attacked like this."

"Mmmmm. I thought we had joined forces. But here you are dismissing me once again."

Daya rinsed the plates in silence, then turned off the tap. "I've done quite well for myself, thank you, simply by staying away from Indians. No other men seem to have a stake in humiliating me in this way."

"I understand," Sahil nodded. "But I don't like you lumping me with them. I would never humiliate you the way they do. I've suffered at my uncle's hands before."

"And still you come back for more?"

He shrugged and pursed his lips. "Funny thing, this relationship with Uncle. It's because Rohit and Veena have no children of their own. You know how it is."

She shook her head. "No, actually, I don't. Why don't you tell me?"

Sahil thought for a moment. "Ever since my mother died, Rohit and Veena have been our real family. Rohit is a bit out of control; sadistic even. He can't help it. But he did save our lives."

"You're going to inherit a packet of money, right?" Daya crossed her arms on her chest.

"What?" He was caught off guard. "Oh! Er . . . some, I'm sure."

"So that's why you put up with Unk."

Sahil's jaw tightened. She knew she had hit a nerve.

"Must be nice being an Indian son. Everyone wants you like you're going out of style!" Daya snapped her fingers and walked out of the kitchen.

"Now Sahil, you're in charge of the burglar alarm. Don't forget to turn it on before going to bed. Good night."

Daya lay on her bed in the dark, listening to Rohit's instructions in the hallway below. She heard him climb the stairs to his bedroom and shut the door. She heard Ranjan leave the bathroom in the hallway. He slowly walked over to Daya's closed door. She could feel him hesitating outside. The floor boards squeaked with his every move. He might even have raised a hand to knock, but then he turned around and walked back to the room he was sharing with Subhash. He shut the door.

Gathering courage, Daya thought idly, staring at the ceiling. Her parents had not called. Risking their wrath she had tried their number, but there was no answer. Probably out to a lavish family dinner, celebrating the double pregnancies of their young brides or something.

It was up to Daya. Should she take up Sahil's offer and go stay with his friends? Or should she stay in the house and go on the attack against the men?

She had visions of grabbing Ranjan by his crotch and forcing him to his knees, while his father and uncle pleaded for his life. She imagined grabbing Sahil in the same way and suddenly felt hot. She pushed the image out of her mind.

Daya was incensed that Rohit had ordered his nephews to fly to New York. But what really made her burn was the realization that her parents must have given their blessings to this matchmaking. She had been unleashed into exactly the kind of situation she feared most. She had been preparing for this betrayal for years, and now the moment was upon her.

Choosing her own boyfriends had not sent a strong enough signal to her parents. They apparently could not let go of the fantasy that their daughter needed an Indian man. And a nephew of Rohit, their old friend! A coup, no less. they would be delirious with excitement if she reported back to her parents that the matchmaking had worked. Overnight, their attitude toward her would change, become more generous, more respectful, more relaxed. Her mother would hover around her, laughing, joking, confiding in her as she prepared Daya for being a wife. *You're lucky,* she might say. *You don't have to deal with a mother-in-law in this case.* Or, *Rohit and Veena are wealthy. They will buy you everything, starting with your very own house!* And perhaps even, *Make sure and use birth control so that you can finish your studies in peace. Don't have any children until you're ready to, otherwise it will be the end.* On and on went the imagined dialogues in her head. Fantasizing intimate moments with her mother was something Daya could do for hours. Finally she sat up and massaged her tense shoulders. *I need to look at this differently,* she cautioned herself. *Because I know I'm not about to get married.*

The thought of another gin and tonic felt good. She put on her clothes and shoes. She hoped Rohit didn't lock the liquor cabinet at night the way her parents did. She walked noiselessly down the stairs to the kitchen. The kitchen door was closed, the same way it had been earlier that day. What a nightmare of a day it had been. She pulled angrily on the door. It swung open silently. She walked right to the liquor cabinet and, with the help of the pale moonlight, located the bottle of gin. She opened the refrigerator and pulled out a bottle of tonic water and a tray of ice. In the vegetable bin she found half a lime.

She quickly poured her drink over the ice, squeezed in the lime and sucked on her wet fingers. She shut the refrigerator door, and walked towards the kitchen table, sipping on her drink. She stopped short, the hair rising on her arms. Her throat tightened with the now familiar anger.

"You've come to join me." Sahil's warm voice floated over to Daya.

Sahil's legs were stretched out on the tabletop and his hands were tucked behind his head. His silk shirt was open to the waist and his sleeves rolled up almost to his shoulders.

"Sorry," Daya said coldly. "I didn't know you were in here."

She stood for a moment, undecided. Should she take her drink up to the room? The room was like a prison. Better just to stay and talk to him. In the light of the moon, the hair on Sahil's chest glinted silver.

"You're catching a moon tan?" she asked dryly as she sat down.

"The truth is, I'm always warm in this house," he grinned. "Hot, actually."

She sipped on her drink then pushed the glass across the table to Sahil. "Have a sip," she offered. "Cool yourself down."

He drank out of the glass, then pressed its cool surface against his forehead. "Do you come here often?"

"Third time this year."

"All because your dad wants to move to New York?"

Sahil looked up in surprise, then smiled knowingly. "Is that what Ranjan's been telling you? We have no intention of moving here. It's just that Rohit has been very active in searching out a wife for Ranjan."

"Just for Ranjan? What about you?"

"Ranjan's older, so he goes first."

"Yeah, but after he's found one, you'll want one too. That's how brothers are." Sahil nodded noncommittally.

"So," Daya snorted, "I'm the third guinea pig this year?"

Sahil tapped on the table with his fingertips. "You really mustn't be Indian. You seem to have nothing but contempt for family obligations."

"It's only fitting," she murmured, "since Indian families show little more than contempt for their daughters."

She took a gulp of her drink. "Were you sitting here thinking about your mother?"

He took the glass from her hands and looked into the liquid. He ran his finger dejectedly around the rim of the glass. Daya sensed an overwhelming sadness in him and felt sorry.

"You don't have to answer that," she murmured.

"Actually, I was. It happened twenty years ago, you know, in this house."

"What!" Daya started in her chair. "Here? In this house?"

He nodded. "Right here."

She felt her stomach muscles knotting with shock. "I don't understand why no one's ever told me about his."

"Oh, they never talk about it. Ever."

Sahil paused.

"My mother killed herself when I was six. I was at the supermarket with Veena. Rohit was at work. Dad was in Africa."

Daya forced her eyes to stay open, forced her ears to listen. "She had planned to take Ranjan with her, to heaven, according to him. She didn't want *me*, again, according to him. At the last minute, Ranjan ran from her bedroom. She had already swallowed all the pills. She called for him but he wouldn't go to her. She called for him again and again, but you see, Ranjan refused to go without . . . ," his voice broke. He swallowed and coughed. "He . . . wouldn't . . . go . . . without . . . me. He's alive today because of . . . of me."

Daya watched as Sahil locked and unlocked his fingers in quick jerking movements. In the darkness his hands rose and subsided like netted birds. Slowly, she placed her hand on top of his. He exhaled loudly and squeezed her hand gratefully. "Quite frankly, Ranjan has never recovered. He's still afraid . . . he doesn't trust women . . . he has nightmares that any wife of his . . ." He shook his head sadly.

"Oh no! Why is he insisting on getting married, then?"

Sahil chuckled, despite himself. "He's thirty years old. He's never been with a woman. He's right on the edge!"

Daya pressed her lips together grimly. "I was right the first time. Someone should get him to a prostitute."

He patted her hand and pulled away. "My brother won't find Mum in a whorehouse." He tucked his hands back behind his head.

"I'm sorry," she mumbled. "I feel so stupid. I wish I'd known earlier. I feel bad about the way I treated your brother . . . I . . . I'm sure I would have been more sensitive if I'd known . . . "

Sahil flashed her a wry smile. "But I've enjoyed every minute of your headstrong company. You're . . . you're so *committed* to life."

She felt the hair rise alarmingly on the back of her neck. "Is that . . . ," she began hesitantly. "Is that what you're trying to determine? Which women might kill themselves?"

He looked at her blankly. His breathing slowed. His forehead shone with perspiration. He licked his dry lips, and wiped the sweat off his face. "I suppose I am," he admitted finally. "I've never framed it quite like that before." He struggled for a moment before adding, "But I know you're right."

"And this has only to do with *Indian* women?"

He nodded, brows knit with pain. The conversation was over.

The kitchen clock rang loudly. Daya looked up. It was four a.m. She stood up from the table. Immediately Sahil got to his feet and came around. She knew instinctively what he would do next, and the anticipation of his touch carried her forward into Sahil's embrace.

They walked side by side up the stairs. At the door to her room, they embraced once more. Daya stepped into her room and shut the door quietly. She slid under the covers and sank into sleep.

"So how many other eligible girls have slept in my bed?"

"A few, but we've changed the sheets since then!"

Daya and Ranjan sat at a corner table in the dimly lit Victoria Palace. The restaurant was furnished like a Victorian doll house, with ruffled curtains on the windows, candy-stripe wallpaper and pink and white chairs with high backs. The waiters wore formal tails and high-collared shirts. The menu consisted entirely of meat dishes. Ranjan had insisted that she order a filet mignon or at least a rack of lamb. Ranjan meanwhile had ordered only a baked potato and a salad for himself. She found the situation extremely funny, and Ranjan was relaxed because Daya was having a good time.

Daya had awoken late that morning with the clear knowledge that she should accept Ranjan's invitation to lunch. She had dressed and descended the stairs, and much to her relief, Ranjan was the only one around. He was in the kitchen, and got up hurriedly when Daya walked in. Ranjan was sure that she would shout at him again. He almost burst into tears when instead Daya said she'd be happy to have lunch with him. But there was one condition, she had informed him: they had to speak honestly about themselves.

"Why are you so sure you want to marry an Indian woman? Are they somehow better than other women?" Daya popped another piece of red meat into her mouth, savoring the tenderness.

"I think so," Ranjan answered. "And anyway," he blushed visibly and concentrated on his salad, "they're the most beautiful women in the world."

"You think?" she asked with surprise. "Funny, I feel the same way. Those big dark eyes and lips. . . . "

"You're extremely attractive," Ranjan interrupted quickly. "And rather intelligent. I saw that at once."

Daya smiled kindly and touched his hand.

"I'm not the one for you," she stated. "Don't waste your time."

Ranjan nodded silently and picked at his salad.

"Do you like my brother?" he asked, still looking at his plate.

She sighed and wondered how to answer.

"Your brother isn't looking for a wife. It . . . makes things a little easier between us."

Ranjan pushed the lettuce around his plate.

"He's stolen every girl I've been interested in. Once they meet him, they won't have anything to do with me. It's not fair."

Daya frowned impatiently.

"That doesn't sound like your brother. Where are these girls? What happened to them?"

"I don't know. He doesn't tell me anything. All I know is that he slept with Rachna, my . . . my . . . the girl I was engaged to."

Oh no, she groaned to herself. *More intrigue. These two are obsessed with each other.*

"Why are you telling me this?" Daya asked in irritation. "She obviously never loved you."

"She didn't love Sahil either." Ranjan cried bitterly. "But she slept with him and not me!"

Daya felt a headache coming on. She was still exhausted from the previous night. The steak sat heavily in her stomach. She suddenly wanted to lie down.

"Let's go," she said tiredly, pushing her plate away. "I feel terrible. I need a rest."

"Won't you finish your steak?" Ranjan blurted in a panic. "You don't have to waste good food on my account."

When Daya opened her eyes, it was dark outside. She was surprised. Her watch read 10:40 p.m. She had slept right through dinner! *Well, no big loss,* she thought, *the boys can manage their soap opera without me.* She smelled the armpit of her t-shirt. The sour smell reminded her immediately of her lunch with Ranjan. She sat up and reached for her jeans in the dark.

"You're awake." Sahil's soft voice floated up through the darkness.

Daya jumped off the bed in fright, clutching her pants to her body.

"What are you doing here?" she hissed. "Why are you here?" As her eyes adjusted, she saw Sahil was sitting on the floor by the dresser. "How long have you been sitting there?"

"Not long," Sahil smiled. "I didn't want to go to bed without seeing you. There's been a change in our plan and we're leaving early in the morning."

"Oh?" Daya quickly pulled on her jeans and shirt and sat on the bed. "Where are you going?"

"Home. To London."

"Why so suddenly?" Daya asked, irritated. "Is there a girl waiting for Ranjan?"

Sahil chuckled and stood up. "There could be, for all I know. We have relatives coming in from India. From my mother's side. We haven't seen them in years."

"You're looking forward to meeting them?" Daya asked with disbelief.

"I am, actually. They've always spoiled us rotten. My gran's a brilliant cook, and full of funny stories."

"About your mother?" Daya interjected.

"Yes, but so much more. She's as solid as a rock."

Daya looked at the ceiling, struggling with a sense of sadness.

"I'll miss you," she said finally. Sahil squatted at the foot of the bed.

"I was just thinking the same thing," he murmured. "I feel happy with you. Light. Something's opened up in me." Sahil ran a finger between Daya's toes and her foot jerked back.

"You're ticklish?" Sahil grinned.

"Very," Daya whispered hoarsely. She stopped herself from adding, *Except when I'm aroused.*

Daya and Sahil looked at each other. Sahil's jaw was tense. His amber eyes shone eerily like cat's eyes in the moonlight. Daya swallowed hard. Her chest was so tight it hurt.

"Aren't your relatives wondering where you are?" Daya drew her legs under her and leaned back.

"Even if they knew, they would never come in here."

"Why? Are they all afraid of you?"

Sahil opened his palms to her and motioned for her to extend her legs. "No, that's not it," he replied. Daya unfolded her legs and wiggled her toes. Sahil caught hold of them and pulled her down the bed. He cradled one foot in his palms and put his mouth on her small toe. The intensity of his touch shot through Daya like a spark. She gripped the side of the mattress. Sahil switched to the next toe and Daya bit her lip to keep from crying out. She willed her body to relax, willed the surface tickling to move deeper, down, down into her belly where it flared and burned slowly.

She lay quieter, allowing Sahil's tongue to stroke her feet, arousing her. Her face felt hot, as though she had just sneezed. *Even if it's just once,* she said to herself, *I want him.*

Daya unbuttoned her jeans and pulled her t-shirt over her head. Sahil carefully eased her jeans and underpants off her body. He kissed her ankle and licked up the side of one leg, all the way up inside her thigh and then back down the other until he was at her toes again. Daya felt her body shivering in response. She watched Sahil licking and massaging her feet. His head was bent over in deep concentration. Daya wiggled her toes and Sahil looked up.

"Hi," she greeted him softly, her voice thick with arousal.

Sahil threw off his clothes and climbed over Daya. His entire body was covered with the thick soft hair that covered his chest. Daya pulled Sahil to her and they embraced in a long luxurious hug.

"It's so good to be holding you at last," Sahil whispered, running his fingers through her hair. "I've been sitting on an erection for an hour!" he laughed. "I tried talking to it, but it knew better."

Daya reached down with her hand. Sahil dug his face into her neck and bit her earlobe. Daya struggled out of his grasp and pinned his arms against the headboard. She straddled him and sucked hard on his left nipple, feeling it stiffen. His body spasmed as she ran the edge of her teeth across the rigid flesh.

"Christ," he sighed happily. "You're a tigress."

"And you," she teased, "are not Indian."

Sahil pulled her face up to his and kissed her. He buried his mouth in her armpit and she pressed him hard against her to keep from crying out.

"You smell so good," he whispered between strokes of his tongue, "I want to taste you, put my mouth on you."

He slid down the bed. She guided his hand between her legs, then his head. He tasted her flesh with long strokes of his tongue. She closed her legs around his head.

"Has anyone told you what you taste like?" he asked, raising his head to look at her.

Daya smiled at him lazily.

"Tuna fish?" she asked jokingly.

Sahil shook his head vehemently.

"The cream inside a freshly cut lady finger," he corrected her solemnly. Daya gaped at him.

"Lady finger? You mean, okra?" She shook with silent laughter. "A vegetarian right down to the sex!"

Daya awoke with a start. Dawn was just breaking. She could hear footsteps on the staircase, and then below in the front room. She remembered that the London Patels were leaving that morning. She remembered her time with Sahil. The events of the previous night rushed through her head. She relived their tenderness together over and over in her mind. She felt exhausted and alive. Sahil had told her before leaving that she need not wake up to say goodbye in the morning. It would be awkward to exchange mere formalities after being so intimate together. She heard the car start, heard the car doors open and shut, and then the car drive away.

Daya looked at the rising sun. It felt like the sun was setting already, the end of a long day. It was time to go back to sleep, to get some rest. She wondered if there was another pillow in the room. She looked around. There was a wardrobe next to the chest of drawers into which she had thrown her clothes. She climbed out of bed and pulled on the door of the wardrobe. It wouldn't open. Great, she thought. Like good Indians, the Patels keep all of their cupboards locked. She pulled again on the door. This time the door opened a crack.

She pried the door open with her nails. The hinges moaned as she pushed each door to its limit. Folded neatly and hung on thick steel hangers were dozens of saris. She ran her fingers along the folds. She could tell immediately from the designs that the saris were dated: they were chiffon with loud multicolored geometrical designs. Late '60s or early '70s. She smiled. Veena Auntie must have saved all her old saris, loathe to throw them out. Daya's mother was the same way, with piles of saris that she refused to wear but was unwilling to give away. At the end of the row of saris hung a dozen or so sari blouses of different colors. Daya disliked saris, but loved the blouses for the midriffs they so wonderfully bared. She pulled out a green silk blouse and held it against her. It looked like it might fit. She imagined Sahil's fingers slowly undoing each hook that ran down the front of the blouse, she wanted to feel the soft material against her flesh. She pulled the blouse off the hanger. Was Veena really that thin in those days? A label sewn onto the inside of the blouse caught her eye. Similar white labels were sewn into every one of her mother's blouses. They had all been stitched in India.

Daya read the label, Manjuri S. Patel. Manjuri? She wondered who that could be . . . S. The middle initial stood for the husband's first name in the full name of a married Indian women. S . . . could be S for Subhash. . . .

Daya threw the blouse onto the bed. *It can't be! It can't be.* She looked around her at the walls of the bedroom. There were water stains on the ceiling. There were cobwebs in the corner. The window sills were caked with dust.

Suddenly Sahil's words hit her in the face.

"They would never come in here."

Daya flung open the door and leaped out of the room before she realized she was naked. She stepped back into the room and grabbed her clothes off the floor. Her hands were shaking. Her legs got stuck in the jeans. She pulled them on with sheer force. Her arms were sweating. They got stuck in the sleeves of her t-shirt and she pulled the shirt roughly over her head. She ran into Rohit's bedroom, picked up the phone, and asked the operator to call her home collect. Her mother answered. The operator asked if she would accept the charges.

"I'm sorry but Daya is not home right now!"

Daya listened to her mother's vigorous denial to the operator. This was the arranged system to signal she wanted her parents to call back. Daya hung up the phone and waited. She looked around Rohit's room. The neatness of the room made her want to throw things about, empty the cupboards and dresser onto the floor, splash perfume and aftershave on the walls. A minute passed and the phone remained silent.

Mother! fumed Daya. *For god's sake, take this seriously and call now. Not after you finish your conversation, not after you finish your cooking. Now!*

Another minute passed.

Betrayed again and again. Lies everywhere. Who was to blame?

The phone rang. Daya snatched it off the cradle furiously.

"Why the hell must you take so long to return my call? First of all you promised to call the day I arrived. Today is the third day. What excuse could you possibly have? You have no sense of time once your darling sons arrive in the house. I could have been killed by now!"

There was silence on the other end. Daya couldn't believe her mother's callousness.

"Do I mean so little to you? Did you have any thoughts for my feelings when you set me up with these morbid nephews of Rohit's? What in hell was going through your mind? Do you have any idea what sickos the two brothers are? Answer me, mother! I have a right to know." Daya fought back the tears of rage that choked her throat.

"Daya, sweetheart, is that you?" Her mother's voice sounded strange, differently pitched, very far away. "It's me, Auntie Veena, calling from Bombay. What is going on? What have those two naughty boys done now?" Daya pulled the receiver away from her ear.

Oh no, Veena! Not now. Where were you when I needed you?

"Daya!" Veena cried urgently. "Speak to me. Are you all right? Did they hurt you? Isn't your uncle around? Talk to him, darling, tell him everything. He loves you like a father. Daya, answer me!"

Daya felt the tears burning her face. *Why? Why in his mother's deathbed?*

"Sweetheart, those two boys are basically good at heart. They would never do anything to hurt you. Whatever happened, happened. Let it be now, let it go. I'm sorry I called when you were expecting your mother, but I'm sure she would say exactly what I'm telling you. You're young still, you have your whole life ahead of you. Forget it ever happened. Daya, are you there?"

She held her hand over her eyes and shook her head slowly.

"It's okay if you can't talk now, darling. I'll be home in two days. Uncle and I will take you out for a nice dinner, and then you can tell us everything . . . "

Daya put the phone down. Immediately it rang again. She walked into her bedroom, snatched up all her clothes and stuffed them into her bag. She walked down the stairs and out of the house. Daya checked her pocket for change. It would be a dollar or so to get to Manhattan. She should have gone the first day, should have gone and done what she came to do, instead of getting caught up with the men. When she arrived at the bus stop, a bus was pulling up. She asked the driver if he went down Museum Mile and he nodded.

Daya stared out of the window, concentrating on every shop name, every road sign, every hoarding. The intimacies of the night before tumbled through her head. She combed the images one by one to locate even a single dishonest touch, look or action. They had held each other for so long, in so many different ways. Not once had he pulled away from her. Not once had his loving attention flagged.

"Here's where the museums start, miss!" the bus driver called cheerfully to Daya. She sprang out of her seat and hurried off the bus.

Museum Mile on Fifth Avenue. Not a soul on the streets. She had hoped to encounter crowds of people, had envisioned losing herself in the rushing bodies of New Yorkers. She walked quickly. She would tire herself out.

How many women had been condemned to that bed? Daya felt numb with grief. She waited for the familiar anger to rise through her once again, but the memories of the previous night were still locked in her groin, glowing like coals. The warmth in her body moved upward and outward, comforting her. She felt his gentle hands on her face. And it was then that she understood. He'd had to do it. In some strange way, it had broken the spell that hung over him.

She walked past a hot dog vendor. He had big drooping eyes, chubby jowls and a bushy moustache. He looked Greek. He caught her eye and waved enthusiastically. His gaze was inquiring. Two blocks down he was there again. "You are Greek?" he shouted, arms in the air. "Come, come!"

Daya walked on.

"Armenian? Turkish? Palestinian?" he called frantically. She ducked into a museum.

The security guard at the museum addressed her before she had even crossed the gate. "I am from Guyana. You are also from Guyana?"

"No!" Daya snapped at the guard and rushed in.

"Trinidad? Jamaica? Fiji?" he called after her. "I'm sure I know you!"

Daya didn't know what museum she had walked into. There were old oil paintings in heavy gold frames. They were portraits of pale people, with faces brightly lit; the rest of their bodies were in darkness. The faces were expressionless and looked like they had been painted off cadavers. She decided to leave through a side exit, to avoid another encounter with the security guard.

As she pushed open the door, the hot dog vendor was right there again. He opened his hands wide and pleaded with her. "You are Lebanese? Egyptian? Iraqi? Come, come, I feed you!"

She frowned at him and turned away. The hot dog vendor followed at a trot, and walked alongside her. "Very nice!" he smiled, framing Daya's face in the air. "Woman," he added emphatically, "where are you from?"

Daya stopped and scowled at him.

"Isn't it *obvious* that I'm Indian?"

The hot dog vendor clapped his hands.

"Ah, Indian!" he repeated with delight. "India! Most beautiful woman in India. Most wonderful woman in India. I see movies. Happy, happy, dancing, singing!" The Greek sprang from leg to leg and snapped his fingers in the air.

"Every man love Indian woman! Whole world love Indian woman!"

Daya took a long look at the singing shaking jowls and the merry twinkling eyes. She started laughing. This man was insane. Stark raving mad.

The Greek danced toward her, then away from her, then whirled around and around, encircling her. She watched the man through tired eyes. She drew in deep gulps of warm spring air.

"Beautiful, beautiful Indian woman! Happy, happy Indian woman!" The Greek danced on, lost in his hymns of praise.

Daya watched him shout out his joy.

This is what I came for, this is what brought me here.

When he finally stopped, she clapped for him. He came up to her and saluted her, bowing low to the ground. Daya shook his hand. "Thanks for the reminder," she said softly.

The Greek smiled at her, not understanding. He snapped his fingers and leapt in the air one last time, then retreated to his hot dog stand. Daya waved to the Greek, but his back was turned to her as he resumed pushing his cart down the street.

So many years of anger, Daya mused, *and this man sees only beauty in my face.* She looked at her reflection in the window of the museum. Her smiling eyes shone back at her, gleaming with a mischievous light.

Women in Exile: Gender Relations in the Asian Indian Community in the U.S.

Sayantani DasGupta and Shamita Das Dasgupta

Charting the Chasm

"It would be much easier if you were a lesbian," my friend Sanjay[1] recently suggested in response to my queries about available Indian men. "There are so many wonderful Indian women, political and progressive, who would fit you perfectly," he added, "Can't think of one man though!" I sighed. Being heterosexual, I thought, was clearly not all it was cracked up to be.

Despite raising her with strong feminist values, and trying to inculcate in her the importance of women's self-sufficiency, it became apparent early on that my daughter intended to eventually marry a man and have children. I suppose my own example, as a wife, mother, and feminist activist, was a stronger motivator than all my warnings. However, as my daughter grew older, it became clear that finding a partner would not be very easy. Her pride in and identification with her Indian heritage inclined her towards choosing a compatriot, yet, there were invisible obstacles that seemed to thwart this sympathy at its roots. Often, to my judicious inquiries about why she would not go out with Indian men, she exasperatedly replied, "You don't seem to understand, Indian men don't like women like me."

I recently saw the movie "Waiting to Exhale," adapted from Terry Macmillan's novel, in which four African American women mourn the lack of 'good' (read: educated, sensitive, kind, honest, loving, truthful, steadfast) African American men. Despite being awed by both Angela Basset's superb acting and phenomenal biceps, I hated the film. Having been brought up on strong feminist ethics, I have no patience for the idea that women, in this case, strong, intelligent, beautiful women, are somehow unfulfilled without men. I also have minimal tolerance for conversations that begin with the query, "Where are all the good (insert the relevant ethnic group) men out there?" Yet, as an Indian American woman in my mid-twenties, I find myself holding my breath, waiting to find a 'good' (read: all that MacMillan's characters were searching for, plus politically progressive/socially conscious) Indian American man. And many of my fellow heterosexual Indian American activist women friends are doing the same. Yet, what's going on is more than a mere man hunt. There is an interesting dynamic at work among heterosexual Indian American men and women, and only by analyzing and defining the parameters of this dynamic can we fully exhale. .

More and more young women of Indian descent complain that they are unable to find a partner within the community who is supportive and encouraging of their independence, assertiveness, activism, and ambition. Although statistics are not yet available, there seems to be a greater number of South Asian women marrying outside the community than their male counterparts. An immigrant mother once remarked ruefully about this phenomenon, "All the accomplished young women in our community seem to be leaving the fold by marriage!"

Indeed, the phenomenon of female exogamy in the Indian American community appears to be predominantly among outgoing, outspoken, and often activist young women. While many highly achieving second-generation women are becoming exogamous, many more of their male counterparts are voluntarily returning to their parents' natal land to find brides. There is obviously a mutual vote of no-confidence being cast between the genders in the second generation of heterosexual Indian Americans. The question is, why?

As two members of the Indian American community, an immigrant mother and a U.S.-born daughter, we have witnessed this gender interplay with both personal and professional interest. While it clearly affects our own lives, the phenomenon of female exogamy also illuminates pivotal community issues such as gender role recreation, consolidation of male power, heterosexual relational models, and finally, community integrity. Our different perspectives and life experiences have allowed us, as collaborators, to view these issues from varied vantage-points. Thus, we have jointly written this essay examining heterosexual relations and gender roles within the Indian American community, while maintaining our different voices through changes in the typeface. We are, however, only two unique voices: a mother and a daughter, a psychology professor and a medical student, a community activist and a writer. We do not presume to dictate any answers, rather, to introduce questions and ultimately, to open a dialogue through which we can recognize the phenomena at work around us, and strive to define them rather than allow them to define us.

Recreating Gender Roles

The Indian American community as we know it today is comprised primarily of those immigrants who came to this country after the relaxation of immigration laws in 1965. There is no doubt that these immigrants have found economic and professional success quickly in this country.[2] As a result, Indians, like other Asian immigrant communities, have been labeled as the "model minority," an idea created in the 1970s when journalists publicized the high educational levels and median incomes, as well as low crime rates among Asian Americans. At the time, this brand of "model minority" was an argument against social welfare programs; however, it has ultimately created political schisms between Asian Americans and other minority communities. Indeed, it is the "model minority" myth which is responsible for propagating the notion that Indians are free from social problems such as unemployment, poverty, racism, and delinquency. Popularization of the myth has not only colored the political and social attitudes of the mainstream, but it has also been deeply internalized by Indians themselves. Consequently, Indian immigrants have become preoccupied with living up to, as well as participating in the creation of the image of a perfect group.

On a recent trip to Nashville, where I had been invited to facilitate a series of gender workshops at an Indian American 'Youth' Conference, I came face to face with a breakdown of the 'model minority' stereotype. As a daughter of immigrants who came to the U.S. in the late 1960's for graduate studies, the Indian community I know is comprised basically of 'first wave' immigrants: white collar and professional workers. Having been raised in primarily white professional towns, the overt racism I faced during my life was confined almost entirely to the schoolyard. As soon as I grew older, the prejudice I faced based on culture or skin color was definitely insidious. "I don't even think of you as a minority," white Americans would say to me, "I mean, Asians are just like us." During my recent trip to Nashville, however, I was shocked to hear my workshop participants describe stereotypes pertaining to themselves. "Americans think we're all motel and 7-11 owners," commented the men, "They think we're cheap." The women added, "American men think Indian women are ditzy and stupid, that we're only good for having babies and cleaning the house." As a daughter of the 'first wave' immigrants, I had been protected from these stereotypes. Indeed, I had always struggled against the idea that Indian Americans were nothing but upwardly mobile, asexual, nerdy doctor/engineer/computer programmers. Never did it occur to me that Indian American women of different communities were being labeled as 'ditzy' or 'stupid'. I was deeply startled as the 'model minority' myth crumbled before my eyes.

When the post-1965 immigrants moved to America, they left behind a familiar world of relatives and friends along with cultural institutions and information. Settling down in the U.S. not only required finding economic stability, but reinventing immigrant identities in the new context. Without any established standards and reference points, everything had to be renegotiated, and Indian American immigrants proceeded to rebuild the "familiar essentials" in their new home.[3]

The Indian American community's reconstruction of itself has been based primarily upon a reinvention of what it means to be a 'good Indian'. Faced with the external threats of racism, assimilation and cultural dissolution, as well as the internal pressures of maintaining a 'good face' consistent with the model minority image, the Indian American communities of the U.S. have closed ranks. Their redefinition of self involves an extremely rigid notion of 'Indian-ness' which homogenizes diversity, rejects variety, and silences dissent.

Construction of this exemplary public face has been dominated by the wealthy and powerful Indian male bourgeoisie which controls the community's religious, political, informational, and cultural institutions. This bourgeoisie created certain representations to embody the integrity of its idealized community. Primary among these icons is that of the Indian woman as chaste, modest, nurturing, obedient, and loyal. According to Anannya Bhattacharjee, ". . . [T]he woman becomes a metaphor for the purity, the chastity, and the sanctity of the Ancient Spirit that is India."[4] Through this creation of an unblemished Asian Indian public face, the immigrant patriarchy has rested the validity of the entire community upon the submissiveness of the community's women. Thus, the 'proper' behavior of both first- and second-generation Indian women in America has become a litmus test of community solidarity. In turn, women deviating from this idea of traditional Indian womanhood are considered traitors to the community. There is, thus, a general denial of feminist activism and women's strength as a part of Indian traditions.

As I became active in feminist groups and domestic violence work in my new home, many of the men I knew became alarmed that their wives were acquainted with me. Many declared jokingly (!) that they did not want their wives to be corrupted by me. Some even renamed our South Asian woman's group, Manavi[5] (which means primordial woman), 'danavi' or demoness. A few more sympathetic souls tried to unearth the reasons for my untoward preoccupations. "What happened to you to make you this way? Were you abused as a child or something?" The subtext was loud and clear that such activities are possible only by women who have somehow been warped. I became a thorn in the community's side.

Feminists and other activists are systematically marginalized from the Indian American hegemonic construction of 'community,' exemplified by incidents such as the 1995 barring of all women's groups, gay/lesbian groups, and other 'political' organizations from the India Day Parade in New York City organized by the FIA (Federation of Indians in America). While it is well protected from all hints of diversity or dissent, the reinvented identity of the Indian American hegemony is also being kept intact through its inculcation in the community's sons and daughters. Indeed, although community festivals initially served immigrants' own nostalgia, they have become vehicles for cultural training of the 'second generation.' Since Indian American youth often have no real connection to the subcontinent beyond their immigrant parents, their cultural teachings are not only anachronistic, dating back to the India of the 1960's and 1970's known by the immigrant parents, but also heavily entrenched in the idealized, reinvented 'familiar essentials' of the hegemony.

"The central task of any youth conference," reads a 1992 opinion letter in India Abroad, "is to inculcate in the young our values, traditions and heritage . . . (however) due to the failings of their parents and due to their own nonchalance, (Indian American youth) fail to appreciate the richness of their ancient heritage and its timeless values. At the same time, like adolescents everywhere, they succumb to imbibing the undesirable elements in American society."[6] The 'undesirable elements' referred to here undoubtedly are what Nita Shah calls "the American culture of drugs, promiscuity, and rebelliousness."[7] However, there is a gender discrepancy in the community's response to such threats. Indeed, since it is the icon of the perfect Indian woman which upholds community integrity, so too are the daughters of the community disproportionately burdened with the preservation of culture in the form of religion, language, dress, food, and child-drearing.

Throughout my life, I have been involved in Indian community dances, poetry recitals, musical festivals, and pujas. While I and countless other little Indian girls were sari-swathed, paper-flower-garlanded, primped, and prodded for most of our youth, our male counterparts got off, for the most part, scot-free. The young women I met at a recent Indian American 'Youth' Conference perhaps said it best. "We girls are expected to deck out in Indian clothes at every bhangra," they complained, "But the guys can just wear their baggy jeans and backwards baseball caps. They dress like homeboys and no one says anything."

Of central importance in the cultural schooling of community 'youth' is the careful preservation of gender roles. To this end, the 'chastity' and 'purity' of community daughters is much prized, evidenced by unequal parental restrictions the autonomous dating behavior of daughters, and the increased vigilance against exogamy of girls.[8] As second-generation women are expected to be 'chaste' and 'pure,' so too are they expected to be 'docile' and 'obedient.' Indeed, most 'second-generation' community members are taught to believe that Indian culture and political activism do not go together. Young women are raised to believe feminism and ultimately, perhaps, women's strength, is anti-Indian.

Heroines and Strong Women

In a community whose integrity is based upon the iconography of women's passivity, history must be rewritten. Indeed, in order to maintain its flawless community facade, the Indian American hegemony has ignored the rich history of Indian women's contributions to various social change movements. Yet, as Indian women, we carry a long history of activism and social awareness, both within and without the subcontinent.[9]

My father, who had participated in the Indian nationalist movement, filled my childhood with stories of the revolution. In most of these anecdotes, women were integral. In many, they were heroines. I myself would later observe women in the thick of various other political movements, such as the Naxalite movement of the late 1960s. My own lifelong and active involvement in fighting for women's rights, therefore, was never a surprise, nor an anomaly. Both my family in India and I considered it to be a natural progression of my thinking and beliefs.

From politics to the environment, from indigenous people's rights to health issues, from displacement of families to workers' rights, Indian women have always played an active role in social movements. Interestingly, most such activist women did not embrace either activism or family in their lives, but combined their multiple roles successfully. By choosing the path of activism, women did not forego the happiness of having a family.

My role models emerged from mythology and real life: goddesses, queens, freedom fighters, participants in social and political movements— women who were at the center, rather than the margins of society. My upbringing, although quite traditional in many ways, never convinced me that being a wife and mother and a social change agent were oppositional to each other. Although my parents had arranged my marriage when I was sixteen, they had not emphasized only the traditional "good wife" role to me. I was raised on Mahatma Gandhi's proclamation, "A woman who does not raise her voice against social injustices is committing injustice herself." Thus, when my daughter was growing up in the U.S., my goal was to raise a socially conscious and active person, someone with a sense of justice and integrity.

One of my earliest memories is of a 'Take Back the Night' march. I must have been five or six. I remember holding my mother's hand as we marched among throngs of other women, holding candles and raising their voices to illuminate the darkness. Later, frustrated with the racism inherent in the mainstream American women's movement, my mother would found the first South Asian women's organization in the U.S., Manavi. I was fifteen, and by that age, extremely familiar with and comfortable within women's organizations. I was brought up marching. Yet, activism was not something 'American' to me, nor was it something unique to my mother. I had grown up seeing a strong tradition of women's strength in India: from the mythical ferocity of the warrior goddess Durga to the very formidable presence of the women in my family. While I grew up hearing stories about my great-aunts, who fought and died in the Indian Independence Movement, I was able to meet in person my grandmother's friends: elderly white-sari-clad ladies who turned out to be Black Belts in Judo, double Ph.D.s and international language experts. I had no doubt that I came from a heritage of insuperable women.

A strong tradition of women's strength has most strategically been lost in the process of immigration and self re-creation. For many Indian American women raised in the West, being 'Indian' and being 'feminist' are antithetical concepts.

More than once, young women have come up to me after one of my talks on college campuses and remarked, "But, you look just like my mother!" The declaration is not about my age, but a comment on the apparent incompatibility of my appearance and work. How could I, a married, middle-aged mother carrying the symbols of sari and bindi, be an activist? These symbols marked me as a traditional woman and thereby, complacent and compliant.

The common assumption among Americans is that only "westernization" leads women to be involved in politics, social change movements, or any kind of social activism. We Indian American women are seen as essentially passive, subservient, conservative, dependent, slavish, oppressed, and tradition-bound (read: backward). It is only by coming to the West and internalizing its culture that we can be free and emancipated. This characterization of Indian women is unambiguously articulated in Bharati Mukherjee's novel, *Jasmine*.[10] Mukherjee's heroine undergoes transformation from Indian/eastern to American/western and thereby is delivered from the tyranny of patriarchal oppression.[11] Thus, when Asian Indian women do become active forces, westernization is given credit for it. Too many academics and lay people alike believe that immigration is responsible for Indian American women's liberation, that acculturation to western culture has made Indian American women 'progressive'.

"What do you consider yourself?" I was asked by a 'progressive' white American woman, "An Indian or a feminist?" It is this mainstream notion, that progressive politics and Asian heritage are somehow irreconcilable, that has maintained the silence around Asian women's activism. For the Indian American community, this attitude is not only an external one, but an internal one as well. Feminists in the community risk being considered 'un-Indian' community betrayers. My mother, a long-time activist in the Indian American community, has managed to confuse community nay-sayers by maintaining a happy thirty-year marriage and stable position in the mainstream Indian American community while continuing her work with issues of domestic violence. Half the time, neither mainstream Americans nor mainstream Indian Americans realize exactly how subversive

a person she is, since they are somehow lulled into security by her 'proper' Indian appearance, attire, and almost ever-present bindi. I am lucky in having her example. I know that while my feminism arises from a long tradition of Indian women's strength, my very Indian-ness is dependent upon my being a feminist. Yet, with my short hair, Western education, clothes and accent, my activism risks being attributed to my westernization, a betrayal of my heritage.

While I was teaching a course on Third World women, a young Indian woman student stayed back after one class. The class discussions that day had been bleak, elaborating the various injustices women face on a day-to-day basis. When the other students had left, this young woman came up to me and said dejectedly, "I am so upset! We are doomed unless we learn from the West." She is not the only person who has expressed these sentiments. Another young woman student asked me once whether my daughter was politically active. On hearing my affirmation, she proudly declared, "My family is very traditional. I live within my heritage. I would never do something like that."

Those with this ahistorical perspective and understanding of Indian women have dismissed our work and labeled activists as traitors to the community. Consequently, many young men of the community dispute the femininity as well as the 'Indian-ness' of activist women.

"Indian men hate us," my friend Preeti, a fellow outspoken Indian American woman and frequent Indian 'Youth' Conference speaker, told me recently. "They just don't like the package." She added, "You may confuse them at first. You look all demure and sweet from the outside, but then you open your big mouth and the illusion crumbles. The fact is, most Indian American men just can't deal with a strong Indian woman." I've had this discussion with many other Indian women and my experiences confirm these sentiments. At a recent conference, I met an interesting, smart, funny and warm Indian American man— a fellow writer. However, our day-long chummy camaraderie turned around 180 degrees as soon as this young man attended my workshop and heard me speak. Since he seemed a fairly liberal person, I don't think it was my politics that offended him. Rather, I believe I somehow intimidated him. While there are politically progressive, even feminist, Indian American men, it seems that many of our heterosexual male counterparts have more stringent and usually more unrealistic expectations for us than for non-Indian women. As my friend Preeti says, "It's okay for their American girlfriends to be whatever they are. But

as soon as an Indian guy dates an Indian woman, she's no good unless she can cook 'daal' just like his Ma."

Rather than encouraging and accommodating women's activism, post-colonial conceptualizations deny variability in women's roles. In the West, there are basically two dichotomous models of women: the goddess and the whore. In fact, the ubiquity of these images has drowned out the existence of any other models from our minds. Similar to the image of the Western goddess, South Asian Hindu cultures have Devi, the chaste and benevolent ideal woman who supports and upholds the patriarchal order. There is also the 'whore'-like fallen woman. However, between these two extremes is another powerful model available in the Asian Indian schema: Shakti. In real life, this image has been translated into the Virangana, the brave warrior woman. Viranganas are the numerous women leaders, from the Rani of Jhansi to Indira Gandhi, who throughout history have led battles against the enemy and struggles against injustice. Although the gentle Devi is the one all parents hope their daughters will emulate, the virangana is not marginalized in South Asia. She is very much respected and worshipped. Furthermore, she is not just a Hindu image. Within Islamic culture also, there are many women leaders who we can claim as our models including Khadija and Ayesha from the time of the prophet; Noorjehan, Jahanara and many others from the Mughal times; Rokeya Sakhawat Hossain, Halima Khatun, Badrunnessa Begum and numerous other freedom fighters from the nationalist movement. This tradition of viranganas and activist foremothers creates a space within sub-continental cultures for women's strength.

My grandmother, while a fairly traditional woman, has never pressured me to be domestic or docile. Indeed, because I have always been academically successful, she seems to consider me outside of the traditional womanly expectations. "You will be a great doctor," she tells me, "and heal the poor. You don't have time to worry about a household. That will be taken care of by others." Clearly, there is a traditional Indian space for me, as a successful woman, that is beyond the expectations of womanly normalcy.

In their transmigration to the U.S., Indian immigrants failed to bring over these traditional spaces for Indian women's strength. Indeed, the role of the virangana, while alive and well in subcontinental cultures, has been wiped out in Indian American communities in favor of the more constricting 'goddess'/'whore' or 'good Indian girl'/'bad Indian girl' dichotomy. Not only traditional spaces, but Indian women's chronicles of activism in this country are also being denied. Early immigrant women who came here in the 1800s carved out a space for themselves amidst virulent social and legal racism. However, the post-1965 immigrants have rendered invisible the work of these early activists in their struggle to redefine themselves with an unblemished and monolithic public face.

Masculinity Under Fire

Racism is not gender-neutral, but strikes at the essential 'masculinity' and 'femininity' of minority peoples. This fact is recognized in the African American community, where the phenomenon of Black men's 'emasculation' by mainstream America is a galvanizing point for many male activists. Indeed, the recent 'Million Man March' on Washington D.C. was partially an attempt to redefine and reclaim African American masculinity from the jaws of racist parameters. In the Indian American community, racism also plays out in gendered terms. Indeed, for Indian American women's groups, the linking of minority 'otherness' to our femininity is a much recognized phenomenon.

When I was a teenager, if a car-full of white men hooted at me, I was convinced they were making fun of me—ridiculing me as ugly, brown and undesirable. If a car-full of non-white men were to do the same, I would recognize it as sexual harassment without convoluting the incident with my own sexual insecurities. Growing up as the only little brown-skin girl on the block in the heart of the U.S. midwest, I was too often told my brown skin was 'ugly'. The combined effect of this rejection and an omnipresent Farah Fawcett/Cheryl Ladd/Barbie white beauty standard convinced me that I, with my dark skin, black hair, and 'foreign' ways, would never be beautiful. As a college student on a liberal New England campus, my brown skin went from 'ugly' to 'exotic'. It was difficult not to enjoy the 'exoticization' and 'spiritualization' of my sexual self after the ego bruises of childhood.

While the effect of racism upon Indian American women's sexual self-concepts has been explored by our community,[12] the role that racism plays in the development of Indian American masculine self-concepts is perhaps left unexplored. The list of stereotypes given to Indian, and for that matter all Asian American men, include: nerdy, weak, unassertive, sneaky, smelly, sexist, and short. In contrast, the characteristics that form a cluster around Western masculinity are related to instrumentality and aggression. Western macho men are independent, strong, large, go-getters, and fighters. Despite the 'sensitive male' movement of the '60s and '70s, the image of Western man as aggressive, powerful and omnipotent has remained largely unchanged over the years. Since this masculine model is based upon the Western male, Indian and Asian men can hardly hope to measure up to it. In all areas of popular ideals of masculinity such as physique, sexuality, aggression, and athletics, the Asian Indian man falls short of the standards in no uncertain terms.

Thus, Indian men are perhaps 'emasculated' through their very status as a 'model minority.' While African American men are marginalized and rendered impotent through their association with criminality, joblessness, as well as the drug culture, and Latino men are disempowered through their association with laziness, stupidity and slothfulness, both groups of minority men are still considered 'masculine,' if not hypersexual and animalistic. On the other hand, the stereotypes afforded Asian American men are more in accordance with a sexist notion of 'femininity'. Asian American men are weak, delicate, precise, fragile, and ultimately, quellable.

> [The stereotype is] . . . of black and Latino men being sexually
> hungry, ravenous beasts (white men are scared of them);
> and of Asian men as being nerdy, asexual and gay (white men
> patronizing them) . . . . Asian men have 1000 per cent more
> pressure to 'prove' their heterosexuality . . . . Asian men are seen
> as not being capable of having power in general (because they are
> not seen as having sexual power), and black and Latino men are seen
> as not being able to handle power in general.[13]

David Henry Hwang's play *M. Butterfly* explores this emasculation of the Asian man through imperialism and machismo. "The West thinks of itself as masculine," says the character Song, an Asian man who for years fools his French lover into thinking he is a woman, "[B]ig guns, big industry, big money—so the East is feminine—weak, delicate, poor . . . but good at art, and full of inscrutable wisdom—the feminine mystique."[14] To explain why it was so easy to fool his French lover, Song adds, "[Because] . . . I am an Oriental. And being an Oriental, I could never be completely a man."[15]

Although both Asian Indian men and women are victims of negative stereo-types in the U.S., the fundamental gender identity of only Indian men is brought into question. Although Indian women's gender identity is a target for racist assault, they are rarely considered unfeminine. Indeed, through images of exoticism and Eastern mystique, Indian American women are often labeled as hyper-feminine. Conversely, due to the impossibility of reaching western mas-culine ideals, the gender typing of Asian Indian men becomes suspect. As "Oriental" men, Indian Americans can perhaps never be considered 'fully male.'

In contrast to this deprecation of the outside world, most Indian American men are treated at home with special privileges. There they can do little wrong and are allowed concessions in line with traditional patriarchal advantages and the strong subcontinental tradition of son-privilege. In the immigrant commu-nity, however, there is a contradiction between this internal reality and the exter-nal forces of U.S. racism. Even though he is brought up as the 'raja' of his home and believes that such treatment is due to him, the racism and neglect of the external world do not allow the Indian American young man to feel privileged. Thus, cultural identification is a double-edged sword: to be an Indian American in the mainstream community means being feminized. Thus, only through their Indian identity can young men find power in being a community 'raja.'

Many of the young Indian American men I grew up with initially rejected their her-itage. Indeed, since community girls were unequally burdened with upholding cultural continuity, young men were able to reject 'Indian-ness' in dress, food, and language. Many young men I knew tried to be ultra-'American' by lifting weights, participating in sports, joining mainstream fraternities, guzzling beers, and even through dating only non-Indian women. However, I've been noticing a change among the men slightly younger than I am. Perhaps because the men my age were unable to successfully compete with American stan-dards of masculinity, younger men seem to be finding their sense of manhood through cul-tural identification. "We come from a strong heritage, a good heritage," a young man recently proclaimed at an Indian American 'youth' conference, "Do we really want to be like these Americans, sleeping around, dressing like women, having no morals at all?" As he became more and more agitated, he punched his arms in the air 'bhangra'-style, shout-ing, "Jai Hind!"

This contradiction of an external racist emasculation and an internal 'raja' syndrome leaves only one area where the Indian American male can assert his masculinity: his relationship with community women. Indeed, while discussing the hostility that women's organizations face in the U.S., one of India's foremost journalists, Madhu Kishwar, remarked that she was flabbergasted by immigrant men's negative reactions. She claimed that Indian men had shown her and her women's magazine, Manushi, much more support than we could ever imagine here. This discrepancy between subcontinental and immigrant Indian men's reactions to women's strength can perhaps be traced to the pressures upon Indian masculinity in the new world.

Indeed, this threat to their masculinity from the mainstream community has prompted Indian men to strictly limit their sisters' behavior. It is only by defining their counterparts as passive, docile homebodies that Asian Indian men can ascertain their masculinity. Thus, in order to both secure a homogenous community face and to ensure masculine privilege, women who do not fit the above characterization are exiled from the community. They become branded as unfit to be wives. They are castrating females.

A few years back, my daughter and I were featured on the cover of a feminist magazine as a mother-daughter activist team. My proud husband took the issue to work for a round of 'show and tell.' One of his close Indian immigrant friends gently advised him that if not for his wife, for his daughter this was risky conduct. "She has to find a husband, you know," he observed. "It is going to be hard to find someone if she gets involved with such things. In our community, very few families want 'smart' girls."

Straying from the Fold

Exogamy is not a new phenomenon in Asian American communities. Indeed, according to Tinker (1973) and Kikumura and Kitano (1973), approximately half the marriages in which one person was Japanese American did not involve a Japanese American partner.[16] However, these patterns may have changed with time. A. Magazine cites that "in 1980, 75 percent of different-nationality marriages among Asian Americans were to whites, 20 percent to other Asians and 5 percent to other minorities. Ten years later, 55 percent of the marriages were to other Asians, 40 per cent to whites, and 5 per cent to other minorities."[17] There are further gender discrepancies in Asian American outmarriage. For instance,

Kitano and Yeung's 1979 research of Chinese American outmarriages in Los Angeles County suggested that the outmarriage rate was 44 percent for Chinese American males and 56 percent for Chinese American females.[18] The rationale for such gender disparity suggested by Kikumura and Kitano (1973) is that "Asian American females seem to acculturate faster than their male counterparts" primarily because "in a racist society, ethnic minority males may be viewed as more of a threat than females." [19] Acculturation, here, is directly linked to outmarriage. The 'war bride' phenomenon, when U.S. servicemen began to increasingly bring their wartime Asian brides home, may also attribute to mainstream acceptance of Asian female/White male marriages. Other arguments are that Asian American women have more incentive to outmarry, since many are dissatisfied with traditional Asian female gender roles, while Asian American men may be inhibited from doing the same by "family pressures, the necessity to carry on the family name, 'saving face,' and physical height" [20] Lastly, research on Asian American outmarriage suggests that sex differences in exogamy rates may be a function of stereotypes which label Asian American males as "quiet, shy, passive, and socially inept," while Asian American females are given more 'positive' stereotypes such as being "exotic, sexy, compliant, agreeable, and domestic." [21]

In many ways, this research on Asian American exogamy cannot be used to analyze the Asian Indian immigrant communities. First and foremost, many of these previous studies ignored the huge subpopulation of South Asians when discussing Asian Americans. Findings on Asian Americans are further rendered inapplicable to South Asians due to our different immigration histories and patterns of community re-creation. For instance, Morishima (1980) speculates that the Japanese American community's history of evacuation and detainment led some Japanese Americans to encourage their children to marry Caucasians with the hopes that succeeding generation could become more and more 'American' (the assumption being that internment occurred as a result of not being 'American' enough). In stark contrast, the bulk of the Indian American community is comprised of post-1965 immigrants who, in many ways, consider themselves 'migrant workers' unwilling to give up ties to their motherland, including, most importantly, ties of marriage. Another vital factor differentiating the experiences of Indian Americans from other Asians is that of color. Indeed, while Asian outmarriage may be affected by the fact that "many Asian American groups are light-skinned, which may make them less different from Caucasian Americans," [22] the skin color of Asian Indians, on the whole, does not resemble that of white Americans.

Although much of these previous findings may be inapplicable to Indian Americans, the idea that higher rates of Asian American female exogamy can be attributed to gendered stereotyping does ring true. Indeed, previous analyses of Indian American women's exogamy have focused solely upon the white American 'exoticization' of the Asian woman, the idea being that the hyper-feminine South Asian woman is a fetish-like token for sexual appetites of the white American man. Although Indian American women are clearly exoticized in the main-stream perception, there are also internal community forces determining their exogamy. Indeed, perhaps it is the marginalization and rejection of successful, outspoken, and high-achieving women from the Indian American community-fold that necessitates their seeking partners elsewhere. And perhaps, the mascu-line role confusion of Indian American men is what makes them intolerant of strong Indian American women. Conversely, mainstream American men, whose masculine self concepts are generally relatively intact and under no racist chal-lenge, are perhaps more open to and supportive of their Indian American female partners' strength.

"I was attracted to you because you were so outspoken and strong," my non-Indian boyfriend tells me, "I love the fact that you can argue anyone into the ground." This is a sentiment I have heard from non-Indian American man. "You're going to be famous," he adds, "and I'll be able to brag about you." Whether or not I achieve any type of fame in my life, his support gives me tremendous encouragement. It is true, it would be much eas-ier if he were Indian, but I'd rather have a supportive partner than one who is constantly made insecure by my strength.

Complementarity, Not Competition

This antagonism emerging between the genders may be a function of the dif-ferences in gender role conceptions in India and America. In India, gender roles are visualized as complementary. Despite many other problems, the flexibility inherent in this perception allows the genders to reverse roles at appropriate times. Thus, to the dynamic and militant Kali, there is the supportive and patient Siva. Although their female partners are powerful, neither Siva nor the spouses of viranganas are considered emasculated in the subcontinental context.

My commitment and association in women's rights work gradually converted my husband. For a number of years now, he has been an active member of Manavi. In many Indian parties I have heard his voice explaining the latest feminist doctrine or praxis regarding violence against women to a roomful of unresponsive men. His involvement with Manavi has at times, drawn snide asides from many of our Indian male friends. Yet, my husband has been my strongest supporter and comrade. However, I can hardly claim total responsibility for his understanding of women's activism. His mother was a motivated participant in the revolutionary wing of the nationalist movement.

In contrast to this idea of complementarity, gender roles in the west are considered dichotomous and oppositional. Thus, there is no room for women to be dynamic without the men being passive, for women to be aggressive without the men losing their machismo. Internalization of western gender standards by the Asian Indian immigrants thereby necessitates marginalization of activist and feminist women.

Due to both the heterogeneity intrinsic to South Asian culture and the long tradition of viranganas in the Indian society, there has always been space for autonomous and strong women. However, due to the homogeneity of the Indian American society, artificially shaped by the immigration laws, a 'model minority' myth and the strict standards of community leaders, this recognition of women's power and energy is being effectively denied within our communities.

The intention of this article is not to blame Indian men for all social ills, nor to tar them as ultimately oppressive. However, we believe it is important to recognize the intergender discord that is brewing in our community and begin a conversation towards an amelioration of the situation. It is our contention that the dichotomous conceptualization of gender roles allows little room for the existence of both strong women and men. It is only by accepting role complementarity or androgyny [23] as gender ideals that we can prevent the actual and psychological exclusion of activist and competent women from our ranks.

Notes

[1] All names have been changed to protect the privacy of the individual.

[2] A. W. Helweg & U. M. Helweg (1990); P. Agarwal (1991).

[3] A. Bhattacharjee (1992).

[4] A. Bhattacharjee, p. 30.

[5] Manavi is the pioneering organization in the U.S. that focuses on violence against South Asian women. It was established in 1985.

[6] India Abroad (June 5), p. 3.

[7] N. Shah (1993).

[8] L. Mani (1992); S. D. Dasgupta (in press); S. D. Dasgupta & S. DasGupta (1996).

[9] R. Kumar (1993).

[10] B. Mukherjee (1989).

[11] In *Jasmine*, Bharati Mukherjee's heroine transforms herself from Jyoti to Jasmine to Jane as she moves from Hasnapur to Iowa in search of liberation. In fact, Mukherjee characterizes 'Jyoti' as already a 'Jane' at birth, as she is a "fighter and adapter." Obviously, Mukherjee believes that only a "Jane" could be a "fighter and adapter," as opposed to Jyoti, who is doomed to be the opposite.

[12] S. DasGupta (1993).

[13] The 1995 National Asian American Sex Survey, *A Magazine* (Aug/Sept 1995) p.27.

[14] D. H. Hwang (1986), p. 83.

[15] Ibid.

[16] S. Sue and J. K. Morishima (1982), p.108.

[17] T. Hong (1995), p.21.

[18] As cited in S. Sue and J. K. Morishima (1982), p.109.

[19] Ibid, p.113.

[20] Ibid, p.114.

[21] Ibid, p.115.

[22] Ibid, p.112.

[23]Androgyny as the third gender identity was elaborated by American psychologist Sandra Bem in 1974. According to Bem, androgynous individuals measure high on both 'feminine' and 'masculine' personality traits. The concept of androgyny has been noted in Hindu mythology as the 'ardhanarishwar.'

Bibliography

Agarwal, P. (1991). *Passage from India: Post 1965 Indian Immigrants and Their Children: Conflicts, Concerns, & Solutions*. Palos Verdes, CA: Yuvati Publications.

Bem, S. (1974). "The Measurement of Psychological Androgyny." *Journal of Consulting and Clinical Psychology*, 42, 155–162.

Bhattacharjee, A. (1992). "The Habit of Ex-nomination: Nation, Women, and the Indian Immigrant Bourgeoisie." *Public Culture*, 5, 19-44.

Dasgupta, S. D. (in press). "The Gift of Utter Daring: Cultural Continuity in Asian Indian Communities." In S. Mazumdar & J. Vaid (Eds.), *Women, Communities, and Cultures: South Asians in America*.

Dasgupta, S. D. & DasGupta, S. (1996). "Public face, private space: Asian Indian women and sexuality." In N. B. Maglin & D. Perry (Eds.), *'Bad Girls'/'Good Girls': Women, Sex & Power in the Nineties*. New Brunswick, NJ: Rutgers University Press.

DasGupta, S. (March/April, 1993). "Glass Shawls and Long Hair: A South Asian Woman Talks Sexual Politics." *Ms.*, III, 76–77.

Hong, T. (August/September, 1995). "Tying the Knot." *A Magazine*, 16–21, 38.

Hwang, D. H. (1986). *M. Butterfly*. New York, NY: New American Library.

India Abroad. (June 5, 1992). "Letters to the Editor," 3.

Kikumura, A., & Kitano, H. H. L. (1973). "Interracial marriage: A Picture of the Japanese Americans." *Journal of Social Issues*, 29, 67–81.

Kumar, R. (1993). *The History of Doing: An Illustrated Account of Movements for Women's Rights and Feminism in India*, 1800–1990. New York, NY: Verso.

Morishima, J. K. (April, 1980). "Asian American Racial Mixes: Attitudes, Self-Concept, and Academic Performance." Paper presented at Western Psychological Association convention, Honolulu.

Mukherjee, B. (1989). *Jasmine*. New York, NY: Grove Weidenfeld.

Shah, N. (1993). *The Ethnic Strife: A Study of Asian Indian Women in the United States*. New York, NY: Pinkerton and Thomas Publications.

Sue, S. and J. K. Morishima. (1982). *The Mental Health of Asian Americans*. San Francisco, CA: Jossey-Bass Inc.

Tinker, J. N. (1973). "Intermarriage and Ethnic Boundaries: The Japanese American Case." *Journal of Social Issues*, 29, 49–66.

Yang, J. (August/September, 1995). "The 1995 National Asian American Sex Survey." *A. Magazine*, 22–1, 47.

Defend Yourself Against Me

Bapsi Sidhwa

"They are my grandparents," says Kishen. I peer at the incongruous pair
mounted in an old gold frame holding an era captive in the faded brown and gray
photograph. I marvel. The heavy portrait has been transported across the seven
seas; from the Deccan plateau in India to the flat, glass-and-aluminum-pierced
horizons of Houston in Texas. The tiny sari-clad bride, her nervous eyes wide,
her lips slightly ajar, barely clears the middle-aged bridegroom's ribs.

"Your grandfather was exceptionally tall," I remark, expressing surprise;
Kishen is short and stocky. But distracted partly by the querulous cries of his
excited children, and partly by his cares as a host, Kishen nods so perfunctorily
that I surmise his grandfather's height cannot have been significant. His grandmother was either exceedingly short or not yet full-grown. I hazard a guess. She
could be ten; she could be eighteen. Marketable Indian brides—in those days at
least—wore the uniformly bewildered countenances of lambs to the slaughter
and looked alike irrespective of age.

We hear a car purr up the drive and the muted thud of Buick doors. The
other guests have arrived. Kishen, natty in a white shark-skin suit, tan tie and
matching silk handkerchief, darts out of the room to welcome his guests loudly
and hospitably. *Aiiay! Aiiay! Array bhai*, we've been waiting for you! *Kitni der
laga di*," he bellows in the curious mix of Urdu and English that enriches communication between the inheritors of the British Raj, Indians and Pakistanis
alike. "I have a wonderful surprise for you," I hear him shout as he ushers his
guests inside. "I have a lady friend from Pakistan I want you to meet!"

I move hesitantly to the living-room door and peer into the hall. Flinging
out a gleaming shark-skinned arm in a grand gesture of introduction, Kishen
announces: "Here she is! Meet Mrs. Jacobs." And turning on me his large, intelligent eyes, beaming handsomely, he says, "Sikander Khan is also from Pakistan."

Mr. Sikander Khan, blue-suited and black-booted, his wife and her three sisters in satin shalwar-kamizes and heavy gold jewelry, and a number of knee-high

children stream into the living room. We shake hands all round and recline in varying attitudes of stiff discomfiture in the deep chairs and sofas covered, desi style, with printed bed-spreads to camouflage the stains and wear of a house inhabited by an extended Hindu family.

Kishen's diminutive mother, fluffed out in a starched white cotton sari, smiles anxiously at me across a lumpy expanse of sofa and his two younger brothers, unsmiling and bored, slouch on straight-backed dining room chairs to one side, their legs crossed at the ankles and stretched right out in front. Suzanne, Kishen's statuesque American wife, her brown hair falling in straight strands down her shoulders and back, flits to and fro in the kitchen. As comfortable in a pink silk sari with a gold border as if she were born to it, she pads barefoot into the room, the skin on her toes twinkling whitely, bearing a tray of potato samosas, fruit juices and coke, the very image of dutiful brahmin-wifedom. A vermilion caste mark spreads prettily between her large and limpid brown eyes.

I know her well. Her other-worldly calm and docility are due equally to her close association with her demanding and rambunctious Indian family, and the more private rigors of her job as a computer programmer in an oil corporation.

I make polite conversation with Mrs. Khan's sisters in hesitant Punjabi. They have just emigrated. The differences from our past remain: I, an English-speaking scion of Anglican Protestants from Lahore; they, village belles accustomed to draw water to the rhythm of Punjabi lore. They have very little English. Tart and shifty-eyed, their jewelry glinting like armor, they are on the defensive; blindly battling their way through cultural shock-waves in an attempt to adapt to a new environment as different from theirs as only a hamburger at McDonald's can be from a leisurely meal of spicy greens eaten in steamy village courtyards redolent of buffalo dung and dust-caked naked children.

Observing their bristling discomfiture and the desultory nature of the conversation, Sikander Khan moves closer to me. He is completely at ease. Acclimated. Americanized.

Our conversation follows the usual ritual of discourse between Pakistanis who meet for the first time on European or American soil. He moved from Pakistan eleven years ago, I too. He has a Pakistani and Indian spice shop on Richmond uptown, I teach English at the University of Houston downtown. Does he have U.S. citizenship? Yes. Do I? No, but I should have a green card by December.

Mr. Khan filed his mother's immigration papers two years ago: they should be through any day. One of his brothers-in-law will bring Ammijee. It will be his mother's, Ammijee's, first visit to America.

Mr. Khan speaks English with a broad Pakistani accent that is pleasant to my ears. "I went to the Dyal Singh College in Lahore," he says courteously when he learns I'm from Lahore. "It is a beautiful, historical old city."

All at once, without any apparent reason, my eyes prickle with a fine mist, and I become entangled in a web of nostalgia so intense that I lose my breath. I quickly lower my lids, and the demeanor of half a lifetime standing me in good stead, I maintain a slight smile of polite attention while the grip of sensation from the past hauls me back through the years to Lahore, to our bungalow on Race Course Road.

I am a little child playing hop-scotch outside the kitchen window. The autumn afternoon is overcast with shadows from the mighty sheesham trees in the front lawn. There is a brick wall to my right, a little crooked and bulging in places, and the clay cement in the grooves is eroded. I keep glancing at the wall, suppressing a great excitement.

Spellbound I sit still on Kishen's lumpy sofa, my pulse racing at the memory. Then, clearly, as if she were in the room, I hear mother shout: "Joy, come inside and put on your cardigan."

Startled by the images I snap out of my reverie. I search Mr. Khan's face so confusedly that he turns from me to Kishen's mother and awkwardly inquires of her how she is.

I have not recalled this part of my childhood in years. Certainly not since I moved to the U.S.A. Too enamored of the dazzling shopping malls and technical opulence of the smoothly operating country of my adoption, too frequent a visitor to Pakistan, I have not yet missed it, or given thought to the past. Perhaps it is this house, so comfortably possessed by its occupants and their Indian bric-a-brac. It takes an effort of will to remember that we are in the greenly-shaven suburbs of an American city in the heart of Texas.

Bending forward with the tray, smiling at my abstraction, Suzanne abruptly brings me to earth. "Joy," she asks, "would you like some wine?"

"I prefer this, thanks," I say, apologetically for a glass of coke.

"I used to know a Joy . . . Long, long ago," says Mr. Khan. "I spent one or two years in Lahore when I was a child."

Suzanne has shifted to Mr. Khan. As his hand, hesitant with the burden of choice, wavers among the glasses, I watch it compulsively. It is a swarthy, well-made hand with dark hair growing between the knuckles and on the back. The skin, up to where it disappears beneath his white shirt sleeve, is smooth and unblemished.

There must be at least a million Sikanders in Pakistan, and several million Khans. The title "Khan" is indiscriminately tagged on by most Pakistanis in the U.S.A. who generally lack family names in the western tradition. The likelihood that this whole-limbed and assured man with his trim mustache and military bearing is the shy and misshapen playmate of my childhood is remote.

But that part of my mind which is still in the convoluted grip of nostalgia, with its uncanny accompaniment of sounds and images, is convinced.

Having selected a glass of orange juice Sikander Khan leans forward to offer it to a small boy whimpering half-heartedly at his feet. I glance obliquely at the back of Mr. Khan's head. It is as well formed as the rest of him and entirely covered with strong, short-sheared black hair.

My one-time playmate had a raw pit gouged out of his head that couldn't have grown hair in a hundred years! Still, the certainty with me remains and, not the least bit afraid of sounding presumptuous, I ask, "Was the girl you knew called Joy Joshwa? I was known as Joy Joshwa then."

Holding the glass to the child's lips Sikander looks at me. My body casts a shadow across his face. His dark eyes on me are veiled with conjecture. "I don't remember the last name," he says, speaking in a considered manner. "But it could be."

"You are Sikander!" I announce in a voice that brooks no doubt or argument. "You lived next to us on Race Course Road. You were refugees . . . Don't you remember me?" My eyes misty, my smile wide and twitching, I know the while how absurd it is to expect him to recall the sharp-featured and angular girl in the rounded contours and softened features of my middle-aging womanhood.

"Was it Race Course Road?" says Sikander. He sits back and, turning his strong man's body to me, says, "I tried to locate the house when I was in Lahore . . . But we moved to the farm land allotted to us in Sahiwal years ago . . . I forgot the address . . . So it was Race Course Road!" He beams fondly at me. "You used to have pimples the size of boils!"

"Yes," I reply, and then I don't know what to say. It is difficult to maintain poise when transported to the agonized and self-conscious persona of a boil-ridden and stringy child before a man who is, after all these years, a stranger.

Sitting opposite me—if he can ever be said to sit—Kishen comes to an explosive rescue. "You know each other? Imagine that! Childhood friends!"

Kishen has squirmed, crab-wise, clear across the huge sofa and is sitting so close to the edge that his weight is borne mostly by his thick legs. Half-way between sitting and squatting, quite at ease with the restless energy of his body, he is radiant with the wonder of it all.

"It is incredible," he booms with genial authority. "Incredible! After all these years you meet, not in Pakistan, but on the other side of the planet, in Houston!"

Triggered off by the fierce bout of nostalgia and the host of ghost-memories stirred by Sikander's unexpected presence, the scenes that have been floundering in the murky deeps of my subconscious come into luminous focus. I see a pattern emerge, and the jumble of half-remembered events and sensations already clamor to be recorded in a novel I have just begun about the Partition of India.

Turning to Sikander, smiling fondly back at him, I repeat, "You're quite right; I had horrible pimples."

Since childhood memories can only be accurately exhumed by the child I will inhabit my childhood. As a writer I am already practiced in inhabiting different bodies; dwelling in rooms, gardens, bungalows and spaces from the past; zapping time.

Lahore: Autumn 1948. Pakistan is a little over a year old. The Partition riots, the arson and slaughter, have subsided. The flood of refugees—12 million Muslims, Hindus, and Sikhs fleeing across borders that define India and Pakistan—has shrunk to a nervous trickle. Two gargantuan refugee camps have been set up on the outskirts of Lahore, at Walton and Badami Bagh. Bedraggled, carrying tin trunks, string-cots and cloth bundles on their heads, the refugees swamp the city looking for work, setting up house on sidewalks and in parks— wherever they happen to be at sunset if they have wandered too far from the camps.

A young Christian couple, the Mangat Rais, live on one side of our house on Race Course Road; on the other side is the enormous bungalow of our Hindu neighbors. I don't know when they fled. My friends Sheila and Sam never even said goodbye. Their deserted house has been looted several times. First by men in carts, shouting slogans, then by whomever chose to saunter in to pick up the leavings. Doors, sinks, wooden cabinets, electric fixtures and wiring have all been ripped from their moorings and carried away. How swiftly the deserted house has decayed. The hedges are a spooky tangle, the garden full of weeds and white patches of caked mud.

It is still quite warm when I begin to notice signs of occupation. A window boarded up with cardboard, a diffused pallid gleam from another screened with jute sacking as candles or oil-lamps struggle to illuminate the darkness. The windows face my room across the wall that separates our houses. The possession is so subtle that it dawns on me only gradually; I have new neighbors. I know they are refugees, frightened, nervous of drawing attention to their furtive presence. I know this as children know many things without being told, but I have no way of telling if children dwell in the decaying recesses of the stolen bungalow.

Although the ominous roar of slogans shouted by distant mobs—that nauseating throb that had pulsed a continuous threat to my existence and the existence of all those I love—has at least ceased, terrible new sounds (and unaccountable silences) erupt about me. Sounds of lamentation magnified by the night—sudden unearthly shrieks—come from a nursery school hastily converted into a Recovered Women's Camp six houses away from ours. Tens of thousands of women have been kidnapped and hundreds of camps have been set up all over the Punjab to sort out and settle those who are rescued, or "recovered."

Yet we hear nothing—no sound of talking, children quarreling or crying, of repairs being carried out—or any of the noises our refugee neighbors might be expected to make. It is eerie.

And then one afternoon, standing on my toes, I glimpse a small scruffy form through a gap in the wall (no more than a slit really) where the clay has worn away. I cannot tell if it's a boy or a girl or an apparition. The shadowy form appears to have such an attuned awareness that it senses my presence in advance, and I catch only a spectral glimpse as it dissolves at the far corner of my vision.

Impelled by curiosity—and by my loneliness now that even Sheila and Sam have gone—I peep into my new neighbor's compound through the crack in the wall, hoping to trap a potential playmate. A few days later, crouching slyly beneath the wall, I suddenly spring up to peer through the slit, and startle a canny pair of dark eyes staring straight at me.

I step back—look away nonchalantly—praying the eyes will stay. A stealthy glance reassures me. I pick up a sharp stone and quickly begin to sketch hopscotch lines in the mud on our drive. I throw the stone in one square after another, enthusiastically playing against myself, aware I'm being observed. I am suddenly conscious of the short frock I have outgrown. The waist, pulled by sashes stitched to either side and tied at the back, squeezed my ribs. The seams hurt under my arms and when I bend the least bit I know my white cotton knickers with dusty patch where I sit, are on embarrassing display. Never mind. If they offend the viewer, I'm sure my skipping skills won't. I skip rope, and turning round and round in one spot I breathlessly recite: "Teddy bear, Teddy bear, turn around: Teddy bear, Teddy bear, touch the ground."

And again, I sense I'm alone. I rush to the wall but my phantasmal neighbor's neglected compound is empty.

The next few days I play close to the damaged wall. Sometimes the eyes are there, sometimes not. I look toward the wall more frequently, and notice that my glance no longer scares the viewer away. Once in a rare while I even smile, careful to look away at once, my lids demurely lowered, my expression shy: trying with whatever wiles I can to detain, disarm and entice the invisible and elusive object of my fascination.

It is almost the end of October. The days are still warm but, as each day takes us closer to winter, the fresher air is exhilarating. People on the streets smile more readily, the tonga horses snort and shake their necks and appear to pull their loads more easily, and even the refugees, absorbed into the gullies and the more crowded areas of Lahore as the camps shrink, appear at last to be less visible.

One such heady afternoon, when the eyes blocking the crack suddenly disappear and I see a smudge of pale light instead, I dash to the wall and glue my eye to the hole. A small boy, so extremely thin he looks like a brittle skeleton, is squatting a few feet away, concentrating on striking a marble lying in a notch in the dust. His skull-like face has dry, flaky patches, and two deep lines between his eyebrows that I have never before seen on a child. He is wearing a threadbare shalwar of thin cotton and the dirty cord tying the gathers round his waist trails in the mud. The sun-charred little body is covered with scabs and wounds. It is as if his tiny body has been carelessly carved and then stuck together again to form an ungainly puppet. I don't know how to react; I feel sorry for him and at the same time repulsed. He hits the marble he was aiming at, gets up to retrieve the marbles and as he turns away I see the improbable wound on the back of his cropped head. It is a raw and flaming scar, as if bone and flesh had been callously gouged out, and my compassion ties me to him.

Suzanne is in the kitchen and Kishen is flitting between the dining table and kitchen filling stainless-steel glasses with water and arranging bowls containing a variety of pickles. He places a stack of silvery platters, their rims gleaming, next to the glasses. The smell of mango pickle is strong in the room and, seeing our eyes darting to the table, Kishen's mother says, "We have made only a vegetarian thal today." She sounds apologetic as if their hospitality will not stand up to our expectations. I know how much trouble it is to prepare the different vegetables and lentils that add up to the thal. Glancing at his sisters-in-law, Sikander says, "The girls refused to eat lunch when they heard you were serving the thal Maajee." The sisters-in-law solemnly nod. "I've been looking forward to the food all day," I also protest.

Turning from me to Kishen, who is folding cutlery in paper napkins, Mr. Khan declares, "I say *yaar*, you're such a well trained husband!" and at that moment, involuntarily, my hand reaches out to lightly feel Mr. Khan's hair. Startled by the unexpected touch Sikander whips around. He notices my discomfiture—and the unusual position of my hand in the air—and passing a hand down the back of his head, dryly says, "I'm wearing a wig. The scar is still there."

"Oh, I'm sorry. I didn't mean to . . ." I say, almost incoherent with embarrassment. But Mr. Khan grants me a smile of such indulgent complicity that acknowledging my childhood claim to his friendship, I am compelled to ask, "What about the other scars . . . are they still . . . ?"

Wordlessly opening the cuff button Sikander peels his shirt sleeve back. The scars are fainter, diminished, and on that strong brown arm innocuous: not at all like the dangerous welts and scabs afflicting the pitiful creature I saw for the first time on that mellow afternoon through a slit in the compound wall. With one finger, gently, I touch the arm, and responding to the touch, Sikander twists it to show me the other scars.

"You want to see the back of my head?" he asks. I nod.

Sikander turns, and with a deft movement of his fingers lifts up part of the piece to show the scar. It has pale ridges of thick scar tissue, and the hair growing round it has given it the shape of a four-day-old crescent moon.

Sikander smoothes down his hair and notices that, except for the children shouting as they play outside, the room has become quiet; even Kishen has come from the dining table to peer at his famous scalp.

"I think I'm out of cigarettes," Sikander says patting his empty pockets with the agitation of an addict desperately in need of a smoke. "I'll be back in ten minutes, *yaar*," he tells Kishen, getting up.

While Sikander is out, Kishen and his mother sit close to me, and Suzanne, drawn from the kitchen by the hushed tone of their voices, joins them in pressing me with information and plying me with questions. Could I tell them what Mr. Khan looked like as a little boy? Do I know what happened to Ammijee? No? Well, they noticed Mr. Khan's reticence on the subject and stopped asking questions . . . But they suspect she has been through something terrible . . . Except for Mr. Khan, her entire family was killed during the attack . . . Do I remember her? Was she pretty?

The focus of interest appears to revolve around Ammijee. They have known Sikander for a long time and his mother's anticipated arrival has caused a stir. I search my memory. I dimly perceive a thin, bent-over, squatting figure scrubbing clothes, scouring tinny utensils with mud and ash, peeling squashes and other cheap vegetables, kneading dough and slapping it into chapatties . . .

The ragged cotton chaddar always drawn forward over her face, the color of her form blended with the mud, the ash, the utensils she washed, the pale seasonal vegetables she peeled. This must be Ammijee: a figure bent perpetually to accommodate the angle of drudgery and poverty. I don't recall her face or the color of her dusty bare feet, the shape of her hands or whether she wore bangles.

All I knew as a child was that my little refugee friend's village was attacked by some Sikhs.

I did not understand the complete significance of the word "refugees" at the time. I thought, on the nebulous basis of my understanding of the Hindu caste system, that the "refugees" were a caste—like the brahmin or achoot castes who were suddenly pouring into Lahore, and it was in the nature of this caste—much as the achoots or untouchables were born to clean gutters and sweep toilets—to be inexorably poor, ragged, homeless, forever looking for work and places to stay.

Sikander had described some of the details of the attack and of his miraculous survival. His account of it, supplied in little, suddenly recalled snatches—brought to mind by chance associations while we played—was so jumbled, so full of bizarre incident, that I accepted it as the baggage of truth-enlivened-by-fantasy that every child carries within. Although I realized the broader implications of what had happened, that the British Raj had ended, that there were religious riots among Hindus, Muslims, and Sikhs, and the country was divided because of them, I was too young to understand the underlying combustibility of the events preceding Partition that had driven my friends away and turned a little boy's world into a nightmare.

But I had heard no mention at all of Ammijee's ordeal. Excited by my ignorance, and the spirit of instruction burning in us all to remedy this lack, Mrs. Khan and her three sisters also move closer; dragging their chairs forward, or settling on the rug at my feet. The entire ensemble now combines to enlighten me in five languages: English, Punjabi, and Urdu, which I understand, and Kannada and Marathi—contributed by Kishen's mother in earnest by brief fusillades—which I don't.

The boys and some of the men in the village, I am informed, were huddled in a dark room at the back of a barn when some Sikhs smote the door shouting: "Open up. Open up!"

And, when the door was opened, the hideous swish of long steel swords dazzling their eyes in the sunlight, severing first his father's head, then his uncle's, then his brother's. His own sliced at the back because he was only nine years old, and short. They left him for dead. How he survived, how he arrived in Pakistan, is another story.

"Ammijee says the village women ran towards the Chaudhrys' house," says Mrs. Khan in assertive Punjabi. Being Ammijee's daughter-in-law she is permitted, for the moment at least, to hold center stage. "They knew what the Sikhs would do to them . . . women are the spoils of war . . . no matter what you are—Hindu, Muslim, Sikh—women bear the brunt . . ."

"Rather than fall into the hands of the Sikhs, the poor women planned to burn themselves. They had stored kerosene . . . but when the attack came they had no time. Thirty thousand men, mad with blood lust, waving swords and guns!"

Mrs. Khan casts her eyes about in a way that makes us draw closer, and having ascertained that Mr. Khan is still absent, whispers, "Ammijee says she went mad! She would have killed herself if she could. So would you, so would I . . . She heard her eleven-year-old daughter screaming and screaming . . . she heard the mullah's sixteen-year-old daughter scream: "Do anything you wish with me, but don't hurt me. For God's sake don't hurt me!"

We look away, the girls' tormented cries ringing unbearably in our ears. Suzanne and the youngest sister brush their eyes and, by the time we are able to talk again, Mrs. Khan's moment is over. The medley of languages again asserts itself: "God knows how many women died . . ." A helpless spreading of hands and deep sighs.

"Pregnant women were paraded naked, their stomachs slashed . . ."

"Yes-jee and the babies were swung by their heels and dashed against walls."

Much shaking of heads: God's help and mercy evoked.

"God knows how many women were lifted . . . but, then, everybody carried women off. Sikhs and Hindus, Muslims women. Muslims, Sikh and Hindu women."

A general clucking of tongues, an air of commiseration.

"Allah have mercy on us," says Mrs. Khan, and in resounding Punjabi again asserts her authority as chief speaker. "His mother had a bad experience, very bad. Ammijee never talks about it, but those who knew her when she was recovered, say . . ."

Mrs. Khan stops short. Having second thoughts about disclosing what her mother-in-law never talks about, she makes a deft switch and in a banal, rhetorical tone of voice says, "She saw horrible things. Horrible. Babies tossed into boiling oil . . ."

Sikander Khan, having bought his pack and smoked his cigarette outside, quietly joins us.

Half-way through dinner two handsome, broad-shouldered Sikhs in gray suits join us. I gather they are cousins. Their long hair is tucked away in blue turbans, and their beards tied in neat rolls beneath their chins. Again there is an explosion of welcome, a flurry to feed the late-comers and a great deal of hand-slapping and embracing among the men. Considering what I heard just a few moments ago, I am a little surprised at the cordiality between Sikander Khan and the young Sikhs. I hear one of the men say in Urdu, "Any further news about your Ammijee's arrival?"

His back is to me, but the sudden switch from Punjabi to Urdu, the formality in his voice and his mode of address, catch my attention. There is no apparent change in the volume of noise in the room, yet I sense we have all shared a moment of unease, an incongruous solemnity.

And then the Sikh men move to greet the women from Mr. Khan's family in Punjabi, inquire after their health and the health of their children and indulge in a little light-hearted teasing. The unease is so dispelled, I wonder if I have not imagined it.

"You haven't invited us to a meal in almost a month, *bhabi*," says the stouter of the two men to Mrs. Khan. "Look at poor Pratab. See how thin he's become?" He pulls back his cousin's arms the way poultry dealers hold back chicken wings and, standing him helpless and grinning in front of Mrs. Khan, asks, "Have we offended you in some way?"

"No, no, Khushwant *bhai*," says Mrs. Khan, "It isn't anything like that . . ."

"She's concerned about your health, brother," pipes up the eldest of her three sisters, "You're too fat and fresh for your own good!" She must be in her mid-twenties.

Khushwant releases his cousin good-naturedly and the sisters, hiding their smiles in their dopattas, start giggling. They have perked up in the presence of these young men who speak their language and share their ways, their religious antagonisms dissipated on American soil.

On surer ground, the same sister says, "What about the picnic you promised us? You're the one who breaks promises, and you complain about our sister!" Her face animated, her large black eyes roguish, she is charming, and I suddenly notice how pretty the sisters are in their pleasantly plump Punjabi way.

"When would you like to go? Next Sunday?" asks Khushwant Singh gallantly.

"We'll know what's what when Sunday comes," says another sister, tossing her long plaited hair back in a half-bullying, half-mocking gesture. She has a small, full-lipped mouth and a diamond on one side of her pert nose.

"I'll take you to the ocean next Sunday. It's a promise," says Khushwant Singh, "But only if *bhabi* makes parathas with her own hands."

"What's wrong with my hands?" the pert sister asks. "Or with Gulnar's hands?" she indicates their younger sister who promptly buries her face in her dopatta. Gulnar is the only sister not yet married. I guess she is sixteen or seventeen.

"Have either of you given me occasion to praise your cooking?" Khushwant asks.

"They'll give you occasion on Sunday," intervenes Mrs. Khan. "But, tell me brother," she says, "what will you feed us? Why don't you bring chicken korma to go with the parathas?"

"No chicken korma till you find me a wife."

"*Lo!*" says Mrs. Khan. "As if you'll agree to our choice! There are plenty of pretty Sikh girls, but you fuss!"

"I want some one just like you, bhabi," says the handsome Sikh, and turns slightly red. "A girl who knows our ways."

"That's what you say, but you'll end up marrying a white-washed *memsahib*!" At once realizing the folly the pert sister springs up from her chair and, abandoning her dinner, hugging Suzanne and holding her cheek against hers, says, "Unless it is one like our Sue *bhabi*. She's one of us. Then we won't mind."

Suzanne takes it, as she accepts the smaller hazards of her marriage to Kishen, in her twinkle-toed and sari-clad stride. She told me about a year back, when we were just becoming friends, that she felt content and secure in her extended Indian family. She tried to describe to me her feeling of being firmly embedded in life—in the business and purpose of living—that she, as an only child, had never experienced. Suzanne comes from a small town in New England. Her father teaches history at a university. I haven't met her family but I gather they are unpretentious and gentle folk.

It is the Sunday of the picnic. Kishen and Suzanne give me a ride to Galveston beach. It is a massive affair. Innumerable kin have been added to the group that met for dinner at Kishen's. Mr. Khan, in long white pants and a blue T-shirt, staggers across the hot sand with a stack of parathas wrapped in a metallic gray garbage bag. Khushwant Singh and Pratab have brought the food from a Pakistani restaurant on Hillcroft.

Later in the sultry afternoon, exhilarated from our splashing in the ocean and the sudden shelter of an overcast sky, we converge on the durries spread on the sand. Mrs. Khan and her three sisters flop like exotic beetles on a striped durry, their wet satin shalwars and kamizes clinging to them in rich blobs of solid color.

413

The parathas are delicious. Sikander heaps his plate with haleem and mutton curry and, crossing his legs like an inept yogi, sits down by me. I broach the subject that has been obsessing me. I would like to use his family's experiences during the Partition in my novel.

As we eat, sucking on our fingers, drinking coke out of cans, I ask Sikander about the attack on his village, trying, with whatever wiles I can, to penetrate the mystery surrounding Ammijee.

I gathered from the remarks Mrs. Khan let slip on the night of the party that Ammijee was kidnapped. But I want to know what Mrs. Khan was about to say when she checked herself. I feel the missing information will unravel the full magnitude of the tragedy to my understanding and, more importantly, to my imagination. Instinctively I choose Sikander Khan, and not Mrs. Khan, to provide the knowledge. His emotions and perceptions will, I feel, charge my writing with the detail, emotion, and veracity I am striving for.

Sikander's replies to my questions are candid, recalled in remarkable detail, but he balks at any mention of Ammijee.

I don't remember now the question that unexpectedly penetrated his reserve, but Sikander planted in my mind a fearsome seed that waxed into an ugly tree of hideous possibility, when, in a voice that was indescribably harsh, he said, "Ammijee heard street vendors cry: 'Zana for sale! Zana for sale!' as if they were selling vegetables and fish. They were selling women for 50, 20, and even 10 rupees!"

Later that evening, idling on our durries as we watch the spectacular crimson streaks on the horizon fade, I ask Sikander how he can be close friends with Khushwant and Pratab. In his place I would not even want to meet their eye! Isn't he furious with the Sikhs for what they did? Do the cousins know what happened in his village?

"I'm sure they know . . . everybody I meet seems to know. Why quarrel with Khushwant and Pratab? They weren't even born . . ." And, his voice again taking on the hard harsh edge he says, "We Muslims were no better . . . we did the same . . . Hindu, Muslim, Sikh, we are all evil bastards!"

Mr. Khan calls. His mother has arrived from Pakistan. He has asked a few friends to dinner to meet her on Saturday. Can I dine with them? Ammijee remembers me as a little girl!

I get into the usual state of panic and put off looking at the map till the last hour. It is a major trauma—this business of finding my way from place to place—missing exits, getting out of the car to read road signs, aggravating—and often terrifying—motorists in front, behind and on either side. Thank God for alert American reflexes: for their chastising, wise, blasphemous tooting.

I find my way to Mr. Khan's without getting irremediably lost. It is a large old frame house behind a narrow neglected yard on Harold, between Montrose and the Rothko Chapel.

Sikander ushers me into the house with elegant formality, uttering phrases in Urdu which translated into English sound like this: "We're honored by your visit to our poor house. We can't treat you in the manner to which you are accustomed. . ." and presents me to his mother. She is a plump, buttery fleshed, kind faced old woman wearing a simple shalwar and shirt and her dark hair, streaked with gray, is covered by a gray nylon chaddar. She strokes my arm several times and peering affectionately into my face, saying, "Mashallah, you've grown healthier. You were such a dry little thing," steers me to sit next to her on the sofa.

Through my polite, bashful-little-girl's smile, I search her face. There's no trace of bitterness. No melancholy. Nothing knowing or hard, just the open, acquiescent, hospitable face of a contented peasant woman who is happy to visit her son. It is difficult to believe this gentle woman was kidnapped, raped, and sold.

The sisters line up opposite us on an assortment of dining and patio chairs carried in for the party. The living room is typically furnished, Pakistani style, an assortment of small carved tables and tables with brass and ivory inlay, handwoven Pakistani carpets scattered at angles, sofas and chairs showing a lot of carved wood, onyx ashtrays and plastic flowers in brass vases. The atmosphere is permeated with the sterile odor of careful disuse.

Kishen, his mother, and Suzanne arrive. Suzanne looks languorous and sultry-eyed in a beautiful navy and gold sari. There is a loud exchange of pleasantries. Kishen notices me across the length of the entrance lobby. "You found your way OK?" he calls from the door, teasing. "Didn't land up in Mexico or something?"

"Not even once!" I yell back.

Some faces I recognize from the picnic arrive. A Kashmiri brahmin couple joins us. They are both short, fair, plump and smug. They talk exclusively to Suzanne (the only white American in the room), Kishen (husband of the status symbol) and Mr. Khan. The sisters, condescended to a couple of times and then ignored, drift to the kitchen and disappear into the remote and mysterious recesses of the large house. I become aware of muted children's voices, quarrelsome, demanding and excited. The sisters return, quiet and sullen, and dragging their chairs huddle about a lamp standing in the corner.

Dinner is late. We are waiting for Khushwant and Pratab. Mr. Khan says, "We will wait for fifteen minutes more. If they don't come, we'll start eating."

Hungry guests with growling stomachs we nevertheless say, "Please don't worry on our account . . . We are in no hurry."

Conversation dwindles. The guests politely inquire after the health of those sitting next to them and the grades of their children. We hear the door bell ring and Mr. Khan gets up from his chair saying, "I think they've come."

Instead of the dapper Sikhs, I see two huge and hirsute Indian fakirs. Their disheveled hair, parted at the center, bristles about their arms and shoulders and mingles with their spiky black beards. They are wearing white muslin kurtas over white singlets and their broad shoulders and thick muscles show brown beneath the fine muslin. I can't be sure from where I sit, but I think they have on loose cotton pajamas. They look incredibly fierce. It is an impression, quickly formed, and I have barely glimpsed the visitors, when, abruptly, their knees appear to buckle and they fall forward.

Mr. Khan steps back hastily and bends over the prostrate men. He says, "What's all this? What's all this?" The disconcerted tone of his voice, and the underpinning of perplexity and fear gets us all to our feet. Moving in a bunch, displacing the chairs and small tables and crumpling the carpets, we crowd our end of the lobby.

The fakirs lie face down across the threshold, half outside the door and half in the passage, their hands flat on the floor as if they are about to do pushups. Their faces are entirely hidden by hair. Suddenly, their voices moist and thick, they begin to cry, "Maajee! Maajee! Forgive us." The blubbering, coming as it does from these fierce men, is unexpected, shocking, incongruous and melodramatic in this pragmatic and oil-rich corner of the western world.

Sikander, in obvious confusion, looms over them, looking from one to the other. Then, squatting in front of them, he begins to stroke their prickly heads, making soothing noises as if he is cajoling children. "What's this? Tch, tch . . . Come on! Stand up!"

"Get out of the way." An arm swings out in a threatening gesture and the fakir lifts his head. I see the pale, ash-smeared forehead, the large, thickly fringed brown eyes, the set curve of the wide, sensuous mouth and recognize Khushwant Singh. Next to him Pratab also raises his head. Sikander shuffles out of reach of Khushwant's arm and moving to one side, his back to the wall, watches the Sikhs with an expression of incredulity. It is unreal. I think it has occurred to all of us it might be a prank, an elaborate joke. But their red eyes, and the passion distorting their faces, are not pretended.

"Who are these men?"

The voice is demanding, abrasive. I look over my shoulder, wondering which of the women has spoken so harshly. The sisters look agitated; their dusky faces are flushed.

"Throw them out. They're *badmashes*! *Goondas*!"

Taken aback I realize the angry, fearful voice is Sikander's mother's.

Ammijee is standing behind me, barely visible among the agitated and excited sisters, and in her face I see more than just the traces of the emotions I had looked for earlier. It is as if her features have been parodied in a hideous mask. They are all there: the bitterness, the horror, the hate. The incarnation of that tree of ugly possibilities seeded in my mind when Sikander, in a cold fury, imitating the cries of the street vendors his mother had described, said, "Zana for sale! Zana for sale!"

I grew up overhearing fragments of whispered conversations about the sadism and bestiality women were subjected to during the Partition: what happened to so and so—someone's sister, daughter, sister-in-law—the women Mrs. Khan categorized the *spoils of war*. The fruits of victory in the unremitting chain of wars that is man's relentless history. The vulnerability of mothers, daughters, granddaughters, and their metamorphosis into possessions, living objects on whose soft bodies victors and losers alike vent their wrath, enact fantastic vendetta, celebrate victory. All history, all these fears, all probabilities and injustices coalesce in Ammijee's terrible face and impart a dimension of tragedy that alchemizes the melodrama. The behavior of the Sikhs, so incongruous and flamboyant before, is now transcendentally essential, consequential, fitting.

The men on the floor have spotted Ammijee. "Maajee, forgive us: Forgive

417

the wrongs of our fathers."

A sister behind me says, "Oh my God!" There is a buzz of questions and comments. I feel she has voiced exactly my awe of the moment—the rare, luminous instant in which two men transcend their historic intransigence to tender apologies on behalf of their species. Again she says, "Oh God!" and I realize she is afraid that the cousins, propelled forward by small movements of their shoulders and elbows like crocodiles are resurrecting a past that is best left in whatever recesses of the mind Ammijee has chosen to bury it.

"Don't do this . . . please," protests Sikander. "You're our guests. . . !"

But the cousins, keeping their eyes on the floor say, "Bhai, let us be."

The whispered comments of the guests intensify around me.

"What's the matter?"

"They are begging her pardon . . ."

"Who are these men?"

". . . for what the Sikhs did to her in the riots . . ."

"*Hai Ram.* What do they want?"

"God knows what she's been through; she never talks about it . . ."

"With their hair open like this they must remind her of the men who . . ."

"You can't beat the Punjabis when it comes to drama," says the supercilious Kashmiri. His wife, standing next to me, says, "The Sikhs have a screw loose in the head." She rotates a stubby thumb on her temple as if she is tightening an imaginary screw.

"I turn, frowning. The sisters are glaring at them, showering the backs of their heads with withering, hostile looks. And, in hushed tones of suitable gravity, Mrs. Khan says, "Ammijee, they are asking for your forgiveness. Forgive them." "Then, she forgives you brothers!" says Mrs. Khan loudly, on her mother-in-law's account. The other sisters repeat Mrs. Khan's magnanimous gesture, and, with minor variations, also forgive Khushwant and Pratab on Ammijee's behalf.

"Ammijee; come here!" Sikander sounds determined to put a stop to all of this.

We shift, clearing a narrow passage for Ammijee, and Kishen's mother darts out instead looking like an agitated chick in her puffed cotton sari. She is about to say something—and judging from her expression it has to be something indeterminate and conciliatory—when Kishen, firmly taking hold of her arm, hauls her back.

Seeing his mother has not moved, Sikander shouts, "Send Ammijee here. For God's sake, finish it now."

Ammijee takes two or three staggering steps and stands a few paces before me. I suspect one of the sisters has nudged her forward. I cannot see Ammijee's face, but the head beneath the gray chaddar jerks as if she is trying to remove a crick from her neck.

All at once, her voice, an altered, fragile, high-pitched treble that bears no resemblance to the fierce voice that had demanded, "Who are these men?" Ammijee screeches, "I will never forgive your fathers! Or your grandfathers! Get out, *shaitans*! Sons and grandsons of *shaitans*! Never, never, never!"

She becomes absolutely still, as if she will remain there forever, rooted, the quintessence of indictment.

They advance, wiping their noses on their sleeves, tearing at their snarled hair, pleading, "We will lie at your door to our last breath! We are not fit to show our faces."

In a slow, deliberate gesture, Ammijee turns her face away and I observe her profile. Her eyes are clenched shut, the muscles in her cheeks and lower jaw are quivering in tiny, tight spasms as if charged by a current. No one dares say a word; it would be an intrusion. She has to contend with unearthed torments, private demons. The matter rests between her memories and the incarnation of the phantoms wriggling up to her.

The men reach out to touch the hem of her shalwar. Grasping her ankles they lay their heads at her feet in the ancient gesture of surrender demanded of warriors.

"Leave me! Let go!" Ammijee shrieks, in her shaky, altered voice. She raises her arms and moves them as if she is pushing away invisible insects. But she looks exhausted and, her knees giving way, she squats before the men. She buries her face in the chaddar.

At last, with slight actions that suggest she is ready to face the world, Ammijee wipes her face in the chaddar and rearranges it on her untidy head. She tucks the edges behind her ears and slowly, in a movement that is almost tender, places her shaking hands on the shaggy heads of the men who hold her feet captive. "My sons, I forgave your fathers long ago," she says in a flat, emotionless voice pitched so low that it takes some time for the words to register, "How else could I live?"

On the way home, hanging on to the red tail lights of the cars on the Katy Freeway, my thoughts tumble through a chaos of words and images, and then the words churn madly, throwing up fragments of verse by the Bolivian poet Pedro Shimose. The words throb in an endless, circular rhythm:

Defend yourself against me
against my father and the father of my father
still living in me
Against my force and shouting in schools and cathedrals
Against my camera, against my pencil
against my TV-spots.

Defend yourself against me,
please, woman,
defend yourself!

Romantic Stereotypes: The Myth of the Asian American Khichri-Pot

Anuradha M. Mitra

For those of us who have never tasted *khichri*, I can state without superfluity that our souls have been denied a foretaste of heaven. On a monsoony day, when the rain comes roaring down in great blanketfolds of memory, reminding us that there is indeed reprieve to be had, khichri is the delicacy that is unguently prepared over a simmering flame. Half of rice, one quarter *toor dal* and one quarter *urad dal*, this steamy mirage of starch restores our soul like very few foods can. Throw in a few greens, chosen fingers of the hottest Peruvian peppers, a hint of coriander, a slimy sliver of ghee, and indeed you have a meal like no other. It is complete, el finito, the end, namaskar; the celebration of a history that is complete unto itself. What is truly great of this recipe, maneuvered at will and fluid to possibilities of an endless variation, is just that: it will stand the test of time, of whimsical fashions, of overspiced taste buds, of overextended souls. It will give us wholesomeness in the end. It will provide a sense of home that is more becoming than any address in North America. The khichri-pot, as you can see, renders us one person. It is the *e unum pluribus* among us, cooking into perfection our many facets as one. It is the national anthem of foods, restoring our abilities to become as one people, defying Lord Mountbatten's dicta at India's irreparable divorce from the British empire in 1947: that India was and is a conglomerate of different entities, to be governed only by the force of sundering, splintering, making the one many.

Transport this nation of twenty-three sovereign states, if we are to take Governor Mountbatten seriously, and what do we have in North America. We have a community of Asian Americans of Asian Indian origin. This distinction is important because it clarifies us from the cooking-pot of another variety—the Native Americans, the first of this land, who have been tethered to their outpost in a singular act of concession. In a similar gesture of aggression, of cultural arrogance, of a power within us that would cry out for annihilation of our spirit rather than assimilation into a homogenous, blanched, strained, and refined oneness, the Asian American of South Asian origin stands out like a pod of distinctively flavorful tamarind.

According to sociologist Juan Gonzales (in *Racial and Ethnic Groups in America*, 1990), the first flood of Indian immigrants searched the frontiers of North America in the early 1900s, first looking for easy gold and then its obvious replacement—golden wheat. They settled in the outreaches of California and the open states of Canada, working the lands and yielding abundant harvests of corn, maize, and wheat, and on the side, as soul-food, delicate Indian herbs and spices, strains of eggplants that tickled the taste-buds, and gourds whose seeds had to be wrapped in fine muslin and stolen out of our once homes like careful contraband. The first immigrants adjusted to the ways of the land, working hard in quiet pride, yet holding on deftly, strongly, arrogantly to the rituals that now separated them from India. From our first ancestors in North America, we got hint of a race of people that flaunted the customs of the host country, that refused to fit in, that insisted on their ethnic heritage as one does one's birthright. Our ancestors gave concreteness to our daily struggle to assimilate. They gave expression to what it is like to mimic the mainstream, to talk like them, to walk like them, in fact, as much as possible, to be them. And it was through their spirit that we got hint of the fact that perhaps for South Asians, the many who had been rendered as one, it was an act of double indemnity to take on the persona of yet another, and to try and be like them.

The next flood of Indians came to the United States from the late 1960s through the early 1980s. They came gushing out of the rural municipalities and clogged cities that had contained their ambitions into the open landscape of America. They came from all directions, overwhelming the staid, tobacco-chewing, silently-ruminating Immigration official, who in a fit of nightmare, saw his white country growing into shades of wheat, yellow, and brown with varying stages of ripeness. Like Benjamin Franklin before him, who had not been able to withstand a similar flood of "dark-skinned Germans and their alien ways," the Immigration Officer reconfigured his software. As far as he was concerned, things just didn't add up right. The geography was different. The displacement of people from one terrain to another was unnatural, according to him. Such an exodus was only granted validity during epochs of war, of unnatural ravages of nature, of calamitous scourges. But, during peacetime, this warm effluvia of peoples flowing into his pristine nation was a fact that was not to be tolerated sitting down. He decided to commit his observations to paper and send it off to his Congressman.

While he worked on his letter and translated it into officialeze, South Asian technocrats, engineers, doctors, and left-brained others came rushing in through the flood-gates. With them, they brought the artifacts of their culture as fetishes. These warded off the evil eye, circumscribed one within the safe boundedness of the familiar, and kept away from intimate embrace objects that personified this foreign first world. Thus, an ancient sitar that had been handed down through generations of foremothers, a stone Ganesha whose hands in the *abhaya-mudra* position radiated magic, a pot that could—on command—make the best curry in the world, snippets of ghost stories dragged out from almirahs of patri-archal homes, found their way into immaculate American homes framed by the white picket-fence, 2.3 healthy children, and a Range Rover that took them places. They brought all of this to the Midwest, to the shore homes of Long Island and New Jersey, to the steamy interiors of Texas, to the *khichri*-cooked kitchens of California. And in these spaces, they negotiated the terms of their living arrangements. They decided, in that linear moment of time of which they had a startling recollection, that theirs was a history that was macroscopic, engulfing in its broad arms both the range and the vista of events, of which, for instance, epic movies are made. They decided, staring at their very own kitchen god who tasted the *khichri* much before the rest of the household, that they were not going to surrender their memories with their citizenship. Being an Asian American was a state of soul, and, as much as possible, they would cleave to this particular strain of soulfulness deeply immanent in their national character.

The Family

Writing to his wife, and, only by inference, to his daughters, in Calcutta, India, who were waiting for that symbol of acceptance into American life—the green card—Rahul wrote:

"Dearest Sunila:

As I write to you on this murderously lonesome Sunday afternoon, the smells of our kitchen, of our home, of you back home in India, overpowers my senses. For in this country of shining laminate and sparkling surfaces, the soul seems so much at the top that it shies of being scratched. I have noticed that the overpowering smell of America is Lysol: it cleanses, sterilizes, and purifies without affirming one's own idiosyncratic smell.

Let's consider the ways in which we are able to imagine ourselves. I am a prototypical South Asian in America. What does that mean? It means that I am framed by the notions of my national character. In simple English, I am truly ghost-like in my invisibility and what is visible is what others will believe. I am *khichri* incarnate, being indeterminately molded into whatever pot will contain my shape. My individuality lies awash in the saffron flavored soft texture that invokes forgetfulness of one's essential nature. In this country, the outward accoutrements of my identity are constantly drawn upon to give me a locatable belonging, a sense of the generic 'me.' My national, racial, and ethnic identities work overtime to render me visible. Yet, they do entirely too much to conceal rather than reveal.

As you can see, in terms of image, I have a stereotype that precedes my reputation. I am the Mercedes Benz, no less the 800 series, of manhood, providing only the best and protecting my woman and children against the onslaughts of the world. I am the container of all virtues, performing the dharma of the committed householder on whose turn of phrase relies the outcome of daily life. In my knowledge of how things work, I am the creator supreme, rivalled only by the Koreans. I am all that a man could ever want to be. Many a white woman when asked why she fell in with a *desi* guy will invariably suggest: "In spite of their incomprehensible accents and sing-song cadences, they seem to have a one upmanship over the Western man. They epitomize financial success and are supreme providers of families, leaving nothing to be desired. Hands down, they are the best."

But, what about those ghost stories that would put a streak through the painstakingly laundered Mr. Clean image? The more pertinent question is: have you ever heard of an Indian unearth his horde of ghost stories? In all my wanderings both in India and in the Western world, I have yet to come across an honest embracing of one's past, of the secrets haunting the dark spaces of familial memory, the ghosts rattling imaginary bones well past the living have been rendered to dust. The facade is so guileless, so serene as to resemble a rippleless pond unmuddied by needless industry. Questions that probe to the heart of the matter are summarily deflected with: "Everything is fine in our family."

I want to remind you of the many ways in which we South Asians perhaps don't fit the notion of our best self. I want to urge you, even at the stake of inviting pain, that we are infinitely much less than what we are given to believe. And, yet, that is precisely what helps us sketch in those penultimate master strokes that define our individuality. I recognize with glee that we are simultaneously our disgusting selves and more.

My love, dredge from your memory bank those unspeakable incidents of your male cousin forcing himself on you, not once, not twice, but a hundred times over, till you began to feed into his frenzy with equal passion. Those were your words, not mine. What about our young neighbor, a version of Omar Shariff, who was sexually violated by the very reverend Jesuit Father in his school. It wasn't till years later, much after he was unhappily married, that he recognized himself as a homosexual who had received intimations on his identity from a freakishly unholy source? What about the silent quarters of extended families in upper class homes and the stealthy night walk to the other's bedroom where women are given repeated lessons in sexual politics? What about those among us who would beat, torment, and silence one of our own, if necessary, to express an incomprehensible aspect of our well-guarded self? Are these stories about ourselves, our shadow-side, our nether world, ever exposed to the light? Are they addressed in a way to ease our shame? Are they invoked to give fullness to our selves, our character, separate from the identity that has been tailor-made for us by a master craftsperson?

We are much more interesting than our successful facade will give us to believe. My love, as your Air India plane taxis off into the Western skies, toast a glass of champagne to the mysterious, smooth-faced behemoth in us. Don't pay attention to the side glances that you will get from your fellow countrypeople. Drink to yourself, to me, to the kids, to us all, and pray that we are given a chance to locate that space within and around us that will bring forth the richest in us. And, by the way, make sure that the girls have a generous sip of that champagne. They will sleep better on the plane.

Go to sleep, lover, and when you awaken, you will be lying naked in my soft embrace. Rahul.

The Community

"Dear, dear, Shantapishi," Sunila wrote to her favorite aunt, the one who had cradled her on the day she was born.

"Rahul was at the airport on the day of our arrival. It took forever to get to him. The tradition of welcoming foreigners into this country is an oxymoron. How are we to welcome into our lives those with whom we feel no singularity? Behind the picture perfect facade of this welcoming committee, the Naturalization official and his cohorts in Customs, I could sense the gritted remembrance of prejudice, of a long-ago sense of superiority perhaps taught across the kitchen table. Armed with olfactory detector that will smell out even the most camouflaged of coconut shreddings, tamarind paste thickened with molasses, stuffed chillies, and whole garlic pickle, the committee wrought havoc to my sense of person. I watched myself being stripped as everything that I render inviolate was dumped in a nearby rubbish heap. One of them caught me yearning for my lost sensations of taste. He moved the rubbish heap beyond the unexpressed longings of my soul. Can you believe that?

For now, I must share with you my amazement at what I see in our community in New York. Because of the confabulations of geography and its uncertainty of where a country begins or ends, most Indians establish solidarity with South Asians—such as Pakistanis, Bangladeshis, Sri Lankans, Burmese, Nepalese, and so on. But the distinguishing factor of this group seems to be the complex manner in which they manage to (dis)connect. Indeed, the ancient enmities marking historical relationships between the countries somehow spills over into relationships forged on streetcorners in Jackson Heights or Elmhurst or whatever place you would care to name in this hugely impersonal vastland.

When we describe ourselves as South Asians, we are also separating ourselves from that other group of Asians who happen to share memory space with that continent of ours, but who seem to be infinitely more comfortable with their cultural identity. This perception is from the outside looking in. Who knows what a one-way mirror will reveal from the inside. I continue to be amazed at the sloppiness with which ancient civilizations are dump-heaped, dismembered limb upon uncertain limb, in the comprehension-box of the mainstream. For judgment that is so vastly uncritical or unrefined, our nuns at Loreto College would have slapped our knuckles. According to this Western tally, Koreans and Taiwanese, Chinese and Japanese, Filipino and Malay, are incoherently glued together in one starch-cooker of *khichri*. I ask myself constantly: do they not have their own separate legacies, historical remembrances, their specific rendering of their very individual national character?

And then, off course, there is the entire business of engaging South Asians and East Asians in conversation with each other. In determining how they come to terms with their living arrangement in North America, a space entirely dissimilar from any of the other topography, is a matter that would drive any ethnographer to samadhi. Tell me, dear aunt, how are we to relate to others if we are unsure of our self-definitions. Can we forgive the transgressions of history and bring resolutions to our fears as we get to know ourselves in unknown ways? It must take a lot of courage to do that.

In all of this activity, I see ourselves disengaging with greater glory rather than coming together into any kind of redemptive space. I find us, South Asians, and specifically those of Indian origin, standing apart from the generic Asian American umbrella under which we have been put. I am fascinated at our resoluteness not to assimilate and to become as one. Our search for that true path, whatever that might happen to be, is a solitary wandering toward that part of ourselves which we are trying to locate in memory.

Why is it that we have to search for ourselves so relentlessly? Why is it that the burden of self-definition has been placed so squarely on our shoulders? Why are we trying so hard? Why? Why? Why? Is it because our self-creation has always been patterned on negative identification: that we are *not* black; we are *not* Hispanic; we are *not* mestiza; we are *not* illiterate; we are *not* working class, for the most part? Is it because we are not the *us* of the mainstream, and, by a process of exclusion, we have to be the *them* of the periphery? Is it because our sense of self is established in opposition to rather than in partnership with the rest of white or black or yellow America? Is it this that makes us crumble and grow weak inside so that we become strangely inarticulate in expressing who we are?

I keep asking myself these questions as I fold my clothes in the laundromat and observe the sea of faces around me. What is it about us, South Asians, that will not allow us to get along with others, and least of all, with ourselves? What urges us to dissimilate, to stand apart, to straddle several cultures without making a commitment to one way of life or the other? What about a compromise? Is that conceivable in our way of thinking? What is it about our ambiguous embrace of our new home as we summarily reject its stereotyping in the same breath? Why are we so perplexed about not being able to fit in even as we reject the notion of assimilation?

I remember clearly a piece on the diaspora that Dan Rather once did on television. (He is a newsanchor for CBS News.) I remember him saying that he had never met a more arrogant group of people than Indians. I couldn't have agreed with him more. Haven't I witnessed, first hand, this 'arrogance' emerging from a sense of perhaps having lived in an ancient, sophisticated, and progressive culture that has evolved and fine honed itself through centuries of development? There is something about our cultural cartography that has territorialized us in the way in which Lord Mountbatten predicted fifty years ago. Why else do you think that South Asians would hesitate in playing activist to their own causes? Why would they not wish to change the status quo? Why would they not make greater attempts to fit in or get along or both unlike the other East Asian groups who seem to integrate with greater ease?

What are our cultural objectives in this new frontier of ours? Why are we here? I have to admit that my questions far outweigh my understanding of

things. I don't know why things are just so right now. But I know that they are. Within the group naming itself South Asian, I am appalled at the prejudices that lie dormant at the edges of our relationship. In our new-found sophistication associated with our new world, we mask our name-calling, fire-spitting cursing of those who are different from us even by the width of a hair. Yet, we think nothing of describing ourselves as progressive, liberal, broad-minded. We have terminology to distinguish the Sikh from the Jain, the Bangladeshi from the Pakistani, the sunni from the shia. Yet, we rarely use those descriptors that bring us together in good faith. In our rush toward building our trust funds and force-feeding into our estates, we miss the untidy hullabaloo of life. We do not once reach after those aspects of ourselves that we have left unexamined? We do not form real bonds across generations, cultures, and groups of people, which are simultaneously alive with the pain of too much joy and some agony.

I have also seen a similar crushing of spirit, a halting of the songbird's melody at the moment that it begins to soar. The South Asian way in which parents bring up into personhood their own children is so often two-faced. I am unsure of the backdrops framing the events of the parents' lives. But from seeing them project their self-image, you would believe that perfection belonged to them alone. They give no slack. They turbo drive these children away from a true sense of who they are. They destroy the slow, easy, meandering path of character-formation. And then they force these children into reprehensible acts: like making career decisions that are based on earning capacity, or choosing life partners modeled on a system that is not pertinent in the new world any longer. It is not surprising then that wife-beating or divorce or violent ways of dealing with incompatibility are on the rise. Among the kids, many of whom are grown, there is needless compliance with the double-standards. Tell me, dear aunt, is this the stuff of which important relationships are forged? Is this how parents are to know their children? Are we being true to our inner-most selves when we daily militarize our children to go against our grain?

Shantapishi, I long to hear one of those songs that you sing, that has articulated unknown parts of me and given them loving names. I long for you by my side as I welcome these huge transformations in my life. Have I ever told you that I think of you every day, and especially at those times when I am truly myself.

Love, Sunila."

Excerpt from

Untitled

Ghalib Dhalla

There are only two things in life worth living for. Passion. And truth.

Passion came to me in plenty, but the truth it seems, eludes me still.

I am driving down the Los Angeles snake, trudging along at twenty miles per hour in a sea of cars. It's seven fifty-nine and I am afraid that I will miss the first half of "Melrose Place." That is all that concerns me at this moment.

Yesterday, it had been that I might be unable to afford my insurance premium, and the growing temptation of surrendering my cynicism to join the "Pyramid." The night before, which was a Saturday, it had been the search for the bed of yet another stranger to wake in, only to roll out into another mechanically meaningless day ahead.

On the radio the news reports of another drive-by shooting, and then of the murder of two young men that was possibly a hate crime. I switch the station to some dance music and revert to modern man's shield against the tyranny of the city—apathy. Too depressing. It doesn't concern me. It's not my problem. I have my own to worry about.

I gaze at the American flag that is hoisted up on some building on the side of the freeway as I begrudgingly bring the car to a standstill again. For some inexplicable reason, the image of the Kenyan flag with its brilliant red and green colors flashes through my mind and the traces of an indelible smile tease the gauntness of my twenty-eight year old face. I think about all that the flag in front of me has meant to people everywhere. What it had meant to me. Its impregnable promise of everything altruistic and benevolent.

It occurs to me that this flag was very much like those three-dimensional prints that everybody gazes at in the malls these days. Squinting, waiting, hoping for a vision to appear. It was only when the tentativeness gave way and you were pulled into its panoramic window that your heart began to sink. The mesmerizing specks of color integrated to reveal an unexpected horror.

I remember seeing that flag up-close eight years ago. I must have been on what might have been the fifteenth floor of a building in Kenya at the American embassy, applying for my visas. My mother sat close to me, half dreading the impending departure of her only son, and I, quite insensitive in my exhilaration, sat transfixed at its sight from a window in the lobby. I could see it flapping itself authoritatively in the wind, imbuing me with such hope, I had felt as if I were already there.

It was a moment, I felt, that all my life until then had been leading up to. The new beginning to a life of adventure and possibilities that Kenya would never be able to offer me. A place with people I had never met and far away from those I had known. I would miss them all, of course, but how exciting that chance to forge an identity independent of them all. It was all waiting there for me, this unconfined life, and the door was about to open up and let me in.

I look at that flag now and it doesn't conjure the same feelings anymore.

Perhaps because I'm no longer a spectator gazing at the print. I've leapt into its dimension and I'm one of those little colored specks that constitutes the big picture now. It stands there, stealing some of the light from the bright Arco gas station sign behind it. The red and blue and white are still there in all their majesty. But I am done gazing at it long and hard. And now, interwoven in the same fabric, I have been able to see something else that does not stand for freedom or compassion or courage. It has failed in its noble intentions to those who lionized it. The magic has dwindled. Its promise withers. There is only this flag, brandishing itself petulantly in the wind, flapping and employing its most critical acting talent to appear immaculate in the putrid L.A. smog.

The line to get into The Cellar is going out the door and the new members are taking so long getting registered, you're turning from a nymphomaniac into a psychotic. Although you want desperately to run past them, you inhale deeply and try to calm yourself.

Then there is *that* someone who has forgotten his membership card, and another whose membership has expired and he is wondering how that can be possible and if he can pay by Mastercard, while he keeps pulling out these little promotional fliers from his pocket. All the time people are coming out and going home and they look sinister and unappealing. This is not how most of them look inside. Is that a trick of the light? Or rather, the lack of it? Perhaps these are just the worms wriggling their way home. Your man may still be in there, and the sound of the creaking floorboards over your head just may be his footsteps pacing from room to room until you find him. The dexterity with which you swipe your card through the scanner tells you you've been there much too often, as if the familiar faces of the check-in clerks don't.

Inside, you are immediately struck by the number of people anticipating an arrival through the door. You want to go to the bathroom but there are a million people waiting in line and someone is already grumbling about what the hell might be going on in there.

Frantic at first, you calm down after making a few rounds. Then oddly enough, you hear the strains of an Indian film song in your mind as you walk. Some song that film star Rekha sang as a courtesan in *"Umrao Jan Ada."* *Yeh kya jagaa he, dosto. Yeh kon sa dayaar he . . .* Christ, of all the things that should be going through your mind! Strange phenomenon, but even Faizal has admitted to singing some classic filmi songs to himself while wandering through the labyrinth on his own.

You wonder if this is a South Asian thing. A way of steadying yourself, as you swagger through this lair of carnality. To hold on to something culturally rooted as you stumble your way through the uncertainties of rampant salacity. Or maybe you're just feeling dramatically tragic again. Aware with much regret that despite all your apparent potential, you are still here in this place. Dateless. Nothing but an empty bed waiting for you at home.

Up the staircase you go. Into a musty room. Doing this dance of the blind. Not quite able to see. Not really wanting to either. Only touching and feeling. Limbs. Hair. Mouths. Tongues. Fingers. Someone brushes your hand rudely off him. You feel momentarily startled. Broken from the erotic spell you were in. He has just reminded you that even here, away from the nightclubs and mushrooming coffee houses, there awaits rejection.

Your expulsion agitates you enough to want to find the manager and get the s.o.b. kicked out. *You know, some ass-hole up there is being really obnoxious! I mean, he's just like, rudely pushing people away and I think he's going to start some trouble . . .* This kind of behavior is unacceptable here. Just a little squeeze on the probing fingers. Maybe a pat on the hand before gently pushing your hand aside would be sufficient. Anybody who persisted *after* that, deserved what they got. But not before that, you ass-hole! Not before that.

Maybe you could tell them you felt him picking your pocket. That would really do it. That's always a problem here. Every few hours that announcement. Watch your pockets. Pickpocket in the house. But you just decide to let it go. There is no more alcohol and the last thing you need is to get overexcited and blow the little high you are on. So you call him an asshole under your breath and go back down and into another room instead.

On your way in, there is a little more light and you recognize some people from the club you just came from. There they had been acting all conceited and too self-absorbed to entertain just anybody's advances. Here they were panting around like dogs in a pound, all gropes and grinds.

You attempt to walk all the way to the back of the room. Gently, yet persistently pushing your way through warmth and sweat. There is a strong odor here. A stench of urine, semen, stale cologne and perspiration all mingling into one. But it's not so bad. You've smelt worse. Without even thinking, you stifle your breath and inhale spasmodically until you've gotten through the throng of people.

At the end of the room, you allow your hands to carelessly wander over the chest of someone standing against the wall. He doesn't move or seem to mind so you move closer and then up against him. Your lips search him out hungrily and he responds with the same urgency. Although you can't see his face in the dark, you like the way his body feels. Strong and reciprocating. He would do just fine.

You ask him if he wants to fuck you.

"What?" He asks.

"Do you want to fuck me?"

"Yeah," he says. "Sure."

Even as the words leave your lips, you were aware of how cold and vulgar they may sound. But what you know more assuredly is that because your behavior is devoid of any bullshit, it is quite apropos. They are the only words that have been spoken with any genuineness tonight. In the cold light of day, nothing else that two people will have confessed or revealed through the course of the night will matter.

A week down the line, when the two of them run into each other at an ATM somewhere in West Hollywood, even less will be remembered. The chance that either one of them will even want to recognize each other is still more questionable.

As they say in Hindi, *Raat gayi, Baat gayi . . .* So you might as well get the show on the road. Within minutes, you have walked out of the club and are racing in Adrian's black Accura down Wilshire Boulevard and into the heart of Santa Monica. On the way, you never look back to make sure he's following you, but frequently ask Adrian if he can still see him from the rear-view mirror.

"He's keeping up, baby," Adrian assures you more than once, his voice tinged with excitement. "He's right behind us."

After we have sex, I light up a cigarette as I lie on his bare chest. I don't generally smoke, but at times like these it feels glamorous and appropriate. The amber glow as I inhale illuminates his beautiful young face, and for a moment I feel caught up in an almost film noir-like moment.

"You're *so* passionate," he says. "So intense! God, what were you on?"

"You mean, what am I on? I could still be on it, you know."

"Oh, yeah. I know," he laughs nervously.

"Nothing," I shrug. "Why do I have to be on anything?"

I realize my inflection is tinged with hostility. That the wonder in his face and the naiveté in his eyes came from what he had been accustomed to all his life. What most Americans knew of as being sex—the orgasm-oriented, routine, blow me, jack me off, "you got some poppers?" kind of sex. A means to an end. Not the kind of sex where people simply fed off of each other's bodies for hours without even possibly ever satiating the hunger that brought them together. Sex where one may seek a temporary lease from the other but not complete redemption. Then again, did anybody else have a need for that kind of sex? Was there any point to it, but to foolishly extend the torment of unquelled urges and to seek pleasure from deprivation?

He tells me the incense that is burning reminds him of Paris, and that he loves the "classical" music playing on the stereo.

"It's a film score," I tell him, suppressing the "For Chrissake" part.

"Oh, it is?"

"Yeah." I exhale. "Bugsy."

"I think I saw that film."

"Mmm," I respond, unimpressed. "So, you've been to Paris?"

"Yeah. A couple of years before I joined the military."

"Did they know about you there?"

434

"Where? In Paris?"

Oh, God, please don't let me roll my eyes around. "In the military, of course."

"What, are you kidding?" he laughs. "We won't ask and you don't have to tell, remember?"

Clinton's face goes through my mind and I grunt.

"Where are you from?" he asks.

I tense up. *That* question again. I'm unsure if he's asking me this because he's so taken with my passion or because he's just unfamiliar with South Asian men in general. I snub the cigarette out on a silver condom wrapper lying at the edge of the bed. The image of him savagely tearing it open with his teeth as he mounted me flashes through my mind. I feel a stirring in the pit of my belly again.

I can feel his eyes on me and he is still waiting for me to reply.

Where are you from? Who are you? Where have you been?

Such a little mystery I've become to him. Maybe he is trying to make sense of what has just transpired between us. Of how I had compelled him to give up so much of his control and inhibition. But I remain silent. Evasive. I don't want to answer him. Maybe it's because I don't think it should matter what I am or where the hell I come from. None of his damn business. Just because he has just fucked me does not mean that he has a right to know everything about me.

But maybe it's because what I am matters too much to me.

South Asian.

Indian.

I decide to leave him unanswered. To spare myself from my shame.

I roll off him and allow Adrian to have his turn.

I lay on my stomach, entwined in the soiled and crumpled sheets as he walks back into the room after taking a shower. He hovers awkwardly around my bed—just a mattress thrown over a spring box. I can sense that he is nervous and doesn't quite know what to do or say because I am making no effort to turn around. I just lie there. Not looking at him. And more importantly, not letting him see me.

He mumbles something about having to drive back to Anaheim and thanks me for everything. I am curt to the point of being cruel. Adrian says something about it being a long drive.

He offers his number and even then I ignore him.

"Adrian, could you get his number and give him ours?" I slur.

They leave the room and I start to feel relieved. I know that I have been insensitive and have probably made him feel like trash. But what was I supposed to do? We had met in some dark corner at a sex club where he could barely have made out what I was. I might have even seemed Latino to him at some point. But now, with daylight intruding through the blinds, and him all showered and satiated, he might have seen me for the South Asian I am. And that would be embarrassing, wouldn't it?

All those images of 7-Eleven salesmen and heavily accented, sing-song dialects would come flooding into his mind and maybe he would cringe. He would realize his exotic passion flower was just the basis for a Simpsons' cartoon character. He would see my typical South Asian features and realize that I looked nothing like him. Large unmysterious eyes. The long bony nose. Skin, dark not from tanning on the beach, but from birth. And then what if he felt cheated? Defiled?

And what of my body? How, in this culture of gym-bodies would he feel about having had sex with someone whose body didn't look like he spent at least two hours in a gym daily, and possibly only looked good in drag on a Halloween night? Swathed in my sheets, now that neither the night nor his lust could have obscured me, I found solace in being ironically passionless and cold to him.

Do you know of such fear?

Is this not the curse of every South Asian whose standards of beauty were in conflict with his own appearance?

No, no, he couldn't see all this. I couldn't have let him see that I was Indian.

I can't seem to remember exactly when it all started. This shame. All I know is that it must have happened a long time ago. Long before I knew what was happening or had any control over it. Perhaps it's all the result of being born in the shadows of colonialism.

Imagine growing up in a country where being "white" automatically meant that you were brilliant, more competent, and entitled to the privileges that everybody else had to struggle for. Even the South Asians and the Africans who warred against each other with class and economic prejudices cast everything aside to act as subservient as they could when the *"goras"* or *"dhorias"* came into view. There were many of them, some of them expatriates who had had to unwillingly relinquish the luxuries of colonial, pre-independence Kenya, but had decided to stay on, or had come back with the hope of educing anything reminiscent of their golden era.

I remember how excited my mother was at the prospect of taking me to see a *"dhorio"* doctor by the name of Dr. Diamond, who had his office in the tallest building in Mombasa island, all fifteen stories of it. He was by no means inexpensive, and had expatriated from England, so naturally he had to be the best around. He would perform virtual miracles on me since his knowledge on medicine had to be superior to any colored doctor. The women in her community circle would raise their brows and drop their jaws because they would be so impressed that Parin had taken her son to none other than the Dr. Diamond.

"He looks *just* like our Hazar Imam," she would enthuse, referring to the spiritual leader of the Ismaili community, and inexplicably feeling more comforted by the resemblance in their accent and Caucasian appearance. Ironic as it was, even the spiritual leader believed to be the direct descendant of the Holy Prophet, and whom most of my community regarded as God's very incarnation on earth, looked nothing like his followers and more like the intimidating white man that commanded such awe-inspiring respect.

It is no wonder, therefore, that by the time we had excitedly clanked the grill shut and ridden the elevator up the fifteen floors and I stood in front of him in my underwear and the thermometer in my mouth, both my mother and I felt as if we were standing in front of God Himself. Moses had found the burning bush. We had found Dr. Diamond.

As an African-Asian you learnt to live by certain principles. Imported was always better than local. Ready-made was always better than tailor-made because it came from abroad. A four week vacation in London or Canada, two of the most popular vacation places for East African Asians, was enough justification to come back with a ridiculously self-imposed accent so that you sounded more like them and less like yourself.

And a fair complexion was always more desirable than a dark one. That was obvious from the class structure that had based itself through centuries on how light- or dark-skinned you were. Even religious conversion into the Muslim faith could not completely eradicate the traces of this predominantly Hindu belief.

Remember Shehnaz, who lived in the same flats as your family did? And how everyone always referred to her as *"masoto"* or dirt rag? How your grandmother had often mentioned to you that her family had descended from a sect of "untouchables," a lower-class people in India that had been subjugated to serve the others? Shehnaz *"masoto"* they had called her. And the snooty women in the community would often grimace behind her back when considering her eligibility as a daughter-in-law, and to her face they would give one of those superficial smiles. No teeth. Just upturned lips stretched thin in an effort to be civil.

It was no wonder that mothers were constantly urging their daughters not to stay out too long in the sun from fear of turning dark. Who will marry you if you turn as dark as coal, stupid girl?

But most important of all, despite the alarming similarities in both races, you learnt that you were always better than the *"golas"* or blacks. The darker to *"masoto,"* the lower your class. No question about it. Simple law of nature. An apparent hierarchy of pigmentation had been a fact of life difficult to miss. The *"dhorias"* at the top. The *"muindhis"* in the middle. And the *"golas"* right at the bottom like the dirt they resembled.

My mother calls me from Kenya. There is an echo in the connection and she acts like she's stuck in my answering machine and is trying desperately to get out. The notion that the machine is on because I will not, or cannot, come to the phone does not enter her mind, so she continues to call out in her most dramatic tone. Her pleas to be recognized start to irritate me.

"Ali, are you there? This is Mummy! If you are there, can you please pick up the phone? Ali, it's Parin, it's Mummy! Ali? Ali? Ali, are you there?" This goes on for a few expensive minutes until she sounds more resigned.

I continue to lie in bed, recuperating from a terrible hangover. I don't feel like talking to her. Hardly ever do these days. She and all the rest of my family have the unique talent of driving me up the wall by repeating what they have to say incessantly until you want to shut your ears and scream. *I heard you! You've said it fifty times, already! Just stop bladdy nagging me!* Then naturally you've hurt their feelings and they claim you don't give a shit about them anymore and perhaps they shouldn't have bothered to call you to begin with. Enter guilt and feeling more like shit.

She confirms her dates for her upcoming trip to Los Angeles. As I am listening in deep silence, I'm not sure that I want her to come. Apprehension fills up inside me. I just don't think I can deal with her. Listening to her, I am reminded of how much that voice had meant to me once. I think about when I first came here and how I would break down crying every time I heard that voice on the phone. How miserable it made me feel to be away from her. All I wanted to do was run back home and be smothered from the demons of this city. Lay my head down in her lap and let her gently caress all of my fears and troubles away as the familiar scent of her perfume calmed my senses.

That was so long ago. Seven years have gone by. Somehow I have learnt to detach myself from that need. One tends to do that after a while of missing someone terribly. After twenty-six years, I had finally extricated from the umbilical cord myself.

Now here she was, making plans to come and see me. Trying, albeit in futility, to tangle me back into such dependency. How would I accommodate her in my life as it precariously stood today?

Where in between Richard and drinking would she stand?

Where was there any room, any need—for yet another to identify myself through?

In thinking of Richard, I think about all the other men that have drifted through my life. All created from the same mold it seems. Having successfully auditioned to be the able benefactors to a hungry dysfunction, they had somewhere along the line ceased to become individuals and become the sludge of a distinct personality instead.

It was different with Richard only because, for reason of exorcising his own ghosts, he had decided to stay. Most others had always been in too much of a hurry to stick around long enough and burst the bubble themselves. Maddeningly unstructured, it was within the pockets of such precarity that we found the fuel for everything that attracted and eventually repelled us from each other.

Passion thrives on many annihilating emotions. It's fueled by catalysts so fickle, so fleeting, that the promise of lasting love is never one of them. Richard's affection for me bore such fugitive traits. Unpredictable. Capricious. Ephemeral. It swallowed all of me up alive.

Little in my life has come close to being as passionate as this indefinable relationship.

Except perhaps my relationship to my father, or that of his to my mother. Who know what experiences in early life form the indelible scars that sear in the years to come? Propel you into recreating the familiar scenes that have an uncanny ability to convince you that this time you would have control in manipulating the outcome. As if you ever really did. Often you start out with almost mythical bravado and end up as a pawn instead.

My earliest memory of being in kindergarten is not of the playground or the finger painting. It is one of deep yearning. It's of myself running behind some five-year old, calling him inexplicably by the same nickname my Mom had for my father. Shila. That's what she called him. Why I was calling Munir or Sandeep by this nickname as I chased him relentlessly around the slides and seesaws on the sand playground would have given any psychotherapist a multiple orgasm.

It seems there was always somebody I was trying to hold back from going away. Always somebody without whom it just didn't feel right. On the playground. In the class room. At home. In life. Somebody should have seen it then. But my mother was too busy making a living and smothering me in the little time she could spare, and my father busy being faithless to her, and compensating her affections with his wrath. *Don't treat him like a girl, for God's sake! He's a boy, can't you see that? You are bringing him up to be a goddamn sissy! No son of mine is going to grow up to be a bladdy sissy!*

My grandmother, who I learnt to call "Mummy," tried even harder to make up for the anomaly for both her own life and the absence of my feuding parents, only to exacerbate the belligerent convictions of an only child in the most tempestuous of surroundings. In later years, she often told me of how as a child, I had never crawled from her fear of bruising my knees. I had gone straight from her arms to learning how to walk as she had held onto my hands carefully.

She told me about the ordeal she had to undergo whenever it was time for me to take a bath. I refused to take one unless my closest friends gathered and watched. She would laugh and say that I had needed an audience even then. Adrian says that I might have been too afraid to let them out of my sight lest they disappeared and didn't come back.

It was no surprise therefore that when my father left to settle matters with his mistress in the capital city of Nairobi, and promised to come back but wound up having his blood splattered all over her room instead, I was determined that nobody would ever leave me again. The consummation between father and child that comes from spending intimate moments that last more than a couple of hours every few weeks never came. Teaching me how to water paint as I sat in his laps and then disappearing for months at a time suddenly became a mercifully acceptable notion compared to not being able to see him again.

No, it would not happen to me again. This abrupt and unjust abandonment. Perhaps if I hadn't failed him in some way. Disappointed him. Held on to him tighter. Appeased him by comprehending signs that he surely must have emitted.

No, never again. I would love him as nobody ever had. He would never have to look elsewhere. I would manipulate any circumstance. Experience as an only child had taught me how to maneuver situations. Offer any sacrifice. Grant any kind of freedom. Keep him by my side. Never find myself in a situation that required reclaiming him. He would be the father they had killed. The mother who had worked too hard. The siblings she had aborted. He would make everything alright.

Enter Richard.

You started to cry over the phone. Couldn't understand why he was treating you this way. Deep inside you must have had a notion.

Richard was the perfect boy. Twenty-two and the object of everybody's desire. He had the kind of muscled, athletic body that everyone gawked at. That the fantasies of dark, lonely nights formulated themselves upon. A prototype of physical beauty in the flesh. Those deep-set dark eyes under the heavy brows, slaying every heart they peered into. A smile that could illuminate the darkest of despairs. A scowl that could condemn you infernally. What could he possibly see in someone like you? Nothing. You were fortunate enough just to have him in your life in some warped, disfigured way.

Often Adrian and Faizal had asked you exactly how he had managed to conquer your most rational and independent spirit. Why, time after time, he had treated you like a book on the shelf, only to be taken out when he had been in the mood to read you, and yet you had remained with unbridled anticipation on that dusty shelf, waiting to be picked out and read again.

The problem, you had attempted to explain, was that Richard had been unable to disenchant you. Yes, you had been disarmed by the lure of his random beckon. But you had also been seduced by the confident rebuke of his shrug. It was precisely his indifference, his unpredictability that had struck the familiar cord that hooked you. That made his attraction that much more irresistible. He could do without you. Walk away without as much as a backward glance.

You had been unable to change that about your father.

Could you change that in him?

Occasionally he even found it possible to say that he loved you, and it's at such moments that you became optimistic again, and felt that you were making strides in your efforts at a ridiculously pre-destined consummation. You had, in reveries, and dreams insuppressible by self-help books and wisdom dispensed by friends, envisioned the very moment when the jousting would end, and a mutually impassioned loving begin.

But most of the time, what your ears hungrily devoured, your heart could not interpret no matter how hard it tried. His words and his deeds spoke different languages and they threw all your fantasies in disdain and turmoil. It drove you insane. All these voices and words and images and so much confusion.

There was that one voice that could have been the voice of reason, begging you to break away from his beguiling eyes. And there was that other one, that must have been your martyred heart, reminding you that Mummy had stayed through the end, and that you must stop being selfish and be selfless, like her. That you too, must give time and time again if you were to claim that you truly loved him.

Hadn't she tried to get away but ended up taking him back every time he had cried? Isn't that how the Hindi films you had seen religiously over the years portrayed all the heroines that triumphed in the end? Suffering? Penance? Patience? Tears from desertion until the joys of being needed again, and being re-claimed?

Images from these Hindi films have often flashed through your mind. Jaya Bachaan in *"Silsila,"* lamenting in song until tall and handsome Amitabh comes back to her from carousing with his mistress. . . Faces of actresses whose names you knew so well. Scenes from movies, the titles of which you have long forgotten . . . And those songs. Yes, those filmi songs with the poignant lyrics that epitomized the suffering of love. They are all there in their pomp and melodrama. Directing you. Reminding you. Unfolding within you in their systematic chaos. How can you help but heed their instinctual direction? It's become a hopeless situation. Just like scores of Indian women who have learnt to identify with the martyred heroines of the Hindi film, you have also learnt to relate to them instead of the independent, free-spirited hero.

You don't burst out into song and dance but you have come to believe in the melodrama. That good has to win. Patience is a virtue that always pays back. And that those who love the most, and are willing to suffer for it, always get the object of their affection to realize that they belong together.

Penance is a prerequisite to romantic fulfillment. Life without the one you love quantifies death.

This has always been evident to you. You've seen it for yourself as you were growing up. On the screen and around you. Remember Gulzar, your mother's friend, who had given you that beautiful blue tote bag from the airline company she used to work at? Hung herself. Depression is what they had called it at first. All those Valiums she constantly devoured. But some time later the rumors started to surface. *He had been seeing some Arab woman, that husband of hers.* In a town like Mombasa, talk about "other women" spread like wildfire. *They had been fighting all the time!* Remarked the women in the community during their ritual gossiping after the evening prayers.

The "*bankara* committee" they had been called. *Bankara* from the benches that skirted the mosque grounds. Most of these women were ailing from arthritis or simply old age, and were unable to climb the flight of stairs leading up to the mosque. The elevator that had been talked about for the last few years had yet to be installed. So they just sat around on the *bankaras* and pretended to observe the prayers that were being cast out over the P.A. system while avidly discussing the state of community affairs. Their bodies had given up on them a long time ago. But their faces. Their faces were like operas. Completely animated. Eyes squinting. Frowning. Brows arched up in exaggerated shock. Mouth gasping away. And their hands. That was another thing. Their hands were constantly in motion. Like they were creating, molding in the air. Gesticulating. Slapping their foreheads. Jabbing and pointing. It was as if the words that were being spoken were incompetent without the body language.

And now, what about their poor eleven-year old daughter? What will become of her? Men! They are such dogs, I tell you! She should have left him a long time ago, the bastard, but instead what does she do? Hang herself!

And Shainoor? *Yah, Khudda! Alnoor and she had been high school sweethearts, imagine that! Do you remember how beautiful that girl was? That long black hair all the way down to here! Tsk, tsk, tsk . . . beautiful fair complexion . . . And that magnificent voice when she sang at all the music parties! Attended mosque daily too! Such a pleasant girl. Truly the pride of the community . . .* Rat poison! That was her response to his seeing another woman. Not a separation. Not a divorce. Not to cheat on him in rebellion. But to drink up poison. Rat poison, no less!

You wonder if any of them had had a choice, really, being in love and bound to their traditional notions of love. What could have been expected of them? To endure faithlessness would have meant to have hope. To meet the wager with an affair? Every woman who had rebelled and indulged in an extra-marital affair had ended up being dubbed as the community whore. Soon, everybody's husbands called her at home with lucrative offers to spend a night at some beach hotel. Many had given in, unable to ever absolve themselves from such a reputation.

You've known, much to your dismay, that in situations both turbulent and trivial, you have always played the role of the victimized heroine in plight. It's what has kept you from telling him to fuck off, turning around and walking away first for a change. You've watched the melodrama unfold on the silver screen avidly through the years. Jumping on top of your seat as a child to applaud the formulaic celebration of a jubilant struggle in love. And now your life has become one.

Men could leave. But if you had the misfortune of relating to the women, or being one, the respectable thing to do was stay. It was in waiting patiently as he treaded and realized the error of his ways, in having the opportunity to be there when he returned, to forgive him and take him back, that you had to find your meaning and validation.

How ever would you deviate from such cultural conviction?

How else was love for an Indian male that related to the psyche of his mother meant to be?

You have been torn apart by these voices before. Familiar strains of lyrics and voices fanned out from an abyss in your heart. It was these voices that you heard again as you clutched the phone in fear of unraveling disaster.

Four weeks ago you had planned to see this movie and now thirty minutes before the show, he called you to say that he had changed his mind. Simple. Changed his mind. Didn't feel like it. Wasn't up to it. Not in the mood.

It should have been quite simple. People change their minds all the time. It was their prerogative. So you take a rain-check, stifle your disappointment, and try to articulate an understanding, "Oh, no problem, Richard. I was feeling a little pooped myself. We'll just do it next week. It's really no big deal. . ."

But not for you. For you it suddenly became a matter of life and death. He had just yanked the life-line away from your desperate grip.

How could he have known of the ceremonies you had observed to prepare for that evening? Of the fact the every time you had felt reason to feel dismayed with life, you had shaken off the bleakness with this evening to look forward to? Of the reverie of having him next to you and smelling him and feeling his warmth. Of listening to his laugh. That full-bodied, robust laugh like he could take hold of life and just swallow it whole. How could he know such longing?

Instead he had even admitted to wanting to go "visit," as he so discreetly put it, some guy called Louis that he had met just a few days ago at some private party.

You would have done anything for him to keep his promise. Made bargains that were impossible to keep. *Please Richard, just this time, don't cancel on me. We don't have to see a movie again for as long as you wish. But just this time . . .*

In the forty-five minutes that he had tormented you, you had tried to cajole him with humor to remind him of how witty and how much fun you could be, shifted to emotional blackmail by reminding him of his promises, and finally capitulated to the most basic of human techniques—begging. Nothing mattered except him showing up at your door.

When he told you that he needed some more time to think about it because he didn't feel like being around you in such a desperate and needy state, you sat by the phone and prayed as you had night after night for some requiting. Bent down on your knees, you looked up at the framed picture of the Aga Khan with teary eyes and commenced to bargain petulantly with his spiritual worth.

Why would you deny me this? You, who we all look upon as God! What was so wrong about wanting Richard? That, after all is not materialistic. It's not like I'm praying for a car or money or anything. All I want it Richard to love me back. How can you just stand there in that damn picture smiling down at me and do nothing to grant my wish?

As a child, Mummy had rhapsodized about how prayers could move mountains. She had neglected to tell you that the Richards of this world would be an exception to this phenomenon.

More Precious Than These Hands

Shivani Manghnani

There are three women in my family—two of whom are very beautiful. My mother was named Meera after the first liberated Indian woman, a Rajput princess who left her husband to sing in temples and devote her life to Lord Krishna—the god she believed was her true husband. Meera's in-laws tried twice to kill her because of the shame and scandal she brought to their family, first by sending her a snake in a basket and then a poisonous drink. These attempts were unsuccessful, for Meera was under Lord Krishna's protection. She won the admiration of even the Muslim kings, who would disguise themselves to hear Meera sing or to watch her dance.

But my mother was not always so fair and graceful. When she was little my *masees* would make fun of her because she was the tallest of the six sisters, and walking to school they would poke her in the ribs and say, "How's the weather up there?" Meera got her height from her father, although she was the only sister who had inherited her mother's thick legs. She did well in school, math especially, so well that after college she wanted to come to America. "I could work for Sunder Uncle," Meera begged her father. But he would not send my mother to America by herself, especially to New York, to work in his brother's engineering firm. So Meera refused to eat, and for five days she was able to keep this fast. Her father was beginning to weaken, but, in the end, it was my grandmother who kept her in India. "You cannot go to a strange country and work with machines and numbers, especially since you are finally becoming beautiful and have the chance to marry well," her mother had told her, for it was true. Meera had always been the daughter with the lightest complexion, and at last her eyes and nose had grown to fit her full lips. Meera had grown her hair long, so that it now reached her waist. Her mother oiled her thick, black locks every night before she went to sleep, and in the morning they fell like streams of silk down Meera's back. The big space between my mother's long, buck teeth, which had made her even more vulnerable to her sisters' cruelty, never did go away because the family could not afford to see the white dentist who knew how to fix such deformities. But Meera was soothed by her father who told her that the gap between her teeth meant that she would one day be wealthy and provide some man's family with a handsome dowry.

Since she could not go to America to become an engineer, Meera did the next best thing. She married a professor of engineering who lived in Hawai'i. My mother did not want to marry my father when she first saw him for tea at the Taj Hotel. First of all, the man was shorter than she was, and he was also darker skinned. Worse, Meera could tell that in ten years her husband would be completely bald, for while sipping his tea or munching on a samosa, he would pause to brush wisps of hair over his expanding forehead. Although my mother did not enjoy staring at my father for these long periods of time, she married him anyway, thankfully leaving the crowded Bombay streets for America.

When Meera first came to Hawai'i and walked along the streets full of bronzed, curvy women, she was surprised that the calls from the men behind their pineapple stands were for her. She knew she was different and many times more beautiful than these island women whom she thought were a bit heavy and much too outspoken, yet she never got used to the beckoning voices, "Girl, you know you're fine!" they would shout, their hands waving to her like palm trees. Once when my mother was in a Waikiki grocery store a barefoot man wearing an obnoxious aloha shirt asked her to model for his calendar, "You could be the next Sophia Loren," he said, running his hands over the heap of ripe tomatoes, coming and breathing so close that the onions my mother had been gathering fell from her hands, rolling to the floor.

Meera's first child was not a son. Meera did not care because she wanted a girl anyway, a girl who would grow up to look like her, though she dreaded facing her relatives and the other Indian women who still worshipped anything with a penis. When my mother first saw the right hand of her child she burst into tears—the child had no thumb, just a garish knob of flesh that sloped downwards from the base of her index finger. My mother could not figure out what she had done wrong during her pregnancy, or her life, to deserve this. She was so shocked and limp after giving birth that she could not name the child. She lay listless on the hospital bed, poking her soft, empty stomach with her fingers, pinching the jiggling flesh with glazed eyes. The white doctor came to her room, sat down and spoke to her quietly and slowly. My mother still could not bring herself to speak and so my father named the child, "Poonam," night of the full moon.

This second woman in my family was also very beautiful, and even as a child Poonam was blessed with a high forehead, wide eyes, and a head of stubborn, curly hair. Meera loved Poonam fiercely, wanting to protect her child from the cruel world outside her playpen. She taught Poonam only English, and made her use her knife and fork instead of her hands when eating. My sister was to grow up American, my mother insisted, there was no reason for her to be different in any other way. My mother joined Easter Seals and stayed away from the other gossipy Indian women, those rotund wives stuffing themselves and their sons with burfi and other pure ghee delights.

Poonam was an angel for the first two years of her life, the years when she was the only daughter. She was weaned off baby food quickly and learned to eat the spicy curries my mother spent hours preparing. All her limbs, save her right arm, were strong, and so when Poonam waddled about the house in her diapers, my mother did not worry about her falling. When Poonam was old enough to begin school, my mother refused to put her in a "special school", because in those schools the children had slanted, wandering eyes. They chewed their fingers and drooled on their desks. Poonam was too clever and much too beautiful to be surrounded by such *helpless* children.

As Poonam grew older she became even more stunning. There was a dark skinned boy named Steven who would follow close behind Poonam on his bike as we walked home from school together, calling out, "Hey Thumbelina! Hey freaky paw, wanna kiss?" Poonam's hand was wrapped like a knot under her t-shirt, and hugging her book bag across her body she would look at me expectantly, like I should go over there and knock him off his bike or something. Steven was a handsome boy, with a cute smile and tight, curly lashes. When he saw me his eyes traveled up and down over my body only once before he yelled, "Flat chest!" and sped away laughing.

My sister did many things that devastated my mother as she grew older. She pierced her nose, dyed her hair an awful blue-black color, and, when my mother refused to look at her, consumed most of the contents in my father's liquor cabinet before escaping into a coma. My parents found my sister's sprawled body on the bathroom floor the next morning, and I found them on their knees, bent over Poonam and the half-empty bottle of José Cuervo rolling aimlessly on the white tile. Poonam's eyes were only half-closed, a thin line of drool escaping the corner of her open mouth. The worst part was that her right arm was sort of reaching up in the direction of the bottle, as if she had tried, while falling, to catch it before it slipped from her grip. Like she was sorry for the whole hair and earring thing and did not want to make a mess of the bathroom floor on top of it all. When the ambulance guy came to whisk my sister off to the hospital my mother was tense, biting her lower lip,

"Everyone has problems you know," she said loudly as he strapped Poonam onto the stretcher, "What are you looking at?" she demanded, turning to my father and me, "What the hell is everyone looking at?" Shaking and moaning, she made one last attempt to save my sister's dignity, throwing a blue bath towel over her bare hand. My father held my mother from behind like a straight-jacket, and soon they were in the back of the ambulance with my sister.

I am the third woman in my family, and although I was born with all limbs in tact, my mother still had to hold back her tears when she saw that I had a short neck, and did not possess the fair, round face of my sister. My mother nicknamed me Chippy, because, she said, I came out shriveled and furry and wet. *The first word that came to my mind*, she always says, *Chipmunk*! raising her hands to emphasize the point, *Really*! When I was still very young my mother gave me heaps of blocks to play with and puzzles to figure out, because, she said, if I was ugly I might as well be smart. She calmed down a little when my braces came off and the Farah Fawcett haircut grew out, but still, I would not have the chance to marry well and inspire envy from other women like my sister.

When I was ten years old my mother enrolled me in ballet lessons. *You have long legs and such good posture*, she said. When I used to pack my pink duffel bag for class, Poonam would finger the elastic ties of my ballet slippers and stare longingly at the peach colored shoes before I could grab them from her and stuff them hastily into my bag. A few years later when my mother's hips erupted from my body and I had the urge to quit, my mother told me that I was a dancer, something my sister could never be. I started going to class early to change into my leotard before the other girls arrived. *It is the discipline that will keep you on top*, my dance teacher would tell me, pleased when she saw me stretching at the barre before class; *those who have well-defined goals and who do not get distracted will succeed.* So I refused food for days, and at dinner my sister would watch me cut my meal into little bits with a look of annoyance. When I would take my hardly touched plate to the sink I could feel her eyes on me, hot and questioning.

Still my mother was not convinced, even when I fainted in the middle of ballet class, right after a perfectly executed triple pirouette from fourth position. Later I got a trip to the nutritionist and reassurances from my bereft mother, "You are the lucky one. You should thank God for a perfect, complete body." I stepped off the scale in the doctor's office and put my clothes back on, cursing God. I cursed him for this completeness, that had robbed me of something more precious than these hands.

I set my mother's china down carefully on the coffee table, placing three tiny, white teacups rimmed with gold in their respected saucers. Under each set I place a folded white napkin fringed with gold colored lace—these I have already ironed for my mother's afternoon tea party.

When our family began to frequent these Indian get-togethers, and this was years after my mother's hiatus during which she dedicated herself to raising my sister, the three women in my family were quite a sight—my blue-haired sister with her hand knotted up in her blouse, my mother in a sari too tight and revealing, and I, tired and bony in something four sizes too large and usually black. I am sure we provided much entertainment for the chattering women covered in gaudy jewels and yards of magenta and orange polyester cloth. My mother would pretend she did not notice the whispering voices that commented on our clothing and wondered where our father was, dragging us past the women exchanging recipes and into the men's circle to talk politics.

Today, our home is soon to be graced by two other Indian women, both older and heavier than my mother, who is busy in the kitchen, frying batches of pakoras for her robust guests. When I ask her if she needs help mixing the batter she says, "Do you think this is enough for your Aunties?" gesturing to the heap of round, crispy dough, glistening with oil.

"Probably not," I reply, and my mother rolls her eyes,

"Go pick some flowers from the backyard."

I take a pair of scissors and go outside. The afternoon sun is hot on my shoulders, already darkened to deep brown from my days spent at the beach. "You will become a blacky if you stay in the sun so long!" my mother always shouts at me, muttering under her breath complaints as to why my father chose Hawai'i of all places in America to settle down. I think silently that if I were in college, far away on the East Coast like my sister, I too would have a fair complexion.

I cut stalks of plumeria from the tree in our backyard, the sticky milk from the stems spilling onto my hands. I place one behind my ear and head back to the house, where Kamla and Sumedha Aunty have just arrived.

"Bahut patali hai," Kamla Aunty says loudly when I enter carrying the bunches of white and yellow flowers, "You're still not eating your *khana* properly, or what?" she asks, handing me a pakora, "Meera, I thought this girl was getting better, no?" When I shake my head, refusing, she pops it into her mouth.

"Yeh ladki bahut kaali hai," Sumedha Aunty adds, running her eyes over my bare shoulders, and I wonder if I should turn around to give the women full view of my body, my skin color.

My mother takes the flowers from me, "Give your Aunties something to drink," she says, motioning for her guests to sit down in the other room. I pour two glasses of guava juice and make my way into the living room, where the three women are already chatting away, not in Hindi that I cannot understand, but in English. "How is the other girl?" Sumedha Aunty asks, dipping a pakora into the coconut chutney before popping it into her mouth, "she is getting old Meera, *hai naa*? Ready for *shadi*?"

"She's not old enough, yet," my mother answers, "Soon, I will take her to India for the jewelry".

"Yes, she is *bahut sunder*, like you Meera, very fair, she will have no trouble," Kamla Aunty says, darting a quick glance my way before brushing crumbs from the gold border of her purple sari.

"Well, not everyone can have the fortune of looking like an Italian movie star," my mother half-laughs, and before she can tell the I-could-have-been-a-cover girl story, I set down the glasses and head back into the kitchen. I take a paper towel and squeeze the fresh batch of pakoras, feeling the oil moisten the towel, then my skin. I head for the sink and pile of dirty dishes, turning the faucet on as far as it will go. My mother speaks loudly, over the sound of the rushing water. "And Poonam, everyone thought she should have been a model too," my mother goes on, "so many of the mothers in the school would tell me that I should get someone to take pictures of my daughter, even pictures of the two of us together, can you imagine?" I start banging the pots and pans together in the sink, sending soap suds flying to the floor. My mother fails to mention that these women would say such things with sincerity that lasted only a brief while, until their eyes dropped from my sister's face, moving downward to her hand.

"See now Meera," Kamla says, just loud enough so I can hear, but soft enough so that I will think she is trying to take my side, "now you have the two sisters always fighting."

"Arre, you think they need me for that? *Hari Om*!" I can just see my mother throwing her hands up to the heavens as she speaks. "Haven't I told you enough about these *bad'mash*?" Let me guess, I think, wringing a dish dowel around my hands, the ballet recital ordeal. I leave the dishes in the sink, standing behind the wall that separates the kitchen from the living room. My mother pours tea into the waiting women's cups, the appropriate signal that a story is soon to be told. She picks up a pakora from the waning pile, kneading the small piece of dough with her fingers before nibbling on its edges. She chews slowly while the women wait, breathless.

I was going to be the Black swan in the ballet recital. I had come home from dance class one afternoon, weary but anxious to try on the costume my mother was sewing. I had to see how I looked in it, how it smoothed out my curves, if my butt stuck out, before I wore it in front of an entire audience. My mother promised to have it ready by the time I came home, but I didn't see it next to the sewing machine in my mother's study.

I remember running to the bedroom my sister and I had been forced to share, throwing open the door in anticipation. On the floor between the two identically sheeted beds was a crumpled, shredded pile of black satin. My eyes moved instantly to Poonam's bed, to the glinting metal edge of a pair of scissors. I was rooted to the floor, numb and suddenly dizzy. Poonam jumped out from behind the closet and giggled, covering her mouth with her hands.

We were on the floor, rolling. I dug my fingernails into her back, she kicked me in the ribs. I was screaming between sobs while Poonam laughed even louder. Soon I was gasping because her hands clutched at my neck, but even then I managed a bare whisper, those hateful names only the kids at school called her,

"Thumbelina! Freaky paw!" I felt better, and watched my sister's pretty face crumple and then twist with hatred.

My mother of course leaves out the name-calling part, and, according to her, the costume was not "shredded" just kind of diced up, and it wasn't so horrible that I had to wear the costume of the girl who danced the part last year, even though the girl was a stick and I was busting out of the seams.

I hear the women laughing in between mouthfuls of pakoras. My mother calls, "Chippy? Bring out more tea please, beti," satisfied that she has properly entertained her guests. Now when I serve them their chai they can take another look at me and imagine my sister and I clawing each other's eyes out. I back away from the wall and head for the stove, where the tea kettle is sitting, empty. I fill the kettle with water, adding two heaping spoonfuls of dark tea leaves. The telephone rings and when I pick up the receiver with an irritated "Hello?," my sister answers,

"Chip? It's me, Poonam . . . ," her voice soft and radiating this peacefulness, like her face when she paints my nails at the kitchen table, admiring my slender fingers while the rest of the family sleeps I leave the kettle on the stove and hop onto one of the wooden stools, setting the phone down on the counter.

"Hi Pooni," I say, twirling the phone chord around my fingers, "Thank god you saved me from the Bombay tea party." I roll my eyes at the chattering voices.

"Is mom feeding the undernourished Aunties again?" my sister laughs,

"Yeah, and its not just the oil off the pakoras that are keeping them satisfied," I let myself smile and rest my feet on the other stool.

"Oh, right," she says, not surprised. There is a pause before she continues in a light but strained voice, "So what story did she tell today? The one about me throwing up all over you in her pink German import, and how the smell never got out of the leather?"

"Thanks for playing. Come on Poonam, you know what comes after the Sophia Loren story."

"Right," she says, softer now, like it has just dawned on her. She clears her throat, "the Black Swan thing."

"Yeah, that thing," I try to keep the hurt out of my voice.

"Chippy, come on. You know I'm sorry about that. How old was I anyway? I mean, really—"

"Look, just forget it."

"Chiiiipppp!" my mother calls from the living room, "the tea kettle is boiling!"

"Shit, mom's calling me." My mother enters the kitchen, her eyes widening when she sees me cradling the telephone against my ear.

"Who are you talking to?" she demands.

"My sister," I answer curtly, not looking in her direction.

"Oh, sorry sorry rani, forget me, the woman who carried her for nine months." My mother gives me a long, cool stare. In living room the Aunties are persuading my mother to join them for the last of the pakoras. "Bring the tea, Chip," my mother orders tersely, and I remove the whistling kettle from the stove.

"What was that about Chippy?" my sister's voice is concerned.

"Oh, the usual. Don't be surprised if she yanks the phone away from me any minute now." I manage a stiff giggle.

"Well in that case, let me tell you about my incredible weekend. You won't believe what happened . . ."

Poonam tells me about the guy she met after she and her friends paid twenty bucks to get into some club. It turns out he's a thirty-year old lawyer and drives a forest green Land Cruiser and thought that Poonam was, take a wild guess, a model. The second my sister walked by him in the crowded club he stopped her and asked her to dance. She said she wanted to finish her drink and he said fine, let me buy you another and then we can dance. Poonam tells me all this, along with how he kissed her goodnight and her knees started shaking.

"Girl, he is a man, you know what I mean? When he holds me in those arms, and he looks at me really deep and all, you know what I'm talking about? That feeling you get in the pit of your stomach when everything is perfect and you can just picture yourself rolling around naked with the guy . . ."

"Poonam!" My cheeks are suddenly warm and I dart a guilty glance towards the living room, "please!"

"Sorry, sorry, I was just trying to tell you what it's like when, well, you know . . ." There is an awkward silence.

. . .

After Poonam had her stomach pumped my mother insisted that she "see someone." So for a few weeks my sister spilled her guts to this old Jewish woman with a nice purple bean bag in her office, and then she discovered other avenues of rebellion. I remember waking up in the middle of the night, feeling my sister's heavy body on my bed as she hoisted herself out through the top window of the room. I always kept my eyes tightly shut and my breathing heavy, so I wouldn't have to hear about all the boys I knew she was sneaking out to see.

One day I came home from school to find Poonam in the backyard, reclining on a lawn chair in short cut-offs and a string bikini top, her left hand dangling a cigarette. I remember her flesh just bubbling out of the skimpy outfit. Poonam exhaled this thin line of smoke and smiled, waiting for me to say something. As I headed to my room Poonam asked me if I wanted a drag. I didn't, but I took one anyway. I handed back the cigarette, coughing and afraid that my mother would smell the smoke on me. Poonam sighed and told me about Steven, and how last night was a big night, because she and Steven had made it to second base. I listened with fascination that made me angry with myself, to Poonam's stories of French kissing Steven in his pool. Every night after this I felt my sister's escape, and in exchange for the details of her late night adventures with the neighborhood boys, I did not tell my mother.

. . .

I take the bag of sugar from the cupboard and empty a cupfull into the tiny silver jar my mother uses when she does her morning puja. A holy man once told her, after hearing the heart-wrenching story of Poonam's birth, that if my mother offered water to the gods each morning, she would become strong. My mother did this every morning, despite the rumors that this man who claimed to be Brahmin was an undocumented ex-con.

Poonam's voice begins again, this time soft and questioning, "So, how's everything with you?"

"Everything's fine."

"Have you met anyone?"

"No." I pull the telephone chord, stretching it out until it bounces back into coiled ringlets.

"You must be concentrating really hard on your studies. God, I wish I could be so disciplined. How's ballet going?"

I pause before answering, "I quit."

"But why?" she asked, her voice raising in surprise, "you were getting so good!"

"Poonam," I sighed, "I really don't want to talk about it. I was just getting tired of it all . . . I just don't have the time anymore." As I say this I know what's on the tip of my sister's tongue, the words she spoke to my mother before leaving for school, *Ma, she's drowning in her clothes and she won't talk, doesn't smile anymore because she's too tired*, Poonam had mumbled between sobs before her sadness turned to anger, *I bet it's her freaky ballet teacher and those prepubescent girls in her class! Making her sick, making her disappear when she has everything.*

And all the while I was seething, my ears hot when I heard my sister's betrayal. *I have kept your secrets*, I wanted to scream, *I have not said a word about your late night rendezvous with Steven, your teenage weakness for nicotine.* My mother had soothed Poonam, assuring her that I would eventually snap out of this phase. What with my older sister going off to school, I was just trying to get myself some attention.

"Chip, I just worry about you, that's all. All by yourself over there with mom. I've been thinking about you Chip. I think you'd be happy here. You could dance here, there are a lot of dancers here, you know? Big ones, with real meat on their bones." She laughs nervously.

"Poonam, I said I didn't want to talk about it." I slosh the milk around in its carton before putting it back in the fridge. It is a while before her voice takes on its lively tone again,

"So should I call that guy or do you think I would look too eager?" In the background I can hear the Aunties asking my mother to see the photo album. Just before the women arrived my mother went through the shelves in my father's study and selected the three most handsome leather-backed photo albums, one of which my mother bought soon after Poonam was born. She had Poonam's name engraved in tiny gold lettering, filling it with pictures that captured my sister in sunlight, at the beach without any clothes on, in the backyard dancing in a sprinkler. Wherever the camera found her Poonam always wore the same mischievous grin, holding her right hand behind her back as if to hide something a little girl should not have in her possession.

I can hear my mother's voice, feigning modesty, "Do you *really* want me to show you the album?" She's probably holding the damn thing in her hands, making the other women drool first before she does them the honor, "Oh, all right, all right, but only because you want me to . . ."

"Poonam, I don't know."

"Well, do you think I should get a tattoo? I really want to get a lotus flower on my right shoulder."

"A tattoo? Mom would kill you!"

"Yeah, well its not like she didn't flip about the nose hole thing. Like her own mother doesn't have one."

"Well Nani doesn't exactly have a nice flower forever imprinted on her back either. And if I recall correctly, you couldn't exactly deal with mom's reaction to your 'new look.'"

"Oh, nice joke Chip."

"Come on Poonam, . . . Okay, now it's my turn to be sorry," I pound my fists against my thigh during my sister's long silence, "Pooni, I didn't mean it like that."

"The lotus is a holy flower, Chip, you should know that," Poonam finally says, and in her voice there is no trace of the bitterness I had spoken with earlier, "You know I've started going to Temple here? There's so much to do here Chip, so many people from all over the place that no one cares about stupid, small differences." I imagine my sister's head of curls floating in the sea of colorful faces. "I have people to practice Hindi with in the dining halls, and you can't walk for two blocks without seeing something like 'Vik's Chaat House.' It's really nice. Cold, though, but not really, not in a bad way. You should come see me Chip, I think you'd like it here."

I hear the clack of my mother's gold chappals against the floor before she marches into the kitchen,

"Let me talk to Poonam," she says, reaching for the phone.

"Let me say good-bye first." I swivel my stool around so that my back is to my mother.

"Chip, don't go, tell her I'm like helping you with your math homework or something."

"Nice try. 'Bye Pooni, love you."

"Love you too. Write me okay? She can't interrupt you if you write."

"Sure. See you." My mother grabs the telephone from my hands,

"Hi Poonam, what's going on?" she demands, inquiring about Poonam's health—what is she eating and is she getting enough sleep? What color is her hair now? When my mother is satisfied that things are going according to plan, she lets my sister go and turns to me, "What did she say to you?"

"Nothing much. It sounds like she's getting adjusted to the big city life, but I'm sure she told you that." My mother narrows her eyes, convinced there is more,

"Has she met anyone?" Once again, the big life determining question.

"I guess no one worth mentioning, because she didn't say anything to me."

"Mm-hmm," my mother nods, turning around, "no one worth mentioning." I follow her out to the living room, where she takes her place on the couch among the Aunties gathered around the family photo album.

"And this was when I was so thin," my mother says, pointing to an old black and white photograph of her in a chiffon sari. She is standing next to a palm tree, the sheer cloth of the sari showing her slender, cinched waist. She must have been sad because she is not smiling. "Before I had children." And the women nod and perhaps think back to thinner days themselves.

In the early days of her marriage, my mother spent generous amounts of money to keep herself very beautiful. She had facials and deep conditioning for her hair once a week, and when my father entertained professors from Tokyo, Frankfurt, or London, she would have her hair set and her nails done as well. Her hands were still soft, because she hired a Japanese woman who came three times a week to help with the laundry, the vacuuming, and chopping vegetables.

I feel just a little sorry for the women as I head down the hall to the room my sister and I used to share when we were younger. I close the door, grateful for the silence, and remember the room when it was much larger, even with my sister here, with the two beds and play corner littered with Barbies and puzzles. The room and all its space is so small now, the half bare walls with scattered photographs shrink around me, the floors are cold beneath my feet.

When my parents decided that it was time to separate my sister and me, they had this room completely remodeled. Poonam took my parents' room, and they moved into the section being constructed upstairs. The new bathroom was huge, floored with peach marbled tiles, two sinks with gold rims, and mirrored closet doors. There were more mirrors, lined with those dressing room type light bulbs, greeting you as you stepped dripping from the shower, because, as my mother noticed, I was growing more dedicated to my dance lessons.

I enter the bathroom, and stand before one of the four full-length mirrors, sideways, so that the reflection of my body is a straight, flat line. I turn to face the mirror, the line disappearing into an hourglass. I raise my hands above my head in second position and feel tall, evidence that not all my dancing days have been forgotten.

When I hear silence, sure that the Aunties are gone and my mother has retired to her room for a long nap, I go back to the living room. My mother's collection of statues, bronze and teak representations of Lord Krishna, Lord Shiva, the Goddess Parvati, all line the shelves, newly dusted and polished. I relax on the large leather sofa and pick up one of the photo albums, now covered with tea cups and a few pakora crumbs. I flip through the pages quickly, I have seen these many times. But only now do I notice that in all of my mother's pictures, whether she is posing next to the used German car my father painted pink for her, because my mother had always wanted a pink car like the women in Hollywood movies drove, or whether she stands in front of sandy beaches, her long hair waving in the breezes, in all of these never once is my mother smiling, and if she is it is with a tight, pursed-lip smile, one that is slight and never shows her teeth.

I hurry through the solemn, smile-less pictures of my mother, hoping that just maybe there is at least one photograph of me. Turning the last page, I do find one photograph, but it is turned face down so that only the date when the picture was taken is visible in scrawled blue ink, *September 2, 1975.* I tear back the sticky plastic covering and turn the photograph over.

It is a picture taken at my sister's fifth birthday party, which I remember my mother had been planning for weeks. It was more like Poonam's "coming out" party, as if my mother had finally agreed to let the neighborhood children see her freaky daughter. When my mother brought out the double-layered chocolate cake, Poonam became so excited—maybe it was the loud, discordant voices of the children singing "Happy Birthday," or the dancing flames of the candles, that caused my sister to pounce on the cake with both hands as soon as it was within her reach. My father had been standing in the background with me, taking pictures, while my mother threw herself into a hysterical frenzy, pulling the cake away from my sister, reaching for a napkin to wipe at her hands, yelling at my father to put the camera down. I remember my mother reaching forward to clean away the layer of frosting from my sister's hand—but either she was not quick enough or Poonam had nudged her aside with her arm.

Poonam's eyes are not looking at the camera, but searching for something next to my father, on his right side, where I am standing. I have not held Poonam's gaze as I do now, I have not taken her hand, extended to me as it is in this instant, to hold her and allow her to carry me across the mess of cake and napkins, across the table and the ocean of my mother's sobs. At that moment, my father holds up his camera to catch Poonam with her right hand, smeared with chocolate icing, raised above her head in salute, a triumphant, glowing smile across her full, moon face.

Afterword
Identity Politics and the Politics of Identity

Sucheta Mazumdar

The corner-store radio used to blare a popular 1950s Hindi film song in the Indian town where I was born: *mera juta hai japani/ patloon angrezani/ ser pe lal topi rusi/ phir bhi dil hai hindustani* (My shoes are Japanese/ my pants English/ on my head sits a Russian hat/ but my heart is still Indian). Reading the stories and poems in this anthology I found myself humming that song. But who or what is the "Indian"—or "Pakistani," "Sri Lankan," "Bangladeshi," or "Nepali"—"heart"? And can there be a "South Asian" identity in North America, force-fed and engorged as we all are on our separatist nationalist constructions of identity?

Constructions of identity are simpler at some levels when one is "back home." For the secular segments of the old urban middle classes in South Asia, secure in their privileged elite positions, one casual version of identity consists of shared foods, good Scotch and cricket scores, and sub-continental English. Our own variety of English, part of that world of Commonwealth English entombing British imperialism, is a part of our common bourgeois culture; unlike a Chinese, a Japanese, and a Korean, who are separated by differences of language, a Sri Lankan, a Pakistani, and a Nepali can have a conversation overcoming the separations imposed by three thousand miles and three national flags. But lurking not very far below the surface of this urbane façade are the specific histories of colonialism, nationalist movements, and post-colonial nationalisms.

The process of national identity formation is always cannibalistic; regional bourgeoisie selectively savage fragments of local cultures, religions, and languages and serve them up as national identities that they then promote as universal and normative values. Cannibalism also kills. The first victim in South Asia was Hindu-Muslim amity. In the nineteenth or even the early twentieth century, it was not unusual for Hindu and Muslim families to send presents and share in the festivities of Id and Diwali, for Hindus and Muslims from the same village to see themselves as members of a community, for Sufi Muslim holy men (pir) to receive both Hindu and Muslim devotees, or for a Muslim to greet a Hindu neighbor with "Ram Ram."[1] The long drawn out nationalist movement on mainland South Asia under upper-caste Hindu hegemony, however, led to the creation of political religions; being Hindu or Muslim was no longer a personal and private matter. Religious affiliations began to define community. The British colonial state abetted this seemingly ancient divide between the two communities. Drawing on the Euro-American discourse on Orientalism predicated on the phobia of an imagined pan-Islamic world, British colonialists found ready allies among Hindu nationalists. The medieval period, when most of India was ruled by kings who were Muslim, was portrayed as a chronicle of rape of Hindu women, defilement and looting of Hindu temples, and the slaughter of cows; the period prior to the coming of Islam to India was portrayed as the golden age of Hinduism. In the subsequent writing of nationalist histories, the rapes of Hindu kings looting Buddhist temples and monasteries were obscured; the voices of untouchables forced to wear pots around their necks by upper-caste Hindus, so that some accidental spit would not defile the ground, were silenced. Some even sought to portray the British as liberators of the Hindus from the Muslims.[2]

The politics of national identity-formation are predicated on the notion of homogeneity. The nationalist movements of South Asia—social movements seeking to establish the hegemony of the bourgeoisie—spawned political parties that sought to unify diverse cultures, languages, and religious beliefs into monolithic entities. In the post-independence period, language, culture, religion, and nation acquired an indivisibility as a marker of national identity in the nation-states of Bangladesh, India, Pakistan, Nepal, and Sri Lanka. History text-books were written and rewritten; propaganda and myth-making created an essential-ized identity called "Indian"/"Pakistani"/"Bangladeshi"/"Sri Lankan"/"Nepali." Like all national identities, these identities are built on the silencing of differences, the erasure of histories, and the surreptitious washing of blood-soaked daggers.

But despite the efforts of segments of the state and political parties, official versions of national cultures and histories are not easily made sacrosanct to all the people who live there. Today, for many women's rights activists, union-organiz-ers, and Dalits (as the former untouchables are called), the writing of these offi-cial histories is increasingly contested territory. Academics, activists, journalists,

media pundits, politicians, and preachers are all aggressively engaged in challenging particular interpretations; writers like Taslima Nasreen draw vicious
sanction precisely because their writing upsets official versions of nationalist history and opens up frightening fissures. In these struggles, alternative spaces are
forged, new social movements can breath life. As immigrants, however, we come
to North America with only a carcass in our baggage that we proceed to mum-
mify as "Indian" or "Pakistani" culture. Time and history stand still from the
day we first boarded that plane. And it is this mildewed and outmoded version
of "cultural heritage" that we hope to pass on to the generations born and raised
in North America.

Quantifying, categorizing, and classifying populations has been one of the
primary systems of bureaucratic control of all modern states. The governments
of the United States and Canada are no exception. Census categories in the
United States have divided South Asians into Asian Indians, Pakistanis and
"Others," and we are all part of that category called "Asian American." Privately,
of course, South Asian dualities spill over: we are not only Bengali-Indian-Hindu-
Indian Americans, Gujarati-Pakistani-Parsee-Pakistani Americans and so on if
we happen to have emigrated from South Asia, but are also Asian-African-
Ismaili-Indian Americans, Bengali-Bangladesi-Muslim-British-Bangladeshi
American, and Indo-Guyanese-Caribbean-Muslim-Indian Canadians. Publicly,
with a stroke of the pen, "ethnicities" based on "national origins" become fixed
public entities. Much-touted projects of multiculturalism, celebrating sanitized
ethnic cultures and bestowing instant credentials on all claiming ethnic authenticity, freeze us in our national-origin categories. The state both creates and
manipulates ethnic identities; at assigned times and in allotted slots, immigrants
are encouraged to unpack that carcass from home. The immigrant bourgeoisie
nosily jostle each other for the tiny spaces allowed for displaying "ethnic pride"
oblivious to the politics of managing diversity.

There is also collusion. The South Asian immigrant bourgeoisie have a direct
and vested interest in preserving and promoting "Indian heritage." Essentialized
constructions of homeland cultural identity help preserve patriarchal authority
and discipline rebellious American-born teenagers; for after all the parent born
in South Asia or Africa or Guyana is the final authority on "authentic" culture.
Never mind the fact that most of these parents, who are doctors, engineers and

scientists, have never read an entire book on South Asian history since the eighth grade, when the inherited British imperial curricular structure tracks children into "science" and "humanities" categories, and that their notions of "India," "Pakistan," etc. are based on their own narrow regional linguistic and religious proclivities. For the state and for their children, they are instant experts, pre-servers of homeland cultural purity and integrity. Neither the "community lead-ers" of Indian, Pakistani, Indo-Guyanese, or any other groups, nor the U.S. or Canadian state are interested in rebellion and challenges to authority. Control of those little sanctioned slots for displaying "heritage" and national cultures, marching in parades and deciding who will be allowed to participate in the "international fairs," legitimizes the immigrant bourgeoisie's social and political standing among other immigrants and in the family.

State-mandated identity politics become even more complicated when South Asians collide with East Asians under the category of Asian American. There is no common vocabulary, for Asia as a continent has been stripped of its own his-tory. Carved up into "spheres of interest" by British, American, French, Dutch, Spanish, and Portuguese colonial authorities, centuries of imperialism and lega-cies of orientalism have contributed to the creation of post-colonial national cul-tures that glorify the uniqueness rather than the commonalities of Asian peoples. Each group of new immigrants from Asia brings its own nationalist cultural bag-gage while American-born Asians wallow in the Mayflower-syndrome, "I was here first and am therefore more Asian American than you." Asian Americans Studies with its pathetic eagerness to prove its American origins and disdain for learning about Asian history, has proved incapable of disentangling how colo-nialism has warped its own world view. For the second- and third- and fourth-generation Asian Americans, mostly of Chinese American and Japanese American origin, who emerged as the progenitors of the Asian American movement in the late 1960s, "Asia" was easily and readily identified with the homeland of their parents. Radical politics did not translate into radical rethinking of national-ori-gin categories; there was no perceived need to redefine the "Asia" in Asian American, or to reach out to strange black and brown peoples. Orientalist con-structions of the cultures of Japan, Korea, and Vietnam as derivative from China and Confucianism easily provided the vocabulary with which to reconstruct a pan-East Asian American identity. Phenotype-based identity politics, a grotesque reminder of how racialist discourse has permeated the very core of all consciousness, has formed the basis of self-identification of East Asian Americans as the bonafide "Asian Americans." South Asian Americans watch from the sidelines in an American replay of the cultural rhetoric of imperialist Japan's "Asian Co-prosperity Sphere" holding forth the promise of a virile East Asia rising to lead all other brown-skinned colonial subjects (Filipinos, Indonesians, Indians etc.) to freedom and economic prosperity under its tutelage. In the uneasy alliances that have emerged on college campuses, it has been easier for practitioners of Asian American Studies to reify national differences among immigrants and include token Indian Americans and other South Asians on the cultural periphery rather than examine the ideological core of Asian American history. We are all implicated in managing diversity.

Beyond campus walls, for South Asian middle-class immigrants travelling the slippery road of upward mobility, it is easier to imitate the hegemonic culture of Anglo-EuroAmerica than explore other Asian cultures. After all, almost two hundred years of British colonialism have prepared us for this. So why bother to link up with all these other Asians when we can sit at the feet of the masters themselves? And yes, a few of us wore turbans, long after the fashion had passed in India, just so that no ignorant person would mistake us for Black, and we do take care to wear a bindi and a sari or salwar-kurta where there are lots of Hispanics and Puerto Ricans, for god knows these Americans are not very good at distinguishing features. But how does it matter to us if Chinese Americans and Japanese Americans and Filipinos have struggled in the Civil Rights movement? Our temples, gurdwaras, jamatkhanas, mosques, and churches do not need to teach the history of Black struggles; one does not need to know the history of African America to be an engineer or a doctor. For most of us, immigrating after the Civil Rights movement, the United States is indeed the promised land. Accustomed as we are to social hierarchies of class and gender and the daily discriminations and exclusions practised in South Asia (e.g., Untouchable and Muslim in India, Ahmedi and Mohajir in Pakistan, Chakma and Hindu in Bangladesh, Tamil in Sri Lanka, women in general, and so on), the notion of equal citizenship is indeed a new concept, and the politics of challenging inequality a fearful one. And so if some people want to link up with the group that calls itself Asian American, and some young people want to go and

465

argue about the rights of minorities, let them, as long as they do not ask for money. Money we keep for the Republicans and for photo opportunities.

Like other Asian Americans dubbed the "model minorities," South Asian Americans can be used to discipline working-class Blacks, Puerto Ricans, and Latinos, by touting how our communities enshrine "family values" (and let's not mention homophobia, sexual harassment, domestic violence, abandoned wives, and child abuse, for these of course never happen in "our" families). We can slip into the comfortable position of "wannabe whites," avoid looking in the mirror and seeing our black faces, and become the more acceptable minorities. As long as we do not make waves we will enjoy a seat at the table.

At another level, middle-class South Asians and the EuroAmerican middle-classes do have some things in common; class politics creates ideological con-gruities. As members of the middle-class, the bourgeoisie share certain values worldwide. These include knowing how to invest capital, marshalling resources, finding loopholes to avoid paying taxes, educating the children in the right schools, exercising patriarchal privileges, living in the suburbs, and keeping a safe distance from working-class minorities; in other words ensuring the cultural and political hegemony of the bourgeoisie. It also includes knowing how to voice one's angst, disguise one's smugness, and manage multiple hypocrisies and con-tradictions. But, unlike the more securely-placed EuroAmerican middle-classes, and despite many of the trappings of material success, the South Asian immi-grant bourgeoisie also knows that it is living on the peripheries of the cultural heart of North America. So they work on their accents and work out, change their hair-styles and even hair color, modify their first names, and embark on that tricky process of balancing "westernization" and "national cultural authen-ticity" in alien lands. It is frightening to have to reinvent oneself.

The balancing act can take many forms. In the present climate of extolling diversity, a touch of unoffensive exotica, a nudge to Orientalist fantasy never hurts. Have you not noticed at social events, in the innumerable photographs appearing in the community newspapers, how the women are always wearing "traditional" clothing while the men are dressed in dark western-style business suits? Women are forever the bearers of culture, the preservers of heritage; they must after all look the part. On college campuses, South Asian academics quote religious mythology and Derrida in the same breath and recreate an identity

based on fragments of homeland religio-cultural nostalgia; one can be applaud-
ed for displaying"ethnic chic" while at the same time retaining one's safe space in
amorphous middle-class America. Jetsetting intellectuals and business elite,
whose cosmopolitanism is a ticket to upward mobility, smile weakly at other
brown-skinned faces so as not to compromise their urbanity by hanging out with
compatriots, and reify how airport transit lounges are their own sites of identity-
formation. Their identity as members of the ruling class is after all quite secure.

Retaining "cultural authenticity" by straddling both worlds can also have
other types of cash value. As NRIs (Non-Resident Indians), for example, the
Indian immigrant bourgeoisie share a certain privileged node regarding the
homeland governments, especially now that central and state governments have
recognized the value of remittances and expatriate investments. In India, a middle-class entrepreneur may be kept waiting for months before getting an interview with a minister. But here, even cabinet ministers come courting and wine
and dine the NRI. The economically successful overseas communities have considerable clout. When the World Bank, for example, under pressure from environmental and humanitarian groups decided to abandon building the Narmada
Dam in Gujarat, the overseas Gujarati community raised bonds to complete the
project, for their kin in India, who are rich farmers, stood to benefit from the
dam. Even if Indians cannot have dual passports, keeping dual identities is convenient and indeed necessary.

And then one can also try to import the imagined worlds left behind. Many
furiously build temples, gurdwaras, and mosques as if these concrete structures
can give them the trappings of social status dislocated by immigration; hopefully such activity has the bonus of adding merit in this world and after. Of course,
to make sure that everybody in the community at least knows who are the most
religious, donations are recorded and published in community newspapers. The
temples, gurdwaras, and mosques help in other ways; they provide social control
over unruly youngsters while keeping them apart in the guise of religio-cultural
difference. In hundreds of temples and mosques and gurudwaras dotting the
landscape of North America, Amar Chitra Katha versions of Hindu mythology
are passed off as Indian history; maulanas try to etch a pan-Islamic Sunni history stripped of all local contexts; preachers hold forth to remake Sikhism into the
only acceptable version of Punjabi identity. All befuddle the mind and reinscribe

467

notions of primordial differences between second-generation South Asian Americans who have little opportunity to question the categories imposed by priests and parents.

For the thousands of taxi-drivers, newspaper vendors, and grocery-store clerks whose seemingly sudden appearance in metropolitan centers across North America has changed the class composition of the South Asian immigrant community, the politics of identity formation present very different challenges. Many come from rich peasant backgrounds from regions that have done well in the Green Revolution, like the Punjab province in both India and Pakistan. Others are young men escaping civil wars and the massive, chronic unemployment of urban South Asia. Products of post-independence nationalist educational institutions and third-tier government colleges that mushroomed with clientalism and political corruption, these immigrants arrive only to realize they have no real marketable skills that will allow them entry into the U. S. or Canadian white-collar labor force. Thwarted in their personal and familial ambitions and working at jobs they find demeaning, salvaging self-respect requires aggressive strategies of separating themselves from all other members of the working class. Keeping their Indian, Pakistani, or Bangladeshi national identity-politics alive crucially allows them to separate themselves from Blacks and Latinos; they can have the small comfort of knowing that they are at least not at the bottom of the social scale and that they too have the power to exclude. Subject to the daily abuses of racism, they are virulently racist; recent immigrants from the countryside and small-town boys adrift in terrifying megalopolis, they turn to religious zealotry and social conservatism to discover their new moorings. A potential scenario with South Asian taxi drivers, Black hospital workers, and Chinese American garment workers marching together in New York City maybe a union organizer's dream, but its very thought is a nightmare for many, not just Mayor Guiliani.

Yet, for me, reading these stories and poems was like the sudden pleasure of meeting another desi when one's senses have been assaulted all day by the unfamiliar. At a safe distance from the homelands where national armies and ancestral mobs have butchered each other's grandmothers, these stories opened up ways of talking about the Partition and wars. Away from suffocating relatives and prying eyes, they also told of sexual pleasures, and about silenced rejections and rapes, subjects that the bourgeois puritanical constructions of culture have little room for. Like children sharing a special toy with that one special friend, the stories reveal bits of one's soul to others from the subcontinent. But then I also felt a claustrophobia; of worlds peopled only by other South Asians and an occasional white. So many of the stories are set indoors. Is this how we really live? What are the faces and names that we are blocking out in this retelling? What are the politics of our self-indulgent narratives?

Forging a South Asian identity in North America that is not burdened with Hindu-Indian chauvinism, or the casual superficiality of the old South Asian elite, has to be a political project, not a vocabulary of convenience. Living in the United States in the 1990s when apolitical "difference" is fetishized and identities born of work-place experiences are made seemingly ephemeral, finding a political identity as the core is difficult. Without a conscious political project, however, using the term "South Asian" merely becomes a façade for perpetuating arrogant Indian American cultural hegemony. I, for one, have no desire to be an accomplice in projects of the immigrant bourgeoisie. The stories and autobiographical notes move me to ask, does my identity have to constructed by what I have inherited and not by what I have struggled to make of myself? Am I doubly doomed by my genes and country of ancestral origin? Or do politics that struggle for social change, for social justice for all—not just the people with whom one may share a certain ancestral affinity—matter at all? I cannot subscribe to a philosophy touting the illusory nature of all phenomena, identities included. Identities are indeed created and constructed and reconstructed; but hiding behind the multiplicity of identities and the chameleon-like display of the most suitable self for the moment seems to beg the question: if one ceases to struggle to find the core of one's politics and one's political identity, what will we see when we look in the mirror?

Notes

[1] British officials and scholars working on the Indian countryside noted this in many places: see William Crooke, *The North-Western Provinces of India*; Malcolm Darling, *Rusticus Loquitar*; Charles Alfred Elliot, *Laborious Days*; Lytton, (Second Earl of), *Pundits and Elephants*; and Edward John Thompson, *The Reconstruction of India*; to name just a few.

[2] Several essays in David Ludden, ed., *Contesting the Nation* (Philadelphia, 1996) take up this issue; see in particular, Tanika Sarkar, "Imagining Hindurastra" and Mushirul Hasan, "The Myth of Unity."

About The Contributors

Jaishri Abichandani was born in 1969 in Bombay, India. Most of her work is situated in Queens, New York where she has lived since 1994. She uses photography as a tool to express her (dis)comfort with and pride about being a South Asian/person of color in this society. She is interested in using photography as a non-traditional, non-Western folk art.

Meena Alexander, most recently author of *The Shock of Arrival: Reflections on Postcolonial Experience* (Boston: South End Press, 1996), *River and Bridge* (poems) (Toronto: TSAR Press, 1996) and the novel *Manhattan Music* (San Francisco: Mercury House, forthcoming January 1997), is Professor of English and Women's Studies at Hunter College and the Graduate Center, CUNY.

Agha Shahid Ali, Kashmiri-American-Kashmiri, is Director of the MFA Creative Writing Program at the University of Massachusetts, Amherst. His seventh collection, *The Country Without a Post Office*, will be published by Norton in 1997. He is also the translator of Faiz Ahmed Faiz's *The Rebel's Silhouette: Selected Poems* (University of Massachusetts Press).

Vivek Renjen Bald is a New York based film and videomaker. Taxi-vala/Autobiography, his first full-length work, was completed in late 1994, and is distributed by Third World Newsreel (NYC). **Saleem Osman** is a former staff organizer for the Lease Drivers Coalition, a South Asian taxi drivers' organization in New York. **Irfaan R.** is a former driver who has left New York and returned to his home city in Pakistan. **Jasvinder Singh** is a former part-time taxi driver who now works as a computer programmer.

Himani Bannerji was born in Bangladesh and came to Canada from India in 1969. She teaches in the sociology department at York University and has written poetry, short stories, and essays on racism, feminism, culture, and politics. Her publications include *The Writing on the Wall: Essays on Culture and Politics* (1993), *Doing Time* (1986), and *Colored Pictures* (1992) and she has edited Returning the Gaze (1993).

S. Bari arrived in the U.S. when she was a few months old. Of Bangladeshi descent, she is the child of a Muslim father and a Hindu mother. She grew up in the U.S.A. and Switzerland, and is currently based in Texas, trying to finish a novel.

Marina Budhos is the author of *House of Waiting* (1995) and is working on a non-fiction book, *Remix: Conversations with Immigrant Teens*, that will be released in 1998. Her fiction and non-fiction have appeared in *The Nation*, *Kenyon Review*, *Ms.*, and *Ploughshares*. She received the Kenyon Review's 1993 Emerging Writer Award, was a 1992-93 Fulbright Scholar to India, and has recently won a grant for women writers to complete her second novel.

Darius Cooper is professor of literature and film at San Diego Mesa College. His poems and stories have appeared in *Critical Quarterly*, the *Massachusetts Review*, *Enclitic*, *Chelsea*, *Helix*, *Greenwood Review*, and *Emergences*. His essays on Indian cinema have appeared in *Film Quarterly*, *East West*, and several anthologies. He has just completed a book on Satyajit Ray.

Rienzi Crusz was born in Shri Lanka and came to Canada in 1965. Educated at the universities of Ceylon, London, Toronto, and Waterloo, he was a Senior Reference and Collections Development Librarian at the University of Waterloo. Anthologized and widely published in Canadian and international journals, he has seven volumes of verse, including *Beatitudes of Ice* (1996).

Shamita Das Dasgupta is Assistant Professor of Psychology at Rutgers University. She is a founder member of Manavi, an organization that focuses on violence against South Asian immigrant women and the author of *In Visible Terms: Domestic Violence in the Asian Indian Context*. She is a recipient of the 1992 "Woman Leader" award from the Y.W.C.A. of Central Jersey. Currently she is editing a book on South Asian women in America.

Born in Columbus, Ohio in 1970, **Sayantani DasGupta** earned her B.S. in Health and Society at Brown University. She is now enrolled as a medical student at Johns Hopkins University and plans to graduate in 1998 as a M.D., M.P.H. Sayantani's articles have appeared in *Ms.*, *Z*, and *A* magazines, and she has co-authored *The Demon Slayers and Other Stories: Bengali Folk Tales* with her mother, Shamita.

Anjalee Deshpande, a director/actor residing in New York, is a part-time poet/creative writer, born in Michigan, Anjalee received her Bachelor's degree in 1995. Since then, she has been acting professionally for stage and film in Atlanta and New York. Currently, Anjalee is an artistic director at La Belle Epoque Theatre in Manhattan.

As a native of Kenya, **Ghalib Dhalla** sold his first article when he was fifteen and has freelanced since. He makes his home now in Los Angeles as a banker, and is currently working upon the completion of his yet untitled debut novel. This is an abridged excerpt from that novel-in-progress.

Born in India, **Chitra Banerjee Divakaruni** teaches creative writing at Foothill College and is president of MAITRI, a South Asian women's helpline. Her work has appeared in *Ms.*, *ZYZZYVA*, *Indiana Review*, *Toronto Review*, and *Calyx*. She has three books of poetry, *Dark Like the River*, *The Reason for Nasturtiums*, and *Black Candle* and her awards include an Allen Ginsberg poetry prize and a Pushcart Prize. Her latest book is a fiction collection, *Arranged Marriage*.

Sucheta J. Doshi is a native of Boston, Massachusetts and graduated from Wellesley College in 1994 with a B.A. in political science and history. She has a Master's in Public Health and is currently pursuing a fellowship at the Center for Disease Control and Prevention. She remains active in South Asian women's organizations and hopes to someday be able to work on health projects in India.

Minal Hajratwala is a newspaper journalist in San Jose, California. Her poems appear in various literary journals and in three anthologies. She was raised in New Zealand and Michigan by a father from Gujarat, India, and a Gujarati mother born in the Fiji Islands. She graduated from Stanford University.

Naheed Islam is a Ph.D. candidate of Sociology at the University of California, Berkeley. She is currently working on a dissertation on Bangladeshi immigrants in Los Angeles. Her research focuses on race, ethnicity, and immigration.

Litu Kabir was born in Bangladesh in 1959, came to the USA in his teens, and is a software engineer by profession. Among his previous works is "The Return", included in the anthology *Living in America* (1995). He is married to Nasima Khatoon and they divide their homes between Cambridge, Massachusetts, and Dhaka, Bangladesh.

Ginu Kamani is the author of *Junglee Girl*. She has contributed to *On A Bed Of Rice: An Asian American Erotic Feast, Traveler's Tales: A Taste Of The Road, au Juice: the journal of eatin drinkin & screwin around, Dick For A Day* and *Herotica 5*. She lives in Northern California.

Amitava Kumar teaches in the English Department at the University of Florida. He is columnist for *Liberation* (India) and a member of the progressive photographers' co-op, Impact Visuals. *No Tears for the NRI*, his book of poems has recently been published from the Writers' Workshop, Calcutta. Kumar is currently working on a book, *Passport Photos*.

Sunaina Maira is a doctoral student at the Harvard Graduate School of Education who is doing her dissertation research on the ethnic identity development of second-generation Indian Americans.

Shakti Maira, who contributed the cover art for this book, came to the United States from India sixteen years ago. He delights in the convergence of multiple cultural influences in his life and work, and use many mediums—paintings on canvas, etched stone, and sculpture in bronze, terra-cotta, and stone. He has exhibited widely in the U.S. and India, most recently at the Island Gallery, Portland, Maine; Perry House Galleries, Washington, D.C.; the Contemporary Arts of India Gallery, New York; and the Village Gallery, New Delhi. He received the 1994 Hitchiner Award for sculpture at the Annual New Hampshire Arts Association Currier Gallery Show.

Sharmili Majmudar lives in Chicago where she writes, creates pottery, attends the Loyola University Graduate School of Social Work, and participates in a number of social and political community projects with pride.

473

Shivani Manghnani was born and raised in Honolulu, Hawai'i. She has just completed her sophomore year at Wellesley College, where she majored in English. This is her first time being published, and she writes in memory of her grandmother, Hari Chandiram Devnani, and for her mother and two sisters.

Bakirathi Mani, who was born in Bombay and raised in Tokyo, developed her interest in the South Asian diaspora while an undergraduate student at Georgetown University in Washington, D.C. At present, she is completing her M.A. in modern Indian history at Jawaharlal Nehru University, New Delhi, and exploring the 'displacement' of the diaspora on the sub-continent.

Ashok Mathur has published one book, *Loveruage: a dance in three parts*, and his novel, *Once Upon on Elephant*, will be released in 1997.

Sucheta Mazumdar teaches Chinese history and Asian American studies at Duke University. One of the co-editors of *Making Waves: An anthology of Writings By and About Asian American Women*, she is the co-founder and co-editor of *South Asia Bulletin*, now called *Comparative Studies of South Asia, Africa, and the Middle East*. Sucheta is currently working on two book projects, one on South Asians in the U.S., the other on Chinese and Chinese American garment workers.

Ameena Meer is an Indian of the diaspora, living and writing in New York City. Her journalism has appeared in *Harper's Bazaar*, *Interview*, and *Spin*, among other publications. Her fiction has been anthologized in *The Flaming Spirit:; New Writing 3: New British and Commonwealth Writing* ; and *On A Bed Of Rice* ; and her first novel is *Bombay Talkie*.

Diane Mehta received her masters in poetry at Boston University and won Kansas State University's Joel Climenhaga Creative Writing Award. Recent publications include poems in *Living in America: Poetry and Fiction by South Asian American Writers*, *the Formalist*, and the *Journal*.

Like Abraham Lincoln, **Jaykumar Menon** was born in Kentucky and raised in Illinois. He now lives in New York City, where he is a civil rights lawyer.

Anuradha M. Mitra, Ph.D., is Director of Communications and Adjunct Faculty Member at The Union Institute, a progressive higher education institution for adult students. The interrelationship of voice and culture is the focus of her current work. She lives in Cincinnati with her husband and two children.

Shani Mootoo is an Indo-Trinidadian-Canadian writer who lives in Vancouver. Her writing has been featured in several Gallerie Women Artists' Monographs, in *Fuse* magazine, and in *The Skin on our Tongues*. *Out on Main Street* (1993) is her first book of short fiction. She is also a visual artist and video-maker, having exhibited in many solo and group shows and written and directed four videos.

Sunita Sunder Mukhi's doctoral dissertation, for the Performance Studies department at New York University, is on the ways in which the Indian community in New York City defines and negotiates Indianess through community cultural productions. Of Indian origin, but born and reared in the Philippines, she has been a performer, director and choreographer, and writer in productions both in Manila and in the United States.

Hema Nair was born in Jammu and raised in Pune, Bangalore, Vishakapatnam, and New Delhi, and now lives in Ewing, New Jersey. In 1989 she won the Best Woman Journalist of the Year Award, an all-India prize for outstanding writing on women's issues. She has been published in *The New York Times*, *Ms.*, *New Directions for Women*, and *The Women's Review of Books*. She is currently a freelance journalist and is working on a collection of short stories.

Tahira Naqvi is originally from Pakistan and is now settled in the U.S. with her family. She currently teaches English at Western Connecticut State University. Her short stories have appeared in the *Journal of South Asian Literature*, the *Massachusetts Review*, *The Forbidden Stitch: An Asian American Anthology*, and *Living in America*. Her collection of short stories, *Attar of Roses and Other Stories from Pakistan*, is forthcoming from Three Continents Press.

Sanjay K. Nigam was born in New Delhi but grew up in the American Southwest. His stories have previously appeared in *Grand Street*, *The Kenyon Review*, and *Quarry West*.

Saleem Peeradina is the author of two books of poetry, *First Offence* and *Group Portrait* and edited *Contemporary Indian Poetry in English: An Assessment and Selection*. He has two more books awaiting publication—a poetry cycle, *Meditations on Desire*, and a prose memoir, *The Ocean in My Yard*. He is currently Associate Professor of English and Creative Writing at Siena Heights College, Adrian, Michigan.

Vijay Prashad is Assistant Professor of International Studies at Trinity College in Hartford, Connecticut. He is a member of the Forum of Indian Leftists (FOIL) which combats social intolerance (the bandwagons of such things as Hindutva) and economic arrogance (IMFundamentalism); for information, contact him at 55 Tremont Street, Hartford, CT 06105 or at vijay.prashad@mail.trincoll.edu.

Mahmud Rahman was born in Bangladesh and has lived his adult life in the U.S. He is a jack of many trades, still master of none. Having written in one form or another since he was twelve, he is now working at fiction. A wanderer at heart, he now lives in Providence, Rhode Island.

Aly Remtulla was born in Kenya to parents of Indian extraction. He now lives in Canada and is currently an anthropology major/ biology minor at Stanford University in California. Aly is co-editor of Stanford's largest literary and arts journal and is also compiling an anthology of international youth poetry.

Sandip Roy grew up in Calcutta and now lives in San Francisco where he edits *Trikone Magazine*. His work has appeared in *India Currents Magazine* and *Christopher Street*, *A Magazine*, as well as in anthologies such as *Queer View Mirror* and *Men on Men 6*. When the rent is due he also writes software.

Roshni Rustomji-Kern's short stories have appeared in *The Journal of South Asian Literature*, *The Toronto South Asia Review*, *The Massachusetts Review*, *Our Feet Walk The Sky: Women Of The South Asian Diaspora* (1993), and *Her Mother's Ashes And Other Stories* (1994). She is the coeditor of *Blood Into Ink: South Asian And Middle Eastern Women Write War* (1994) and editor of *Living In America: Fiction And Poetry By South Asian American Writers* (1995). She is Professor Emerita, Sonoma State University.

Shyam Selvadurai was born in 1965 in Colombo, Sri Lanka. *Funny Boy* is his first novel and is published in the U.S.A. by William Morrow and in Canada by McClelland and Stewart. It won the Smithbooks/Books in Canada First Novel Award and spent more than four months on Canadian bestseller lists.

Somini Sengupta is a writer living in Brooklyn, New York. She adores Nusrat Fateh Ali Khan.

Vijay Seshadri was born in Bangalore and came to America at the age of five. He was educated at Oberlin College and Columbia University, where he was also a Ph.D. student in Middle Eastern studies, focusing on the history of Islam in India and on Urdu and Persian poetry. In his early and mid-twenties, he worked in the fishing and logging industries of the Pacific Northwest, from which experiences the details of the poem, "Lifeline," are drawn. A collection of his poetry, *Wild Kingdom*, was published by Graywolf Press (1996). He is currently on the editorial staff of *The New Yorker*.

Purvi Shah was born in Ahmedabad, India. As secretaries laboring within tiny, windowless cubicles in an anxiety-rich department at the American Foundation for the Blind, a friend and I would hastily scribble poems to restore imagination to our days. What she has included in this anthology is a "work" poem from this series.

Sejal Shah was born in Rochester, New York and received her B.A. from Wellesley College. She is the recipient of a 1994 Academy of American Poets Prize and a 1995 New York State Artist Residency Exchange fellowship for fiction. She is currently at work on a first collection of poems.

S. Shankar is the author of a novel, *A Map of Where I Live*, a collection of poems, *I As Man*, and various works of criticism. He teaches in the English Department at Rutgers University, Newark, and is a founding member of the editorial collective of the periodical *SAMAR*.

Kavita Sharma is completing her M.F.A. in Creative Writing at the University of Alabama, where she also teaches. Her poetry has been heavily influenced by her bicultural heritage. Presently she is completing a book-length collection of poems which addresses these issues.

Reena Sharma was born in the Fiji Islands and migrated to the U.S. at the age of five. She holds an M.A. in English Literature and is teaching English composition at Mount San Antonio College in CA. Her favorite activities include sleeping, eating, reading children's books, sleeping some more, overanalyzing (but still trying to live in the moment), and teaching her two year-old niece, Kharisma, how to share and blow bubbles.

Bapsi Sidhwa grew up in Lahore, Pakistan and now resides in Houston. She has published four novels, *An American Brat*, *Cracking India*, *The Crow Eaters*, and *The Bride*, in addition to several short stories. Sidhwa received the Lila Wallace–Reader's Digest Writers' Award in 1993.

Natasha Singh is currently working on a collection of short stories. She wishes to give thanks to the Great Mother from whom all creativity comes.

Rajini Srikanth teaches literature in the Boston area and is co-editor of *Closing the Gap: South Asian Americans in Asian America* (Temple University Press).

Abraham Verghese was born in Ethiopia to parents from Kerala, India. He has studied and lived in Ethiopia and India before coming to the United States in 1980. His memoir, *My Own Country: A Doctor's Story of a Town and Its People in the Age of AIDS* (1994) is an account of his experiences as a physician treating AIDS in the small town of Johnston, Tennessee. He lives in El Paso, Texas, where he is professor of medicine and chief of infectious diseases at the Texas Tech Health Sciences Center. He is currently working on a novel that also draws on his experiences as a doctor.

Nisma Zaman has been working in documentary film for the past four years, and is producer/director of Beyond Black and White, a personal exploration of bicultural identity. She was the curator of the photography gallery at Ithaca College and earned a B.F.A. in Film, Photography, and Visual Art.

Credits

The editors and the publisher would like to thank the following authors for their kind permission to reprint copyrighted material in this book:

Alexander, Meena. "San Andreas Fault." From *River and Bridge*. Toronto: TSAR, 1996. First published in this version in Amerasia Journal 22.1: 232-237.

Ali, Agha Shahid. "In Search of Evanescence" and "Snow on the Desert." From *The Nostalgist's Map of America*. New York: Norton, 1991.

Budhos, Marina. "Jumbee Curse." From *Caribbean Writer*.

Cooper, Darius. Excerpts from "An Archive of Myself." From *Emergences 5/6*.

"Under the Gravity of Some Thirty Odd Years." From *Chelsea* 46: 236-239.

Kamani, Ginu. "Just Between Indians." From *Junglee Girl*. San Fransisco, CA: aunt lute, 1995.

Mootoo, Shani. "Out on Main Street." From *Out on Main Street and Other Stories*. Vancouver: Press Gang Publishers, 1993.

Naqvi, Tahira. "Beyond the Walls, Amreeka." First published in *Journal of South Asian Literature*, 1984.

Peeradina, Saleem. "Michigan Basement II." First published in *Group Portrait*. Oxford University Press, 1992.

Remtullah, Aly. "emerald's bubble." First published in *Trikone* January, 1996.

Seshadri, Vijay. "A Sketch from the Campaign in the North." From *Wild Kingdom*. St. Paul, Minn.: Graywolf, 1996.

"Lifeline." From *Wild Kingdom*. St. Paul, Minn.: Graywolf, 1996.

Selvadurai, Shyam. "Excerpt from *Funny Boy*." From *Funny Boy*. New York: William Morrow, 1994.

Sidhwa, Bapsi. "Defend Yourself Against Me." First published in *Colours of a New Day: Writing for South Africa*. Eds. Sarah Lefanu and Stephen Hayward. New York: Pantheon, 1990.

Singh, Natasha. "Miss Vindaloo." First appeared in an earlier version in *Fireweed: A Feminist Quarterly of Writing, Politics, Art, and Culture* 51/52, Early Spring, 1996.